THE **AFIRE** GUIDE
TO U.S. REAL ESTATE INVESTING

THE **AFIRE** GUIDE
TO U.S. REAL ESTATE INVESTING

What global investors need to know about commercial
real estate acquisition, management, and disposition

4th EDITION

Edited by Will McIntosh, PhD

New York   Chicago   San Francisco   Athens   London   Madrid
Mexico City   Milan   New Delhi   Singapore   Sydney   Toronto

1 2 3 4 5 6 7 8 9   LCR   28 27 26 25 24 23

ISBN   978-1-265-41346-0
MHID   1-265-41346-0

e-ISBN   978-1-265-41708-6
e-MHID   1-265-41708-3

This publication is designed to provide accurate and authoritative information in regard to the subject matter covered. It is sold with the understanding that neither the author nor the publisher is engaged in rendering legal, accounting, securities trading, or other professional services. If legal advice or other expert assistance is required, the services of a competent professional person should be sought.

—From a Declaration of Principles Jointly Adopted by a Committee of the American Bar Association and a Committee of Publishers and Associations

Library of Congress Cataloging-in-Publication Data

Names: McIntosh, Will (Real estate consultant), editor. | Association of Foreign Investors in Real Estate, issuing body.
Title: The AFIRE guide to US real estate investing : what global investors need to know about commercial real estate acquisition, management, and disposition / edited by Will McIntosh, PhD.
Description: Fourth edition. | New York : McGraw Hill, [2024] | Includes bibliographical references and index.
Identifiers: LCCN 2023036891 (print) | LCCN 2023036892 (ebook) | ISBN 9781265413460 (hardback) | ISBN 9781265417086 (ebook)
Subjects: LCSH: Real estate investment—United States.
Classification: LCC HD255 .A59 2023 (print) | LCC HD255 (ebook) | DDC 332.63/240973—dc23/eng/20230809
LC record available at https://lccn.loc.gov/2023036891
LC ebook record available at https://lccn.loc.gov/2023036892

CONTENTS

SECTION 1

Introduction: *Preparing for Investment in the US*

SECTION 2

Introduction: *The Commercial Real Estate Life Cycle*

SECTION 3

Introduction: *Commercial Real Estate Finance and Partnerships*

SECTION 4

Introduction: *Tax and Regulatory Issues*

FOREWORD

Here Be Dragons

Gunnar Branson, CEO, AFIRE

The Hunt Lenox Globe was created in 1504 with three Latin words printed near the east coast of the Asian continent: *hic sunt dracones*, or "here be dragons." The mapmaker presumably lacked detailed information about the region. Since then, the phrase has become a kind of shorthand sometimes used for unknown regions yet to be discovered. As far as anyone knew at that time, the region mostly unexplored by Europeans might as well have been filled with dangerous mythic creatures.

Operating in distant places around the world is not easy. It's especially challenging without a good map. Usually over time explorers create and refine guides for those that follow. Repeated experiences and connection to local communities eventually make the mysterious familiar. Risk becomes quantifiable and more certain. Opportunity becomes prudent. Today's maps, Google and otherwise, have far fewer blank spots than they did 500 years ago, and certainly there's less room for *hic sunt dracones* to be written, even in the smallest typeface.

Thirty-five years ago, as institutional real estate investors in Europe and Asia continued to explore the US property markets, they might have been tempted to write those Latin words in their own notes or investment proposals. US regulations and tax policies were different enough from home rules to trip up the best real estate deals. Metrics and accounting principles worked with different sets of assumptions. Even the markets and dealmakers had their own rules and customs. Transparency and certainty were scarce.

Much like the geographic explorers centuries before, global investors had to physically go to the places they sought to understand. They had to meet the locals and learn from experts. They slowly gained experience one project at a time. In the late 1980s, global investors came together to create AFIRE (Association of Foreign Investors in Real Estate) to share insights and help penetrate the mysteries of the US property market.

Instead of dragons, AFIRE members discovered meaningful expertise in their new world.

They began to fill in map details through meeting with each other, sharing insights, and building trust in the landscape. They shared essays, thought pieces, and research. Their collected material grew as their knowledge expanded. Shared "samizdat" style (self-published) in emails and newsletters, the articles were eventually added and updated in three-ring binders and then eventually published as a bound book.

Like ancient maps, the AFIRE guide grew organically, piece by piece, reflecting the acquired wisdom of every explorer.

The first full edition of *The AFIRE Guide to US Real Estate Investing* was edited by Richard Crystal of Winston & Strawn and released in 2003. Right from the start, it was essential reading for global investors ready to see beyond imaginary dragons to understand the actual landscape of US property markets. An updated version was completed in 2009, edited by William B. Freyer of King & Spalding, followed by Hebrew and Mandarin versions in 2012. The third updated edition, edited by Willys H. Schneider of Arnold & Porter Kaye Scholer, was released in 2017.

Over more than 20 years, *The AFIRE Guide* expanded its readership beyond institutional investors and advisors to include academics, students, and noninstitutional investors needing a "good map" of the terrain. Every edition gained new readers as the details became more accurate and more helpful for participants in the US property markets.

You now hold in your hands the fourth edition of *The AFIRE Guide*. No longer samizdat, this version published by McGraw Hill is fully revised and updated by the AFIRE research committee led by Will McIntosh of Affinius Capital and AFIRE Editor-in-Chief Benjamin van Loon. New guidance on topics that range from technology, ESG, and changing asset types, to evolving tax law and regulations are included in full.

The AFIRE Guide is free of dragons. It includes the collected wisdom from 35 years of exploration. It will evolve further, and there will likely be more editions in the future as we continue to explore and learn. As you venture into the US real estate market and invest in property for those at home, remember to study this, our latest map, *The AFIRE Guide to US Real Estate Investing*.

ACKNOWLEDGMENTS

For the fourth edition of *The AFIRE Guide,* AFIRE thanks AFIRE's Managing Director and Editor-in-Chief, Benjamin van Loon, for his work managing the creation of this entire volume; Lauren Richey, for her help with the glossary, author biographies, and other elements; Braydon Campbell with Campbell Symons Design for his design support and counsel; and the entire AFIRE membership, for making this new edition possible.

AFIRE also thanks Jim Fetgatter, founding CEO of AFIRE, for guiding the initial concept and iterations of *The AFIRE Guide*, as well as all previous *AFIRE Guide* editors, including Richard Crystal (2003), William B. Fryer and Sebastian Kaufmann (2009), and Willys H. Schneider (2016).

INTRODUCTION

The Association of Foreign Investors in Real Estate (AFIRE) is pleased to present a fourth edition of *The AFIRE Guide to US Real Estate Investing*.

Much has changed since we published the first edition of this book in the early 2000s. In 2007, we experienced the Global Financial Crisis—often referenced in this new edition—which produced extreme distress and permanent alteration in the global financial markets and the banking system. And more recently, starting in 2020, the COVID-19 pandemic sent shock waves through the world economy and triggered the largest global economic crisis in more than a century. Both events have significantly impacted the regulatory environment, lending, and the real estate markets, lending to the evolution of this book and the necessity to create a new edition, suited to the current climate.

In response to the pandemic, federal, state, and local governments in the US took steps to mitigate the spread of the virus, such as significant lockdowns, that limited economic activity, leading to a sudden and deep recession with millions of jobs lost. The US Federal Reserve took action to try to ensure that credit continued to flow to households and businesses, preventing financial market disruptions from intensifying the economic damage. Federal policymakers enacted five relief bills that provided an estimated $3.3 trillion of relief and the American Rescue Plan in 2021 added another $1.8 trillion.

As expected, the impact of the US government's significant monetary and fiscal response helped stabilize the economy but eventually led to higher inflation, peaking at 9.1 percent in 2022. The Federal Reserve then turned its focus on inflation and getting it back down to its 2 percent target range. The Fed began increasing the federal funds rate to a range of 5.25–5.5 percent in late 2023, which significantly impacted borrowing costs and the capital markets, bringing the economy back to a slower growth environment.

Higher interest rates have ultimately impacted the housing market and have translated into higher capitalization rates in the commercial real estate markets. We are currently experiencing a repricing in the US real estate markets that has yet to play out. In addition, we are seeing increased interest in investing in the more nontraditional or alternative real estate, including data centers, life sciences, and affordable housing, as well as providing debt to fill the gap created by tighter lending by the traditional real estate lenders.

The AFIRE Guide includes topics relevant to investing in institutional real estate in the US, including both direct and indirect investments. The intent is to provide the knowledge needed to assist AFIRE members in deploying their capital in the US real estate markets—even amid changing marketing conditions. *The AFIRE Guide* covers subjects from various perspectives and is intended to provide a relatively general overview of the covered topics, in practical rather than technical terms. Investors should consult specific professional advice as needed.

We have attempted to include a broad spectrum of topics pertinent to non-US-based investors in US real estate within *The AFIRE Guide*. It should be useful to those new to investing in the US real estate market as well as a valuable resource for seasoned US market investors. We trust that our members and practitioners from across the industry will find it helpful.

Substantially revised since the last edition of this book, self-published by AFIRE in 2017, *The AFIRE Guide* focuses on the current knowledge needed to prepare for investing in the US real estate market. It provides information on the commercial real estate life cycle, commercial real estate finance and partnerships, and tax and regulatory issues.

AFIRE is fortunate to have individuals among its membership with extensive experience with investing in the US real estate market. Many of these individuals have contributed as authors to this guide. AFIRE is very grateful to these authors and thanks them for their contributions. As editor, I would also like to thank Benjamin van Loon for his tireless efforts in helping bring this publication to fruition, and the leadership of AFIRE CEO Gunnar Branson and the McGraw Hill team in the publication process.

Will McIntosh, PhD,
Global Head of Research, Affinius Capital

Introduction

Preparing for Investment in the US

For decades, the US has served as a leading global destination for foreign institutional investment. Some of the main criteria supporting this role include:

1. **Stable Political and Economic Environment:** The US has a stable political and economic environment, which makes it an attractive destination for investors who seek stability and predictability in their investments.
2. **Large and Diverse Market:** The US has a large and diverse real estate market, which offers a wide range of investment opportunities in various property types, such as office buildings, apartments, industrial facilities, and retail centers.
3. **Strong Legal System:** The US has a strong legal system that protects property rights and enforces contracts, providing a high level of security for foreign investors.
4. **Favorable Tax Regimen:** The US tax regimen offers several incentives and benefits for real estate investors, such as tax deductions for mortgage interest and property depreciation.
5. **Transparent Market:** The US real estate market is transparent, with reliable data and information available to investors, making it easier to make informed investment decisions.
6. **High Returns:** The US real estate market has historically provided high returns for investors, relative to other nations, making it an attractive destination for foreign institutional investment.

With these criteria in mind, this section of *The AFIRE Guide* serves as an introduction to the US investment landscape.

In Chapter 1.1, the authors present a four-section approach that covers the basic purpose of an investment strategy, the foundational elements of a successful investment strategy, a methodology for creating an investment strategy, and lessons learned from investors who have spent many years selecting or formulating investment strategies.

Chapter 1.2 provides a broad overview for international investors, discussing the ownership rules, legal systems, and customs applicable to US real estate, which is necessary to assimilate advice and assemble the correct team of experts for a successful investment strategy. The most common forms of interests in US real estate are fee-simple absolute ownership, leases and leasehold estates, and easements and licenses.

Chapter 1.3 outlines the tax considerations, including blocker corporations and real estate investment trusts (REITs), associated with a real estate fund, which can vary depending on the level of the property, property holding company, fund, investor, or fund manager/general partner.

Chapter 1.4 introduces the main variances of US real estate markets, generally labeled by the investment community to be primary (or gateway), secondary, and tertiary markets, and why investors typically focus on subsets of these markets, how to best approach each market, and related benefits and challenges.

Chapter 1.5 discusses the integration of environmental, social, and governance (ESG) factors into real estate investment decision-making. Incorporating ESG considerations into commercial real estate asset valuation can help investors and asset managers make better-informed decisions, reduce risk, and drive long-term value creation.

Chapter 1.6 details the property types and sectors that generally attract institutional-scale investment in the US, including the four "main" types—multifamily (or residential), industrial, office, and retail—as well as growing nontraditional sectors, such as data centers, life science, self-storage, healthcare (senior living and medical office), and student housing.

Chapter 1.7 explains the role of a broker and investment advisor for US real estate transactions. International investors almost always have different needs than domestic sources of capital. To be successful, the investment advisor must have the ability to understand the transaction from the perspective of the cross-border investor.

Similarly, Chapter 1.8 explains the role of an attorney and tax advisor in these same processes. The purpose of this chapter is to describe these roles and outline the various factors non-US-based investors should consider when selecting legal and accounting advisors for real estate transactions.

Finally, Chapter 1.9 discusses the role of professional and trade associations in providing an entry point for non-US investors into US real estate. This chapter explores some of the main commercial real estate associations and other groups in the US and how they can benefit institutional investors based outside the country.

Formulating an Investment Strategy

Sound Decision-Making, Conviction, and Creativity

Andy Lusk, Chief Investment Officer, Lionstone Investments

Hans Nordby, Head of Analytical Research, Lionstone Investments

At its essence, formulating an investment strategy is the art of seizing opportunity while mitigating risk. It is one of the biggest challenges faced by investors.

From a wide array of information, an investor must determine how to achieve attractive returns relative to risk, usually in the face of stiff competition.[1] The purpose of this chapter is to briefly lay out an approach to formulating an investment strategy for US real estate.

We have organized this chapter into four sections. The first section explains the basic purpose of an investment strategy. The second section suggests the foundational elements of a successful investment strategy. The third section offers a methodology for creating an investment strategy. And finally, the final section summarizes lessons learned from a large sample of investors who have spent many years selecting or formulating investment strategies.

THE PURPOSE OF AN INVESTMENT STRATEGY— SOUND DECISION-MAKING

The basic purpose of an investment strategy is to provide a firm foundation for your decision-making structure; that is, a rationale upon which to make decisions with conviction, regardless of whether other market participants agree.[2]

In today's world, we have instantaneous access to massive amounts of information and data. A successful investor must know how to cull the best, most relevant information; analyze that data; and then convert it into a strategy. Once information turns into strategy, it can lead to sound decision-making during market cycles, providing immunity from the herd mentality that often suffocates independent thinking. Information synthesis requires frameworks and a focus that generally is only possible with a well-articulated point of view that inevitably underpins a good investment strategy.

Due to the generally fragmented nature of the real estate industry, many decisions are based on relationships formed through private transactions and/or with localized players. However, well-constructed, clearly defined investment strategies can also reinforce those relationships while achieving better investment results. In other words, great ideas support great relationships, while great relationships do not always support great ideas.

THE FOUNDATION OF AN EFFECTIVE INVESTMENT STRATEGY—BUILDING CONVICTION

An effective strategy leads to investments that collectively produce attractive **risk-adjusted returns**.[3] Every investment strategy should have three foundational elements: an overarching investment philosophy, informed intuition born from experience, and the ability to process information into knowledge faster than the rest of the market.

Investment Philosophy

A profitable investment strategy should be supported by an investment philosophy that defines the purpose of an investment and the basic principles for making decisions. The investment objective (e.g., preservation of capital vs. maximization of capital) will point to the most appropriate strategy.

In terms of decision-making principles, traditional value investors might say that the number one goal of investing is never to lose capital. More contemporary investors might adhere to the principle of only investing in underestimated assets or massive arbitrage opportunities. There is not necessarily a single correct purpose or set of decision-making principles, but an effective investment strategy is better if it rests upon a well-understood **investment philosophy**.

Informed Intuition

A fundamental element of an effective investment strategy is what we call "informed intuition." Some call this experience. Others call it pure gut instinct. In either case, a successful investment strategy is often rooted in historical realities, recalling the past to predict the future more successfully or accurately. Market cycles are inevitable; a good investment strategy contemplates, anticipates, and prepares for this reality. As Mark Twain said, history does not always repeat itself, but it often rhymes.

Processing Information into Knowledge

The best investment strategies are based on a thorough knowledge of the underlying drivers of value and risk for any given industry. In real estate, this requires understanding the supply and demand for assets and for capital.

The opportunity and curse of our time is instantaneous access to ubiquitous data: the market knows everything and nothing at the same time. The challenge of today's competitive, data-driven environment is to process that information quickly and accurately to seize lucrative opportunities and avoid those that are unprofitable. Accomplishing this requires a data-sorting process that is rapidly becoming the norm in the real estate industry, especially as more market participants realize that approaches to real estate investing can be as analytical and sophisticated as the tactics long employed for other asset classes (i.e., stocks, bonds).[4]

In the end, an investment strategy built on these three foundational elements leads to one critically important result: conviction. Conviction is the ability to go forward (or not) when one is alone at a moment of truth. That is how a well-constructed investment strategy—one built upon an investment philosophy informed by intuition and knowledge—can lead to success.

FORMULATING AN INVESTMENT STRATEGY— A CREATIVE AND DISCIPLINED PROCESS

The formation of an investment strategy is a fundamental skill of an investment firm. This is, first and foremost, a creative process. However, it is also a disciplined step-by-step procedure to construct powerful conclusions. A well-defined approach increases the probability that ideas are considered, properly vetted, and ultimately converted into strategies that can be executed. This process mimics the scientific method: start with a thesis, test it with data and research, refine it, and test it again. If the thesis proves to have merit, then execute it by matching the appropriate talent, capital, and structure to that strategy.

Step 1: Idea Generation—Explore Data

Ideas for new investment strategies can come from many places. Some are formed out of experience, others from our knowledge of demand drivers or capital market inefficiencies that we see in our existing portfolios, and even others come from market research.

Whatever the source, it is wise to enable and encourage the creative process to flourish, thereby allowing good ideas to surface. It's a best practice to start the process by asking questions that lead to understanding where demand is strong for real estate—especially in the long run—and where capital markets may not fully understand these trends.

Questions that can help at the idea-generation stage include:

- What changes are happening that may usher in a new era in the environment for real estate investing? In other words, how will the future differ from the past in terms of society, capital markets, and demographics?
- What industries and locations in the country are producing goods and services that are demanded globally?
- What industries and locations are vulnerable to disruption due to major technological changes?
- What are the real estate preferences of the people working in thriving industries? Where do these people prefer to live, work, and play?
- Which of these trends do capital markets not fully understand so they misprice them?

The first question is overlooked by many who act as if existing patterns will continue indefinitely. However, the answers to this question were essential to navigating the shift that began in 2020 with the advent of the pandemic and the aging of millennials into a different phase of their lives.

During the 2010 to 2019 **economic cycle**, **millennials** had an average age of 26, and they displayed the real estate habits of young, single people. In contrast, in the 2020s, they have generally reached an inflection points in their lives with an average age of 36 over the decade, and their preferences drive which submarkets get the population and income growth that boost real estate values. At the same time, the pandemic made remote work viable, accelerating the move of millennials from the coastal cities that suited them in their twenties to states that suited them better with milder weather, more affordable housing, shorter commutes, and other characteristics valued by knowledge workers in their thirties. The combination of the pandemic and the millennials "growing up" changed demand for space in the built environment in such profound ways that real estate investment in the 2020s has become distinctly different than in previous decades. As a result, setting your investment strategy solely based on historic analyses would have been a bad strategy. As we conduct research to answer these questions, we develop hypotheses for new investment ideas. The next step is to test these ideas.

Step 2: Test the Idea—Find Sustainable Patterns

As noted, there is a tremendous amount of data on real estate markets that can be mined to test the ideas generated in step one.

We can test whether an asset or set of assets with particular geographic and/or physical attributes outperforms or underperforms the market on the basis of occupancy or growth of rental income and value. We can use sophisticated software to overlay a wide variety of demographic, economic, and real estate market data to identify national niches trending toward higher or lower long-term demand.

By identifying patterns, we can predict the evolution of a submarket with characteristics similar to those in a submarket across the country. With this information, we can derive conclusions that give us confidence in a thesis.

Of course, epoch-making changes in the economic environment can't be back-tested. That's why we identify themes to reflect where those changes will start contributing to cities' economic strength and higher real estate valuations. That means looking at the broader economic and property-use environment, economic growth of different cities, and the property investments and submarkets within a city best positioned to benefit from that growth.

Step 3: Refine the Idea—Create an Effective Investment Strategy

Once a hypothesis is tested and validated by research, then it moves to the next phase: converting it into a repeatable strategy, preferably on a large, national scale. If it turns out that the idea is good—but not repeatable or large-scale—we may not pursue it. If it does fit these criteria, we will ask a series of questions about our suitability in executing the strategy. For example, do we have access to all the skills required to be successful? Can our investors avail themselves of this particular strategy in a more efficient way? Who will our competitors be, and what advantages will we have that they lack? If we conclude that the strategy works, we proceed to the next step.

Step 4: Transform Patterns into Framework—Language Is Power

Once we have vetted a good idea, we develop a framework and common language to determine where we devote our time, energy, and investment decisions. Effective frameworks have all or most of the following components:

- Clear, written parameters based on market, location, and product type
- Screening methods for efficient sourcing (i.e., focus and market expertise)
- Pricing discipline (i.e., constantly comparing market price vs. intrinsic valuations based on our knowledge of the market, including replacement costs and rental growth prospects)

An investment language to guide discussions and ultimately actions is integral to executing at the highest level.

Step 5: Align Strategy with Capital—Form an Optimal Team

With a framework and investment language established, the next step is to determine the form of capital and structure that best suits the strategy. Considerations include the optimal time period for the investment strategy, the overall risk of the strategy, and tax implications—all of which are covered elsewhere in this book.

Both managers and investors benefit from starting with a few fundamental questions to point us in the right direction:

- Is the strategy best suited for a perpetual or shorter-duration vehicle?
- What structure best aligns the interests of all parties?
- What is the best decision-making structure?

In most cases, investors and managers will operate in a highly competitive marketplace. Acting with conviction and urgency will require team alignment and streamlined decision-making. All internal staff, service providers, and everyone on the investment and management team—from board members at the capital provider to accountants at the property level—must be aligned in decision-making and execution. The simpler and more elegant the strategy, the more unified and nimble the entire team will be.

Step 6: Check Investment Strategy—Three Essential Qualities

Once an investment strategy has been created, it is necessary to check for three essential qualities of successful strategies: market cycle sensitivity, scalability, and competitiveness.

Market Cycle Sensitivity: Real estate investing is subject to dramatic swings in both rental and cap rates. Effective strategies need to consider market cyclicality.

Scalability: Whether one chooses public or private market vehicles or debt or equity investment structures, the execution of a strategy should be straightforward and large-scale enough to merit the infrastructure needed to field a winning team.

Competitiveness: An investment strategy ultimately must produce investment returns that are competitive on a risk-adjusted basis with other opportunities.

Finally, a viable investment strategy must generate excellent results at each step of the investment process—great ideas, efficient sourcing, attractive pricing, competitive capital structure, and risk-focused execution.[5] A strategy meeting these criteria will earn a position in the marketplace and attract investors.

A NOTE TO INVESTORS—KNOW THYSELF

The most successful commercial real estate investors have a well-understood purpose, a clear governance structure, and a consistent culture. They know themselves well at all levels, and they tend not to change significantly in these three categories. They have stable balance sheets, their staff turnover is low, and their judgments are mature throughout cycles. As a result, they create or select investment strategies that are consistent with their purpose, align with partners who understand that purpose and culture, and then simply repeat the strategies as opportunities present themselves. Great ideas then support great relationships.

Some of the unifying principles shared by successful investors are based around purpose, governance, and culture:

Purpose: Emphasize the ultimate purpose of your capital. Everyone benefits from being reminded that we are serving teachers, universities, pensioners, and others who depend on our fiduciary duty and investment acumen.

Governance: Clear decision-making structures that are well understood internally, as well as by outside partners, lead to better execution. Opacity is confusing and creates friction.

Culture: People who allocate capital generally tend to spend much more time evaluating the culture of the recipients of their capital than nurturing their own cultures. As such, the most successful investors have well-developed cultures that attract and retain high-quality people internally and hire the best managers in the business.

DEFINING STRATEGY

The goal of this chapter was first to state the prerequisites and the critical characteristics of any investment strategy and then describe the creation of an investment strategy.

The definition of "strategy" demands the use of all forces (in this case, resources of time, talent, and "treasure") for large-scale, long-range planning, and development to ensure investment success. Ultimately, the formation of a strategy is both art and science, as it incorporates market data and investor characteristics to achieve success, which is internally and externally defined.

On the one hand, the current age offers the challenge of unlimited data and instantaneous communications. On the other hand, economic and social disruptions now occur at a rate unprecedented in modern civilization. The way that space is used, its related value, and the vehicle in which it is owned will no doubt adapt. It is a stock pickers' market, but it is also a market where investors will win and lose on a large scale. Pursuing well-developed investment strategies aligned with an investor's purposes dramatically increases the odds of long-term success—especially in US real estate.

NOTES

1. Miller, Norman G., and Peng Liu. "Risk-Adjusted Performance Measurement for Commercial Real Estate." *Journal of Real Estate Research 22*, no. 3 (2001): 239–266.
2. Fisher, Jeffrey D., and Robert White Jr. "A Framework for Real Estate Investment Management." *Journal of Real Estate Research 16*, no. 3 (1998): 309–326.
3. Hartzell, David, John S. Hekman, and Mike Miles. "Real Estate Returns and Inflation." *Real Estate Economics 14*, no. 3 (1986): 363–384.
4. Ling, David C., and Andy Naranjo. "The Integration of Commercial Real Estate Markets and Stock Markets." *Real Estate Economics 28*, no. 1 (2000): 5–35.
5. Miles, Mike, and John R. Ezzell. "The Weighted Average Cost of Capital, Perfect Capital Markets, and Project Life: A Clarification." *Journal of Financial and Quantitative Analysis 20*, no. 3 (1985): 367–375.

The Basics of US Real Estate Law

Rules Applying to Investment and Operations

Kris Ferranti, Partner, Shearman & Sterling

Jonathan Newman, Partner, Shearman & Sterling

For many international investors, forays into US real estate markets force a confrontation with an unfamiliar set of laws and government regulations and common practices. An adequate understanding of these is necessary to implement a successful investment strategy. While a prudent investor will engage attorneys, brokers, accountants, engineers, architects, and other real estate experts to render advice, the investor also must have a basic understanding of the ownership rules, legal systems, and customs applicable to US real estate in order to assemble the correct team of experts and to assimilate and understand the experts' advice.

TYPES OF REAL ESTATE INTERESTS

The most common forms of interests in US real estate are **fee-simple absolute ownership**, **leases and leasehold estates**, and **easements and licenses**. With a few limited exceptions, these interests are obtained by grants or conveyances contained in legal documents.

Fee-Simple Absolute Ownership

A fee-simple absolute interest in real estate (also known as **fee simple or freehold**) is the most comprehensive form of ownership and is conveyed by deed. In its purest form, fee simple absolute ownership is perpetual and includes all rights and interests in the owned real estate, including ownership of the land, all buildings and structures attached to the land, and all rights to minerals, timber, and other products. However, fee simple is often acquired subject to certain preexisting rights of others in the real estate, usually consisting of easement rights, rights of tenants under leases, and rights of third parties under other written agreements. Typically, a purchaser of US real estate will obtain a search of the title to the property to identify these preexisting rights and will obtain title insurance ensuring that the state of title is as shown on the title search.[1]

For example, a common US real estate transaction will involve an investor acquiring fee-simple ownership of a land parcel that contains a multifloor office building with multiple occupants. In such a transaction, the acquisition will typically be subject to the rights of the building occupants (and their respective leases), rights of utilities providers (e.g., electricity, water, natural gas, and communications), and services to the building under easements granted over the real estate. The parcel may also be subject to certain restrictions on its use provided for in private agreements with neighboring landowners or other third parties. Most often, such third-party rights are beneficial, adding value to the real estate because they provide income and services to the owner and impose orderly use requirements on both the owner and surrounding landowners.

However, other rights to which fee-simple ownership may be subject—such as liens by providers of materials and services; rights of lenders under mortgages and other security instruments; and easements, restrictions, and other rights potentially incompatible with a new investor's proposed use—are often detrimental and should be eliminated prior to acquisition.[2]

Leases and Leasehold Estates

While fee-simple ownership typically has unlimited duration, a **leasehold estate** is an interest, usually granted by a fee-simple owner, that entitles the leasehold estate owner to possession of the real estate only for a specified "term." In its purest form, a leasehold estate entitles its owner, during the duration of the term, to all the rights of possession and use that are held by the fee simple owner.

Most US leasehold estates, however, are created by lengthy lease agreements that provide (1) for the rights and obligations of the landlord and tenant and (2) for restrictions on the uses and activities that can be conducted on the leased real estate. While a leasehold estate is a powerful real property interest, it may not survive a landlord or tenant bankruptcy because the bankrupt party may have the right to accept or reject the lease in bankruptcy.[3]

Leases may take many forms, including ground leases, space leases (which may be gross or net leases), and subleases.

A **ground lease** is a lease of land, usually undeveloped, on which the tenant has the right to erect buildings or other structures. Under this arrangement, the tenant will have fee-simple ownership of the buildings and other structures it erects, and upon the expiration of the ground lease, the fee-simple ownership of the buildings and structures will revert to the landlord (unless the ground lease grants to the tenant the right to remove them at the end of the lease term). Ground leases are useful vehicles for fee-simple owners of real estate who desire to hold their land in connection with long-term financial planning and want to produce income from the land, but do not possess either the will or the expertise to construct and operate income-producing improvements on the land. Ground leases are also commonly used for the development of land owned by state and local governments that want a private party to construct and own facilities they need, or for development or rehabilitation of land that a government is restricted or prohibited by law from selling to a private party. Ground leases are useful to developers of real estate because they eliminate large up-front land acquisition costs.

Ground leases usually have lengthy durations so that development costs invested by tenants can be fully recouped, with profits, over the useful life of the buildings and structures erected on the land. Depending on the type of development, typical terms of ground leases range from 20 to 99 or more years, with 40 to 60 years being common. Most tenants with ground leases will insist that their leases be "financeable." This entails separate rights in favor of the tenant's lenders to receive written notice of, and cure defaults by, the tenant under the ground lease, prior to any landlord action that may terminate or cause a forfeiture of the tenant's leasehold.

While ground leases serve a useful purpose in US real estate activities, leasehold estates are most often created in improved real estate. A lease of improved real estate may cover a parcel of land and all land improvements, or it may cover only a portion of a building located on the land. Many leasehold estates created in both land and improvements are called **triple-net leases**, under which the landlord generally has no obligations other than to ensure that the tenant's possession of the leased property is not interfered with by third parties. In these types of leases, the tenant has all indicia of ownership, aside from legal fee-simple ownership, and is required to perform all responsibilities and make all payments relating to the leased property that otherwise would be the responsibility of the landlord. Under a triple-net lease, the landlord is to receive the rent "net" of costs relating to the real estate, such as taxes, utilities, and maintenance costs—all of which are paid by the tenant.

Space leases, which are leases of portions or spaces within a building, are the most common form of leasehold estates. They are used in buildings with more than one tenant, such as multitenant office buildings, shopping centers, industrial parks, and apartment buildings. These leases are usually on a "gross lease" basis and require the landlord to provide certain utilities and services (e.g., electricity, water, HVAC [heating, ventilation, air conditioning], and general maintenance), with the tenant being required to reimburse the landlord on a periodic basis for its *pro rata* share of the costs of these services (usually determined by reference to the size of the tenant's leased space).

Finally, **subleases** are leasehold estates granted by a tenant under an **overlease**. A tenant cannot grant any more rights to a subtenant than are granted under the overlease. As such, the sublease will be subject to the terms of the overlease, will not extend beyond the term of the overlease, and unless a separate agreement is made between the subtenant and the overlandlord, the sublease will terminate upon any termination of the overlease.

Easements and Licenses

While a fee-simple absolute ownership or a leasehold estate in real estate usually entitles the owner to exclusive use and possession of the real estate, the holder of an **easement or license** typically has no such rights. Easements and licenses are granted for specific purposes, such as the installation and use of utilities or the use of roadways and accessways. Unless the document creating the easement or license expressly states otherwise, the owner of any estate in the real estate may continue to use and occupy the real estate covered by the easement or license in any manner consistent with the rights granted in the easement or license.

Easements and licenses can be either exclusive or nonexclusive, granting a person or entity (or multiple persons or entities) easement or license rights in the same real estate.

Easements are generally considered as *interests* and not *estates* in land and are usually perpetual in duration, although they may also be of limited duration. Such **appurtenant leases** are granted as appendages to fee-simple or leasehold estates and provide additional rights, such as access or utility services, to benefit the fee-simple or leasehold owner. Easements not granted to benefit a particular parcel of land are commonly called **easements in gross** and are usually granted in connection with the provision of public utility or telecommunications services.

Licenses generally are not considered to be interests in land and are commonly described as the right to enter on the land of another and perform acts that would otherwise constitute trespass. Licenses are usually limited in duration, and if they are not, are revocable by the granting landowner at any time.

Real Estate as a Security Interest

Although it is not typically considered to be an interest in land, an investor may make a loan that is secured by US real estate (commonly referred to as a **mortgage**) rather than making a direct investment in real estate. If the borrower fails to make payments on the mortgage or otherwise defaults on other terms of the loan, the lender may force a sale of the property through a foreclosure procedure. In the US, procedures for foreclosure differ by state. Some states require a court procedure, or a **judicial foreclosure**. Other states allow a **nonjudicial foreclosure** by a public auction without a court proceeding, unless the borrower contests the sale. The timeline for a foreclosure also differs significantly among each state and even among jurisdictions within a state. Some courts are notoriously backlogged in foreclosure matters, particularly during times of economic distress.

Where the lender and borrower agree to avoid a foreclosure proceeding, the borrower may turn the real estate over to the lender through a deed in lieu of foreclosure. If a foreclosure proceeding is contested by the borrower, a court may consider a number of equitable common law and statutory defenses. As such, it may be difficult to obtain a foreclosure judgment for a nonmonetary default unless it is clear there is significant impairment affecting the value of the real estate securing the loan.

OWNERSHIP OF CERTAIN PORTIONS OF REAL ESTATE

Air and Subterranean Rights

Generally, the owner of a parcel of real estate in the US owns not only the surface of the parcel, but also all rights to the sky in a direct vertical line above and in the earth in a direct vertical line below the surface of the parcel. The owner of a single parcel may divide these rights into subparcels and convey them separately to others. For example, it's common for an owner of a parcel of land to retain fee-simple absolute ownership of the surface *and* the air above the parcel, to a specified height, in order to construct and operate a shopping center. This owner may also convey fee-simple absolute ownership of the remaining air rights above that specified height to another entity (or entities) for the construction and operation of an office or apartment building.

While not unusual in the US, this transaction is extremely complex and requires comprehensive agreements among the various interest owners to govern the construction, use, and operation of the portions of the real estate owned by each of them, as well as the assistance of a highly qualified engineering firm to properly create the subparcels.

Mineral, Timber, and Similar Rights

Owners of real estate in the US may also separate and convey independently the rights to the **emblements** or products located on and produced from the real estate, such as crops, timber, and mineral and resource rights (e.g., oil, natural gas, coal, precious ores, metals, sand, and clay). These emblements are often conveyed by means of **farming**, **timber**, or **mineral rights leases**, which are specialized leases that do not grant the full set of possessory rights provided in a customary leasehold estate. These specialized leases often more akin to licenses that allow the lessees to enter onto the real estate for a specified purpose. In some states where mining activities are abundant, it is common for rights to oil, gas, coal, and other minerals to be owned, sold, conveyed, and otherwise dealt with separately from surface rights.

TYPES OF COMMON OWNERSHIP

Tenants-in-Common

Real estate may be owned by multiple parties through ownership as **tenants-in-common**. In this arrangement, each tenant-in-common owns an undivided percentage interest in the real estate. Each tenant-in-common has the right to possession of all of the real estate, and no tenant-in-common may use or occupy a portion of the real estate to the exclusion of other tenants-in-common. Each tenant-in-common is entitled to receive a portion of the rents, other income, and emblements derived from the real estate. A tenant-in-common may convey or transfer its undivided percentage interest to another party without the consent or joinder of the other tenants-in-common, but the transferring owner cannot legally convey more than its own percentage interest.

Tenants-in-common may choose to enter into a written agreement among themselves that governs the use and operation of the real estate and establishes a procedure by which they can make joint decisions relating to the real estate. Because of a variety of legal and practical considerations, however, persons who desire to own commercial real estate jointly are likely to avoid a tenancy-in-common and form a corporation, partnership, limited liability company, or other legal entity.[4]

Joint Ventures, REITs, and Other Entity Ownership

Common ownership of investment real estate in the US frequently is done via a joint venture (JV) among parties who will have specified percentage interests in the venture. The JV may take the form of a partnership, a limited liability company (LLC), a corporation, or other legal entity. JVs are common where parties wish to enter into a business together only for the purpose of owning and developing or operating a single property and to exist only during the period of such ownership.[5]

Real estate investment trusts (REITs) may also be attractive to non-US investors as an investment mechanism that minimizes or avoids US federal income tax liability. A REIT is an entity that owns or finances income-producing real estate, and the entity qualifies as a REIT by meeting specific requirements as to the assets it owns, the sources of its income, its ownership composition, and its distribution of funds.[6]

Commingled Funds

As an alternative to a direct investment in real estate, an investor may choose to invest in a commingled fund that invests in real estate. Funds may be open-end or closed-end funds and may invest in real estate equity or debt.[7]

Condominium Ownership

The condominium form of ownership is another type of common ownership of US real estate. Unlike most others, this form of ownership is created through a statutory scheme, rather than pursuant to common law, and has similarities to strata schemes in other countries.

Although different in each state, the process for creating a condo typically consists of creating units of space within a parcel of real property by filing certain condo plats and building plans in the public real estate records. Units thus created are treated for legal and tax purposes as separate "parcels" of real property and can be sold and conveyed to third parties.

All portions of the real estate that are not units, typically called common areas, are reserved for the joint use of all the owners of units. Condo statutes also typically include "special" or "limited" common areas (e.g., parking areas, balconies, and porches) that are reserved for the exclusive use of individual unit owners. Each unit owner in the condo owns, in addition to its unit, an undivided percentage interest in the common areas.

Condos are typically governed by a condo association whose members are the unit owners and subject to the provisions of the condo's declaration, by-laws, and rules and regulations covering permissible uses and activities within the units, common areas, and limited common areas.

REAL ESTATE TITLE RECORDS AND TITLE INSURANCE

US Real Estate Title Records

As a general rule, documents that affect title to or ownership of real estate are recorded in the public real estate records of the county or city within a state where real estate is located. A properly executed deed from a transferor to a transferee is the document used to transfer real estate. The transferee is not required to record such a deed but almost always does because the recording of the deed in the public records perfects the transferee's ownership interest by providing legal notice to all third parties of such ownership. Absent such recording, most jurisdictions will not enforce property rights against a subsequent purchaser who acquires the property for value, without notice of the unrecorded property interest and who records their interest first. To obtain title insurance, the insured property right must be recorded.

Prior to purchasing real estate or making a loan secured by an interest in real estate, a purchaser or lender will request a title insurance company to perform a search of the public real estate records to identify the legal owner of the property and any matters that affect title to the property.[8] The title examiner will identify who has received the most recent conveyance of title, as well as any other recorded instruments that affect title to the parcel. After the examination is complete, the attorney or title examiner will usually prepare an abstract or certificate of title that contains the name of the record owner and any other matters affecting the record owner's title.

Because of the potential for human error in the indexing and examination of the public real estate records, almost all investors in US real estate now obtain **title insurance**.

Title Insurance

Upon closing the purchase or mortgage loan transaction, a title insurance policy will be issued by the title insurance company in reliance on the comprehensive title examination described above. The title insurance policy ensures that the condition or state of title to a parcel of real estate is as described in the policy.

The policy issued to a purchaser is the **owner's policy** while the policy issued to a lender is a **loan policy**. Where the transaction involves a leasehold interest, such as a ground lease, it is common for the ground tenant to obtain a leasehold insurance policy and for the lender to obtain a loan policy on such leasehold.

The fee for the title insurance policy is in the form of a one-time premium based on the amount insured (i.e., the purchase price in an owner's policy or the amount of a loan in a mortgagee's policy). Title insurance premiums in **published-rate states** are established by regulatory officials, and companies may not charge premiums less than the published rates. In **negotiated-rate states**, companies are free to negotiate premiums. Customs differ among jurisdictions as to whether the purchaser or the seller pays the premium. Coverage under a title insurance policy continues for an unlimited time and provides coverage for claims for which the insured party may have legal liability to others even after the insured party no longer owns the insured real estate.

Pursuant to the title insurance policy, the title insurance company agrees to indemnify the insured party against any losses, up to the amount specified in the policy, if the title to the real estate is not in the condition or state reflected in the policy. For example, suppose an investor acquires a parcel of real property, and then a public utility company begins construction of a large electrical transmission line across the parcel under rights granted by a former owner. The easement rights are not reflected in the investor's title insurance policy because the person who examined the title to the parcel in connection with the issuance of the policy could not locate the easement document, due to an indexing error in the public real estate records. In such a case, the title insurance company would be required to pay the investor for any losses, including loss of value to the real estate incurred by the investor as a result of the existence of the easement.

Title insurance also provides coverage against claims that cannot be revealed by the public records, such as forgeries and unauthorized conveyances that occurred prior to the effective date of the policy. In addition, it provides for the payment of attorney's fees and other costs of defense in connection with any claim, even if the claim is not valid.

Most title insurance is issued based on standard policy forms and endorsements written and maintained by the American Land Title Association.[9] In addition to the basic insurance provisions, each policy excludes from coverage claims arising from certain standard items, such as governmental regulations, police powers, environmental laws, and the rights of creditors. A title insurance policy also excludes from coverage any claims not disclosed by the public real estate records but known to the insured and not disclosed prior to its issuance of the policy.

In addition to the exclusions, each title insurance policy also contains certain exceptions to coverage. These consist of matters affecting title to the insured real estate revealed by the examination of title and certain "standard" exceptions, which generally address certain specified rights affecting title that cannot be ascertained from the public real estate records.[10]

GOVERNMENTAL REGULATIONS GOVERNING ACQUISITION, OWNERSHIP, DEVELOPMENT, AND OPERATION OF REAL ESTATE

Real estate law in the US is generally a matter of state common law. There are many similarities among the real estate laws of the various states, but enough differences exist that it is common practice for an investor's team of advisors to include an attorney in the state in which the real estate being acquired is located. Federal laws and regulations also come into play, particularly when real estate is acquired by a foreign investor. There are state and federal laws that limit or prohibit the acquisition of US real property (or impose reporting requirements) by nonresident foreign persons, or entities that are controlled by nonresident foreign persons. Many of these laws apply only to mineral resources or to agricultural property.[11]

Many of these regulations are covered in greater detail in Section Four of this book, but generally, the following are the most common federal regulations applicable to the acquisition of real estate by foreign investors:

Know Your Client (KYC) Processes

To combat money laundering, illicit finance, and terrorism, US regulations require financial institutions to follow a **know your client (KYC)** procedure to ensure that each financial institution understands the identify of its clients. Borrowing funds for a real estate acquisition will trigger a bank's KYC procedures.[12]

Foreign Investment Risk Review Modernization Act of 2018 (FIRRMA)

The **Committee on Foreign Investment in the United States (CFIUS)** is authorized under FIRRMA to review certain acquisitions of real estate by a foreign person if the acquisition presents a national security risk (e.g., properties in or near US air or seaport facilities, US government or military installations, or locations where a foreign person could obtain intelligence on activities at a military or other government property).

A purchase, lease, or concession of covered real estate by a foreign person may be reviewed by CFIUS if the foreign person will acquire any three of four property rights: (1) the right to access the covered real estate, (2) the right to exclude others from physically accessing the covered real estate, (3) the right to improve or develop the covered real estate, and (4) the right to attach fixed or immovable structures or objects to the covered real estate. It is up to the parties to the transaction to determine whether a national security risk might exist. The parties may then opt to voluntarily submit a filing to CFIUS for review.

Foreign Investment in Real Property Tax Act (FIRPTA)

Under US law, income derived from ownership or disposition of US real estate is generally taxable. This includes rental income as well as any gain on the disposition of real estate. As a mechanism to capture taxes due upon the disposition of US real estate by foreign persons,[13] FIRPTA requires a purchaser of US real estate from a foreign seller to withhold and send to the Internal Revenue Service (IRS) a specified percentage (generally 15 percent) of the amount realized on the disposition. Certain states impose similar taxes and withholding requirements for real estate dispositions within the state.[14]

Federal Reporting Requirements

The **Agricultural Foreign Investment Disclosure Act (AFIDA)** and accompanying regulations provides for the collection of information pertaining to foreign ownership in US agricultural land. The regulations require foreign investors to report interests in US agricultural land to the U.S. Department of Agriculture. The **International Investment and Trade in Services Survey Act (IITSSA)** provides for the collection of information pertaining to international investment in US businesses. If a foreign person or entity owns 10 percent or more of the voting interest in the US entity,[15] IITSSA requires that US businesses report all foreign investment, direct or indirect, to the **U.S. Bureau of Economic Analysis (BEA)**.

Environmental Laws

US environmental laws are primarily under the jurisdiction of the **U.S. Environmental Protection Agency (EPA)** while the **U.S. Army Corps of Engineers (USACE)** regulates water bodies and wetlands, and the **U.S. Fish and Wildlife Service (FWS)** has jurisdiction over matters relating to endangered species.

State and local authorities may have comparable authorities that regulate environmental matters within the state's jurisdiction. And with the current drive for cities to take action on climate change, more and more cities are issuing regulations relating to environmental issues.[16]

Purchasers typically retain environmental attorneys and/or consultants to review the environmental status of the property a purchaser is considering acquiring. Environmental assessments are generally done in phases, and most commercial properties will include a **Phase I Environmental Site Assessment (ESA)**. A Phase I investigation is typically a non-invasive examination of the property and consists of observations at the site; researching relevant federal, state, or other relevant regulatory databases; review of historical property and relevant state and local agency records; and interviews with knowledgeable personnel of the owner, neighbors, and others who may have relevant information concerning the site. Depending on the results of the assessment, further investigation may be conducted in a Phase II ESA, which may include soil, water, and other physical testing.

Zoning and Land Use

Zoning and land-use laws are enacted and administered by municipalities and counties to regulate the use of real estate within their boundaries.

Excepting some sparsely populated areas, almost every municipality and county in the US has enacted a zoning ordinance, most in conjunction with a comprehensive development plan. The zoning and development plans together have the effect of dividing an enacting community into zones or districts within each of which only certain uses are allowed. Common zones or districts are those that may allow for such uses as single-family residential (individual homes); multifamily residential (apartment buildings and residential condo complexes); commercial, office; industrial; and mixed use (combination).

Zoning ordinances usually differentiate as well within these zones or districts. Zoning may also provide for special districts, such as those containing landmarks, historic structures, or preservation measures. In addition to providing for permitted uses, a typical zoning ordinance also imposes minimum requirements for each parcel of real estate. Such requirements can encompass a variety of use and development issues, typically addressing lot size, density of use, parking, building setbacks, height restrictions, ancillary structures, and front-, side-, and rear-yard requirements.

Finally, a zoning ordinance may provide for some special types of uses (e.g., communications towers, cemeteries, junkyards, and landfills) requiring special-use permits, usually obtained from the enacting community only after public hearings and approval by the governing body of the community.

Uses that were legal at the time the zoning ordinance was created or modified to prohibit the use will usually be permitted until the use is discontinued for a specified period, or until any structure on the property is removed or destroyed. Variances and special exceptions from the requirements of the ordinance may be granted to provide relief from requirements that create an unnecessary hardship on an owner because of extraordinary conditions pertaining to the size, shape, or topography of the real estate.

Before making any real estate investment in the US, an investor should confirm that the real estate complies with applicable zoning laws and seek legal advice to determine whether a noncompliant or nonconforming use should lead it to consider abandoning the proposed investment, or whether rezoning, variance, or other remedial action should be undertaken prior to making the investment.

Building Codes/Safety Requirements

In almost all areas of the US, improved real estate must comply with local building and life-safety codes. These codes consist of extremely detailed construction requirements for structural components, electrical, plumbing and mechanical systems, interior and exterior finishes, and building systems (such as fire alarm and sprinkler systems) and provide for the safety of occupants. Most of these codes are prepared by nonprofit trade organizations (such as the International Code Council), formed by and composed of experts in the real estate and construction industries. Local communities adopt these codes, sometimes with modifications to adapt them to local construction practices.

In most areas in the US, construction of a building cannot lawfully be performed unless the company performing the construction has been issued and maintains in effect a valid building permit. One condition to the issuance of a building permit is approval by certain officials of construction plans and specifications that, if followed, would cause the completed building to comply with the local building codes and life safety-requirements. Once a building permit is issued and construction begins, local governmental officials (commonly called building inspectors) conduct periodic inspections to ensure that the building is being constructed in conformity with the approved plans and specifications, building codes, and life-safety requirements. A final inspection will determine whether the completed building has been constructed in conformity with the applicable building codes and can be lawfully occupied and operated, in which case a certificate of occupancy will be issued. In most US communities it is illegal to occupy or conduct business in a building for which a certificate of occupancy has not been issued.

Before making any US real estate investment, a prudent investor will confirm that the real estate complies with applicable building codes and life-safety requirements. Since investors are unlikely to have the knowledge or expertise to make that determination, they should, in addition to requiring evidence of a valid certificate of occupancy, engage a qualified engineer or construction consultant to conduct a thorough physical inspection to determine the extent of any noncompliance.

Transfer Taxes

The transfer of real estate in the US is generally subject to transfer taxes. Transfer taxes may be imposed at the state level, and additional transfer taxes may also be imposed by counties and municipalities within the state. It is a matter of local custom and some negotiation as to whether the purchaser or seller will be responsible for the payment of transfer taxes. In some jurisdictions, the transfer of a controlling interest in the owner of a property may result in a transfer tax obligation. The transfer tax amount is typically a percentage of the price paid for, or value of, the property.

ESG

Environment, social, and governance (ESG) principles are increasingly becoming a part of corporate governance for public companies. These include principles such as measures to decrease pollution and waste and efforts to increase diversity and well-being within all the ranks of a company.[17]

ADVISORS

Finally, when embarking on real estate investment in the US, it is critical to select an integrated team of advisors.

Real Estate Counsel

When entering into a real estate transaction in the US, a purchaser may be encountering a new and foreign culture. As a potential point of distinction from other countries, US real estate counsel is a significant advisor in connection with real estate acquisitions. The attorney may be involved in the early stages and assist in the formation of a team of advisors or may join once a property is selected for acquisition.

Initially, the US attorney may lead the diligence investigation of the real estate and perform a review of legal agreements and title information affecting the property. The US attorney will be a technician advising the purchaser on approaches to structuring the transaction for tax efficiencies, a draftsperson and negotiator for the relevant legal documents required, and a trusted advisor assisting the purchaser in understanding the complexities of what may seem like voluminous and unfamiliar US real estate documentation. As mentioned previously, a purchaser may also consult with specialized counsel such as counsel within the state in which the property is located, including zoning, land use, or environmental counsel.

Brokers

Brokers are valuable advisors in the real estate investment process. It is important to note, however, that initial contacts with brokers may give rise to unintended brokerage claims or competing claims among multiple brokers because in many jurisdictions, brokers may be able to claim commissions on unconsummated transactions, or without a signed brokerage agreement. Prior to working with any broker, an investor should document and fully comprehend the terms upon which the broker is being retained.

Other Advisors

Depending on the circumstances of the transaction and the property, it may be advisable for a purchaser to consult with zoning consultants, engineers or construction consultants, insurance advisors, or special counsel for specific legal issues related to the property.

NOTES

1. See "Real Estate Title Records and Title Insurance" below.
2. See Chapter 2.2.
3. See Chapter 3.9.

4. See Section Three.
5. See Chapters 3.4 and 3.5.
6. See Chapter 4.6.
7. See Chapters 3.6 and 3.7.
8. While public records of title information are increasingly available for anyone to search electronically online, title searches are most often done by experienced title insurance company title examiners.
9. https://www.alta.org/.
10. Such rights might include, for example, those of any person in possession of the insured real estate under an unrecorded lease or other unrecorded document granting a right of use or possession. Standard exceptions also include boundary line disputes, encroachments, and other matters relating to the physical condition of the insured real estate, taxes, and governmental assessments not shown by the public records, as well as rights granted by law to persons who have provided, prior to the date of the policy, materials, labor, or services to improve the insured real estate. In most cases, the prudent investor can and should negotiate the elimination or modification of the exceptions so as to significantly reduce its exposure to claims. In addition, endorsements to the basic title insurance policy are available in most states to provide additional coverage for matters essential to the ownership and use of the insured real estate, such as zoning laws, compliance with private restrictive covenants, and access.
11. In advance of any acquisition of real estate, a purchaser is advised to review the relevant federal laws that apply to the prospective purchaser and the type of property being acquired and to consult with counsel in the state where the property is located for an understanding of the relevant state laws.
12. See Chapter 4.2.
13. See Chapter 2.6.
14. See Chapter 4.4.
15. Unless the investment is less than a $1 million threshold amount, or in the case of real estate is in less than 200 acres of property, or otherwise is for personal use
16. See Chapter 1.5.
17. See Chapter 1.5.

Tax Prep

Structuring Investments for US Tax Law

Michelle Jewett, Partner, Mayer Brown

Non-US persons seeking to invest in the US real estate market often do so by acquiring interests in US real estate funds. However, navigating the tax considerations associated with a real estate fund can be complex, with various and sometimes competing tax considerations at the level of the property, property holding company, fund, investor, or fund manager/general partner.

This chapter provides a high-level overview of these tax considerations and explores potential investment fund structures and their corresponding tax implications, including structures using **blocker corporations** and **real estate investment trusts (REITs)**.

CONSIDERATIONS AT THE PROPERTY AND PROPERTY HOLDING COMPANY LEVEL

Property Taxes

Property taxes are a common measure used by local governments to raise revenue in the US. These taxes are typically levied on the value of a property and are calculated by multiplying the fair market value of the property by an assessment ratio and a tax rate. How property value is determined varies widely. The property owner is usually the person responsible for paying the tax.

Real Estate Transfer Taxes

Real estate transfer taxes may be imposed by state and local governments in the US on the transfer of ownership of real property, and in many cases, the transfer of a controlling interest in an entity holding real property.

The rate of transfer tax can vary widely, with percentages ranging from very small amounts, such as 0.01 percent of the property value in Colorado, to relatively large amounts, such as 4 percent of the property value in the city of Pittsburgh, Pennsylvania. The buyer is typically responsible for paying the tax, although the tax may be divided between the buyer and seller or otherwise negotiated as part of the sales contract.

Use of Holding Companies

Funds typically use a separate legal entity to hold each real property. This is primarily done to isolate risk and to meet third-party lender requirements. For instance, if a person is injured on the property and files a lawsuit, having a separate entity holding the property can safeguard the fund's other assets. Similarly, in the event the fund holds a distressed property through a separate legal entity, the fund's other properties generally would be protected from creditors of the distressed property.

LLCs are a common form of real property holding company. Under the US entity classification rules, an LLC that has a single member is generally classified as a disregarded entity for US federal income tax purposes, unless it elects to be treated as a corporation by filing a "check-the-box" election form with the **IRS**. Classification as a disregarded entity means the LLC is not subject to US federal income tax, and the income or loss generated by the real property is treated as being directly earned by the sole owner of the LLC.

Because state and local tax treatment of an entity may differ from the federal income tax classification, it is possible that state or local taxes could be imposed on a property holding company (or another transparent entity in the fund structure), notwithstanding its treatment as a disregarded entity for federal income tax purposes. Moreover, because some jurisdictions tax income derived by or through LLCs and other forms of state law legal entities (e.g., limited partnerships) differently, it's common for funds to deviate from the typical use of LLCs when determining the optimal holding company structure for a property.

CONSIDERATIONS AT THE FUND LEVEL

Sponsors typically structure the entity that is the "fund" as an entity treated as a partnership for US tax purposes, most commonly a **limited partnership**. A fund that is treated as a partnership for US federal income tax purposes generally is not subject to US federal income taxes. Instead, the fund's partners include their distributive share of the fund's profits and losses in their taxable income.

CONSIDERATIONS AT THE INVESTOR LEVEL

Taxation of Non-US Investors' US Trade or Business Income

Non-US investors are subject to US federal income tax on income that is effectively connected with a trade or business conducted within the US. This is known as **effectively connected income (ECI)**. If a non-US investor is a partner in a fund that conducts business within the US, the investor is thus considered to be engaged in a US trade or business, and their share of the fund's income attributable to that trade or business is considered ECI. The non-US investor is subject to US federal income tax on its ECI at the regular graduated rates applicable to US individuals, corporations, or trusts. The fund must withhold and remit to the IRS a percentage of a non-US partner's distributive share of ECI to the IRS based on the highest federal income tax rate applicable to such a partner.

In addition, all or a portion of any gain realized by a non-US investor on the sale of an interest in a fund that is engaged in a US trade or business is treated as ECI and subject to US federal income tax. To ensure collection of such tax, the seller must generally withhold and remit to the IRS 10 percent of the gross sale proceeds.

Although it is possible for non-US persons to invest in US real estate in a manner that does not give rise to a US trade or business (e.g., ownership of a single triple-net leased property), the activities of a real estate fund are typically sufficient to give rise to a trade or business. As a result, non-US investors that invest directly in real estate funds can generally expect to be treated as engaged in a US trade or business—in the absence of special structuring.

Taxation of Non-US Investors' US Real Property Interests

The **Foreign Investment in Real Property Tax Act of 1980 (FIRPTA)** generally treats gain or loss realized by a non-US investor from the disposition of a **US real property interest (USRPI)** as ECI. FIRPTA applies to the direct sale of real property and to the sale of interests in **US real property holding corporations (USRPHCs)**, which are corporations that own USRPIs with a value that equals or exceeds 50 percent of the value of its total (US and non-US) real estate assets and assets used in a trade or business.

In certain cases, FIRPTA also applies to the sale or redemption of partnership interests where the partnership owns USRPIs. The FIRPTA regime requires the purchaser of a USRPI from a non-US seller to withhold 15 percent of the gross sale proceeds, unless certain exceptions apply. The non-US seller must file a US tax return, report the sale, and reconcile the amount withheld with its actual tax liability. Depending on the amount withheld, the non-US seller or partner may need to claim a refund or pay additional taxes. A partnership, such as a fund, that recognizes gain treated as ECI under FIRPTA must withhold a non-US partner's share of such income in the same manner as if such gain were ECI.

Important exceptions to the application of FIRPTA provide helpful planning opportunities. For example, gain from the sale of REIT stocks that are owned more than 50 percent by US persons (domestically controlled REITs) are not subject to tax under FIRPTA. Relevant exceptions from FIRPTA applicable to fund investments also exist for certain foreign government investors and qualified foreign pension funds.

Branch Profits Tax

When a non-US investor that is classified as a corporation invests in a fund that is engaged in a US trade or business, the non-US investor's distributive share of the fund's ECI is generally subject to the "branch profits tax" at the rate of 30 percent (or a reduced rate under an applicable tax treaty) to the extent such income is not "reinvested" in the US. The purpose of the tax is to replicate the 30 percent withholding tax applied to dividends paid by a corporation to non-US shareholders. However, gain resulting from the sale of a USRPHC is not subject to the branch profits tax, but capital gain dividends are subject to the branch profits tax.

US Withholding Taxes

A non-US investor's share of US-source passive income, such as interest, dividends, rents, or royalties not classified as ECI, will generally be subject to a 30 percent withholding tax. For instance, if the fund owns a US corporation that pays dividends, the US imposes a 30 percent withholding tax on such dividend income, unless a reduced treaty rate applies. The fund is generally required to withhold tax with respect to the non-US partner's share of such items of income, even if the amounts are not actually distributed. Relevant exceptions from US withholding tax on passive income exist for certain foreign government investors.

Notably, portfolio interest is eligible for an exclusion from US withholding tax (the **portfolio interest exemption**). Generally, portfolio interest refers to any interest that is not ECI and is paid on an obligation that meets certain registration requirements. However, portfolio interest specifically excludes: (1) interest received by a 10 percent owner (measured by voting power) of the issuer of the obligation (taking into account shares owned by attribution), (2) certain contingent interest income, (3) interest paid to a bank on an extension of credit made pursuant to a loan agreement entered into in the ordinary course of the bank's trade or business, and (4) interest paid to a controlled foreign corporation from a person related to the controlled foreign corporation.

US Federal Income Tax Return Filing Requirements[1]

A non-US investor engaged in a US trade or business is required to file a US federal income tax return, even if such investor has no ECI with respect to such investment. This filing requirement extends to non-US investors who have invested in flow-through entities, such as a fund, that are engaged in a US trade or business. However, non-US investors who invest in real estate through a US corporation, including a corporation that has elected to be taxed as a REIT, are not required to file tax returns if there is no gain taxable under FIRPTA.

Because non-US investors that do not already file US tax returns may be reluctant to incur US tax filing obligations resulting from their investment in a fund, it is often important for funds to offer non-US investors an opportunity to invest in US real estate through a structure involving a corporate blocker.

STRUCTURING ALTERNATIVES

The "Blocker" Corporation

To mitigate the adverse effect of ECI and FIRPTA for non-US investors, funds often choose to utilize corporate blocker structures, or entities treated as corporations for US tax purposes. To the extent that a non-US investor invests in a real property blocker, the investor generally will not be subject to branch profits tax or requirements to file US tax returns. Instead, the corporate entity will be subject to corporate income tax on such income.

While blockers do not necessarily minimize the aggregate US tax liability associated with an investment in the fund, because the corporation is subject to tax on the ECI, blockers provide the benefit of allowing non-US investors to avoid filing US tax returns with respect to an investment in the fund.[2]

REITs

US real estate funds often use REITs in their fund structures. Although REITs are treated as corporations for US federal income tax purposes, REITs do not pay income tax if they distribute all of their taxable income annually. This ability to eliminate the "double layer" of taxation that applies when investing through regular corporations can make investing in real property through a REIT tax-efficient for non-US investors.

To qualify, the REIT must meet certain organizational, asset, and income tests; invest primarily in real estate and/or real estate-related assets; and make annual distributions equal to at least 90 percent of taxable income within specific time periods. Non-US investors generally are not subject to direct US income tax payment and filing obligations with respect to operating income (also called **ordinary dividends**) derived though a REIT. However, distributions of the proceeds from the disposition of US real property by REITs (**capital gain dividends**) are generally subject to tax under FIRPTA, irrespective of the ownership of the REIT. In addition, a sale of an interest in a fund that utilizes a REIT structure will be subject to tax under FIRPTA unless the REIT is domestically controlled, or if another exception applies.

Debt Investments

Funds utilizing corporate blockers (including REITs) may employ structures pursuant to which non-US investors acquire both equity and debt instruments issued by the blocker. The interest on the debt can generally be deducted by the blocker as it is paid or accrued, subject to certain limitations, which reduces the corporate tax liability of the blocker.[3]

Having a corporate blocker issue debt instruments may also help minimize withholding taxes imposed on non-US investors by allowing them to take advantage of the portfolio interest exception, or to access tax treaty rates that are typically more favorable than the rates applicable to dividend income.

CONSIDERATIONS AT THE FUND MANAGER/ GENERAL PARTNER LEVEL

A fund's general partner (GP), which is typically an affiliate of the management company, is often compensated through the grant of a special interest in the fund that provides the GP with the right to a disproportionate share of fund (**carried interest**) after the fund achieves certain performance metrics.[4]

The GP is subject to tax on its distributive share of the fund's income, a portion of which may be capital gain. For individuals, capital gain is taxable at preferential rates, compared to ordinary income. Section 1061 of the Internal Revenue Code (IRC) generally requires a three-year holding period for a general partner's share of capital gains earned through a fund to be eligible for the lower tax rates applicable to long-term capital gain.

Finally, the fund manager typically receives annual management fees that are treated as ordinary income for federal income tax purposes.

Potential Investment Structures and Tax Implications

There can be a great deal of complexity in blockers and US real estate fund structures in light of the different tax and regulatory considerations for different types of investors, and the following structures reflect the most basic variations.[5]

BASIC FUND

Non-US investors and US investors acquire interests in the basic fund, which is treated as a partnership for US tax purposes (see Figure 1.3-01). The non-US investors can generally expect to be treated as "engaged in a US trade or business" in the US. Rental income and other operating income of the fund is ECI. Gain on the sale of real estate by the fund or gain recognized by non-US investors in connection with a sale of their interests in the fund is treated as ECI and subject to US tax under FIRPTA. Amounts deemed to be repatriated to corporate non-US investors under US tax principles are subject to a 30 percent branch profits tax. In addition, non-US investors are subject to US federal, state, and local income tax filing obligations.

FIGURE 1.3-01 **Basic fund**

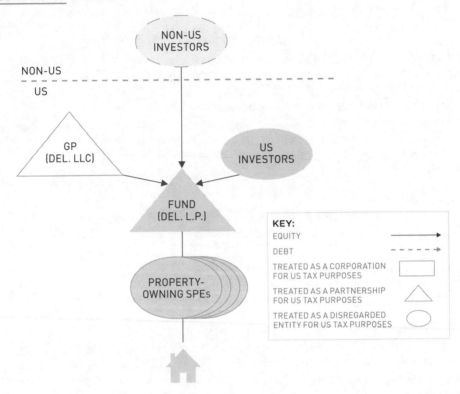

LEVERAGED CORPORATION
US and non-US investors invest in the fund through a US corporation. This leveraged corporation is funded with a combination of equity and debt (see Figure 1.3-02). The non-US investors are not treated as "engaged in a US trade or business."

However, because the corporation is USRPHC, any gain recognized by non-US investors in connection with a sale of their interests in the fund is treated as ECI and subject to US tax under FIRPTA. Dividend distributions and interest payments from the US corporation to the non-US investors are subject to a withholding tax of 30 percent, which may be reduced pursuant to an applicable tax treaty.

The corporation would be subject to entity-level US income tax (and additional state and local tax) on its distributive share of the fund's net taxable income, including gain from the sale of real estate. Interest payments should reduce taxable income of the US corporation, subject to applicable limitations.

On liquidation of the fund, the corporation will liquidate after the fund has disposed of its assets and distributed its share of the proceeds from the sale of the fund's assets. The liquidating distribution should not be subject to US tax under FIRPTA, branch profits tax, or withholding tax.

FIGURE 1.3-02 **Leveraged corporation**

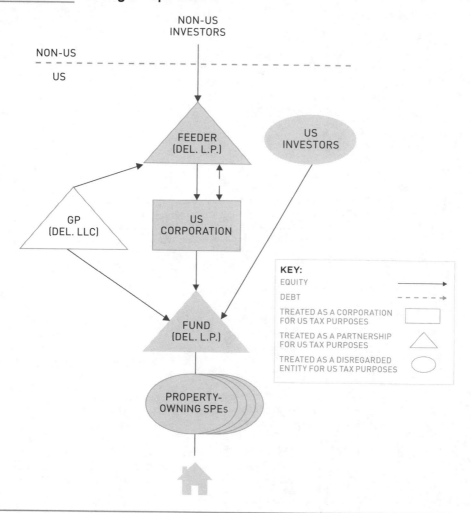

FUND INVESTS IN A REIT
Non-US and US investors invest in a fund, which in turn acquires 100 percent of the common equity in a REIT. In this structure, non-US investors generally are not treated as engaged in a US trade or business, except in the case of a property sale or sale of an interest in the fund (see Figure 1.3-03).

Assuming it satisfies applicable distribution requirements, the REIT should not be subject to US federal income tax. Non-US investors' shares of the fund's dividend distributions from the REIT are subject to a withholding tax of 30 percent, subject to reduction pursuant to an applicable tax treaty. If the REIT sells US real estate and distributes a capital gain dividend, or if a non-US investor sells its interest in the fund or has such interest redeemed, non-US investors generally will be subject to US federal income tax under FIRPTA and will need to file US tax returns. A 15 percent withholding tax will be imposed on the capital gain dividend or sale proceeds, as applicable, as a mechanism to collect such tax.

FIGURE 1.3-03 **Fund invests in a REIT**

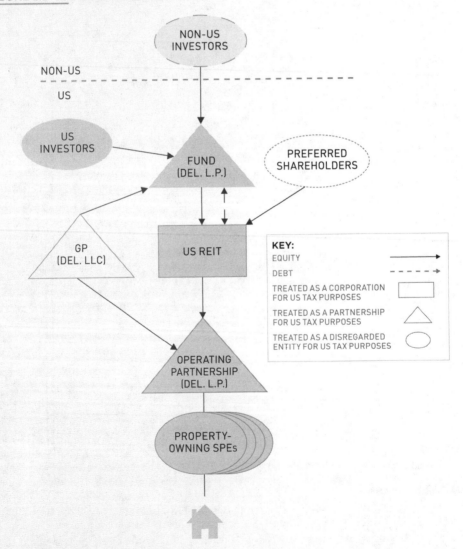

DOMESTICALLY CONTROLLED REIT

Non-US and US investors invest in the fund, which in turn acquires 100 percent of the common equity in a REIT. Non-US investors own less than 50 percent of the fund interests, such that the REIT is domestically controlled. In this structure, non-US investors are generally treated as described earlier for a general fund investment into a REIT, except that non-US investors will not be subject to tax under FIRPTA in connection with a sale or redemption of an interest in the fund.

FEEDER FUND WITH NON-US BLOCKER

Non-US investors invest in a feeder fund that has been established as a limited partnership in the Cayman Islands. The feeder fund then invests in a separate Cayman Islands limited partnership that elects to be treated as a corporation (a **Cayman blocker**) for US tax purposes. The Cayman blocker *and* a feeder fund for US investors then both invest in the fund, and the fund in turn acquires 100 percent of the common equity in a REIT.

The non-US investors will not be treated as engaged in a US trade or business, including under FIRPTA. Instead, the Cayman blocker will be subject to US income tax and file US tax returns with respect to (1) any capital gain dividends paid by the REIT, if the REIT is not domestically controlled, and (2) any gain recognized in connection with a sale or redemption of interests in the fund under FIRPTA.

The Cayman blocker is subject to a 30 percent withholding tax on its distributive share of ordinary REIT dividend income (other than capital gain dividends) from the fund, except to the extent that the Cayman blocker is treated as transparent in a non-US investor's jurisdiction of residency and such investor can claim benefits under a tax treaty between such country and the US.

NOTES

1. In addition to the US federal income tax considerations, investors in funds should be mindful of state and local tax implications. The tax rules and rates vary significantly across different states and local jurisdictions and can affect the tax liability of investors or the intermediary entities involved.
2. If a non-US investor sells an interest in the fund and the blocker is a USRPHC, the investor (other than certain foreign government investors and qualified foreign pension funds) may be subject to tax under FIRPTA.
3. One notable limitation on the deductibility of interest is section 163(j) of the Internal Revenue Code, which restricts the deductibility of certain interest payments to 30 percent of an entity's adjusted taxable income. However, real estate businesses that are subject to the section 163(j) limitation may choose to make a onetime, irrevocable election as a "real property trade or business" that exempts them from the limitation on interest deductions under section 163(j). However, in exchange for this exemption, the business must utilize a slower depreciation convention to depreciate real estate.
4. The carried interest is typically structured to qualify as a profits interest that is not subject to tax upon grant pursuant to Revenue Procedures 93-27 and 2001-43.
5. The illustrations do not address the federal income tax considerations applicable to certain types of non-US investors, including foreign government investors and qualified foreign pension funds. Additionally, they do not discuss state and local tax considerations associated with a fund investment.

1.4

Core and Beyond

Understanding Gateway, Secondary, and Tertiary Markets

Zeb Bradford, CIO, Metzler Real Estate

The US is a large country, presenting an array of opportunities to foreign investors—but this diversity can often seem bewildering to new market entrants.

However, in comparison to other countries, many of which have only one or two cities with the scale needed to be liquid enough for institutional investors (e.g., Paris and Lyon in France, or Tokyo in Japan), the US offers outside investors a range of entry points for institutional-scale investment.

This chapter will provide a description of these US markets, generally labeled by the investment community to be **primary (or gateway), secondary, and tertiary markets**.

While the distinctions between each market type are often subjective, there is a general agreement on what constitutes the main gateway markets in the US (see Figure 1.4-01). But rather than entertaining a lengthy debate on market hierarchies, this chapter will employ a nominal ranking of US cities and ultimately provide a background on the level of investor interest in these markets, including why investors typically focus on subsets of these markets, how to best approach each market, and related benefits and challenges.

FIGURE 1.4-01 Primary and secondary markets—general product types

Because most general real estate product types (e.g., office, multifamily, retail, hospitality) are driven by similar economic and demographic factors, the bulk of this chapter focuses on those markets that reflect these general product types. However, there are other product types currently attracting strong investor interest (e.g., industrial, data centers, and life sciences), and these types use a different set of market rankings. This chapter concludes with a brief discussion exploring these differences.

PRIMARY MARKETS

Foreign investors are generally comfortable making forays into the US markets via primary/gateway cities for a variety of reasons—sometimes for the simple fact that these cities are well-known by their investors and board members.

Investors also consider these markets to be very liquid, making it easier to purchase or exit investments. And importantly, investors also have an emotional affinity to these markets, because they're more like large European or Asian cities, with vibrant and walkable downtown areas and highly developed **central business districts (CBDs)**.

Primary markets are generally cities that have a combination of the following characteristics:

- Long-term economic, educational, cultural, or political significance
- Downtown areas that have remained a primary work destination
- Downtown areas that serve as vibrant, dense population centers
- Coastal proximity supporting international trade

Typical primary markets in the US include the following.

New York City, New York

New York City is the largest US city by population and **gross domestic product (GDP)**. It is the corporate and financial capital of the US, with large technology and media industry prominence. It has a large and diverse residential population, and is home to JFK, the world's seventh busiest airport by departures. Additionally, the New York City port ranks third in the world for overall container traffic, with more than 9 million TEU[1] per year.

Boston, Massachusetts

Boston is a historic city with global cultural, research, and educational significance. It is home to more than 50 colleges and universities, including Harvard and MIT, and the largest life science cluster in the US and a still-vital financial sector. The city also hosts over 250,000 students, according to a recent study by Boston University.

Washington, DC

Washington, DC, is the US capital city, with nearly 364,000 government employees in the greater DC area, according to the Federal Reserve. It is home to thousands of legal and lobbying firms, defense companies, industry associations, and large corporate offices benefiting from proximity to government agencies. The greater DC **metropolitan statistical area (MSA)** also contains the largest global data center hub in the US.[2]

Chicago, Illinois

Chicago is the third-largest city in the US by population, considered the capital of the Midwest, with an extremely diversified economy. A financial leader in commodities and futures trading due to proximity to US agricultural heartland. Home to O'Hare, the fourth busiest airport in the world by passenger volume, and home to global headquarters of companies such as McDonald's, ConAgra, Kraft Heinz, and United Airlines.

San Francisco, California

Historically, San Francisco is the financial capital of the Western US and home to the head office of Wells Fargo, the fourth-largest US bank. It has proximity to prominent universities, including UC Berkeley and Stanford, as well as to the high-tech and venture capital industries of Silicon Valley and the greater Bay Area. It is served by the Port of Oakland, the eighth-largest port in the US (2.4 million TEU per year).

Los Angeles, California

The second-largest US MSA for both population and GDP, Los Angeles has a highly diverse economy and an inimitable role as the media capital of the US. It is home to a growing tech industry, as both media and technology continue to converge. LAX airport ranks fifth in the world for passenger traffic, and the ports of LA and Long Beach are ranked first and second in the US, respectively, in terms of container traffic, handling a combined 20 million TEU per year.

SECONDARY MARKETS

Secondary markets are generally distinct from primary markets for having some, but not all, characteristics of primary markets. For example, a secondary city may not have as much population or GDP as gateway cities do. Some secondary cities are also younger than US gateway cities (i.e., Denver, Colorado, vs. Boston, Massachusetts), which means they have not had enough time to establish comparable cultural or political provenance—an important "soft" factor that distinguishes the two market types.

Notably, secondary markets also tend to have room for population expansion and are not as limited by physical or political boundaries compared to primary markets.

Representative secondary markets that tend to attract institutional investment include the following.

Philadelphia, Pennsylvania

Philadelphia is the seventh-largest city in the US by population. Positioned roughly halfway between DC and New York, Philadelphia has highly rated museums and cultural institutions, including the University of Pennsylvania, Temple University, and Drexel University. Comcast, DuPont, and other notable companies are headquartered in Philadelphia, as well.

Charlotte, North Carolina

This Southern **Sunbelt** city ranks twenty-second in overall population for US MSAs. It is home to more than 91,000 financial services jobs and the headquarters of the second- and sixth-largest banks in the (Bank of America and Truist Financial). Wells Fargo also retains a large presence in the city with more than 25,000 employees. Charlotte Douglas International Airport was the sixth-busiest airport in world by number of departures in 2021.

Nashville, Tennessee

Relatively small (thirty-fifth-largest MSA in the US) but culturally significant, this Sunbelt city is home to country music, media companies, and a large tourism industry (14 million annual visitors). Its size and affordability have made it increasingly attractive for corporate relocations, including AllianceBernstein, which moved from New York to Nashville in 2018, bringing more than 1,000 new jobs to the region.

Atlanta, Georgia

With the eighth-largest MSA in the US, Atlanta is generally considered the economic capitol of the South with a highly diversified economy, and home to the highly ranked Georgia Institute of Technology and Emory University. Additionally, Atlanta is one of country's most ethnically diverse large cities and is home to five Historically Black Colleges and Universities (HBCUs) led by Morehouse, Spelman, and Clark Universities.

Miami, Florida

Miami, Florida, is the ninth-largest MSA in the US with a diverse set of economic drivers, including major port facilities (tenth busiest in the US), cruise ship terminals (busiest passenger terminal in the US, handling 2.5 million passengers), and tourism (more 22 million visitors in 2021). Miami is also important as a financial, medical, and educational hub for Central and South Americans, and is a favored migration destination for many Americans seeking to escape higher taxes, lower growth, and northern cities.

Dallas, Texas

Dallas, Texas, ranks as the fourth-largest MSA in the US and has the beneficial combination of a highly diversified economy, central national location, strong economic growth, low taxes, and the world's second-busiest airport based on passenger traffic. The city has benefited from strong inward migration from the higher tax and regulatory states of the West Coast with major expansions of both tech and financial services companies. Companies headquartered in Dallas include AT&T, Kimberly Clark, American Airlines, and Southwest Airlines.

MARKET TRENDS

As evidence of how the delineations between primary and secondary markets aren't hard and fast, recent data show how some primary markets have been steadily losing population to secondary markets—especially those in the Sunbelt (see Figures 1.4-02 and 1.4-03).

FIGURE 1.4-02 **Net domestic migration (2020–2021)**

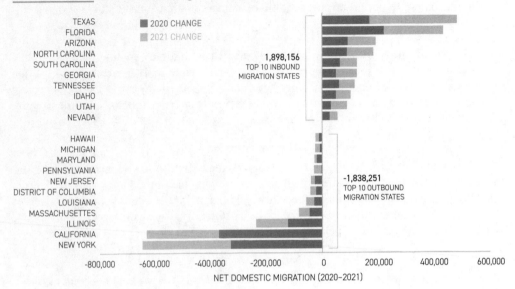

Source: U.S. Census Bureau

FIGURE 1.4-03 **Population growth**

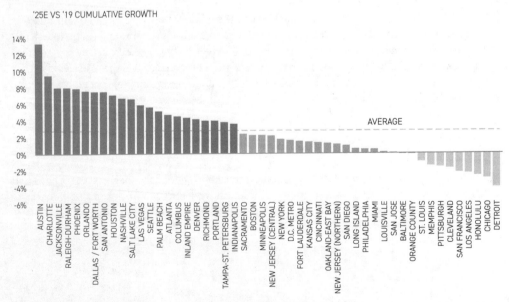

Source: Green Street and Oxford Economics

There are a variety of reasons for this migration, including the massive growth and adoption of remote work spurred by the COVID-19 pandemic, but most observers point to economic fundamentals as primary factors for individuals migrating, including the incentives of better take-home pay and lower taxes (see Figure 1.4-04).

FIGURE 1.4-04 **Gross pay needed to earn the same net pay by state**

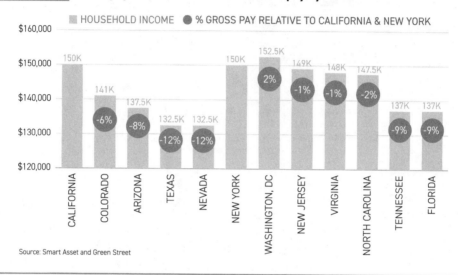

Source: Smart Asset and Green Street

Like individuals and families, the reason that companies are moving to secondary markets is partly to follow their employee and customer bases, and partly to capture reductions in indexed business costs via lower taxes and regulations (see Figure 1.4-05).

FIGURE 1.4-05 **Cost of doing business in gateway and growth markets**

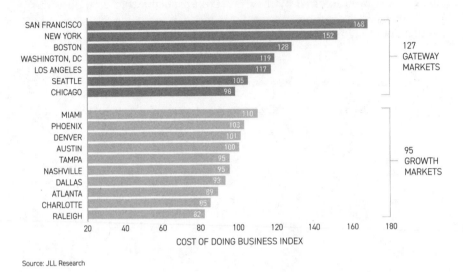

Source: JLL Research

The migration effect on the overall real estate market fundaments has been profound, with a meaningful difference in the office sector, using employment in the Sunbelt states from 2020–2022, in comparison to the more traditional primary markets (see Figure 1.4-06).

FIGURE 1.4-06 **Difference in office-using employment in Sunbelt versus traditional primary markets**

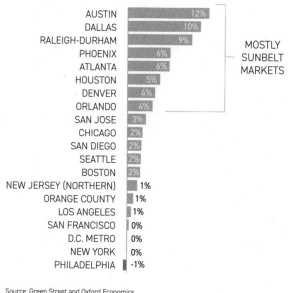

Source: Green Street and Oxford Economics

This increased office usage has also translated into significantly greater rent and occupancy growth in the Sunbelt markets from 2017–2022 (see Figure 1.4-07).

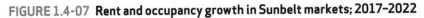

FIGURE 1.4-07 **Rent and occupancy growth in Sunbelt markets; 2017–2022**

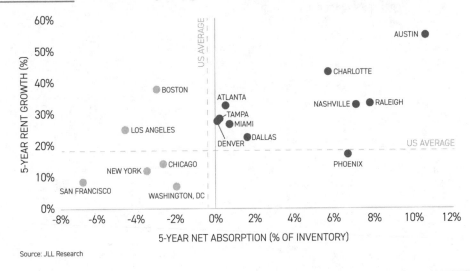

Source: JLL Research

Institutional real estate investors have naturally reacted to these trends in population and economic growth and their effects on real estate fundamentals by prioritizing these secondary markets over the more traditional markets (see Figures 1.4-08 and 1.4-09).

FIGURE 1.4-08 **Overall real estate prospects city rankings[3]**

1. Nashville	**6.** Raleigh/Durham
2. Dallas	**7.** Miami
3. Atlanta	**8.** Boston
4. Austin	**9.** Phoenix
5. Tampa	**10.** Charlotte

<u>FIGURE 1.4-09</u> **Number of markets in Emerging Trends Top 20**
('23E-'27E as % of stock, excludes shadow supply)

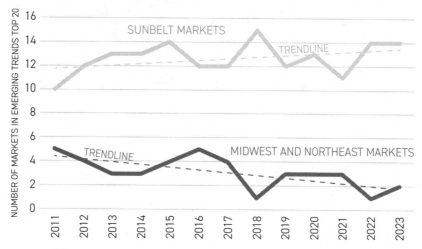

Source: Emerging Trends in Real Estate surveys; compelled by Nelson Economics.

CHOOSING A STRATEGY

While these trends are expected to continue, there are several considerations investors must keep in mind when devising a market selection strategy (see Figure 1.4-10):

- Primary markets remain important economic and cultural centers, and there will always be specific investments in those markets that remain attractive.
- Politicians in the more high-cost/high-tax states, which are home to most gateway markets, may eventually attempt to counteract the draining away of companies and citizens from their states with a lowering of taxation and regulation.
- The infrastructure in many secondary markets is being strained based on recent growth. It is likely that taxes will be raised to help strengthen and expand infrastructure to accommodate this growth. These fiscal changes will narrow the cost advantage of these markets.
- A portion of the migration to the lower cost markets has been driven by individuals capitalizing on remote work opportunities afforded by the 2020 pandemic. While remote work will persist, corporate and individual attitudes toward office use will reach a new balance.
- Many secondary markets have very few physical barriers to growth, such as a mountain range or the ocean. This lack of geographic constraint can quickly lead to overbuilding and keep land values low.

- Climate change risk is expected to be greater in the Sunbelt markets, either through diminishing supplies of water, greater storm intensity and occurrence, or rising sea levels.[4] This will make it more difficult or expensive to insure assets in these markets and could eventually spur another wave of migration.

FIGURE 1.4-10 **Annual supply growth forecast by market**

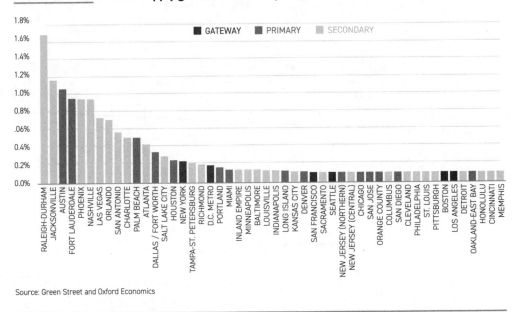

Source: Green Street and Oxford Economics

ALTERNATE PRODUCT TYPES DRIVING MARKET REINTERPRETATIONS

The Industrial Sector

The industrial market (which may be called distribution, warehousing, or logistics in non-US markets) has a different set of market classifications than the general real estate market, because economic and population growth are not as influential for determining industrial market relevance (see Figure 1.4-11).

The ability to efficiently receive and ship goods from both an occupancy and transport perspective are the primary drivers for industrial market selection. Proximity to transport nodes (e.g., coastal and inland ports, rail yards and highway links, multimodal yards, and airports) and the end customer factor into market preference for industrial tenants.

FIGURE 1.4-11 **Industrial market classifications**

Generally, industrial markets can be broken down into the following categories:

- **Gateway:** Traditional core locations near major ports of entry, with low vacancy, strong absorption, high taking rents, and scarcity of developable land.
- **Primary:** Core markets with strong absorption, solid rent growth, but some development opportunities.
- **Strategic:** Emerging markets with growing fundamentals including strong growth rates, rents beginning to rise, but development opportunities.

The life science sector differentiates itself from traditional real estate markets due to the specialized build-out and building systems required for the tenant base with heavy research and development (R&D) infrastructure requirements (see Figure 1.4-12). Additionally, the life science property types need a combination of the following market conditions to be considered worthwhile investments:

- **Institutions** (e.g., research universities, nonprofit research centers, health systems) that can attract government research funding and emerging talent and have the ability to monetize or partner on successful innovation.
- **Talent,** or human capital, which includes executives, engineers, researchers, academics, scientists, creatives, and traditional blue- and white-collar workforces.
- **Capital,** including venture capital, institutional capital, and National Institutes of Health (NIH), philanthropic, and industry R&D expenditures.

There are the following generally accepted classifications of life science markets:

Premier: Boston-Cambridge, San Francisco Bay Area, and San Diego, which are the largest, most mature, lab markets with the most diversity of tenants (pharma, bio, devices)

Primary: Raleigh-Durham; Washington, DC; Seattle; Philadelphia; and New Jersey, which have strong industry presence and a large diversity of tenants

Secondary: New York City, Chicago, Los Angeles, Denver–Boulder, and Houston, which are smaller but growing lab markets with strong industry representation

FIGURE 1.4-12 **Top life science/R&D markets**

The Data Center Sector

The data center market has grown dramatically over the past decade due to the ever-increasing demand for digital data from both companies and individuals (see Figure 1.4-13).

These data centers house hundreds of cabinets full of servers that keep a company's digital infrastructure running. Facilities often feature power feeds from multiple substations, diverse connection points from fiber carriers, redundant battery backups and diesel generators, and robust cooling systems. They are also safeguarded by an array of energy, security, and governmental regulations, and are a highly specialized asset type that doesn't follow traditional real estate metrics.

Two primary factors determine the size and importance of a data center market:

1. **Energy:** Data centers demand access to large, reliable, and efficiently priced power sources in order to keep the data centers running without interruption, at a competitive price.
2. **Latency:** Latency is the time for transmission of data between user and content generator. As such, proximity to and from the suppliers and users of the data is of great significance.

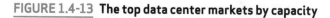

FIGURE 1.4-13 **The top data center markets by capacity**

Premier Market: Northern Virginia, which is by far the most dominant data center market in the US due to its proximity to the US government, is the largest single US generator and user of digital data.

Primary Markets: Northern New Jersey, Columbus, Atlanta, Chicago, Dallas, Phoenix, and northern California all serve as regional hubs for digital data traffic.

Secondary Markets: All remaining markets on the map are emerging data center markets and can be viewed as growing in importance for regional data users.

NOTES

1. A TEU (20-foot equivalent unit) is a measure of volume in units of 20-foot-long containers. Large container ships typically transport between 18,000 and 21,000 TEU.
2. Northern Virginia currently moves an estimated 70 percent of the world's internet traffic daily, according to the Virginia Economic Development Partnership.
3. ULI's 2022 Emerging Trends in Real Estate survey.
4. According to First Street Foundation, the Sunbelt is expected to be exposed to longer, more extreme temperatures of 125°F (52°C) in 30 years' time. It predicts that an "extreme heat belt," in which heat indices exceed such temperatures, will expand from 50 US counties in 2023 to over 1,000 by 2053.

Corporate Responsibility

ESG Expectations in the US

Sunil Misser, CEO, AccountAbility

The integration of environmental, social, and governance (ESG) factors into investment decision-making has gained widespread priority in recent years, especially in the real estate sector. ESG considerations—which come with specific, quantifiable performance goals for everything from corporate governance behavior to asset performance and carbon emissions—are increasingly recognized as essential components of investment analysis and decision-making by real estate investors.

Real estate is a critical asset class that plays a crucial role in the global economy, and as such, it has a significant impact on ESG issues. The real estate sector contributes to approximately 40 percent of global carbon emissions, making it a significant contributor to climate change.[1] Additionally, as the industry sector that serves a core human need—shelter—real estate also has significant effect on (and is affected by) critical social factors, such as housing affordability, community development, and tenant welfare.

And at a more fundamental level, governance issues, such as board diversity, transparency, and accountability, have a meaningful influence over investment theses, philosophies, and performance. Coupled with growing regulatory fervor and governmental expectations for corporate citizenship, energy usage, and carbon emissions, ESG is an increasingly fundamental pillar of investment decision-making, risk mitigation, and long-term value creation.

THE BUSINESS CASE FOR ESG IN REAL ESTATE INVESTING

ESG factors have become a critical consideration for real estate investors, as reflected in the *AFIRE International Investor Survey: Q1 2023 Pulse Report*. The report highlights that ESG and sustainability have been prominent areas of interest to investors in recent years and remain a top-three area of concern, with a significant disconnect in how the industry is pricing climate risks in its proformas and valuations.

Embedding ESG considerations can help reduce risks and create long-term financial value. Buildings that meet sustainable standards tend to have lower operating costs, potential for higher tenant satisfaction rates, and as a result, longer lease terms. This can translate into higher occupancy rates, reduced vacancy rates, and higher rental income. Investing internally to improve ESG performance can attract a wider range of investors and tenants who are increasingly seeking sustainable and socially responsible investments.

ESG investing can help address social issues such as affordable housing, access to transportation, and community development. Investing in affordable housing can provide housing solutions for low-income families, while investments in transportation infrastructure can improve access to job opportunities and reduce carbon emissions. ESG investments can also help create healthy and vibrant communities that foster social cohesion and well-being.

Sustainability strategies help reduce the carbon footprint of buildings and contribute to mitigating climate change. Sustainable building practices such as energy-efficient lighting, HVAC systems, and water conservation can significantly reduce carbon emissions and operating costs. Furthermore, strategic ESG investing can promote the use of renewable energy sources, such as solar and wind power, to reduce reliance on fossil fuels.

Investors who incorporate ESG considerations into their investment strategies can realize financial benefits, address social issues, and contribute to mitigating climate change. As ESG factors become increasingly important for tenants and investors, real estate companies that prioritize sustainability and social responsibility may see higher demand for their properties and greater investor interest.

ESG METRICS FOR REAL ESTATE INVESTMENTS

ESG metrics are quantitative measures used to evaluate the environmental, social, and governance performance of companies, assets, or portfolios. In the context of real estate investments, ESG metrics provide valuable insights into the sustainability and impact of assets, and help investors identify risks and opportunities related to ESG factors.

Environmental metrics measure the environmental impact of a property and on a broader scale, the business ecosystem in which they operate. Scope 1 and 2 emissions reflect those owned or controlled by a company, whereas Scope 3 emissions are a consequence of the activities of the company, but occur from sources not owned or controlled by it.[2]

Some of the most critical environmental metrics for real estate investments include energy and water consumption, greenhouse gas emissions, and waste management. These metrics can be used to assess the sustainability of a building and identify areas for improvement.

Social metrics impacting a property can include factors such as access to transportation, community development, and affordable housing. These metrics can be used to evaluate how a property contributes to the well-being of its residents and the surrounding community. Investments in affordable housing can provide housing solutions for low-income families, while investments in transportation infrastructure can improve access to job opportunities.

An organization's processes, policies, practices, and impact within an ESG construct are captured in governance matters. These may include factors such as board diversity, executive compensation, and corporate social responsibility policies. Governance metrics can be used to evaluate how well an asset is managed and identify potential risks to the investment. Assets with strong governance practices are more likely to have a long-term strategic vision and may be better equipped to navigate potential risks.

ESG frameworks, standards, and rating agencies outline and assess ESG governance criteria, and together with the public disclosure of governance-related policies offer investors insight to determine company performance and impact. Frequently occurring ESG governance criteria, and of the greatest relevance to the commercial real estate (CRE) industry, include compensation policy, ESG reporting standards, board level oversight, governance policies, and risk assessment.

Overall, ESG metrics provide real estate investors with indicators for evaluating the sustainability and social responsibility of their investments. By evaluating a property's environmental, social, and governance factors, investors can identify potential risks and opportunities for improvement, while also contributing to a more sustainable and socially responsible real estate industry.

ESG STANDARDS IN REAL ESTATE INVESTING

ESG reporting is used to inform stakeholders, including investors and rating agencies, about an organization's ESG performance and impact—both financial and nonfinancial—as well as progress toward stated goals and targets.

Within an organization, reporting can serve as a tool to develop an ESG strategy, set priorities, track year-over-year performance against targets, and communicate ESG progress across the organization. Prioritizing ESG topics can form the foundation of ESG disclosure, as it allows organizations to identify and define topics to report against.

Organizations can consider publicly disclosing ESG information using recognized frameworks, such as the Sustainability Accounting Standards Board (SASB) and the International Organization for Standardization (ISO), or under international agreements, including the UN Global Compact, a nonbinding UN pact to get businesses and firms worldwide to adopt sustainable and socially responsible policies, and to report on their implementation.

The Financial Stability Board (FSB) launched The Task Force on Climate-Related Financial Disclosures (TCFD) to develop recommendations on the types of information that companies should disclose to support investors, lenders, and insurance underwriters in appropriately assessing and pricing a specific set of risks related to climate change.

The Global Real Estate Sustainability Benchmark (GRESB) is a global standard for assessing the ESG performance of real estate investments. GRESB evaluates the ESG performance of real estate portfolios and individual assets based on a set of standardized metrics. Investors can use GRESB to compare the ESG performance of different investments and identify areas for improvement.

First introduced in 1993, and formed from the US Green Building Council, Leadership in Energy and Environmental Design (LEED) is a rating system for evaluating the sustainability of buildings. LEED evaluates buildings based on their energy efficiency, water conservation, waste management, and other environmental factors. Properties that meet LEED standards are more likely to be energy-efficient and environmentally sustainable.

The UN Principles for Responsible Investment (UNPRI) is a global framework for responsible investing. UNPRI provides investors with a set of principles for integrating ESG factors into their investment strategies. Real estate investors can use UNPRI to evaluate the sustainability and social responsibility of their investments and identify potential risks and opportunities.

ESG AND FINANCIAL PERFORMANCE OF REAL ESTATE INVESTMENTS

The relationship between ESG factors and financial performance of real estate investments is a topic of increasing interest and research. Studies, including the UN Environment Programme Finance Initiative, are looking at the correlation between ESG performance and financial performance in real estate investments.

Investors increasingly recognize the potential financial risks associated with poor ESG performance. Climate change and social issues can impact the value and performance of real estate investments in the long term. For example, assets located in areas prone to flooding or extreme weather events may experience increased insurance costs or be subject to damage, resulting in lower property values and income.

Tenants are increasingly seeking sustainable and socially responsible properties, and assets that meet these standards may have higher tenant satisfaction rates and longer lease terms.

ESG investing can also attract a wider range of investors who are increasingly seeking sustainable and socially responsible investments. This can increase demand for the property, resulting in higher property values and greater investor interest. This is supported by an EY report indicating that 88 percent of institutional investors surveyed following the pandemic state they will likely pursue more sustainable and resilient investment opportunities.[3]

Moreover, ESG investing can help reduce potential financial risks, regulatory risks, and other risks impacting an organization's reputation. Properties that meet sustainable standards are more likely to comply with environmental and social regulations, reducing the risk of penalties or fines. They are also less likely to face negative publicity from environmental or social issues, reducing the risk of reputational damage.

ESG AND REAL ESTATE ASSET VALUATION

ESG considerations have become increasingly important in commercial real estate asset valuation. Investors and asset managers are recognizing the impact that ESG factors can have on the financial performance and long-term sustainability of real estate assets. ESG considerations may include factors such as energy efficiency, water conservation, waste reduction, indoor air quality, tenant health and safety, community engagement, and ethical business practices.

Incorporating ESG factors into asset valuation helps investors and asset managers identify risks and opportunities that may not be captured by traditional financial analysis. For example, a building with strong energy efficiency measures may have lower operating costs and be more resilient to regulatory changes and energy price volatility. Similarly, a building with a strong community engagement program may have higher tenant retention rates and be more attractive to socially responsible investors.

ESG considerations may also be important for regulatory compliance, as governments around the world introduce policies and regulations aimed at reducing greenhouse gas emissions and promoting sustainable development. In some cases, failure to comply with ESG regulations may result in financial penalties or reputational damage.

Incorporating ESG considerations into commercial real estate asset valuation can help investors and asset managers make better-informed decisions, reduce risk, and drive long-term value creation.

ESG REPORTING AND DISCLOSURE IN REAL ESTATE INVESTMENT

ESG reporting and disclosure have become increasingly important in the real estate investment industry. Investors and stakeholders are interested in understanding the ESG risks and opportunities associated with real estate assets, as well as the actions being taken to manage those risks and create value.

Real estate investment managers are responding to this with a deeper assessment of ESG reporting and disclosure frameworks. These frameworks may include standardized ESG metrics, such as energy and water usage, carbon emissions, waste generation, and social and governance practices. They may also include qualitative information on the management of ESG risks and opportunities, such as sustainability policies, community engagement initiatives, and ethical business practices.

Real estate companies and funds may issue sustainability reports that disclose information on ESG performance, including energy and water usage, waste management, and tenant satisfaction. These reports reflect sustainability goals and targets and form a valuable basis for third-party organizations to provide ESG ratings. These ratings can be used to compare ESG performance across different investments and to identify areas for improvement.

The Global Reporting Initiative (GRI) provides a valuable framework for reporting on sustainability performance across a range of industries, including real estate. GRI reporting typically includes information on ESG risks and opportunities, stakeholder engagement, and governance practices.

According to EY's 2021 survey, ESG performance disclosures are central to investment decisions, with 78 percent of investors reporting that they conduct a structured, methodical evaluation of nonfinancial disclosures. The demand for enhanced disclosure is also triggering the need for more advanced data analytics to produce trusted ESG performance reporting.

In addition to meeting stakeholder demands, ESG reporting and disclosure can help real estate investment managers better manage their assets. By tracking ESG performance and disclosing information to stakeholders, real estate investment managers can identify areas for improvement and implement strategies to reduce risk and enhance value.

ESG reporting and disclosure can also help real estate investment managers access capital. Investors are increasingly looking for investments that align with their ESG values and strategies and may favor real estate investment managers that are transparent about their ESG performance and initiatives.

REGULATORY LANDSCAPE AND ESG IN REAL ESTATE INVESTING

The regulatory landscape for ESG in real estate is evolving rapidly, with increasing attention being paid to sustainability action in the industry. In the US, ESG regulations are impacting commercial real estate investing, and those that can stay ahead of regulatory developments are also able to protect against future risks.

Some jurisdictions have implemented sustainability mandates that require real estate companies and funds to meet certain ESG criteria. For example, the city of San Francisco has a mandate that requires all commercial buildings over 50,000 square feet to meet certain energy efficiency standards.

Green financing is a growing trend in the real estate industry, with lenders and investors offering financing and incentives for sustainable building and renovation projects. For example, the Green Bond Principles (GBP) provide guidelines for issuing green bonds to finance environmentally sustainable projects, including in the real estate sector. Future ESG rules and regulations in this area are anticipated, such as those within SEC disclosure requirements.

Governments may offer tax incentives for sustainable building practices or investments in renewable energy. For example, the US offers tax credits for investments in renewable energy and energy efficiency projects.

In a fast-changing regulatory environment—from the EU's Corporate Sustainability Reporting Directive (CSRD) to the proposed SEC directive on disclosure of climate-related information—the ESG landscape is evolving, and organizations who fall behind are exposed to a significant level of risk.

FUTURE DIRECTIONS FOR ESG IN REAL ESTATE INVESTMENT

ESG considerations are becoming increasingly important in real estate investment. Investors and stakeholders are demanding transparency and accountability in ESG performance, and regulatory frameworks are emerging to support ESG integration.

Real estate investors and asset managers who incorporate ESG considerations into their investment strategies and practices may achieve better risk-adjusted returns, enhance value, and contribute to a more sustainable future. They can also attract investors who prioritize ESG factors in their investment decision-making process.

Looking to the future, ESG considerations are likely to become even more central to real estate investment. As the impacts of climate change and social inequality become more pronounced, investors will expect thoughtful response and action on these issues.

Governments and regulatory bodies are expected to introduce more stringent requirements for ESG integration, and technological advancements will create new opportunities for sustainable real estate development.

Real estate investors and asset managers who stay ahead of these trends and integrate ESG considerations into their investment strategies and practices will be better positioned to succeed in the future. By doing so, they can achieve better outcomes for their investors, their communities, and the planet.

NOTES

1. World Economic Forum. "How We Can Decarbonize the Real Estate Sector," November 8, 2022, https://www.weforum.org/agenda/2022/11/how-we-can-decarbonize-the-real-estate-sector/.
2. World Economic Forum. "Scope Emissions: Why Measuring the Greenhouse Gas Impact of Your Business Activities Is Vital for Decarbonization." World Economic Forum. September 26, 2022. https://www.weforum.org/agenda/2022/09/scope-emissions-climate-greenhouse-business/.
3. EY. (2021). Institutional Investor Survey. https://assets.ey.com/content/dam/ey-sites/ey-com/en_gl/topics/assurance/assurance-pdfs/ey-institutional-investor-survey.pdf.

Asset Trends

An Overview of Commercial Property Types in the US

Will McIntosh, PhD, Global Head of Research, Affinius Capital

Today, many different types of commercial real estate properties are available for investing. They are generally classified across sectors, similar to other investment asset classes, based on their distinct features and characteristics or the end users of space. The four traditional property types have historically been multifamily (or residential), industrial, office, and retail given their high-quality or "core" profile offering stabilized cash flows; however, nontraditional or niche sectors have grown in popularity in recent years and experienced increased investment activity from institutional investors. These emerging sectors can include areas like data centers, life science, self-storage, healthcare (senior living and medical office), and student housing.

MULTIFAMILY RESIDENTIAL FOR RENT

The typical for-rent apartment in the US is part of a multifamily structure with five or more units. Institutional investors tend to focus on properties with 150 to 500 or more rental units. Apartment structures can be classified by density, architectural style, and class (such as A, B, or C). High-rise apartments tend to be located near urban centers where land is more expensive and vertical development is necessary. Buildings classified as high-rise typically have 10 to 15 stories and a variety of amenities, including a staffed front desk. Mid-rise apartment buildings range in height from four to nine stories and can be located either in urban areas or the suburbs. Developments may offer a wide range of amenities, including onsite management and other services. Garden-style apartments are relatively low-density and typically located in suburban areas where land is less expensive. They may include numerous two- to three-story buildings along with a separate building containing a management office and amenities. The larger garden apartment developments are likely to offer a selection of amenities that include a swimming pool, exercise room, tennis courts, and walking trails.

The most common apartment lease term is one year. However, shorter terms may be available in some locations. Shorter-term leases tend to require a higher rent and can provide an excellent inflation hedge for investors in markets that are not overbuilt. Long-term apartments as an investment tend to be very attractive in the US, given the underlying national demographics and continuing housing shortage.

INDUSTRIAL/LOGISTICS

Industrial/logistics properties include the following: large single-user buildings, single- and multitenant warehouses, and distribution facilities. Warehouses and distribution facilities have become popular investments. They provide space for storing and distributing goods to support the same-day delivery promise made by online retailers. Warehouses are usually built as single-story structures with fewer design elements than most office buildings and shopping centers. They are relatively simple to construct, have long physical lives, and usually require less management effort than other commercial property types. Older properties, especially those with ceiling heights lower than what many users demand, are finding their property functionally obsolete.

Most new space is built as single-story structures that can be configured to accommodate single or multiple tenants. Industrial flex space is an industrial building that is partially converted into office space. Rents per square foot are lower than traditional office space, and there is ample parking. Tenants can be firms that require large amounts of inexpensive space or firms that need their offices in the same building as their manufacturing and warehouse operations.

Many warehouse/logistics properties are single-user buildings leased to tenants on a **triple net (NNN)** basis, where the tenant pays the operating expenses, including insurance and taxes. Most warehouse space is relatively homogenous and releasing, and moving costs are relatively low. In recent years, the significant increase in online sales, has led to an increase in investor demand for warehouse/logistics properties. This property type has been a leading performer among the traditional property types and with the anticipated strength of online sales in the future, its strong performance is likely to continue.

OFFICE

Office buildings tend to be classified by location (urban or suburban) and class (A, B, and C). Class A office buildings tend to have the best location, high-quality tenants, amenities, and overall desirability. They are usually new structures and command the highest rents. Class B office buildings usually have a less attractive location and fewer amenities; they are overall less desirable that Class A buildings. Rents tend to be lower than Class A. Class C buildings typically were once Class A or B and tend to be older. They have a less desirable location and may be below current standards for one or more reasons. Rents are set to match the ability of lower revenue tenants.

An important determinant of office property classification is age and functional obsolescence. Older buildings can be considered Class A if they are in a great location and do an excellent job of accommodating tenant needs. If a property declines in its ability to provide for the functional needs of current and prospective tenants, its classification will likely deteriorate.

Office rent is typically quoted on a dollar-per-square-foot basis, and accurately and consistently measuring a building's square footage is extremely important. Office leases involving major tenants may have terms as long as 25 years. However, lease terms of 5 to 10 years are more common. Tenants generally share in the payment of operating expenses above a certain limit.

The COVID-19 pandemic and the move to working from home have profoundly affected tenant demand for office space. Many companies have decided to allow their employees to work from home going forward or only require them to be in the office three to four days a week. As a result, as office leases are coming up for renewal, some tenants are announcing that they will not need as much space in the future. Additionally, properties that are older and in less-desirable locations are becoming functionally obsolete and likely to face a change in use (such as conversion to multifamily) or demolition.

RETAIL

Retail properties exist in a variety of forms. The simplest is a freestanding retail outlet (e.g., a fast-food franchise). Today, many retail establishments are in shopping centers or malls.

One of the most popular types is neighborhood shopping centers. This type of center is located for the benefit of the nearby resident population. It contains retail establishments offering mostly convenience goods (e.g., groceries) and services (e.g., barbershops, coffee shops and restaurants, and dry cleaning). A grocery store may anchor these centers. The gross leasable area of the anchor(s) and nonanchored tenant space typically ranges from 30,000 to 125,000 square feet. The trade area of a shopping center is the geographic proximity from which it draws its customers. A neighborhood center's trade area is typically within a two- to three-mile radius of the center.

A similar type of retail is the community shopping center. This is a larger version of the neighborhood center. This type of center may be anchored by a discount department store and may include outlets such as clothing stores, banks, furniture stores, lawn and garden stores, fast-food operations, and professional offices (e.g., dentists). The gross leasable area (GLA) is usually three times that of a neighborhood center. A community center's trade area is usually within a three- to six-mile radius of the center.

Another type is the power shopping center. Power centers typically have leasable areas ranging from 250,000 to 600,000 square feet. The dominating feature of a power center is the high ratio of anchors to ancillary tenants. Typically, power centers contain three or more giants in hard goods retailing (e.g., toys, electronics, home furnishings, and off-price stores). Home Depot and Walmart are prominent big-box retailers that frequently locate their stores in power centers. These centers often draw shoppers from a radius of five miles or more.

Yet another type is regional shopping centers or malls. Regional centers (malls) focus on general merchandise and usually have at least two-anchor tenants that are major department stores (e.g., Nordstrom and Dillard's). Typical sizes range from 400,000 to 800,000 square feet of GLA. Major tenants are national chains or well-established local businesses with high credit ratings and a significant financial position. These retailers draw people from a larger area than the neighborhood or community centers, although 80 percent of their sales are typically drawn from within a 5- to 15-mile radius. Minor "in-line" tenants are located between the anchor tenants to capture customers. Regional centers often contain several stores of one type (e.g., shoe stores). Many include small fast-food outlets arranged in local courts. Many malls, especially those of lower quality and inferior location, have witnessed declining rents and increased vacancies, which will in turn require new strategies to combat.

The last type we'll discuss here is super-regional malls. These centers may have as many as five or six major tenants and dozens of minor tenants. The typical GLA exceeds 800,000 square feet and includes many of the same features as regional centers, but are larger and offer more amenities (e.g., indoor amusement parks) to attract longer foot traffic.

The retail tenant's primary concerns are the availability of adequate space for its business, shoppers' access to their space, the volume of consumer traffic generated by the center, and the visibility of the tenant's location with the center. Rents are quoted based on GLA. The GLA for a particular tenant captures the amount of space occupied and controlled by the tenant, and is therefore similar to an office tenant's usable area.

The lease contracts between retail owners and tenants are often extremely complicated and vary considerably across properties and tenants. Many clauses and conditions that are standard in the leases of regional mall department stores are inappropriate for a hair salon or gift store in a neighborhood shopping center. Small retail businesses often lease space for durations as short as one or two years, whereas larger tenants are often willing and able to commit to much longer leases. Anchor tenants, the large and generally well-known retailers who typically draw most customers to the shopping center, may sign lease terms of 25 to 30 years, with one or more renewal options. Nonanchor tenants often make flat or indexed rental payments in addition to some percentage of their gross sales. All tenants typically share in paying the center's operating expenses.

Retail property performance has been making a comeback. After years of pressure from e-commerce sales and challenging demographic and economic conditions, necessity-focused retail, retail power centers (neighborhood retail centers anchored by at least one large retail tenant and between 250,000 and 600,000 square feet of rentable space), and fortress malls (Class A malls) are performing well. Many tenants have adjusted to compete with online sales by converting to an omnichannel format where they offer their products both online and in stores. Additionally, many offer in-store pickup for online sales.

DATA CENTERS

Data centers make up the backbone of the internet. As such, they house the infrastructure—uninterruptible power supply, fiber-optic cables, servers, racks, cooling systems—critical for data storage, applications, networking, and computing. Historically, the vast majority of corporate computing was performed within data center space built, owned, and operated by the organization itself.

In its simplest form, data center firms are hosting companies that lease servers (or space on the servers) and provide storage capacity to companies. The hosting provider owns and operates the equipment and the data center with three product options: computing capacity, storage, and managed services or on-site support functions. Alternatively, wholesale or colocation providers lease physical space within their facilities to one or more customers. Wholesale customers tend to be larger organizations with data center requirements of 1 megawatt (MW) or more power capacity. The customer maintains operational control over all their equipment used within their controlled space. Multiple customers operate in a single facility in their own private data hall, while sharing the common areas of the building such as the mechanical and electrical equipment, security, the loading dock, and office space.

The cloud has significantly changed the IT landscape in the past decade. In the mid-2000s, as the need for digitization increased and the data sphere grew exponentially (driven by mobile devices and the Internet of Things), cloud computing was created by such organizations as Amazon and Google. Cloud computing generally refers to the delivery of computing services like servers, storage, databases, networking, applications, software, and more over the internet, with the aim to offer flexible resources, economies of scale, and more business agility. Cloud-based delivery and consumption models are now mainstream, powering a new wave of innovation across industries and domains. The cloud-based delivery of infrastructure, platform, and software as a service has enabled companies to focus on solving higher-level business problems by eliminating the need for large upfront investments and enabling business agility through advantageous cost structures.

LIFE SCIENCE

Real estate in the life science space consists of office, laboratory, and current good manufacturing process (cGMP) facilities leased to private, research, university, and government tenants focused on genomics, pharmaceuticals, biotechnology, and cell therapy, among others. Further, the life sciences sector has been experiencing a convergence of secular tailwinds within demographics, quality-of-life innovations, and healthcare spending that is leading to an extremely compelling demand outlook. Fundamentals in the sector are currently strong and driven by acceleration in the pace and level of innovation, technological advancement and leveraging data science, as well as record funding levels, both from venture/private capital and government agencies. These tailwinds have created formidable growth in sector employment, driving demand for lab space.

Private and government funding is the primary demand driver for the life science sector because it capitalizes the early-stage biotechnology businesses that serve as the incubator and pipeline for discovering and developing new approaches and therapies. For life sciences companies and startups in particular, venture capital investment is a crucial funding source and typically coincides with a company moving to a larger space with potentially more sophisticated design requirements. Venture capital investment has grown from under $7 billion in 2011 to $50 billion in 2021—a seven-times increase.[1]

Currently, there is less than 200 million square feet of lab space in the US, just a fraction of the 18.1 billion square feet of industrial and 8.3 billion square feet of office.[2] The three most important markets, which comprise roughly 60 percent of the US investable asset universe, are exhibiting tight vacancy rates as low as 3.5 percent and have experienced rent growth of approximately 30 and 60 percent from 2019 to 2022.[3] These three markets represent the most important research clusters, as they contain the universities and talent, and thus capture the preponderance of funding.

SELF-STORAGE

Self-storage properties are metal-clad warehouses comprised of hundreds of individually leased units that can be climate-controlled. This property type does not include POD, or portable container storage, but rather physically located storage facilities. Lease terms are month-to-month rentals. A typical storage facility is located on a two-to-five-acre lot featuring 5 to 10 one-story drive-up buildings, although select Sunbelt and Gateway city markets can offer two-story or higher construction. These properties offer a variety of different unit sizes with large roll-up doors in addition to outside parking for boats, RVs, and other motor vehicles. As such, these assets tend to receive smaller valuations—usually in the range of $3 to $5 million—and therefore predicate a portfolio/aggregation approach to achieve higher levels of scale economies within a select market area. As of 2021, over 2 billion square feet of rentable self-storage in the US were spread across more than 52,000 facilities.

These assets tend to be located near a dense customer base, usually attracting tenants from a radius of three to five miles. Other considerations focus on the residential unit growth, the ratio of single-family to multifamily residences, the availability and affordability of land, ease of zoning, commuter traffic patterns, and so on. Given their attractive characteristics, publicly traded REITs are the largest owners of self-storage assets in the US and internationally.

The self-storage industry began in the mid-1960s in North America and has spread to Europe and Asia as developed economies have become consumer-centric. Self-storage has become an increasingly popular property type for investors due to its low operating and maintenance costs, high occupancy, and resilient cash flow dynamics even in a recession. Market saturation remains a risk for the space, given some jurisdictions' quick timeline for new development and the generally frictionless permitting process. Overbuilding can result in higher turnover, shorter-term leases, increased vacancy rates, longer lease-up periods, and lower rents.

HEALTHCARE (SENIOR HOUSING)

Healthcare is another specialty property type because it caters to a distinct kind of tenant, which can include senior living, medical office, skilled nursing, and hospital facilities. Senior living communities are designed for the 80 years and older cohort and offer care services across the spectrum of memory care, assisted living, and independent living. Senior housing operators manage these types of communities. Leases are structured as NNN with fixed rent bumps but can also participate in the operational cash flows from care services (i.e., REIT Investment Diversification and Empowerment Act [RIDEA] structures). Physicians or affiliates of healthcare systems use medical office properties.[4] Buildings are multistory and are often located near a hospital, leading to a steady demand profile and lower rental risk compared to traditional offices. Due to the higher tenant improvement costs, medical office leases tend to last 7 to 10 years. Skilled nursing provides around-the-clock patient care on both short- and long-term bases. Demand is stable and needs-based, and offers the lowest cost setting to treat many conditions. This subcategory features high legislative risk around revenues. Finally, hospitals provide the highest level of care for emergency and high-acuity needs. Hospitals benefit from population growth and aging demographics.

STUDENT HOUSING

Based on physical attributes alone, student housing properties are similar to apartments; however, the sector exhibits demand drivers and operational intensity distinct from the traditional multifamily space. As such, market participants tend to be student housing specialists given its added complexity. The different types of student housing structures are dorms/residence halls, purpose-built apartments, cottages, and duplexes.

Properties can be located on- or off-campus around colleges and universities in the US, with on-campus or immediately adjacent housing benefiting from more robust fundamentals. Further, on-campus units tend to have a central location, stronger rent growth, and higher occupancy levels; however, the university may restrict or control the operations in addition to complexities involving ground leases, long procurement times for construction, and limited debt financing. Off-campus student housing typically suffers from inferior fundamentals, although these assets feature full operational control and fee-simple land ownership, and can be easily financed.

The sector's demand drivers focus on broader demographic and enrollment trends, the strength of the labor market, and the availability and cost of obtaining student debt. Operational differences between traditional multifamily and student housing include lease terms running 11.5 months, tighter operating margins, significantly higher tenant turnover, leases by the bed versus unit, fully furnished dwellings, and a small leasing window.[5]

UNDERSTANDING SECTORS

Commercial real estate properties are best understood and described using a sector-based framework, in some respects like stocks. Notably, the various sectors within commercial real estate provide investors with exposure to assets driven by different fundamentals and market participants. While the majority of investment capital remains in the traditional sectors of multifamily, industrial, office, and retail, other niche sectors have emerged and are gaining traction with institutions. Ultimately, real estate is cyclical and sectors even more so, highlighting the value that deeper insight can offer to investors given the individual nuances of each property type.

NOTES

1. JLL Research. 2022 Life Sciences Research Outlook & Cluster Rankings.
2. Per CoStar Industrial and Office Inventory as of Q4 2022, "Life Science Inventory Is Top 12 Markets," from CBRE US Life Sciences Trends, 2021.
3. JLL, CBRE.
4. Green Street. Sector Primer: Health Care.
5. Green Street. Sector Primer: Student Housing.

The Broker/Investment Advisor

A Wide Range of Options for International Capital

Jacques Gordon, PhD, Executive-in-Residence, MIT

U S real estate has been a target for inbound investment flows for decades, if not centuries. A wide variety of different countries have each taken their turn as the largest source of inbound capital[1] over the last several decades; international capital typically accounts for between 15 and 25 percent of all commercial real estate transactions in any given year.[2] The US has a strong reputation for real estate transparency, with attributes such as strong protection of property rights, wide availability of fundamentals and performance data, and an efficient transaction process.[3] Thus, it is not surprising that investors from many different countries regularly allocate significant portions of their annual real estate investment targets to the US.

International investors face a wide range of options when they consider making investments in US real estate. It should come as no surprise that the world's foremost consumer society also offers the widest range of investment products and sources of financial advice when it comes to investing in commercial real estate. The US has 35 metro areas,[4] each with a population of over two million. Ten of these metros appear on the "Global 30" list of the cities with the largest market capitalization of *commercial* real estate in the world, more than any other country by a significant margin.[5] The basic principles involved in setting up an investment program and identifying a team of advisors and service providers in the US have not changed substantially over the last 30 years. However, the US markets themselves are highly dynamic. US labor mobility and population movements are higher than other G-20 countries. New niche property types (such as data centers, life science buildings, and manufactured housing communities) are often introduced in the US investment markets ahead of other countries. Local advice can help a non-US investor identify strong investments and avoid unnecessary risk.

One of the first things any financial manager should do before building a US real estate investment portfolio is to clarify their objectives and how they want to achieve them. A short checklist of criteria is shown in Figure 1.7-01. A professional investment advisor plays a critical role in helping shape an investment program to meet the specific goals of an international investor. Clarification of these goals will narrow the wide range of investment alternatives, which includes listed real estate securities, commingled funds, mortgages, joint ventures, and direct-equity investments. Structured finance—including mezzanine positions, opco/propco investments, and Proptech ventures—are among the channels that international investors have pursued in recent years. The matrix shown in Figure 1.7-02 illustrates the six broad options available to investors in US capital markets. Each cell in this matrix offers different combinations of financial and legal characteristics, which can be matched against the investment criteria checklist.

FIGURE 1.7-01 **Investment criteria**

- TIME HORIZON
- RETURN EXPECTATIONS
- TARGET SIZE OF ALLOCATION TO US REAL ESTATE
- TOLERANCE FOR DIFFERENT TYPES OF RISK
  (SPECIFIC RISK, DURATION RISK, MARKET RISK, ETC.)
- DEGREE OF DISCRETION GIVEN TO ADVISOR
- LIQUIDITY
- INVESTMENT STYLE: INCOME, GROWTH, OPPORTUNISTIC
- DOWNSIDE PROTECTION VERSUS UPSIDE POTENTIAL
- USE OF LEVERAGE
- TAX POSITION IN THE US, ABILITY TO USE TAX LOSSES
- CURRENCY AND CASH MANAGEMENT

FIGURE 1.7-02 **The real estate capital market matrix**

	EQUITY	DEBT
PRIVATE DIRECT MARKET	DIRECT PROPERTY INVESTMENTS PARTNERSHIP AND JOINT VENTURES	MORTGAGES AND SYNDICATED LOANS
PRIVATE INDIRECT MARKET	OPPORTUNITY FUNDS PRIVATE PLACEMENTS COMMINGLED FUNDS	HIGH-YIELD CMBS MEZZANINE DEBT FUNDS
PUBLIC MARKET	REITs REAL ESTATE OPERATING COMPANIES	INVESTMENT GRADE CMBS REIT DEBT

Each cell in the capital-market matrix ultimately derives its financial performance from commercial real estate, yet the financial and legal structure of different investment vehicles create wide variations in risk-reward-liquidity combinations. Figure 1.7-03 illustrates some of the trade-offs associated with the various cells in the matrix. The different combinations of governance, control, diversification, cross-border tax status, and financial reporting offered by each option compel investors to define their own investment objectives, tolerance for risk, reporting requirements, and investment horizon.

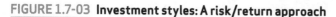

FIGURE 1.7-03 **Investment styles: A risk/return approach**

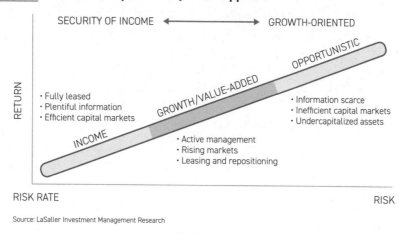

Source: LaSaller Investment Management Research

For instance, a direct equity investing program maximizes an investor's control over each asset, but diversification and liquidity objectives become harder to achieve. When investors allocate less than $25 million to US real estate, real estate securities (stock in REITs) and interests in collateralized mortgage-backed securities (CMBS) offer much greater diversification and higher levels of liquidity than direct investing. For investors allocating between $25 million and $500 million to the US, private equity commingled funds (open- and closed-end) also offer a reasonable degree of diversification, while giving investors the chance to seek more customized strategies than those broadly available to the investing public. These funds do not offer nearly the same degree of liquidity as do publicly traded securities, but many long-term investors are willing to give up some liquidity to avoid the price volatility found in the public markets.

Figure 1.7-04 illustrates that investors will also need to consider how to combine real estate with other asset classes in building their US portfolios. This chart shows that both listed and private equity real estate in the US compare favorably to other asset classes, and that they are not perfectly correlated with stocks and bonds—which pushes out the efficient frontier to the "northwest," which is exactly what institutional investor strive for. Geographic and property-type diversification are important considerations for long-term investors. Some international investors will be looking at US real estate as an extension of their domestic real estate portfolios. Others will be looking at US real estate within the context of a US portfolio of stocks and bonds. Still others will be seeking a safe harbor in US dollar-denominated hard assets. Whatever the context, an investment manager or a professional investment advisor should be prepared to guide a non-US investor toward appropriate levels of diversification at the portfolio level, in addition to offering asset-specific guidance. A diversified portfolio will reduce the risks associated with specific properties or markets. Asset-specific guidance is also incredibly valuable given that off-shore investors may not be familiar with the nuances of local US markets.

FIGURE 1.7-04 **30-year risk/return comparisons**

US real estate earns competitive risk-adjusted returns relative to other asset classes

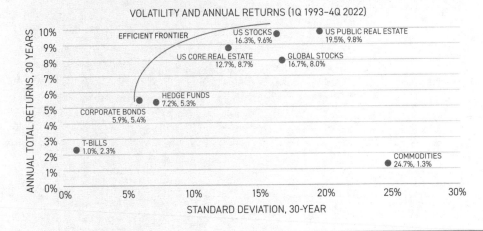

VOLATILITY AND ANNUAL RETURNS (1Q 1993–4Q 2022)

How much diversification is required? Using the latest statistical techniques applied to over 10,000 properties in the NPI (NCREIF Property Index) suggests a portfolio of 18 to 20 properties will typically eliminate a majority of the idiosyncrasies associated with direct investment. As portfolios approach 30 or 40 properties, this idiosyncratic risk falls to levels equivalent to 70 to 90 percent of the overall index.[6] Listed REITs provide the most efficient means of diversification, as many well-established REITs own hundreds of properties. On the debt side, commercial mortgage-backed securities (CMBS) also provide an efficient means of diversification. It is important to remember, though, that in a CMBS diversification can expose the subordinate tranches to any problems first, while the higher-rated tranches are well-insulated and harness the power of diversification.

CHOOSING AN ADVISOR

Many intermediaries, advisors, and consultants specialize in one or more of the different investment vehicles described in the real estate capital markets matrix. However, it is rare to find an investment professional who can cover every cell in this matrix with equal levels of expertise. Moreover, geographic and property-type expertise is useful in a large, diverse country like the US. As a result, an international investor faces a seemingly overwhelming number of choices when first investigating the options. How should an investor begin? As in any country, it is important to understand the players and define their roles. Figure 1.7-05 lists the major sources of investment services found in the US for direct investing in equity real estate.

FIGURE 1.7-05 **Sources of investment advice for private equity**

PROFESSIONAL	SERVICE PROVIDED	WHO PAYS?	PAID HOW?
BROKER	ACCESS TO ASSET FOR SALE		
	SELLER'S AGENT	SELLER	COMMISSION
	BUYER'S AGENT	BUYER	COMMISSION
CONSULTANT	ASSET ALLOCATION AND MANAGER SCREENING	INVESTOR	TIME AND EXPENSES OR RETAINER
INVESTMENT MANAGER	PORTFOLIO MANAGEMENT AND STRATEGY	INVESTOR	PERFORMANCE & AUM
ASSET MANAGER	ASSET-SPECIFIC BUDGETS, REPORTING	FUND MANAGER	PERFORMANCE & AUM
PROPERTY MANAGER	LEASING AND RENT COLLECTIONS	FUND MANAGER	COMMISSIONS & AUM OR % OF GROSS/NET INCOME

NOTE: AUM – Assets Under Management

Although each of these functions is quite distinct, in some cases they can be carried out by the same investment team or firm. Many US real estate service providers have different divisions capable of carrying out each of these important functions, or they have long-standing relationships with service providers that international investors can take advantage of. When embarking on any investment program an international investor should clarify which functions are to be carried out by whom. In the world of direct investing, all five of these functions are required for the smooth operation of a large portfolio. In some cases, more sophisticated international investors may retain some of the strategic, portfolio-level decisions for themselves, or they may open a US-based office tasked with learning the market and sifting through deal flow. In others, a US-based investment manager takes on responsibility for the portfolio mix. Typically, offshore capital relies on a mix of both local and "home-office" guidance to get a US-directed investment program up and running. Specialized functions like property management or debt advising are often outsourced to local US firms, while strategic investment decisions are best handled by a combination of US-domestic expertise working closely together with overseas staff who are most familiar with the specific, tax, legal, and asset/liability mix of each investor.

Providers involved in the securities and debt sectors have similar roles and functions, although the names may differ. For instance, a placement agent for debt capital is often called a correspondent or mortgage banker, while the debt asset manager is called a servicer. There is no property management function in a debt context, unless there is a default, which then becomes the responsibility of a special servicer. In a REIT, the asset and property managers are typically all employees of the trust while the strategic investment management functions are carried out by its chief executive officer, chief financial officer, and board of directors. By contrast, a direct investment program typically hires third parties to execute various leasing or management functions and is more likely to be diversified by property type and geography, whereas REITs tend to specialize in a specific sector.

Brokers in both the private market and publicly traded vehicles are required to have the proper licenses and both are regulated. However, the brokerage function for the real estate securities market, unlike the private market, requires the services of a market maker and of investment bankers to facilitate the issuance of shares. Although commission structures are vastly different between the public and private markets, the brokerage function is very much the same—to act as an intermediary between buyers and sellers. Experienced advisors typically have experience in both the listed and the private equity markets.

ADVISORS, CONSULTANTS, AND MONEY MANAGERS

The title "advisor" can legitimately be applied to any of the functions listed in Figure 1.7-05, but there are several important distinctions to keep in mind. First, investors must understand exactly who is paying for the service and advice being offered. A buyer needs to be aware that seller's agents, sell-side securities analysts, and rating agencies who opine on the merits of a specific asset or the creditworthiness of mortgage-backed securities or unsecured REIT debt are all paid by the owner or the entity raising capital. The turmoil in the US debt capital markets (2007–2009) was due in part to inadequate regulation, weak oversight of the rating agencies, and aggressive tactics used by issuers of debt securities. The rating agencies' reputations were damaged, and a new system has been put in place that requires securitized debt issuers to undertake "risk retention" by holding a residual tranche of each debt security. Renewed confidence in the debt markets by investors has been achieved through more transparent reporting on all aspects of the securitized debt issuance and rating process. By the same token in the direct equity markets, seller's agents know that their reputations for truthfulness and full disclosure are among their most valuable assets. Nevertheless, the fact that property owners are paying commissions to capital market intermediaries should raise a caveat emptor signal to any investor.

COVID-19 brought a new set of requirements and skills quickly to the US marketplace. Although "virtual" document rooms and the use of video for touring properties was in use prior to COVID, these practices became the main way that buyers and sellers interacted during the lockdown period. It is remarkable to observe that deal flow in 2021 was at or close to record highs in many sectors (e.g., warehouses, residential markets) despite the persistence of COVID. The rapid emergence of "prop-tech" tools in the decade leading up to COVID made a huge difference in the ability of the capital markets to function, despite restrictions on travel and face-to-face meetings.

Asset allocation consultants, appraisers, and market research firms all charge investors for their services on a time/expense basis much like any other professional firm. For large assignments these firms are often on a retainer, which gives clients access to the top consultants on an as-needed basis. These consulting firms are usually unwilling to put their fees at risk, pending the outcome of their advice.

The services rendered by investment managers and buy-side brokers are quite distinct, although both are paid by the investor. Investment managers act as fiduciaries or money managers and remain involved with the investment through the entire holding period. They expect that a portion of their fee will be tied to the performance of the assets in their custody. The key distinction here is that the investment manager provides reporting and asset management services once the transaction is completed, while the buy-side broker typically focuses on the transaction itself. Investment managers are typically paid for performance over the holding period of the asset. For noncore (value-add) investments investment managers typically coinvest alongside the client. By contrast, buy-side brokers act as placement agents and are paid for identifying, tying up, and assisting in the closing of targeted assets. In the equity markets, seller's agents rarely share their commissions with buy-side brokers, so the services of the buy-side broker must be paid by the investor. However, most cross-border investors do not have their own asset-management staff and require ongoing investment management services. As a result, buy-side brokerage is much less common in the US for equity investors than it is in Europe or Asia where buyers may have extensive networks of cross-border service providers within the region that are already well-established.

PRINCIPALS AND AGENTS

Another important distinction is the difference between an "agent," who represents a transacting party or investor, and a "principal," who is a party to the transaction or investment. Principals either put their own assets at risk alongside the investor or put a significant portion of their fee at risk until the financial outcome of the investment is known. Principals are commonly thought to have a closer alignment of interest with investors than do agents. But agents also have their reputations and repeat business to think about when conducting business on behalf of an international investor. The term "fiduciary" applies to both types of advice, since both are relationships based on trust and adherence to the principle of putting a client's interests ahead of the advisor or the coinvestor.

The notion of a principal also acting as an investment manager for an international investor raises the question of whether the principal has the same time horizon and risk tolerance as the investor. Going back to the investment criteria in Figure 1.7-01, investors should not be surprised to find several differences between their own investment objectives and those of their coinvestment partners. Rarely are two sources of capital exactly alike when it comes to taking and avoiding risk. Nevertheless, the coinvestment model, in conjunction with a back-ended performance fee, remain powerful tools available to international investors to ensure the alignment of their own and their US partners' financial interests. Investors should remember that the amount of the coinvestment is less important than the relative significance of the coinvestment amount to the sponsor of the investment vehicle.

DISCRETIONARY VERSUS NONDISCRETIONARY INVESTMENT PROGRAMS

As suggested in the checklist from Figure 1.7-01, the degree of discretion granted to an investment manager is a key choice to be made by the investor early in the process. At one extreme, an investor may prefer that all investment decisions be approved by the capital source, while at the other the investment manager may make all the decisions, subject to parameters previously agreed to. To an investor, the advantage of retaining discretion is control over the investment program and the outcome. The disadvantages include a reduction in nimbleness and a steep learning curve on each transaction that can slow down decision-making. Moreover, the accountability for success and failure is less clear than in a discretionary program.

IN-HOUSE VERSUS OUTSOURCE

A growing group of money managers are now based in more than one country. Some of these institutions face the choice of doing their US investment activity themselves or outsourcing it to a specialist. Several investment management firms specialize by working exclusively with capital from one country and putting it to work in US real estate on behalf of that country's investors. Others have established a global platform and are capable of working with both assets and capital sources across multiple countries. Offshore institutions without US staff always face the decision of whether to put some of their own people into the market to help with investment activities. The approach of building an entire organization capable of buying, managing, and reporting on US-based assets is an expensive option. Nevertheless, firms from Australia, Canada, China, Germany, Japan, the Middle East, and Sweden have all success- fully followed this model. Most non-US-based sources of capital elect to outsource some portion of their investment activities, depending on their own capabilities and needs.

Due Diligence

Ultimately, the international investor seeking real estate advice in the US should apply the same tests they would use with their local advisors and investment managers. The acronym STEP (skills, trust, experience, and performance) reminds an investor to evaluate an advisor from four important perspectives.

First, skills: the right blend of skills—strategy, execution, and reporting—must match the nature of the assignment. A regional or property-type specialist will have valuable insights within that range of expertise, but may be less versatile for a broad assignment. Excellent communication and listening skills are also critical. International investors should look for advisors who are adept at dealing with non-US clients and who can demonstrate a commit- ment to high levels of service across time zones and across cultures. A tendency to offer advice first and to listen second (if ever) marks some US-based advisors as more interested in their own welfare than that of the client.

Second, trust: a deep and enduring level of trust must be established between inves- tor and advisor. Trust can only be built up over time, of course. Nevertheless, evidence of high ethical standards should be examined, such as the way an advisor handles confidential information and treats its employees. Lawyers and accountants who regularly deal with the advisor can provide important insights, especially to an international investor unaccustomed to US business practices.

Third, experience: the credentials of the individuals handling the account must be exam- ined, especially with respect to their experience with cross-border transactions and non-US entities doing business in the US. References from recent clients should be sought. Turnover statistics among senior staff can also be requested. Non-US investors should keep in mind that US professionals do change employers more frequently than their European or Asian counterparts. A cumulative turnover rate of less than 10 percent over several years demon- strates a reasonable level of stability in the US.

Fourth, performance: ultimately, an investor needs to be confident that the advisor knows how to make money in commercial real estate. Three- and five-year track records of each candidate's performance should be sought. This performance should be compared to a rele- vant (investable) universe with a similar risk-return profile. Investors should confirm that the individuals who created this performance are still with the firm. Performance of discretionary assets is more telling than the performance of nondiscretionary assets but both are important, especially to an investor seeking a nondiscretionary relationship. Investors should also make sure that the statement of this performance is compliant with the international guidelines laid down by the International Accounting Standards Board and described in the International Financial Reporting Standards.

Last, in the aftermath of recurring credit crises (2001, 2008, 2023) it has become imperative to ascertain the financial soundness of any investment advisor. The near-collapse of many major banks and financial institutions has taken its toll on a wide variety of real estate organizations in the US over the last 20 years. An investor should inquire about the exposure of any firm to balance sheet problems or debt-refinancing problems that could lead to bankruptcy or to the departure of key individuals.

A LOCAL BUSINESS GOES GLOBAL

It is often said that the key to success in cross-border real estate investing is the ability to think globally but to act locally. An advisor who can excel at both will best serve the interests of a cross-border client. International investors almost always have different needs than domestic sources of capital. To be successful, the investment advisor must have the ability to understand the transaction from the perspective of the cross-border investor. An advisor who has learned how to "walk in the moccasins" of a cross-border investor will be best prepared to give truly useful advice and to help execute this advice on behalf of non-US investors.

In 2023, cross-border investors face a new set of challenges compared to prior periods of financial volatility. Access to dependable sources of debt that are accretive to the cash flow of new investments has become a challenge as interest rates rise and lenders get more conservative. These credit availability issues are also present in other countries. The tendency of financial institutions in the US to stay one step ahead of the regulators has produced a mixed blessing: a country with great sources of financial innovation, but also a country whose banking system is prone to "Minsky"[7] moments.

Already one of the world's most transparent markets, the US has plentiful sources of online data and mapping tools suitable for taking virtual property and neighborhood tours. Moreover, as *The AFIRE Guide* demonstrates, the US has a large selection of tax advisors, law firms, and accounting firms with deep experience helping structure tax-efficient cross-border transactions. Off-shore capital routinely figures in the country's real estate transactions (both large and small), and the US tax changes to the **Foreign Investment in Real Property Tax Act (FIRPTA)** enacted in 2015 continued to make the US attractive for qualifying non-US pension funds. Investing in the US requires careful attention to the capital markets and the fundamentals, both of which tend to be cyclical. The risks and opportunities of investing at various stages of each property cycle are quite different. Yet developing an investment program with clear objectives and identifying trusted advisors hold the key to unlocking value in the world's largest commercial real estate markets, as shown in Figure 1.7-06.

FIGURE 1.7-06 **The top 30 global markets for real estate investors**

	METRO NAME	INSTITUTIONALLY OWNED REAL ESTATE IN 2022
1.	GREATER TOKYO	$557
2.	NEW YORK METRO AREA	$386
3.	GREATER LONDON	$331
4.	HONG KONG	$303
5.	PARIS / ILE DE FRANCE	$295
6.	LOS ANGELES COMBINED STATISTICAL AREA	$226
7.	SAN FRANCISCO BAY AREA	$217
8.	SEOUL CAPITAL AREA	$171
9.	SINGAPORE	$170
10.	WASHINGTON, DC METRO	$132
11.	SYDNEY GREATER CAPITAL CITY AREA	$130
12.	BOSTON-CAMBRIDGE METRO	$128
13.	GREATER TORONTO AREA	$113
14.	CHICAGO METRO	$113
15.	SHANGHAI URBAN AGGLOMERATION	$104
16.	OSAKA PREFECTURE	$94
17.	GREATER MELBOURNE CAPITAL CITY AREA	$92
18.	SOUTH FLORIDA (DADE, BROWARD, PALM BEACH)	$91
19.	BEIJING URBAN AGGLOMERATION	$85
20.	METROPOLREGION MUNCHEN	$84
21.	SEATTLE-TACOMA METRO	$83
22.	GREATER MOSCOW	$82
23.	HOUSTON METRO	$80
24.	STOCKHOLM EUROSTAT METRO	$76
25.	GUANGZHOU URBAN AGGLOMERATION	$67
26.	SHENZHEN URBAN AGGLOMERATION	$67
27.	BERLIN & BRANDERBURG	$67
28.	FRANKFURT EUROSTAT METRO	$65
29.	ATLANTA METRO	$64
30.	HAMBURG EUROSTAT METRO	$63

Source: LaSalle Investable Universe 2022

NOTES

* The author would like to thank Nobel Carpenter of Banyan Street Capital, who provided contributions to this chapter.

1. According to JLL, the following countries have each taken a turn at being the largest source of inbound investment into US real estate over the past 30 years: Canada, China, Germany, Japan, the Netherlands, Singapore, South Korea, and the UAE. Other countries, including Australia, Denmark, Israel, Kuwait, Norway, Qatar, and the United Kingdom, regularly rank among the top three.

2. Based on RCA data from 2000 to 2020, where international capital was identified as either the buyer or seller. These percentages are an underestimate, given that international capital is not always disclosed in minority positions or in debt transactions. International investing in domestically controlled REITs is one of the most tax-efficient way for overseas capital to invest in US real estate and these transactions are not always easily tracked in RCA data.

3. See the JLL Global Real Estate Transparency Index (1999–2022) https://www.us.jll.com/en/trends-and -insights/research/global-real-estate-transparency-index.

4. As of 2020, Estimates by the US Bureau of the Census website: www.census.gov.

5. See Figure 1.7-06: The top 30 global markets for real estate investors p. 66.

6. Fisher, Jeff. "How Many Properties Does It Take to Diversify Away Risk in Real Estate?" NCREIF Academy 2023.

7. Named for Hyman Minsky, an economist who studied how financial innovation and credit collapses are often closely linked in the financial world, with the US being the prime example of this two-edged sword.

The Attorney/Tax Advisor

Building a Knowledge of the Nuances

John L. Sullivan, Partner, DLA Piper

Shiukay Hung, Partner, DLA Piper

When embarking on real estate investment in the US, it is critical to select an integrated team of advisors.[1] Of these advisors, law firms and accounting firms play a frequently indispensable role for all phases of the real estate life cycle.

The purpose of this chapter is to describe these roles and outline the various factors non-US-based investors should consider when selecting legal and accounting advisors for real estate transactions.

IMPORTANCE OF STRUCTURING

Lawyers and accountants both play an important role in the structuring of US real estate investments, especially for non-US-based investors, who are subject to unique tax and regulatory requirements, including country-specific requirements such as income tax treaty requirements. Accordingly, there is no one-size-fits-all advisory structure for all non-US investors. Rather, an optimal structure is tailored to the tax profile, investment objective, regulatory requirements, and risk tolerance of a particular investor.

Law firms and accounting firms often share responsibility as tax advisors. Non-US investors are subject to an array of US and non-US tax requirements. From a US tax perspective, the objective is to maximize investment returns by minimizing US taxes and compliance obligations. Such tax planning often includes the use of special tax advantaged vehicles, such as **real estate investment trusts (REITs)** and/or blocker entities[2] leveraged with intercompany debt. It may also include structuring the real estate transaction to qualify for certain tax exemptions available to non-US investors.

The structuring of real estate investments for non-US investors is complicated. In 1980, the **Foreign Investment in Real Property Tax Act (FIRPTA)** was signed into law in the US, imposing a tax on non-US investors on the gain from the disposition of US real estate.[3]

Despite its name, FIRPTA is not a self-contained set of rules governing the US taxation of non-US investors. Instead, FIRPTA is one of the many sets of US federal tax rules that form a part of the **Internal Revenue Code of 1986**, as amended, that may apply to a particular real estate transaction. To further complicate matters, depending on the tax profile of the non-US investor, the non-US investor may qualify for preferential tax treatment (e.g., a sovereign wealth fund; a qualified foreign pension fund as defined under the **Protecting Americans from Tax Hikes Act of 2015 (PATH Act)**; a taxpayer entitled to benefits under an applicable income tax treaty with the US). A specific non-US investor may also benefit from special tax structuring such as an entity interest sale of a domestically controlled REIT or an intercompany debt-leveraged blocker entity designed to benefit from the "cleansing exception" and the "portfolio interest exemption."

On top of US federal income tax considerations, legal and accounting advisors also need to evaluate state tax considerations such as property transfer taxes.[4] Last, the legal and accounting advisors will need to consider the non-US investor's home country tax and regulatory laws that may impact the ultimate structure of the transaction, such as the desired level of control over investment and operational decisions, the use of debt-leverage, and/or the selection of a particular special purpose entity (e.g., an LLC or LLP).

ROLE OF THE LAW FIRM

The involvement of a particular law firm can be as extensive as the transaction or client demands. The role may vary depending upon whether the law firm is representing a seller, purchaser, developer, borrower, lender, equity investor, or other participant.

The role of the law firm in a transaction may involve:

- Structuring the transaction to carry out the business objectives in a tax efficient and regulatory compliant manner, including planning and structuring acquisition, disposition, and development.
- Preparing and negotiating letters of intent, confidentiality agreements, and commission agreements, and advising the client on related liability issues, particularly for binding obligations that may arise out of letters of intent or commission agreements, which are attributable to events other than entry into a purchase and sale agreement and/or actual consummation of the transaction.
- Preparing and negotiating purchase and sale agreements and related documents, including escrow agreements and acquisition/sale closing documents; and advising the client on necessary, advisable, standard, or customary contractual provisions on liability issues, particularly those arising out of representations, warranties, and indemnities; their survival beyond the closing of the transaction, and limitations on amounts owed or recoverable for related breaches; and on termination issues, particularly those arising out of unsatisfactory due diligence and changed circumstances (such as casualty, condemnation, and loss of income).
- Conducting due diligence activities, such as review of title, survey, environmental reports, leases, service or operating agreements, local zoning ordinances and codes, and compliance with REIT tax qualification rules.
- Forming the investment entity, including negotiation and documentation of limited partnership agreements, limited liability company operating agreements, REIT organizational agreements, and joint venture agreements through which the essential contractual, economic, operational, and other conditions can be managed.

- Negotiating and documenting any financing for the investment[5] and assisting in the satisfaction of loan closing conditions, including compliance with title and survey requirements; delivery of nonconsolidation and other opinions of legal counsel; arranging for issuance of acceptable reliance letters for environmental and property condition reports; and obtaining or coordinating the delivery of tenant estoppel certificates and subordination, nondisturbance, and attornment agreements.
- Obtaining a tax opinion, private letter ruling, or other advanced tax ruling from a taxing authority; advising on **Employee Retirement Income Security Act (ERISA)** rules; advising the client on compliance with applicable reporting requirements,[6] and assisting with operational matters following acquisition such as preparing office, retail, and ground leases, and property management and leasing agreements, and negotiating the terms thereof.

In addition to the preceding, specialized tax expertise is often central to the overall structuring of the transaction. Experienced tax counsel specialized in representing non-US investors can develop and implement the desired tax structure for a particular real estate investment, select an appropriate investment entity, draft and negotiate the required tax provisions in the relevant documents (such as an entity's organizational documents and the purchase and sale agreement), and render tax opinions or obtain a private letter ruling or other advanced tax ruling from an applicable taxing authority.

Non-US investors often require the use of special tax-advantaged investment entities, such as internal leveraged blocker entities or REITs. In many instances, these entities are formed under the laws of the state of Delaware, and limited partnerships and limited liability companies are favored forms, owing to their flexibility. As appropriate, certain blocker entitics may also be formed offshore in the Cayman Islands, the British Virgin Islands, or the home country jurisdiction of the investor.

SELECTION OF THE LAW FIRM

The factors that should inform an investor's selection of legal advisors include the following.

SINGLE SOURCE OF LEGAL ADVICE
In addition to requiring subject matter experts in real estate, tax, finance, and regulatory matters, a transaction may involve multiple states and require legal advice in each of the relevant states. An ideal law firm should have the resources to advise on these matters and provide non-US investors with a single source of legal advice.

EXPERIENCE IN HANDLING SIMILAR TRANSACTIONS
A law firm with significant experience in advising non-US investors in previous similar transactions can draw on its prior experience and facilitate the consummation of the new transaction expediently and efficiently. Conversely, a law firm that lacks experience advising non-US investors in similar transactions may cause delays, increased costs, and in extreme cases, failure of the deal. Clients are best served by selecting attorneys who operate more like counselors, with a style and attitude that enable them to advance a deal, rather than serving

as mere legal technicians unable to provide practical and commercial advice in the context of the real estate transaction.

REPUTATION OF THE FIRM AND ITS ATTORNEYS

There are many sources available to non-US investors to assist them in investigating the reputation of potential US legal advisors (e.g., *Chambers USA* and *The Legal 500*) to referrals from other non-US investors, accounting firms, brokers, business consultants, and real estate industry groups.[7] In addition, non-US investors should consider law firms that demonstrate their thought leadership and subject matter expertise by publishing articles in trade journals or magazines, speaking at trade and legal conferences, or serving on leading real estate and tax trade organizations..

EXPERIENCE IN REPRESENTATION OF NON-US INVESTORS

Extensive tax planning and analysis involving US tax rules *and* tax treatment in the investor's home country is typically needed for non-US investment in US real estate. US legal advisors would typically advise from a US legal and tax perspective, and coordinate with either its foreign office or the investor's regular foreign legal and tax advisors, as appropriate, as to the laws of the investor's home country. Moreover, it is important for the US legal advisor to be able to communicate easily with and understand the business culture and style of the non-US investor so that the latter can be reflected in the negotiation and structuring of the transaction.

ABILITY TO UNDERSTAND THE CLIENT'S BUSINESS AND LEGAL OBJECTIVES

This factor surfaces in many aspects of a US real estate transaction. For example, the limited partnership agreement and the limited liability company operating agreement will provide much of the contractual basis for an investment transaction. The US legal advisor should be able to negotiate and draft such agreements in a manner that will effectively and successfully attain the desired economic and operational results.

SUFFICIENCY, AVAILABILITY, AND EFFICIENCY OF ATTORNEYS STAFFING THE TRANSACTION

The staffing decision is often dictated by the size, complexity, and timing of a transaction. For example, a large multisite project or a portfolio transaction that is scheduled to close on an aggressive timeline might require a larger team of lawyers than a smaller single-site acquisition that is on a more relaxed closing schedule. If the transaction involves properties in multiple states, engaging a law firm with an office in some or all of those states will create efficiencies and lower costs by reducing the need to engage additional outside local counsel.

FEES AND EXPENSES

Throughout the selection process, fees and expenses should be considered. While US law firms are often reluctant to agree to a fixed fee for a particular engagement, especially when the time required to complete it cannot reasonably be estimated at the outset of the project, most US law firms will prepare a budget of expected costs for the client's consideration.

CONFLICTS OF INTEREST

Non-US investors should also consider potential conflicts of interest. A selected law firm may have represented or may be currently representing another party to a transaction in another matter. Depending on the facts and circumstances, including the nature of the conflict in question, such conflicts may be able to be waived with the consent of the parties involved after full disclosure.

ROLE OF THE TAX ACCOUNTING FIRM

Accounting firms often share responsibility and work together with law firms to create an optimal structure for a particular real estate investment. While the tax attorney is responsible for the legal aspects of implementing the structure, the tax accountant is responsible for tax return preparation and withholding compliance.

Similar to the role of the law firm, the role of a particular tax accounting firm will vary depending on the specific real estate transaction and whether the accounting firm is advising a seller, purchaser, developer, borrower, lender, equity investor, or other participant.

The role of the tax accounting firm may include the following:

- Performing financial and tax due diligence review, including REIT tax due diligence review
- Preparing tax models and projections to evaluate the after-tax **internal rate of return (IRR)**, including analysis relating to tax basis, built-in gain, foreign tax credit, taxable income, and earnings and profits
- Preparing transfer pricing studies to support intercompany debt structures
- Performing cost segregation studies to accelerate the timing of depreciation expenses
- Preparing US and non-US income tax returns, withholding statements, and other tax informational returns, including the provision of an electronic platform for data gathering
- Advising on state and local taxation and preparation of associated tax returns
- And for REITs specifically, performing quarterly and annual REIT tax compliance testing to monitor that a REIT is operating in compliance

SELECTION OF THE TAX ACCOUNTING FIRM

Many of the leading accounting firms in the US have a national tax practice focused exclusively on real estate and REITs. Such accounting firms offer a level of sophistication and expertise not found at general accounting firms without specialized national real estate and REIT practices.

If the non-US investor has US tax accountants in its home country with sufficient US tax expertise in advising on US real estate investments, the non-US investor may prefer to retain them as US tax accountants. Alternatively, the non-US investor may prefer to engage the US office of an accounting firm in its home country or a different US accounting firm.

While an accounting firm would typically offer tax compliance projects that can be reasonably estimated on a fixed fee arrangement, more unpredictable tax advisory projects are typically offered on an hourly basis like a law firm. In addition, some accounting firms may offer outsourcing arrangements to assist a client's in-house tax department with day-to-day or special ad hoc tax projects under a special fee arrangement. Last, most accounting firms offer sophisticated tax technology to help clients simplify the data gathering and tax compliance process.

NOTES

1. See Chapter 1.2.
2. See Chapter 1.3.
3. See Chapter 4.4.
4. See Chapter 4.7.
5. Including loan agreements, promissory notes, deeds of trust, mortgages and other collateral security documents, environmental indemnities, nonrecourse carveout guaranties, deposit account control agreements, cash management agreements, assignment and subordination agreements with respect to property management and leasing agreements, interest rate lock agreements and interest rate swap agreements.
6. Including the International Investment and Trade in Services Survey Act through the U.S. Department of Commerce, Bureau of Economic Analysis, and when appropriate, the Agricultural Foreign Investment Disclosure Act.
7. See Chapter 1.9.

Community Connection

Research Resources, Professional Associations, and Other Tools for Non-US Investors

Gunnar Branson, CEO, AFIRE

Benjamin van Loon, Managing Director, AFIRE

ommercial real estate is fundamentally a compromise. No one person or organization can single-handedly conceive, design, finance, build, manage, or sell an asset. The architect, the debt provider, the urban planner, the government, the equity investor, the property manager, the legal advisor, and even the tenant has a significant leadership stake in any building—each with their own point-of-view, priorities, and leverage. It is rare in the US that any asset is a success through the dictates of a single individual.

Compromise is at the heart of how collaboration happens, but a positive result is neither easy nor ensured. Large amounts of capital must be aggregated and committed for lengthy periods of time. Safety dictates extreme care when building and maintaining a structure. Local governments may or may not be aligned with real estate priorities. Any given deal can take months or years to consummate, and ownership can extend over decades. Trust between parties is difficult to build and easy to destroy. Negotiations become emotional when parties defend positions before discovering mutual interest. Underperformance and mistrust often correlate.

So without existing networks or relationships, how can new "outside" investors even broach the topic of mutual interest?

Professional associations.

WHY GET INVOLVED WITH ASSOCIATIONS?

When investors ask why they should get involved with associations, they have reason for skepticism. Taking time out of a busy schedule to meet with colleagues and competitors may not seem to be a productive task. Costs for additional travel, sponsoring events, or engaging in nonremunerative industry projects can be difficult to justify. Discussing strategy or market observations with potential competitors is not, intuitively, the best thing to do with one's time.

And yet industry associations may be one of the more important tools an investor can use—to build trust, challenge assumptions, and learn about developing trends. It is also a place to hold oneself and one's colleagues to a higher standard of professional behaviors, ethics, and performance. Instead of hiding in the individual silos of a firm, a country, or a region, association meetings are a public square where participants open up to each other in person and share experiences, gain a broader perspective, and build long-term trust relationships. Associations may not always immediately serve an individual's career or strategy—membership cannot guarantee a new client or deal, though both often can be found there. But over time, the network, information, and personal connection found in an association builds long-term business success, assistance when times are tough, and perspective on how to lead through an environment of systemic compromise and change.

Associations represent a dense network of other investors, operators, owners, attorneys, brokers, architects, accountants, government officials, and other thought leaders. When engaged with appropriately, participants will gain knowledge, find potential partners, advocate for real estate, and test out ideas.

In the US there are many organizations focused on different aspects of real estate, and most leaders and organizations are active participants with at least a few of them. It's not a surprise that Alexis de Tocqueville, in his essays about the US in the nineteenth century, wrote "there are no countries where associations are more necessary to prevent tyranny of parties or the whims of princes than those whose social state is democratic."[1] Associations, professional or otherwise, are a central component of US civic and professional life—and all can trace their roots to the actual formation of the US.[2]

Of course, associations are not an American invention, and a case can be made that the US was itself partly invented by associations.[3] The first US president, George Washington, along with a third of the men who signed the Constitution, belonged to a global organization of Freemasonry that evolved from guilds of stone masons in the Middle Ages. Apart from governments or religions, this organization that expanded well beyond support for masons focused on creating better men and a better world through equality, religious freedom, freedom of expression, and individual accountability. The relationships they built through their association were essential to building a new nation, whether it was the conceptualization of a new government or allying it with trade and governmental leaders in Europe.

It is not surprising to see so many associations focused on commercial real estate. After all, the complexity of this industry requires a broad and deep network of colleagues to succeed. Not only were the first leaders of the US proud members of associations like the Freemasons, but many of them, including George Washington, were successful real estate surveyors, developers, and dealmakers.

Joining a commercial real estate association provides a range of benefits, including:

1. **Access to Education and Designations:** Many associations offer education and professional development programs that can help institutional investors stay up to date on the latest trends and developments in the market. These programs can also provide investors with the skills and knowledge they need to make informed investment decisions. Designations relevant to real estate, such as the CCIM[4] or CFA,[5] can also enhance an investor's credibility and marketability in the industry.

2. **Networking Opportunities:** Associations provide institutional investors with opportunities to connect with other industry professionals, including developers, owners, brokers, and service providers. These connections can lead to new investment opportunities, as well as provide valuable insights and perspectives on the market.

3. **Access to Research and Data:** Many associations produce research and data on the commercial real estate market, which can help institutional investors make informed investment decisions. This information can include market reports, economic forecasts, and demographic data.

4. **Advocacy and Representation:** Associations can also advocate on behalf of institutional investors on issues that impact the industry, such as tax policy, zoning regulations, and environmental regulations. This advocacy can help ensure that the interests of institutional investors are represented and protected.

TOP US REAL ESTATE ASSOCIATIONS

Firms investing in the US commercial real estate market should consider participating with one or more groups depending on the association's mission and the focus of different people within a given firm. Attendance at meetings is a first step, but the most productive activity is to volunteer to be part of committees, to assist with planning, and to engage with research and lobbying efforts made by the association.

The following is not a comprehensive list of organizations but should serve as a starting point for institutional investors to be aware of and perhaps participate with.

Urban Land Institute (ULI)

ULI is a global organization with chapters throughout the world. Members include most disciplines within real estate, including design, legislation, planning, finance, and construction. Most real estate professionals have an individual membership and participate in local chapters as well as in national and global meetings. Senior leaders also participate in special product councils of 50 to 75 people that focus on particular asset classes or sectors of the industry.

Commercial Real Estate Women Network (CREW Network)

CREW is a global association focused on supporting women in commercial real estate through networking, research, development, and career outreach. With over 12,000 members in chapters throughout the world, well-attended events, summits, and retreats are focused on advancing the careers of their members.

Institute of Real Estate Management (IREM)

IREM is an international institute with learning, certifications, and networking for property and asset managers. Over 20,000 members are served with publications, education, and governmental advocacy on their behalf.

Building Owners and Managers Association International (BOMA International)

A federation of US local associations and global affiliates, BOMA represents the owners, managers, service providers, and other property professionals of commercial buildings, such as office, industrial, medical, corporate, and mixed use.

National Council of Real Estate Investment Fiduciaries (NCREIF)

NCREIF serves the institutional real estate investment community with a robust and diverse database of country-specific real estate assets. NCREIF produced the first property level return index, the NCREIF Property Index (NPI) captures investment performance records that meet the rigorous scrutiny and review of major investors and academia. Attendance at their meetings primarily include research and accounting professionals from institutional investment firms in addition to real estate–focused academics. NCREIF also offers a variety of educational programs and seminars throughout the year focused on various real estate disciplines.

National Association of Real Estate Investment Trusts (NAREIT)

NAREIT's membership is focused on real estate investment trusts (REITs) and real estate companies throughout the world that own, operate, and finance income-producing real estate, as well as those firms and individuals who advise, study, and service those businesses. NAREIT lobbies on behalf of the industry with US policymakers, with a particular emphasis on the role REITs and REIT investment play in job creation, economic activity, and the lives of millions of retail investors. NAREIT produces and sponsors research on REIT investment used to communicate its benefits—continuing income, diversification, capital appreciation, and inflation protection—to investors, policymakers, and the media, worldwide. They also provide REIT news, data, and real estate industry perspectives and host the REIT industry's primary investor conferences and educational events.

National Association of Real Estate Investment Managers (NAREIM)

NAREIM membership is focused primarily on the operational issues faced by North American–based investment management firms. Small group meetings throughout the year for different peer groups and operational specialties provide opportunities for candid and insightful discussions. Their annual compensation, DEI, and management practice studies are unique and in-depth benchmarks for the entire industry.

National Association of REALTORS® (NAR)

NAR is the largest trade association in the US with over 1.4 million members, including real estate agents, brokers, and property managers. While the NAR is primarily focused on residential real estate, it has a commercial division that provides resources and education for commercial real estate professionals. The NAR offers a range of educational resources and designations, including the Certified Commercial Investment Member (CCIM) designation, which is widely recognized in the commercial real estate industry.

In addition to education and designations, NAR also offers networking opportunities through its annual conference and expo. The conference provides a platform for industry professionals to connect with each other, learn about new trends and developments in the market, and discover new investment opportunities.

International Council of Shopping Centers (ICSC)

ICSC is a global trade association that represents the retail real estate industry. The ICSC has over 70,000 members in over 100 countries, including developers, owners, brokers, and retailers. The association offers a range of educational programs, including the certified shopping center manager (CSM) designation, which is recognized as the industry standard for retail real estate professionals.

The ICSC also hosts several conferences and events throughout the year, including the Recon conference, which is the largest gathering of retail real estate professionals in the world.

National Association of Industrial and Office Parks (NAIOP)

NAIOP represents developers, owners, and investors in the industrial and office real estate sector. The association has over 20,000 members in North America, including developers, owners, investors, and other professionals involved in the industry. The NAIOP offers a range of educational programs, including the Certificate of Advanced Study in Commercial Real Estate Development program, which provides a comprehensive overview of the commercial real estate development process.

The NAIOP also hosts several events throughout the year, including the annual Developing Leaders conference, which is designed for young professionals in the industry. The conference provides attendees with the opportunity to network with industry leaders, learn about new trends and developments in the market, and discover new investment opportunities.

National Multifamily Housing Council (NMHC)

NMHC members include leaders from throughout the multihousing industry. Meetings, webinars, and conferences are scheduled throughout the year, along with research and advocacy with US policymakers on behalf of the multifamily owner, operators, and developers. The industry's most prominent and creative leaders at the helm, NMHC provides a forum for insight, advocacy, and action that enable both members and the communities they build to thrive.

Real Estate Roundtable (RER)

RER is a public policy organization that represents the interests of the commercial real estate industry in the US. The RER has over 150 members, including developers, owners, and investors in the industry. The organization focuses on advocating for policies that support the growth and development of the industry, including tax reform, infrastructure investment, and regulatory reform. Quarterly meetings bring together real estate and government leaders to help understand how to better address the issues impacting real estate.

Pension Real Estate Association (PREA)

PREA includes over 700 corporate member firms around the world, including public and corporate pension funds, endowments, foundations, insurance companies, investment advisory firms, REIT's developers, real estate operating companies, and service providers. Their well-attended events and conferences are outstanding networking opportunities supported by their research and publications.

Association of Foreign Investors in Real Estate (AFIRE)

AFIRE is the association for international real estate investors focused on commercial property in the US. AFIRE's members includes almost 200 leading global institutional investors, investment managers, and supporting partners from 24 countries representing approximately US $3 trillion in real estate assets under management in the US. Three major conferences and several smaller meetings every year allow investors, operators, and service providers to meet, share best practices, and gain insights on the US real estate markets. Their award-winning journal, podcast, and annual surveys provide unique perspectives and information for cross-border investors.

Commercial Real Estate Development Association (NAIOP)

NAIOP membership includes over 20,000 North American–based developers, owners, and related professionals focused on office, industrial, and mixed-use real estate. Members are served through national forums, education, certification, and advocacy with US policymakers.

Institutional Real Estate, Inc. (IREI)

Similar in feel to associations, IREI is a for-profit consultancy and publisher that serves institutional investors, investment managers, and consultants. Their publications provide news and feature articles focused on the firms, events, issues, and trends shaping the market. Throughout the year, their events and conferences collect true thought leaders from across the industry.

* * *

Joining a commercial real estate association provides investors with a range of benefits, including access to education and designations, networking opportunities, access to research and data, and advocacy and representation on issues that impact the industry. Participation, of course, is not a requirement for investors, but investing time and resources in these groups can deliver a commensurate return in knowledge, insight, and the support of professional colleagues.

NOTES

1. Alexis de Tocqueville, Isaac Kramnick, et al. *Democracy in America: And Two Essays on America* (Penguin Classics 2003).
2. Abbott, Andrew. "Professionalism in the Postindustrial Society: The British and American Experiences Compared." *Comparative Studies in Society and History 40,* no. 2 (1998): 296–326.
3. Wuthnow, Robert. "The Organization of American Culture: Private Associations, Professional Bodies, and Public Programs." *American Journal of Sociology 88*, no. 5 (1982): 1188–1214.
4. A Certified Commercial Investment Member (CCIM) is a recognized expert in the disciplines of commercial and investment real estate. The designation is awarded by the CCIM Institute, formerly known as Commercial Investment Real Estate Institute of the National Association of Realtors.
5. The Chartered Financial Analyst (CFA) program is a postgraduate professional certification offered internationally by the American-based CFA Institute to investment and financial professionals.

Introduction

The Commercial Real Estate Life Cycle

Depending on the scale of a real estate investment or product, the general steps of the real estate life cycle include:

1. **Planning and Diligence:** identifying the goals of the project, assessing the feasibility of the project, and creating a plan for moving forward
2. **Acquisition:** acquiring the property, either by purchasing it or through a long-term lease agreement
3. **Development:** designing and building the project, which may include obtaining permits, securing financing, and hiring contractors and other professionals
4. **Marketing and Leasing:** promoting and leasing the property to tenants or buyers, which may include developing marketing materials, conducting tours of the property, and negotiating lease or sale agreements
5. **Operation and Management:** managing the day-to-day operations of the property, including maintenance, repairs, and tenant or buyer relations.
6. **Disposition:** selling or disposing of the property, which may involve finding a buyer or negotiating a sale price

Each phase of the real estate life cycle potentially warrants an entire volume on its own, but for the sake of *The AFIRE Guide*, this section will focus specifically on the diligence, acquisition, management, and disposition of real estate in the US.

Chapter 2.1 provides an overview of the due diligence process. As a formal practice, it helps investors identify the risks and potential of a property through a comprehensive appraisal of the property's value, risks, and potential, as well as assisting in verifying certain legal and financial assumptions, avoiding or mitigating the risk of loss, and increasing the probability of achieving the financial goals for an investment.

Chapter 2.2 explains the various pathways toward US real estate acquisition. Although this chapter focuses primarily on equity investment in US real estate, many of the concepts introduced here will also be relevant to those interested in making, purchasing, or participating in loans for which the collateral (directly or indirectly) is US commercial real estate.

Chapter 2.3 dives further into the states of real estate acquisition, which typically involves three stages: (1) preparation and execution of a letter of intent (LOI), (2) negotiation and execution of a contract of sale, and (3) consummation of the sale at a closing. It also highlights the nuances and pitfalls that need to be navigated throughout the acquisition process, from structuring and taxes to local market customs and practices.

Chapter 2.4 focuses on leasing and occupancy, beginning with a review of the role an owner's leasing broker (or a tenant representative) takes in the normal steps of securing new tenants, as well as negotiating extensions or modifications of lease with existing tenants. This chapter also covers the timing of commission payments and tenant improvement allowances, as well as a typical lease structure for each of the major asset types.

Chapter 2.5 highlights the dynamics of managing a wide range of property types, which are continually evolving, especially as the uses and expectations of technology, physical and human resources, and the overall built environment transform over time. No matter if a real estate portfolio is comprised of office, industrial/logistics, retail, life sciences, or mixed use, there are some consistent aspects of property management that all investors should understand across the commercial real estate spectrum.

Chapter 2.6 discusses the sale, or disposition, of a property as the final stage in the investment cycle. Once the decision has been made to sell an asset, the goal of the disposition process is typically to maximize sale proceeds at the lowest risk. Property owners will typically engage a capital markets broker to assist with the disposition process.

Understanding the Asset

Property Due Diligence

Benjamin van Loon, Managing Director, AFIRE

Due diligence is one of the most crucial components of the investment decision-making process in commercial real estate. As a formal practice, it helps investors identify the risks and potential of a property through a comprehensive appraisal of the property's value, risks, and potential, as well as assisting in verifying certain legal and financial assumptions, avoiding or mitigating the risk of loss, and increasing the probability of achieving the financial goals for an investment. A proper due diligence process will also play a vital role in confirming that the representations made in a contract are true and correct.

This chapter provides a general overview of the property due diligence process, as well as a more detailed look at the legal, financial, and operational aspects of due diligence.

UNDERSTANDING DUE DILIGENCE

In commercial real estate transactions, investors typically prefer to conduct due diligence pursuant to an executed contract. However, sellers may sometimes require that such work be performed prior to contract. This approach can lead to execution risks, where the seller can choose to consummate a transaction with another party. It is, therefore, recommended that the purchaser delivers their due diligence requests early in the process to maximize the due diligence period.

Due diligence periods generally range from as little as 10 days to as long as 90 days, depending on the property and market practices. A time period within which the seller is required to deliver all materials should be stated in the term sheet or contract. Three to five days from the time of request or the date of the contract (whichever is later) is not uncommon. In the event that the seller fails to deliver a complete set of materials by the due date, the contract should provide relief to the purchaser by, for example, extending the due diligence period on a day-to-day basis due to the delay in delivery.

It is essential to consider several issues during the due diligence process, including legal, financial, and physical and operational issues, which should be considered for all asset types. Legal issues include matters such as zoning, land use, and environmental regulations, which may affect the property's value and potential. Financial due diligence should focus on reviewing the property's financial statements, rent rolls, and lease agreements to assess the property's income-generating potential, existing cash flow, and potential for future growth. Physical and operational due diligence should cover the property's physical condition, including inspections of the building's systems and structure, and the property's operational performance, such as the analysis of maintenance and repair history, tenant satisfaction, and vacancy rates.

Some of the leading factors that might affect the intensity of due diligence for commercial acquisitions include property location, property type, seller reputation, and transaction value.[1] Not surprisingly, investors will conduct a higher level of due diligence for properties in riskier locations—such as properties within or near flood zones, or properties adjacent to critical infrastructure that might also be impacted by rulings from the **Committee on Foreign Investment in the United States (CFIUS).**

There is also a strong correlation between the level of due diligence performed on a commercial asset and the subsequent investment performance of that asset.[2] As such, investors should conduct thorough due diligence as a baseline measure for maximizing their returns and minimizing risks. This maximization might also be spurred by considering due diligence as an ongoing process that continues throughout an investment period.[3] This would typically involve regularly monitoring and analyzing the property's performance, financial statements, and operational activities.[4]

LEGAL DUE DILIGENCE

The legal part of the due diligence process includes a thorough analysis of the legal aspects of the transaction, including contract negotiation and review. It also involves assessing the legal title to the asset being purchased, reviewing property leases and service contracts, and examining the certificate of occupancy and zoning, among other things.

In particular, understanding the leases is critical to forecasting the performance of a property. A detailed lease abstract can help summarize all stated monetary and material nonmonetary terms that may affect cash flow assumptions. This includes tenant improvement allowances, renewal options, and termination rights. Proper understanding of the lease agreements is critical to avoid any adverse effects on the availability of space to relet on market terms or reserve requirements to be deposited with a lender as collateral.[5] Therefore, it is recommended to have an attorney review or prepare a form of abstract to spot check the abstracts, especially for tenants occupying a significant portion of the property or whose leases are essential in obtaining financing.

It's also important for buyers to understand the terms of the ground lease, particularly in the case of property held in leasehold rather than fee simple. It is crucial to obtain an accurate understanding of the terms of the ground lease, including permitted use, restrictions, escalations, and operating covenants, if any. The calculation of the purchase price may be determined based on a capitalization rate applicable to the rent in place at the time of exercise or a fair market value appraisal of the land. Therefore, it is essential to understand whether the appraisal includes the improvements and how the appraiser is selected.

Finally, zoning can present a risk, particularly if a legal, nonconforming building cannot be rebuilt in the case of substantial or complete destruction of the property. This type of risk can seriously affect the valuation of the property, insurance coverage, and availability of financing.[6] Therefore, it is recommended to confirm zoning through a third-party zoning report, an opinion of counsel, and/or a letter from a municipality's zoning office.

FINANCIAL DUE DILIGENCE

The financial due diligence of an asset will help determine if the property is financially sound and viable in the long term. This part of the due diligence process typically involves collecting and analyzing information necessary to make informed projections of a property's financial performance.[7] This process typically begins with a review of the property's current rent roll, operating and capital budgets, as well as current and historical income and balance sheets from the past three to five years. These documents provide insight into the current financial position of the property and its performance over time.

To get a more detailed understanding of the property's financial performance, financial due diligence involves reviewing individual leases and tenant files to identify potential risks and opportunities for future changes in income and expenses. This includes evaluating the creditworthiness of tenants and assessing their ability to meet their rental obligations. Further, it involves analyzing market dynamics, including economic trends, supply and demand, and demographic shifts, as well as evaluating comparable properties.[8]

Financial due diligence will also add clarity on the financing options for the property. This might involves engaging a broker who will work with the investor to identify the best financing options based on the property's financial performance, market trends, and other factors.[9] The goal of this process is to secure favorable financing terms that support the investor's long-term investment goals.

PHYSICAL AND OPERATIONAL DUE DILIGENCE

As the most obvious part of the due diligence process, physical and operational due diligence involves an actual *look* at the property.

When acquiring commercial real estate, investors must conduct extensive due diligence to evaluate the physical and operational conditions of the property. Physical due diligence involves a comprehensive property inspection, while operational due diligence involves a review of building procedures, policies, and interviews with property management staff. The purpose of these inspections is to identify any risks and opportunities that may impact the property's value and financial performance.[10]

A **property condition report (PCR)** is a crucial component of physical due diligence. A PCR provides an overview of the building's condition, including the age and condition of various building components such as the roof, windows, and elevators. The report also assesses the life and safety systems, which can impact the property's operating and capital budgets, as well as the level of reserves that lenders may require when financing the property. A PCR can also help buyers anticipate future capital expenditures and maintenance costs, which can impact the property's value.[11]

Environmental due diligence typically forms the other side of the property condition assessment. A Phase I **environmental site assessment (ESA)** report is a comprehensive review of the property and surrounding areas to identify any potential environmental hazards. This report highlights any existing or previous contamination, including soil and groundwater pollution, which may require remediation or abatement before tenant renovations or other work can begin. In some cases, a Phase II report may also be required to assess the extent of contamination or hazardous materials present on the property.[12]

For operational due diligence, it is essential to review building procedures and policies and interview property management staff. An understanding of the building owner's obligations under any collective bargaining (union) agreement that will be binding on sale is especially crucial in urban markets, such as New York City. This is of particular concern with hotel properties, where collective bargaining agreements can significantly impact the property's financial performance and value.[13]

Finally, a crucial issue that affects leasing and the calculation of a tenant's proportionate share of a building is the rentable measurement of the building. An investor should obtain the as-built plans for the property and the Building Owners and Managers Association (BOMA) measurement, which is the standard in most markets for measuring the rentable square footage of office properties. The BOMA measurement provides a consistent and transparent method for determining a property's rentable area, which can help prevent disputes between landlords and tenants over leased space.[14]

These physical and operational inspections, alongside the legal and financial aspects of due diligence, provide investors with a comprehensive overview of the property's physical and operational condition, helping them identify any risks and opportunities that may impact the property's value and financial performance.

NOTES

1. Roulac, Stephen. "Institutional Real Estate Investing Processes, Due Diligence Practices and Market Conditions." *Journal of Real Estate Portfolio Management*, vol. 6, no. 4, 2000, pp. 387–416, DOI: 10.1080/10835547.2000.12089621.
2. Kolev, Diana Bunin, and Megan K. Collins. "The Importance of Due Diligence: Real Estate Transactions in a Complex Land Use World." *Journal*, New York State Bar Association, vol. 84, no. 3, 2012, pp. 24–34.
3. Just, Tobias, and Hermann Stapenhorst, editors. *Real Estate Due Diligence A Guideline for Practitioners.* Springer International Publishing, 2018, https://doi.org/10.1007/978-3-319-62510-2.
4. See also Chapter 2.5.
5. Deloitte. "Legal Due Diligence for Real Estate Transactions." Accessed April 17, 2023, https://www2 .deloitte.com/content/dam/Deloitte/global/Documents/Legal/dttl-legal-deloitte-legal-handbook-for-real -estate-transactions.pdf.
6. JLL. "Real Estate Due Diligence Checklist: What Investors Need to Know." Accessed April 17, 2023, https://www.us.jll.com/content/dam/jll-com/documents/pdf/other/jll-real-estate-due-diligence-checklist -what-investors-need-to-know.pdf.
7. Iezman, Stanley L., and Stephen R. Peterson. "Managing Risk and Creating Value in Real Estate Investments: The Importance of Due Diligence." *Probate and Property*, vol. 14, no. 3, American Bar Association, 2000, pp. 13–26.
8. McDonald, Paul. "Financial Due Diligence in Commercial Property Transactions." *The Valuer & Land Economist*, vol. 34, no. 7, 1997, pp. 582–585.
9. Harp, R. Kymn. "Give Them Their Due: Due Diligence in Commercial Real Estate Transactions." *Probate and Property*, vol. 25, no. 4, American Bar Association, 2011, pp. 40–54.
10. Pagliari, Joseph L., et al. *The Handbook of Real Estate Portfolio Management.* Irwin Professional Pub, 1995.
11. Marks, Kenneth H., et al. *The Handbook of Financing Growth: Strategies, Capital Structure, and M&A Transactions*, vol. 482, Wiley, 2009.
12. Tramm, Kenneth S., and Ernest C. Crosby. *Environmental Due Diligence: A Professional Handbook.* West Conshohocken, PA: Infinity Publishing: 2006.
13. Hennessey, Brian, et al. *The Due Diligence Process Plan Handbook for Commercial Real Estate Investments.* eBookIt.com, 2013.
14. Baum, Andrew. *Real Estate Investment: A Strategic Approach*, 4th ed.. Routledge, 2023, https://doi.org/10 .1201/9781003140283.

Entering the Real Estate Cycle

The Acquisition Process

Richard Grossmann, Partner, Kirkland & Ellis

nvestors with capital to deploy are likely to be presented with commercial real estate opportunities throughout the capital stack, with a range of risk and return profiles. Although this chapter focuses primarily on equity investment in US real estate, many of the concepts introduced here will also be relevant to those interested in making, purchasing, or participating in loans for which the collateral (directly or indirectly) is US commercial real estate.

A SPECTRUM OF OPPORTUNITIES

Within the broad category of equity investments, investment options span projects at different stages of the real estate life cycle—from new "ground up" development to well-established "trophy" assets—across different asset classes and geography, and along a spectrum of involvement, ranging from direct ownership of property (often through a joint venture) to essentially passive REIT and fund investments, as shown in Figure 2.2-01.[1]

FIGURE 2.2-01 **The real estate capital stack overview**

Classification of Real Estate Investments

Real estate investments are traditionally divided into four basic classifications—**core, core-plus, value-add, and opportunistic**—based on the level of risk entailed and returns targeted, as shown in Figure 2.2-02.[2]

FIGURE 2.2-02 **The four basic classifications of real estate investments**

OPPORTUNISTIC INVESTMENTS
- Ground-up development with high debt
- 20%+ returns with high variability

VALUE-ADD INVESTMENTS
- Moderate to high risk
- High upside, but considerable capital needs
- 13% – 15% returns annually with variability

CORE-PLUS INVESTMENTS
- High-quality tenants
- Slightly inferior location
- 9% – 13% returns annually with some variability

CORE INVESTMENTS
- High-quality locations
- High-quality tenants
- Comparable to bond investments
- 7% – 10% returns annually with little variability

OPPORTUNISTIC

VALUE-ADD

CORE-PLUS

CORE

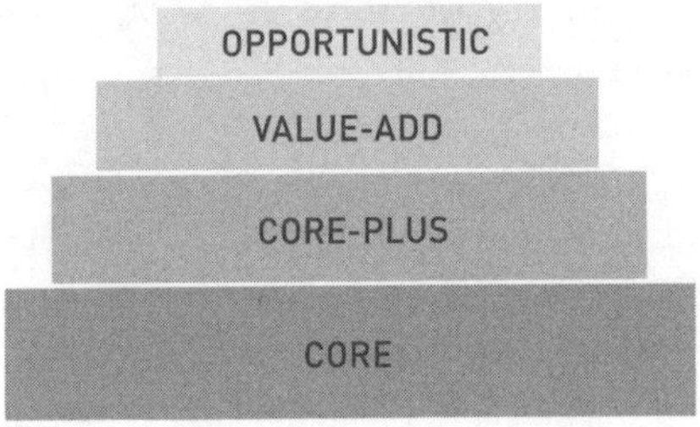

Core investments are those considered safest and are expected to generate asset-level returns in the range of 7 to 10 percent[3] annually, with little variability. Because of their predictable, stable cash flows, they are sometimes regarded as an equity alternative to corporate bonds.

Core assets are in desirable markets[4] and are generally occupied by high-quality tenants under long-term leases. However, shifts in technology, society, and the economy can rapidly challenge or upturn the "core" status of an investment. For example, social and economic pressures catalyzed by the COVID-19 pandemic, combined with improvements to remote working technologies, have upended what was until recently the quintessential core real estate investment: Class A office buildings situated in the central business districts (CBDs) of primary markets, such as New York and San Francisco.[5]

Core-plus assets are those that do not qualify as core due to one or more risk factors. Core-plus buildings may have lower-quality, less creditworthy tenants. Their rent rolls may show multiple leases expiring in close succession, threatening significant vacancy and retenanting costs. There may be deferred maintenance or other property condition issues. Investors in core-plus real estate generally look for asset-level returns of 9 to 13 percent annually.

Value-add investments are appropriate for investors prepared to accept moderate to high risk in exchange for anticipated returns of 13 to 16 percent or higher. The standard profile of a value-add project is one with significant up-front capital expenditures and little or no cash flows during a period where the asset might be repositioned, refurbished, and/ or retenanted with the goal of achieving higher cash flows in the future. An example of a value-add investment would be acquiring a decades-old multifamily property with high vacancy and low rents in order to renovate the apartments and add common amenities with the intent of attracting new tenants willing to pay higher monthly rental rates.

Opportunistic investments are, for the most part, synonymous with new ground-up development, substantial redevelopment, and conversions of properties from one use to another.[6] Investors in opportunistic projects are in most cases targeting asset-level returns of 15 to 20 percent or higher. These investments are typically the most complicated and are appropriate for experienced real estate investors with access to advisors possessing **architectural, engineering, and construction (AEC)** expertise, together with financing, leasing, and other operational capabilities.[7]

Property Types

The five main types of commercial property are office, retail, multifamily, industrial, and hospitality. Although these terms are familiar and their meanings are, by and large, self-evident, within each type there is a myriad of subtypes and specialty products, which, in some cases, may perform very differently from one another. And while these property types remain somewhat distinct, the boundaries between them are somewhat blurred. For example, **mixed-use projects** have become the rule, rather than the exception, especially in markets that bill themselves as **"live-work-play"** locales.[8]

In addition, a proliferation of alternative and specialty assets provides investors with opportunities to invest in other types of real estate investment beyond the five mainstays. Some examples include data centers, self-storage facilities, marinas and boatyards, medical and life science offices and biomanufacturing, student housing, senior housing, and manufactured housing.[9]

Location, Location, Location

It is a truism in real estate investing that the success of any commercial property hinges on its location. Real estate investment capital for a long time flowed primarily into the so-called gateway markets.[10] Yet the migrations and demographic shifts brought on by the COVID-19 pandemic have contributed to trends in real estate capital flows that gone beyond these markets.

For example, the institutional shift into secondary markets, especially in the Sunbelt, has been especially pronounced.[11] Burgeoning demand coupled with less expensive land prices and labor costs, promising attractive returns, have made cities such as Atlanta, Charlotte, Nashville, Raleigh-Durham, Austin, Denver, and Las Vegas magnets for real estate investors.

Another shift, on a slightly different scale, has been the movement of institutional real estate capital into the suburbs, along two different avenues of investment; first, government-supported initiatives and in some cases, legal mandates to densify and diversify inner suburbs have encouraged development of mixed-use residential projects on sites close to public transportation.[12] Second, **single-family rentals (SFR)** have grown from a niche residential investment into big business and may be viewed as a hedge against higher interest rates and a safe haven in an economic downturn.[13]

Tax and Regulatory Considerations

Tax Efficiency. While tax issues are covered in more detail elsewhere in this book, it's important to mention that a given investor's tax attributes and jurisdiction for tax purposes may render some real estate investment options more tax efficient than others. Although some foreign investors may qualify for an exemption, as a general rule, when a foreign investor disposes of an interest in a US real property interest (which is broadly defined to include direct ownership interest in property as well as equity in entities that own US real property), the purchaser is required to withhold 15 percent of the gross proceeds in what is referred to as FIRPTA withholding.[14] A trusted tax attorney or advisor should be consulted to assist with navigating the intricacies of US taxation in connection with real estate investments.

CFIUS. The Committee on Foreign Investment in the United States (CFIUS) is a committee comprised of appointees from multiple US government agencies responsible for reviewing transactions involving foreign investment in the US, including certain real estate transactions by foreign persons, to determine their effect on national security. Properties of concern to CFIUS include those located within or that will function as part of an airport or maritime port or are in close proximity to a US military installation or another facility or property determined by the US government to be sensitive for reasons of national security.[15]

Antitrust. Although most real estate transactions qualify for exemption from US antitrust regulation, investors should be aware that transactions involving certain types of hospitality assets may trigger US antitrust review—in particular, ski resorts and casino/gaming venues.

AN ARRAY OF WAYS TO INVEST

Having read the preceding presentation of the variety of real estate investment opportunities in the US available to foreign investors, one may find oneself wondering how to go about actually investing in US commercial real estate in the first place. In lawyerly fashion, the response is: "It depends." We suggest that an investor begin by answering a couple of questions: (1) What is your commercial real estate experience, what resources and capabilities do you bring, and perhaps most importantly, what must you rely on someone else to handle for you? and (2) How active a role would you like to play in the selection of investments and in strategic and operational decision-making? The answers to these questions will likely point you toward one of the investment vehicles presented in this section.

Real Estate Funds

For the foreign investor seeking diversification and exposure to an important asset class who is happy to have others select which investments to make and how they should be managed, deploying capital by investing in a real estate fund may be attractive. A real estate fund is a pooled investment vehicle that a professional advisor, or "sponsor," creates to pool money from multiple investors. Depending on the sponsor and the specific fund, funds may spread their investments across various asset types (sometimes subject to preset allocations) or focus on a specific asset type that meets a proprietary set of investment criteria (e.g., industrial logistics properties located along key distribution routes). Funds may either be closed-ended (meaning that the fund has a fixed investment period—3 or 4 years—and term—often 10 years—set by the sponsor at the fund's inception, and an investor's capital is committed for that duration) or open-ended (meaning that the fund has no termination date, and investors are permitted [subject to certain conditions and limitations] to enter and exit the fund at regular intervals determined by the sponsor). Closed-ended funds tend toward value-add and opportunistic investments, with expected returns largely arising from asset sales in the later stages of the fund's life, while open-ended funds typically favor core or core plus assets that produce strong, recurring cash flows but lower total returns. Fund investors generally play no role in the management of the fund, although certain large investors may be entitled to representation on an advisory committee. In all cases, understanding the fund's business plan is crucial, as is proper due diligence of the sponsor in whose hands lies the success of that business plan. Because the sponsor will generally be entitled to receive a share of the profits ("promote" or "carried interest") and various fees, these costs, as well as tax implications, must be carefully analyzed in evaluating the overall economics of the investment.

REITs[16]

REITs are a special class of entities (usually trusts or corporations) that have elected to receive certain tax benefits—essentially, avoidance of any corporate-level income tax, because their earnings are passed along to shareholders as dividend payments—in exchange for meeting various tests to qualify as a REIT under the US tax code and related regulations. Only certain types of real estate investments are permitted for REITs—so-called equity REITs primarily own properties, such as office and apartment buildings and warehouses, that are leased out to rent-paying tenants, while mortgage REITs invest in mortgages, mortgage-backed securities (MBS), and related credit products that generate a stream of interest payments. Some REITs are listed on the major US stock exchanges and must comply with the public company reporting requirements imposed by the U.S. Securities and Exchange Commission (SEC); their market value fluctuates as does any other publicly traded company, and their shares can be bought and sold freely. Nontraded REITs are a more recent phenomenon; although registered with the SEC, they do not trade openly on any market exchange (and the investor's capital is typically locked up for a period of two or more years), they are not subject to the same reporting and disclosure obligations as a publicly traded REIT, and their valuations are not subject to stock market movements.[17] In some respects, a nontraded REIT is similar to an open-ended real estate fund, except more broadly accessible by virtue of a much smaller minimum investment.

Joint Ventures[18]

Real estate joint ventures can take many forms, but in essence, all involve a partnership (the common meaning of the word—and usually also in tax terms, though not necessarily in the technical legal sense) between two or more parties formed to execute a particular business plan. Most often, this consists, on the one hand, of a real estate developer or operator/manager, endowed with on-the-ground know-how and supported by a team of experienced real estate professionals, and on the other hand, one or more financial investors who will provide a portion (maybe most or even all) of the capital needed to fund the project(s). In the simplest case, the parties enter into a joint venture in order to acquire, develop, and/or own and operate a single, preidentified site or asset, and this remains the most commonly encountered joint venture format. On the other hand, the past several years have seen growing interest in the establishment of "platform" or "programmatic" joint ventures, where the parties team up with the aim of undertaking a series of projects together on prenegotiated terms. Negotiation and documentation of a platform or programmatic joint venture require a carefully thought-through process for the sourcing, evaluation, and approval of potential investments. Although this negotiation and documentation tend to be significantly more complex than a single-asset joint venture, primary benefits of having dealt with these tricky issues all at once up front include the ability to move quickly in pursuit of desirable assets once identified and the efficiency of legal spend relative to asset value (when compared to entering into one-off joint ventures for each of the assets).[19]

The developer or operating partner will manage the day-to-day affairs of the joint venture, but the financial investor(s) will have more influence on the business than investors in a fund, because the approval of the investor(s) will generally be required for certain actions included on a list of "major" or "unanimous" decisions. This list may be limited to only a few decisions that relate to the most fundamental matters, such as a change of the purpose for which the joint venture was formed. But in many cases investors will negotiate for a more fulsome set of approval rights, for example, over annual budgets and business plans and capital events (such as dispositions and financings). Like a fund sponsor, the developer or operating partner in a real estate joint venture will often capture a disproportionate share of the upside of a successful project as promote (carried interest) and may also be entitled to various fees for services (e.g., development management, property management) provided to the joint venture.

Mezzanine Loans and Preferred Equity

Mezzanine loan and preferred equity investment opportunities may appeal to those seeking to invest capital in a specific property while occupying a position in the capital stock that is less risky than "common" equity in a real estate joint venture. Though often treated together due to similar risk-adjusted returns and hybrid debt- and equity-like characteristics, they differ in terms of accounting and tax treatment, rights in a bankruptcy, and other respects. When considering whether to structure an investment as a mezzanine loan or preferred equity, one should closely consult with an attorney and an accountant versed in these technical areas.

A mezzanine loan is junior in priority to the mortgage loan made to the property's owner. The holder of a mezzanine loan will be paid interest only after operating expenses and debt service on the senior loan have been paid. Due to its secondary priority, the interest rate on a mezzanine loan is typically higher than the interest rate on a mortgage loan. The mezzanine loan is secured by a pledge of the equity interests in the property owner (i.e., the borrower under the mortgage loan), so that in a default scenario, the mezzanine lender may become the equity owner of the property by foreclosing the pledge, subject to the mortgage loan. However, because the mezzanine lender's lien is junior to that of the mortgage lender, a foreclosure by the mortgage lender can result in extinguishment of the mezzanine lender's interest.

Preferred equity is an ownership interest subordinate to all debt (both mortgage and mezzanine) but is entitled to a fixed-rate preferred return, or "pref," on invested capital before distributions are made to the holders of the common equity in the property. Preferred equity holders often do not share in profits in excess of their pref, but preferred equity investments may be structured with an equity "kicker" feature. Due to a tertiary position in the capital stack, the preferred return hurdle will generally be higher than the interest rate on the mezzanine loan, but lower than the target returns for the common equity capital. Preferred equity holders generally have few, if any, rights to approve decisions concerning property operations but may become entitled to assume management of the property if they have not been redeemed—through a return of their invested capital together with the preferred return—prior to a specified date.

PURSUING INVESTMENT OPPORTUNITIES

Zeroing in on what investment method(s) are most suitable and appealing will allow the investor to tailor an appropriate process for seeking out and pursuing specific investment opportunities.

Information Gathering and Networking

Real estate industry newsletters and publications (print and online) are a valuable source of information on the current market and emerging trends.[20] Involvement with real estate industry trade associations is another way to stay informed, as well as to learn of conferences and networking events, attendance at which can strengthen existing relationships and facilitate introductions to new contacts.[21] Many universities, business schools, and academic institutes likewise sponsor real estate conferences and networking events. Finally, relationships with investment bankers, brokers, placement agents, and other professional "connectors" can prove extremely valuable sources of potential investment opportunities.

Due Diligence

Sourcing investment opportunities is, of course, merely the first step; the investor must then perform its due diligence to evaluate the risk-and-reward profile of a particular investment. Once again, the investment method will drive the due diligence process.

The assistance of third-party advisors and consultants can be an enormous help, especially for an investor relatively new to US real estate investing (or a particular investment method). However, the investor must be mindful of potential misalignments of interest between the investor and the advisor or consultant, especially where the compensation takes the form of a commission or fee that is not dependent on the performance of the investment.

For public REITs (both traded and nontraded), due diligence is essentially equivalent to equities research, where the investor will look primarily to publicly available sources of information, such as the REIT's prospectus and annual Form 10-Ks filed with the SEC, as well as market analysis performed by equity analysts.

For real estate funds, on the other hand, publicly available information will be much more limited. Instead, investors will generally be required to establish bona fides (i.e., capability to make a capital commitment of the size required by the fund's sponsor) and sign a confidentiality agreement before obtaining a private placement memorandum (PPM), which will include information about the specific fund offering and strategy, economics (i.e., fees and promote), and other terms of investment, as well as about the sponsor's key principals and track record (e.g., performance of previous funds, though, of course, this historical performance data does not guaranty similar results in the future). The fund's limited partnership agreement—the legal document governing the rights and obligations of the sponsor, acting as general partner, and the investors, as limited partner, will also be made available for review.

Investors considering a joint venture will want to learn as much as possible about the developer or operating partner—much the same information with which a fund investor is concerned regarding the sponsor. But they will also need to closely examine the underlying real estate asset(s), including legal matters such as the state of title and compliance with zoning regulations,[22] as well as physical[23] and environmental[24] conditions and valuation,[25] while also negotiating the specific terms of the joint venture, including fees and promote payable to the developer or operating partner, "major" decisions for which the investor partner's approval will be required, exit and liquidity rights, and more.

Documentation and Execution

Continuing a common theme throughout this chapter, the documentation and execution of a particular investment will vary depending on the investment itself.

Investing in a public REIT is no different from trading in any other publicly traded stock.[26] Shares in nontraded REITs, on the other hand, generally must be purchased on a specific timetable (e.g., on the first day of the month) pursuant to a subscription request. Pricing will in most cases be based on the REIT's net asset value (NAV) per share at that time,[27] and the investor will pay additional charges for transaction fees and commissions.

Investing in a real estate fund is a more involved process. After completing its due diligence of the fund's sponsor and deciding to move forward with the investment, the investor will complete and submit a subscription book, including an investor questionnaire, in order to establish that it is an "accredited investor" or "qualified purchaser" and is otherwise eligible to acquire a limited partner interest in the fund. The sponsor, acting as the general partner of the fund, must formally accept the subscription in order for the investor to be admitted as a limited partner, at which point the investor will be bound by the terms of the fund's limited partnership agreement. However, some investors (especially those making large commitments to the fund) will negotiate side letters that modify and/or supplement the terms of the limited partnership agreement to align with the specific investor's tax and other requirements.

For joint ventures, as well as mezzanine loans and preferred equity investments, the investment process and documentation will be more bespoke and consequently more time-consuming and demanding of the investor's attention. The first step will typically be negotiation of a detailed LOI, which outlines the economic and material noneconomic terms of the subject investment. The LOI should be nonbinding on the parties (except for a few specific provisions, such as confidentiality and if applicable, exclusivity) but provides a framework for the negotiation of the definitive deal documents.

NOTES

* The author wishes to express his gratitude to Steve Tomlinson for extending the opportunity to contribute to *The AFIRE Guide* to a junior colleague and for his insightful comments on the text. Thanks also to associate Tom Michaelides for his contributions to this project. Any errors or omissions are my own.

1. Godbersen, Soren. "Real Estate Equity Investing: What, Why & How." Equity Multiple, July 12, 2019. https://trustabccapital.com/real-estate-capital-stack/.

2. Kastelberg, Tyler. "Difference in Core, Core Plus, Value-Add, and Opportunistic Real Estate." Bullpen, March 24, 2021. https://www.bullpenre.com/insights/core-core-plus-value-add-opportunistic.

3. The target returns cited for all investment types in this section do not take into account recent increases in interest rates generally and should be viewed as spreads relative to the risk-free rate (for which the rate on 10-year US treasuries is often considered a reliable proxy).

4. See Chapter 1.4

5. See, e.g., Eavis, Peter, Julie Creswell, and Joe Rennison. "Why Office Buildings Are Still in Trouble," *New York Times*, March 24, 2021. https://www.nytimes.com/2022/11/17/business/office-buildings-real-estate-vacancy.html; Wong, Natalie, John Gittelsohn, and Noah Buhayar. "New York City's Empty Offices Reveal a Global Property Dilemma." Bloomberg Work Shift + Wealth, September 25, 2022, https://www.bloomberg.com/graphics/2022-remote-work-is-killing-manhattan-commercial-real-estate-market/#xj4y7vzkg.

6. See, e.g., Chaffin, Joshua. "Turning Offices into Condos: New York After the Pandemic." *Financial Times*, February 14, 2023, https://www.ft.com/content/7037a8e0-d396-4563-bb2a-43abea7afe87.

7. A subcategory of opportunistic investments are "brownfields" projects undertaken at former industrial sites, where extensive environmental remediation is required prior to repurposing the property for a new, nonindustrial use. Brownfields projects are often encouraged through federal, state, and/or local government subsidies and benefit programs. See also, "Overview of EPA's Brownfields Program." U.S. Environmental Protection Agency, January 26, 2023, https://www.epa.gov/brownfields/overview-epas-brownfields-program.

8. See, e.g., "Mixed-Use Developments Quadruple Compared to a Decade Ago." Multi-Housing News, June 30, 2022, https://www.multihousingnews.com/live-work-play-apartments-quadruple-compared-to-a-decade-ago/.

9. See Chapter 1.6.

10. See Chapter 1.4.

11. See, e.g., Kobierowksi, John. "Real Estate Trends in the United States and the Sunbelt." *Forbes*, July 26, 2022, https://www.forbes.com/sites/forbesbusinesscouncil/2022/07/26/real-estate-trends-in-the-united-states-and-the-sunbelt/?sh=75409615580a.

12. See also: Barzilay, Omri. "How Major Real Estate Developers Are Experimenting with Co-Living." *Forbes*. January 3, 2018. https://www.forbes.com/sites/omribarzilay/2018/01/03/how-major-real-estate-developers-are-experimenting-with-co-living/.

13. See also, Florida, Richard. "JPMorgan Is About to Spend $1 Billion on Hundreds of Rental Homes Across the US on the Way to Becoming a Megalandlord." Insider, November 17, 2022, https://www.businessinsider.com/jp-morgan-to-acquire-1-billion-of-single-family-rentals-2022-11.

14. Nevertheless, certain types of foreign investors—most notably, qualified foreign pension funds (QFPFs)—are exempt from FIRPTA withholding requirements. Foreign investors that do not qualify for an exemption from FIRPTA may instead seek to structure investments in such a way as to minimize or eliminate FIRPTA withholding and/or other US taxation.

15. "CFIUS Real Estate Instructions (Part 802)." U.S. Department of the Treasury, February 13, 2020, https://home.treasury.gov/policy-issues/international/the-committee-on-foreign-investment-in-the-united-states-cfius/cfius-real-estate-instructions-part-802. Note that certain nations closely allied with the United States, including Canada, the United Kingdom, and Australia, have been granted exemptions from some CFIUS requirements. For investors not exempt from CFIUS regulations, whether the transaction will trigger CFIUS review must be evaluated as part of the due diligence process.

16. Schneider, Willys H. 2016. *AFIRE Guide to US Real Estate Investing*, Chapter 19: Non-US Investment in REITs, Washington, DC: AFIRE.

17. The Two Most Well-Known Examples of Non-Traded Reits Are Blackstone Real Estate Investment Trust (BREIT) and Starwood Real Estate Investment Trust (SREIT).

18. See, e.g., Behler, Albert P., and Eugene A. Pinover. 2016. *AFIRE Guide to US Real Estate Investing*, Chapter 10: Joint Ventures, Part I: Considerations Entering into a Joint Venture. Washington, DC: AFIRE; and Tomlinson, Stephen G., and Kamran A. Bajwa. 2016. *AFIRE Guide to US Real Estate Investing*, Chapter 11: Joint Ventures, Part II: Structures and Terms. Washington, DC: AFIRE.

19. A popular variation on the platform joint venture is the entry by a financial investor into a "GP JV" with a developer or operator, which GP JV, in turn, enters into asset-level joint ventures with other financial investors. Two-tier promotes are typical of this arrangement, whereby the asset-level investor is promoted by the GP JV and then, within the GP JV, the developer/operator is promoted by the "GP JV" investor. By taking a share of the asset-level promote, the "GP JV" investor seeks to achieve a higher rate of return than the asset-level investor; however, in exchange, the "GP JV" investor can expect to take on a greater degree of risk (such as for cost overruns on a development) than the asset-level investor.

20. Examples include *The Real Deal*, a widely read general interest magazine covering real estate news (with a focus on New York City, South Florida, Los Angeles, and Chicago), and PERE: Private Equity Real Estate, which publishes a magazine as well as studies intended for readership by investment professionals in the real estate funds space.

21. In addition to AFIRE, examples include Urban Land Institute (ULI), National Association of REITs (Nareit), and International Council of Shopping Centers (ICSC).

22. A title insurance company will be engaged to provide a title report or commitment, which lays out the status of title to the real property. It will include a "legal description" of the property, names of the title holders, and a comprehensive list of the encumbrances recorded against the property (such as mortgages and other financing liens, rights of way, and use restrictions). A survey prepared by a licensed surveyor identifies the locations of buildings and other improvements, as well as easements, utility lines, setbacks, and other features and also confirms that the legal description matches the actual boundaries of the property. A zoning report, which can be obtained from one of several vendors, confirms the current zoning district, the permitted uses of the property, the current requirements for that particular zone, and whether or not the property is conforming with the current requirements.

23. A physical condition report (PCR) is an assessment of the physical condition of a property prepared by an engineer after conducting an onsite inspection of the property. The report identifies deficiencies and recommendations, as well as estimated costs for repair or replacement of damaged or failing building systems or safety issues. In addition, many investors choose to visit properties in order to assess factors that a PCR does not address, such as whether décor is unattractive or outdated, although improvements in 3-D virtual tours and other assistive technologies that became vital tools during the pandemic have to some extent curtailed the need for in-person tours.

24. Obtaining a Phase I Environmental Assessment is standard practice. It is a report prepared by an environmental consultant that analyzes current and historical uses of a property to assess contamination of the soil and/or groundwater beneath the property and other threats to the environment and/or human health. For certain types of properties (e.g., those presently or formerly used gas stations, industrial plants, dry cleaners), additional, more invasive environmental testing, commonly referred to as a Phase II, may be prudent.

25. Review of rent rolls, operating statements, and utility and tax bills, among other financial data, are critical to making a confident determination of a property's net operating income (NOI) and market value. Other valuation tools include third-party appraisals, broker opinions of value (BOVs), cap rate analysis (a ratio of NOI to value), and cash flow modeling techniques.

26. Another option is to invest through REIT mutual funds or exchange-traded funds (ETFs).

27. A minority of nontraded REITs have a fixed price per share, rather than using NAV–based pricing.

Stages of Acquisition

Letter of Intent, Contract of Sale, and Closing

Zev D. Gewurz, Director, Goulston & Storrs

Sara Wilbraham, Attorney, Goulston & Storrs

International investors have long looked to the US as a leading market for investment in residential and commercial real estate, particularly for the ease of doing business. With limited exceptions, relating to national security[1] and increased reporting,[2] any foreign investor can purchase US real estate. Moreover, the US is well-known for its rule of law and transparency, providing legal protections equally to all investors, and generally reliable information and disclosures, leading to stable and well-settled practices for closing transactions—including the acquisition of real estate.

Acquisition and disposition of real estate in the US typically involves three stages: (1) preparation and execution of a **letter of intent (LOI)**, (2) negotiation and execution of a contract of sale, and (3) consummation of the sale at a closing. It's typical for acquirers to enter into a binding contract of sale to govern the relationship between the parties during the contract period and to provide a roadmap for the closing and remedies in the event of a breach. Although LOIs generally are not binding, they also can serve an important purpose, especially for the buyer.

LETTERS OF INTENT

An LOI can serve several purposes. It can be used by a buyer to formalize an offer to purchase. It can be used by both buyers and sellers to flesh out any "deal breakers" before the parties spend too much time or money on due diligence and negotiations. In this way, it also serves as a vehicle to resolve and memorialize key business terms at an early stage.

Typically, these key business terms include the purchase price, the amount of "good faith" deposit, the length of the due diligence period, the allocation of costs, the status of brokers, and the closing date. Its most important feature, however, can be to provide "exclusivity" for the buyer, meaning that, upon execution of an LOI, the seller will take the property off the market and will not enter into discussions with another prospective buyer. It also can provide "confidentiality" for both parties. If drafted properly and signed, typically, these two terms are the only "binding" parts of an LOI. If the parties intend for these terms to be binding, they also should be made to "survive" the expiration or early termination of the LOI.[3]

Scope of LOI

Some parties prefer not to expend any time or resources on an LOI and elect instead to proceed directly to negotiation of a contract of sale. As noted earlier, some parties will want to know that there is at least a basic agreement on key terms before proceeding to what could be a lengthy and costly negotiation. Other parties—usually the party that believes it has the most leverage—may want to negotiate the details of as many business and legal terms as possible before any deal is awarded. Finding the right balance between these approaches can be critical to a successful execution. In very active and desirable markets, some sellers with significant leverage may even require their final bidders to submit a complete "markup" of a form contract of sale, with comments to every single provision, before they award a deal.

Due Diligence During LOI Stage

In most markets, speed of execution is at a premium. This leads many buyers and sellers to want to start the due diligence period immediately upon agreement of key terms and prior to the execution of a negotiated contract of sale.

While basic mechanics for due diligence can be outlined in an LOI, it is more customary and protective for the seller to enter into a separate **access and confidentiality agreement**, which expands the scope and limitations of permitted due diligence during this period. Typically, a buyer will be granted access to the property, subject to certain limitations.[4] Such agreements will typically expand the nature of the confidentiality obligations, making confidential the terms of the transaction, the identity of the parties, and even the existence of the transaction and all information and materials delivered to or obtained by the buyer— excepting the buyer's advisors and unless such information otherwise is available to the public or is required by law to be disclosed.

Binding and Non-Binding LOIs

Parties should ensure that, except for the limited provisions they want to be binding and to survive, the language of the LOI states that all other provisions are not legally binding obligations, at law or in equity.

To do so, the LOI should contain a clear and unequivocal statement that it is merely an expression of the parties' interest and desire to negotiate a formal contract of sale in accordance with general terms set forth therein and is nonbinding unless and until the parties enter a binding contract. Parties should also state explicitly in the LOI that neither should rely on the LOI or on any discussions regarding the proposed transaction and that nothing contained in the LOI is a commitment, offer, or agreement.

While most courts will look to the language of the LOI as evidence of the intent, even if an LOI is executed and contains the appropriate language, parties should still take care in their negotiations. In most states, there is an "implied covenant of good faith and fair dealing," which infers a duty to negotiate in good faith. Failure to reach an agreement is not, in and of itself, a breach. A party could be liable, however, if the failure to reach agreement results from a breach of that party's obligation to negotiate in good faith. To avoid issues of "good faith negotiation," it is best to clearly state in an LOI that either party can terminate negotiations at any time and for any reason without any liability whatsoever. Some parties, particularly sellers, prefer not to sign LOIs, even once finalized. Even when an LOI is not signed or binding, the key business terms customarily are treated as nonnegotiable during the contract period.

CONTRACTS OF SALE

Real estate in the US is transferred by a simple deed and does not require a contract. Most buyers, however, need time to investigate a property and plan for a closing. They are often unwilling to expend the necessary time and resources unless they are confident that, after their investigations and planning, the seller will sell them the property. Sellers, on the other hand, do not want to take their properties off the market and give buyers extensive time to investigate and plan, only to have a buyer decide after several weeks or months that it no longer desires to buy the property. The parties typically address these issues by committing to each other in an enforceable contract of sale.

What Makes a Real Estate Contract Enforceable

There are several requirements that must be present for a real estate contract to be enforceable. The contract must be in writing, must be signed by both parties, and must have legal purpose and mutual assent, including an offer and acceptance, sometimes referred to as a "meeting of the minds." It must include a recitation of consideration, which need not be in the form of money (it also can be an exchange of other real or personal property or a promise to perform an obligation).

Finally, a real estate contract must identify (1) the parties involved (all of whom must have legal capacity), (2) the subject property (usually through a legal description), (3) the purchase price (or the manner for calculating the purchase price), and (4) the closing date (or the manner for determining the closing date, which must have an outside date). A court should be able to look at the "four corners of the document" and determine the parties' obligations.

OTHER PROVISIONS IN REAL ESTATE CONTRACTS

Beyond the minimal requirements, there are other concepts that can be of critical importance to buyers and sellers and that are often extensively negotiated.

Parties and Assignment

The seller party to a real estate contract is usually the same as the property owner. In the event that more than one party holds an interest in the property, or if there is more than one property with more than one owner, all parties with interests will need to convey to the buyer at closing.

While the seller rarely has a right or occasion to assign a real estate contract, the buyer may want or need this right. A new or different buyer entity may be required by a lender, joint venture partner, or the buyer's organizational structure. The buyer may also want to have the right to "flip" a contract to a third-party buyer at a favorable price. Typically, the seller will want to have the right to consent to any such assignment, unless it is to a true affiliate of the original buyer. The seller also may require that the original buyer remain liable for its obligations under the contract, including the payment of the purchase price, even after a permitted assignment. Real estate contracts are freely assignable by law unless a provision in the contract says otherwise. Most real estate contracts address this provision in some detail.

Property

Care should be taken to sufficiently describe the land and improvements being purchased as well as any personal property and appurtenant rights. While some contracts refer to a street address or even a tax lot number, a metes-and-bounds legal description of the boundary, taken by the seller's vesting deed and verified on a survey, is best practice. The description of the property should also include beds of adjoining public roads, rights-of-way, and subsurface rights (i.e., mineral rights, air rights, and development rights), as well as the improvements located on the land.

Additionally, property descriptions should include detailed descriptions of applicable tangible and intangible personal property, including the seller's interests in leases and contracts and in any names and trademarks related to the property.

Different assets will have their own types of property to be considered and described. In multifamily deals, for example, buyers will want to specify the stoves, fridges, washing machines, and other appliances. In portfolio deals, parties will need to determine whether the transaction is "unitary," meaning that the closing must be on "all or none" of the properties, or if the buyer has "kick-out" rights for one or more properties that fail to meet diligence standards or conditions to closing.

Purchase Price

Real estate contracts must state the sale price for the property and the method of payment. The purchase price usually is expressed as a fixed dollar amount, but can also be based on a price to be determined in the future based on a specific formula or method (e.g., a certain dollar amount per buildable foot approved).

Earnest Money Deposit

Most contracts provide for a so-called "good faith" or "earnest money" deposit. The deposit is, as its name suggests, an expression of good faith and is typically fully refundable during a due diligence period. There is no set formula for the amount of the deposit. For deals with higher purchase prices, the deposit will typically be a substantial number, but not necessarily a percentage of the purchase price. Sometimes, there is an initial deposit that is a lower amount and then a second additional deposit payable by the buyer at the expiration of the due diligence period. If there is a due diligence period, it is critical that the buyer make clear in the contract that the deposit is fully refundable for any or no reason prior to the expiration of the due diligence period. Additionally, the buyer should ensure that a breach of contract by the seller or failure of a buyer condition to closing will result in the deposit being refundable as well. Typically, deposits are held in interest-bearing escrow accounts by the title company or other escrow agent and are disbursed at the closing. While the buyer may desire to select the title company, the seller has an interest in ensuring the reliability of the escrow agent. Typically, interest follows the deposit.

Specific escrow provisions should be set forth in the contract or in a separate agreement between the escrow agent and the buyer/seller. Parties want to ensure that the escrow agent has no discretion, and the escrow agent wants to ensure that it is fully indemnified in the event of a dispute between the parties. The deposit often will serve as "liquidated damages" for the seller in the event of a breach by the buyer. If the deposit is to serve as liquidated damages, the parties must be particularly careful when drafting the contract, stating expressly how difficult it is to estimate damages in advance. Buyers should also make unequivocally clear that these liquidated damages would be the seller's sole remedy and supersede any other remedy, including specific performance.

Due Diligence and Title Review

While most due diligence periods are based on a fixed time period—often 30 to 45 days, depending on the nature of the property and market—it is important to make clear when the period commences. Buyers want due diligence periods to commence only once they have received all due diligence materials. This approach can serve to extend the due diligence period, as buyers can undertake general investigations while they are waiting for materials. Sellers want more certainty and prefer to recite a specific diligence expiration date, regardless of when the buyer receives information or commences investigations. Sometimes, these provisions are addressed in the LOI, as well as in the contract of sale.

One of the most important and detailed parts of a buyer's diligence involves review of title to the property. The scope and process for reviewing title and survey and any encumbrances against the property, the obligations of the seller to remove certain monetary liens, including mortgages and mechanic's liens, and the ability to obtain appropriate title insurance, including all applicable endorsements, as a condition to closing, are addressed extensively in the contract. In short, buyers will want the right to object to any matter believed not to be applicable to the property or that may hinder its development, ownership, or operation.

Buyers will also want to impose on sellers an absolute obligation to remove all mortgages and other monetary liens (such as mechanic's liens) against the property or arising from work performed on the property on behalf of the seller. Finally, buyers will want a provision that entitles them to object to any new matter(s) first discovered after the issuance of the initial report. The seller will attempt to require the buyer to proceed with the purchase if title defects are minimal or "curable" by affirmative title insurance and may negotiate for a cap on the seller's obligation to cure certain monetary liens. Buyers will require a set of endorsements, adding coverage to their policy, including, among others, a zoning endorsement, a "same as survey" endorsement, and a "comprehensive" endorsement. Not all endorsements are available in all states. Title companies will provide affirmative insurance for certain encumbrances that do not pose a high risk of future title loss. Buyers should also search for bankruptcies and violations outside of the title report. While some contracts require the seller to clear any such violations as a closing condition, this can be a heavily negotiated item. Generally, the parties will agree to have the title review and objection/response periods completed prior to the expiration of the due diligence period.

Representations and Warranties

After performance of due diligence, the best way for a buyer to learn about the condition of a property prior to acquisition is by having the seller represent and warrant certain facts about the property in the contract.

The principle of *caveat emptor* (let the buyer beware) is the starting point of every purchase contract. Under the law, the buyer alone is responsible for checking the quality and suitability of the property before purchasing. Sellers usually have few disclosure obligations in commercial transactions. At the same time, sellers are not permitted to misrepresent the condition of the property. If the seller makes a representation that turns out to be untrue, then the buyer will be able to enforce its rights under the contract, which may include the right not to close and the right to seek damages before or after closing. Buyers usually seek to have sellers make representations and warranties about matters that a buyer cannot determine through its own due diligence. For example, buyers often require that sellers make representations and warranties about, among other items, the seller's authority to sell, the status of leases and contracts, and any litigation or violations affecting the seller or the property.

Sellers, by contrast, want to make as few disclosures (and retain as little liability) as possible by limiting the number and scope of representations and warranties. It is here that much negotiation occurs. Most commonly, sellers will try to limit representations and warranties to their actual knowledge or only to the extent of written information they may have received. Sellers will try to further limit the liability for a breach of specific representations by requiring that any breach have a "material adverse effect" on the buyer or the property.

Further, sellers will try to limit the survival period for most or all of their representations and warranties. Under the "merger doctrine," all discussions, negotiations, and agreements, including any representations and warranties made in a real estate contract, are "merged" into the deed at closing. Once the deed is delivered, the only obligations between the buyer and the seller of real estate are those set forth in the deed and those in written agreements that expressly survive the closing. Some parties require that certain fundamental representations, like those relating to the authority of the parties, survive indefinitely. Most other representations will survive somewhere between 3 and 12 months after closing, depending on the market and the parties' respective leverage. Sellers will try to further limit their maximum liability for a breach to a capped dollar amount. Depending on the asset class and the market, the capped amount is generally between 1 and 3 percent of the purchase price.

An important issue for buyers is the question of who will stand behind the sellers' potential liability after the closing. If the seller owned only the property it is selling, after the closing, the seller would have no other assets to support any post-closing liability. Buyers often request that sellers post a guaranty from an asset-backed affiliate or individual, or cash in escrow, or agree to hold back and not distribute the capped liability amount for the survival period.

The most difficult negotiation relates to allocation of risk for representations and warranties that were true when made but which changed during the contract period due to a change in facts or circumstances. For example, a major tenant of the property filed for bankruptcy, or an environmental spill occurred on or near the property during the contract period. Parties argue about whether all or only some of the representations and warranties need to be true and correct, and to what extent, at closing.

Covenants

One way to try to mitigate changes in facts and circumstances relating to the property during the contract period is to include a set of covenants in the contract. A covenant is an unconditional promise to do or to not do something for the period of time described in the contract, the failure of which would create liability on the part of the nonperforming party. The most common seller covenant, aside from the covenant to deliver the deed at closing, is to continue to operate the property in the ordinary course, including maintaining current levels of insurance, throughout the contract period. Other covenants include not taking any major actions, such as entering into new or amending existing leases or contracts, altering the property, or changing the zoning, without the prior consent of the buyer. Covenants also include positive actions such as complying with obligations under leases and contracts and providing the buyer with notice of any events that occur which might have an adverse effect on the property. Sellers want the freedom to operate their property without restraint, especially if the buyer has the right to decide not to close the purchase. Buyers want to make decisions based on their investigations and underwriting and do not want to be obligated to buy a property that has changed prior to closing. One common compromise is to provide sellers with certain rights to act without buyers' approval during the due diligence period and to restrict such rights after the expiration of such period.

Conditions

It is important to distinguish between a covenant and a condition and to make clear in the contract whether a particular term is a covenant or a condition. Unlike a covenant, a condition is a contingency, an event that must occur before the parties are obligated to perform. The failure of a condition does not create liability, but rather excuses a party's performance.

While sellers will seek to narrow buyers' closing conditions, they are particularly important for buyers. Negotiated properly, conditions should describe all the pieces necessary for the buyer to acquire, develop (if applicable), and operate the property. They are also the buyer's last chance to retain its deposit after the due diligence period expires. Typical buyer conditions include delivery by the seller of closing documents and possession of the property, issuance by the title company of a satisfactory title policy, continued accuracy of the seller's representations and warranties, and performance by the seller of its other covenants. Sellers, in turn, care most about delivery by the buyer of the purchase price.

Different deals call for different conditions. Buyers often condition their obligation to close on the receipt of estoppels from tenants or from parties to an easement or other material agreement or instrument affecting the property. In development deals, buyers also may require that all necessary land use and zoning permits and approvals be in place or that certificates of occupancy be issued. This is particularly relevant in so-called forward purchase agreements, in which accurately describing "lien-free completion" of the property as a condition to closing is critical.

Risk of Loss

In some states, common law allocates the risk of loss to the buyer as soon as the contract is signed, but this allocation can be modified by agreement of the parties. In such situations, the buyer will require that a provision be added to the contract of sale to state the modification. If the property were damaged by fire or other casualty, the seller would want to transfer the property to the buyer and assign insurance proceeds without being required to make repairs. If a taking were to occur (i.e., through an eminent domain process), the buyer would want to be able to cancel the contract and receive a return of the deposit, while the seller would want to transfer the property to the buyer and assign condemnation awards.

In most contracts, the parties negotiate a threshold amount of damage to the property, often stated in dollars or square footage. Below this threshold, the contract will remain in full force and effect and the buyer will take title to the property plus insurance proceeds or awards, or the seller will complete repairs prior to the closing. Above this threshold, the contract may be terminated. Such provisions may also establish that, if the loss allows certain tenants to cancel their leases or restricts access to the building on the property, the contract can be terminated.

Default or Breach

The most common remedy for a buyer's failure to take title when the seller has fully performed its obligations under the contract is for the seller to terminate the contract and retain the deposit as liquidated damages. In order for the seller to retain the deposit, the buyer must have breached its obligations under the contract, all of the conditions to closing must have been satisfied, and the seller must be ready, willing, and able to sell the property. This means it is clearly evident that the seller has executed and delivered, or otherwise is prepared to deliver, the closing documents, all in accordance with the terms of the contract.

Buyers typically negotiate for several remedies in the event that a seller breaches the contract or otherwise fails to perform, including the right to terminate the contract and retain the deposit, sue for damages, and obtain specific performance. Some sellers in some markets attempt to limit their liability only to the return of the deposit and try to exclude any right to sue for damages entirely. This is difficult for a buyer to accept, especially in the event of a willful breach by the seller, such as the conveyance of the property to a third party in violation of the contract. In such cases, according to the buyer, its recovery should be unlimited. Even in these cases, however, sellers may be successful in limiting their liability to reimbursement of the buyer's actual, out-of-pocket costs, up to a capped amount, in addition to the return of the deposit. Another way in which sellers seek to limit potential liability is by requiring buyers that desire to seek a remedy of specific performance to commence litigation within a specified period of time following the required closing date, beyond which time the remedy will no longer be available.

Buyers also have post-closing remedies for breaches of the seller's representations and warranties. Those remedies are typically available only during a negotiated "survival period," which is generally between 3 and 12 months, and are made subject to a capped amount, which typically is between 1 and 3 percent of the purchase price in larger transactions. Again, sellers will try to require that buyers commence litigation prior to expiration of the survival period, to preserve this remedy.

Miscellaneous Provisions

These are the provisions at the end of a contract of sale. While they generally do not contain business terms and are largely standardized, they can have significant implications. Some of the provisions addressed previously and later, including the "assignment" provision (addressed previously) and the "time of the essence" provision (addressed later), are generally contained in the "miscellaneous" section. Some of the other provisions found in this section include the "merger clause," which provides that the contract contains the entire agreement of the parties and that all previous agreements, oral or written, are merged into this one document. Before including a merger clause, it is important to make sure there are no other agreements being relied on by the parties. The "severability" clause also can be important, as it allows a court to remove any provision that turns out to be unenforceable by law rather than reject the entire contract. Notice provisions can be important when it comes to duly delivering material communications, like a termination of the contract, and the "business day" provision can be important for counting days in any period, whether it is for due diligence, title review, or closing. Finally, governing law and forum selection will determine where and how the contract will be interpreted in the event of a dispute. It is important to have qualified counsel guiding this part of the contract negotiation.

CLOSING

Escrow Closings

Real estate contracts specify both the time and place of the closing. While the time of the closing can be very important, unlike in many other countries, the place is not. Few parties in the US get together in person in a specific place to conduct a closing. Most closings in the US are conducted by escrow arrangements with the buyer's title insurance company or title agent. In such arrangements, the parties will deliver the closing documents and funds to the title company, which will distribute them pursuant to escrow instructions and a closing statement signed by the parties. While certain documents and other deliverables, particularly documents that are not to be recorded in the public land records, can be distributed by email prior to or during the closing, most states require originals for documents that will be recorded.

Time of the Essence

The time of closing may be a significant issue. The buyer will want sufficient time to complete its due diligence and obtain any required capital and financing. The seller will want to proceed to closing at the earliest possible date. Even if a closing date is specified in the contract, without a provision specifying that "time is of the essence," either party will be entitled to a "reasonable" adjournment of the closing. In determining what is "reasonable," courts may consider the nature of the property and the time period for closing, the experience of the parties, the conduct of the parties, the presence or absence of good faith, and the possibility of hardship or prejudice to either party.

"Time of the essence" clauses enable either party to demand performance by the other on the date specified for the closing without permitting the other party to rely on its legal right to a reasonable extension of time. Courts have strictly enforced contracts containing this language, and failure by one of the parties to perform on the closing date will constitute a material breach and may result in the forfeiture of the deposit, among other remedies.

CLOSING CHECKLIST

As soon as the contract of sale is executed, attorneys for the parties should prepare a closing checklist, including a schedule of critical dates. At the same time, the buyer should arrange to undertake its physical and environmental due diligence, if not already commenced earlier during the LOI stage. The buyer should order an updated title commitment and survey and review copies of all documents affecting title, including any covenants, conditions and restrictions, easements, condominium or homeowner association documents, and development, regulatory, and other governmental agreements. The buyer also should arrange for review of all leases, management agreements, and all other contracts that affect the property. Copies of all such documents should be made available promptly to any institution providing equity or financing to the buyer. Finally, as the closing draws closer, the parties should prepare a settlement statement calculating all of the various prorations and adjustments based on the negotiated allocation of costs relating to the property and the closing.

Local Law and Custom

While most real estate transactions can be handled across state borders, it remains true that some aspects of real estate are truly local. Some states use "special" or "limited" warranty deeds while others use "quitclaim" deeds, some use "mortgages" while others use "deeds of trust," some pay real estate taxes semiannually while others pay quarterly, and some have transfer and/or mortgage recording taxes while others have none. There are state and local taxes and other forms that must be completed and filed in certain jurisdictions, and there are differing practices for which party pays what portion of certain taxes and title, recording, and other fees. Some states have mandatory disclosures that are required to be included in every real estate contract. Finally, it is always important to understand local zoning and land use permits and approvals, especially in a development deal. Buyers and their counsel should make sure to obtain local advice and counsel regarding these and other local laws and customs.

Closing Deliveries

The contract will specify all items required to be delivered by the parties at closing, in addition to the purchase price and possession of the property. Often, the forms of closing documents will be negotiated in advance and attached as exhibits to the contract. The most common closing deliveries include the following, although different states may have different requirements, and different deals may have unique circumstances requiring other documents or instruments:

- Deed
- Assignment and assumption of leases and licenses, together with originals thereof
- Assignment and assumption of contracts and management agreements, together with originals thereof (or evidence of termination thereof)
- Bill of sale and general assignment
- Original security deposit letters of credit, with assignments thereof
- Estoppel certificates relating to leases, contracts, title documents, and other material agreements affecting the property or its owner, as applicable
- Subordination and non-disturbance agreements, if applicable
- Notices to tenants of the transfer of the property, providing addresses to which they will submit rent payments and other notices to the buyer
- Transfer tax returns, if applicable
- Evidence of good standing and authority
- Owner's title affidavit, in the form required by title company, together with documents evidencing the seller's authority to complete the sale
- An affidavit confirming compliance by the seller with the Foreign Investment in Real Property Tax Act (FIRPTA), which requires, under 26 U.S. Code § 1445, the withholding of a certain portion of the purchase price in the case of certain non-US sellers of real property
- Certification by the seller that its representations and warranties in the contract remain materially true and correct as of the closing date

- Settlement statement showing all prorations and adjustments
- Keys to the property and all files related thereto, including guaranties and warranties

There are generally few restrictions on international investors purchasing real estate in the US. Legal protections in the US apply equally to all investors, and practices for closing transactions are well settled. There are, however, many nuances and pitfalls that need to be navigated throughout the acquisition process, from structuring and taxes to local market customs and practices, and from protecting rights and limiting liabilities to ensuring that would-be investors are getting the benefits of their bargains.

NOTES

1. In certain circumstances where foreign persons buy or invest in US real estate, the transaction may be subject to review by the Committee on Foreign Investment in the United States (CFIUS). CFIUS is an interagency committee of the US government that reviews certain foreign investment transactions within its jurisdiction for matters of national security. This kind of CFIUS review has been triggered, for example, in transactions where (1) the real estate was proximate to a US military base or port, (2) a tenant of the property was a US government agency or contractor, and (3) the building was a hotel in which the president of the US regularly stayed. Where parties believe that they may be engaged in a transaction that could be subject to review by CFIUS, they must decide whether to notify CFIUS of their transaction and whether to seek the Committee's approval and safe harbor protections. A CFIUS review can take longer than 90 days to run its course, given the rights of the Committee to extend the review period, and can deter sellers from considering a foreign investor as a buyer.
2. In 1978, Congress passed a law called the Agricultural Foreign Investment Disclosure Act (AFIDA) to track foreign ownership of US agricultural land. The purpose of the act was to gather information regarding any foreign person who buys, sells, or holds a direct or indirect interest in any US land that was categorized as "agricultural" or "forestry" within the previous five years, and to disclose certain information regarding such transactions and holdings to the secretary of agriculture by filing a so-called Form FSA-153 with the local county office of the Farm Services Agency where the land is located within 90 days of the reportable action occurring. While the foreign investor may desire to remain anonymous, AFIDA disclosures are subject to the Freedom of Information Act (FOIA), and are therefore subject to public disclosure. While this is merely an information filing requirement, failure to duly and timely file can subject the foreign investor to significant penalties based on a percentage of the value of the property.
3. While some refer to "term sheets," there is generally no substantive difference between a term sheet and an LOI.
4. Including the timing of access, nature of testing, requirements not to disturb and to restore the property, and provisions regarding both an indemnity and insurance to cover any damage resulting from buyer's investigations.

Building Occupancy

Leasing for Diverse Property Types in the US

Sarah Queen, Head of Equity Strategies, MetLife Investment Management

nternational investors have long looked to the US as a leading market for investment in residential and commercial real estate, particularly for the ease of doing business. Leasing is almost always conducted through a leasing broker. This chapter reviews the role that an owner's leasing broker (or a tenant representative) takes in the normal steps of securing new tenants, as well as negotiating lease extensions or modifications with existing tenants.

This chapter also covers the timing of commission payments and tenant improvement allowances, as well as a typical lease structure (e.g., area [re]measurement, free rent periods, rental rate, operating expenses and recoveries, increases in rent, term, management, fees, options) for each of the major asset types—with additional details included for multifamily leases, which can vary significantly from commercial leases.

Leasing is the fundamental driver of value creation in real estate. Leases are at the core for determining the revenue of an asset, which informs net operating income, cash flow, and asset value. Whether an asset is already fully occupied, stabilized, below market occupancy, or vacant, being able to understand the leasing process, evaluate deals, understand market terms, and successfully negotiate deals are fundamental skills for investment and asset managers.

LEASING PROCESS

In most US markets, once a tenant has determined that it needs to lease space, it will engage a leasing broker. The broker will then guide the tenant through the leasing process, helping them refine requirements, tour potential spaces, review landlord proposals, and ultimately assist with lease negotiations (see Figure 2.4-01).

The tenant will execute an agreement with the broker that delineates the nature of the services and memorializes the fees. The fee is standard across a market (usually based on a fee per year of the lease or a percent of the lease's revenues) and is paid by the landlord when the lease is completed, so there is no out-of-pocket fee for the tenant for commercial leases.

Typically, a tenant's broker is paid 100 percent of a standard commission (also known as *a full commission*) and the landlord's broker is paid 50 percent (*a half commission*), so the landlord is paying 150 percent of the standard commission if there are two brokers. When the tenant does not have a broker, the landlord's broker receives a full commission, not a half commission. Additionally, for large office assignments (e.g., >150,000 sq. ft.), some tenants will structure a fee-sharing agreement with their leasing brokers when the firm is selected. The brokers will send the landlord an invoice showing their calculation of commissions as the lease nears the execution stage, and the invoice is typically paid 50 percent at lease execution and 50 percent upon occupancy.

FIGURE 2.4-01 **Leasing process**

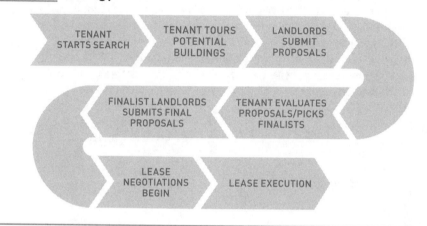

For smaller leases, hiring a leasing broker can be extremely helpful for the tenants, as the brokers will have much more experience highlighting issues that are not apparent to the tenant, but could result in significant costs. For larger tenants, a broker is essential to navigating all the complexities with large leases. If the tenant is already in a property and is looking to expand or exercise a renewal option (including negotiating a renewal outside of its option rights), it can be beneficial to hire a broker to advise the tenant through the process and keep the landlord focused on delivering market terms.

Upon engagement with a tenant, a broker will typically request tenant information, such as how the tenant will use the space (e.g., for officing, R&D, warehousing, retail), how much space is required, the tenant's price range for both rent and build-out, and how long the lease will be. Brokers will also need to discuss expectations. For example, will the tenant build out the space to meet their needs, or do they want it move-in ready? For the building itself, do they want specific amenities, such as conference spaces, food and beverage availability, a gym, outdoor space, covered parking, and other amenities? Do they have specific space needs, such as ceiling height, column spacing, number of dock doors, or anything else?

Even with this information, it can be difficult for brokers to help determine how much space a tenant needs, especially as these needs are impacted by the individual building's configuration and load factor. Working with space-planning professionals, a tenant will need to understand its usable space needs. Then the broker will work with the tenant's specific needs (including space preferences like full, partial floors or multiple floor configurations) to ensure the tenant is looking at possibilities that meet its needs.

Once the tenant and broker have determined their search criteria, the broker will have the potential tenant tour possible buildings, fine-tuning the tenant's criteria. Sometimes the process will start with a virtual tour of many assets and then be pared down to a smaller number of actual tours, and other times the potential tenant wants to tour all the possibilities.

Following the tours, the broker will either send out a **request for proposal (RFP)** to potential landlords or ask the landlords to submit proposals for a specific size or space. The tenant's broker will then compare all the responses, evaluating the monetary and nonmonetary issues and then guide the tenant as responses are sent to multiple landlords, repeating the same process until the tenant makes its selection.

However, even after a landlord and tenant begin exclusive negotiations and engage leasing legal counsel, there are myriad issues that could derail the negotiations. For example, if the tenant and landlord cannot reach a final executed lease, the tenant's broker would then need to restart the process at any point along the continuum in Figure 2.4-01. The broker may be able to simply reengage with the second-choice landlord, but that space may not be available, or the landlord could alter its terms once it understands the other potential deal is not progressing.

TYPICAL LEASE COMPONENTS

In addition to the major lease points detailed in Figure 2.4-02, a few fundamental lease terms impact multiple parts of leasing:

Gross Lease
- Tenant pays its rental rate, which is inclusive of a baseline of operating expenses. Landlords pay all the costs of operating the building (i.e., maintenance, taxes, insurance, and common utilities).
- If a tenant's rental rate was $50/sq. ft. and the operating expenses were $10/sq. ft., the tenant would pay the landlord $50/sq. ft. in rent and the landlord would be responsible for paying the $10/sq. ft. in expenses.

Net Lease
- Tenant's rental rate excludes expenses and in addition to the rent, tenant pays the expenses separately.
- If this was the same market as above, the net rent would be $40 **NNN** with $10 expenses (for an equivalent of $50 gross rent) (See Figure 2.4-03).

FIGURE 2.4-02 Critical components of a lease

PARTIES	Understand the entities signing the lease and their financial wherewithal
RENTAL RATE	• Type of lease (Gross or Net)? • When and how the rent increases? Annual fixed rent amount or percentage increase? Steps? Or combo? • Any spaces not on typical rent (storage etc.)
PERCENT RENT (OVERAGE)	• Percentage rent enables the landlord to share in a retailer's revenues by capturing a percentage of sales above a baseline.
ABATEMENT OR FREE RENT	• The period between Lease and Rent Commencement (months or years free) • Depending on the market, may include construction • Net or Gross free (are expenses free too?) • Typically, free rent is upfront, but it can be during any period
USE	• There can be a lot of variation use, especially in retail, where you are curating a certain mix of retailers. • Sometimes ancillary uses are defined by selling space—i.e., card store selling purses—only X% can be used for purses • Exclusives—limits competing uses (steakhouse vs. steaks on menu vs. Brazilian steakhouse) • Restricted uses—bowling alley or car dealership, etc.
TERM	• Lease commencement to expiry, will usually include a free rent period.
CONDITION OF SPACE OR DELIVERY OF PREMISES	• "AS IS" or is work required • Even if the Landlord is handing over the space "raw" to the Tenant for them to build out the space, there may be landlord work required, like restrooms/lavatories
PREMISES	• Should include floor, suite numbers, and sq. ft. for each suite (if multiple) as well as total sq. ft.
OPERATING EXPENSES	• Tenants will pay a portion of the Operating Expenses spent to run the building. • It may be in addition to the direct costs of electricity, water, etc, billed for individual suites.

FIGURE 2.4-03 **Typical expense spread for the leasing process**

EXPENSES

GROWTH RATE = 3%

NET EXAMPLE					
	YR1	YR2	YR3	YR4	YR5
EXPENSES	$ 10.00	$ 10.30	$ 10.61	$ 10.93	$ 11.26
AMT LL PAYS	$ -	$ -	$ -	$ -	$ -
AMT TENANT PAYS	$ 10.00	$ 10.30	$ 10.61	$ 10.93	$ 11.26

GROSS EXAMPLE					
	YR1	YR2	YR3	YR4	YR5
EXPENSES	$ 10.00	$ 10.30	$ 10.61	$ 10.93	$ 11.26
AMT LL PAYS	$ 10.00	$ 10.00	$ 10.00	$ 10.00	$ 10.00
AMT TENANT PAYS	$ -	$ 0.30	$ 0.61	$ 0.93	$ 1.26

LEASING STRATEGIES

Moving into new space is expensive, so a central issue for leasing concerns how landlords can attract new tenants.

To answer this question, landlords and owners need to understand what type of tenants are expanding in the market: technology, financial or legal services, ecommerce, and so forth. What is motivating these prospective tenants: Do they want more efficient space, to be near busy intersections or specific tenants, access to highly amenitized space, or alignment with employees' homes or commuting plans? Are there areas of newer construction that have created a nexus of food and beverage offerings that are attracting customers or workers? Does the building physically work for the majority of tenants already in the market?

Tenants will usually look at renewal as part of their potential lease negotiation options. Unless a tenant needs to restack or reconfigure, renewing is usually cheaper. Because restacking may involve multiple moves, some tenants may opt to only focus on new options. However, as the existing landlord is the only one that effectively addresses lowering the tenant's current rental rates, the renewal landlord also has the benefit of being able to provide the tenant some immediate incentives.

In addition to focusing on driving occupancy, owners will want to ensure that they have aligned the leasing and asset strategy to maximize asset value. For example, if you are preparing for a large redevelopment, you may want to focus on short-term leasing to tighten your overall expiration schedule to ease redevelopment issues. If you need stronger occupancy to sell an asset, it may make sense to make a few shorter-term deals (3 to 5 years) to boost occupancy instead of waiting for a 10-year lease.

Last, as owners enter negotiations with tenants, they need to understand their own position: How badly do you need this tenant? What leverage do you have with the tenant (i.e., how badly do they want to be in your building)? You will need to prioritize the issues that matter the most to you and then reframe the points of contention to find a solution that results in a lease.

DEAL EVALUATION

Whether you are a landlord or a tenant, you need to be able to compare deals, both across markets and within a market. Additionally, as the lease is being structured, the landlord will need to evaluate terms to determine the impact, working to structure a deal that maximizes value while delivering to the tenant the economics that is required for the tenant to commit to the space.

Typically, the landlord will utilize a **net effective rent (NER)** calculation to evaluate lease proposals. An NER calculation takes all the costs of the deal and amortizes into the deal, so it possible to evaluate the "true rent" being paid. The following are methods that can be used to evaluate lease deals:

- **NPV/sf:** The length of the term can increase the **net present value (NPV)** but could still have low NER or be negative compared to budget.
- **NER/sf:** Leases with positive NERs and large capital outlays (especially if they have a long term) can produce internal rates of return (IRRs) for the property. This is the most common method for comparing across markets/assets.
- **Total Revenue Increase:** This method does not consider deal size or term. Also, this method inherently assumes space was never leasing.
- **Full Valuation:** This method shows if the deal is accretive to budget and gives the impact of the capital outlays as well. However, it does not necessarily allow brokers to compare to other market deals.

When the tenant is comparing deals, it will need to understand the total deal costs, but not only on a square-foot basis, as the tenant may be comparing across buildings with different size suites.

MULTIFAMILY LEASING

Multifamily leases are typically 12 months in length, but some markets may offer some as short as 5 months and as long as 24 months. While commercial leases have many clauses that will be negotiated, there is little room for negotiation in multifamily leases.

The negotiables might only include the rent amount and free rent period (if any) with the rest of the clauses being straightforward. Some markets have multifamily leases governed by government regulations (therefore even less to negotiate), and as more regulations around rent control (and/or rent stabilization) come into being, there will be even less room for lease negotiation. While many of the largest multifamily buildings advertise no-fee leasing and prospective tenants can easily lease space without a broker, if a tenant is interested in leasing directly from a condominium owner, it will be difficult to find those opportunities without a broker.

Operating Terms

Management of Diverse Property Types in the US

Brian Jennings, Senior Managing Director, CBRE

nternational investors have long looked to the US as a leading market for investment in residential and commercial real estate, particularly for the ease of doing business. Leasing is almost always conducted through a leasing broker. The dynamics of managing a wide range of property types are continually evolving, especially as the uses and expectations of technology, physical and human resources, and the overall built environment transforms (and is transformed by) culture. But no matter if a real estate portfolio is comprised of office, industrial/logistics, retail, life sciences, or mixed use, there are some consistent aspects of property management that all investors should understand across the commercial real estate spectrum.

REQUEST FOR PROPOSAL (RFP)

Most large-scale commercial owners and investors outsource property management to firms that specialize in the field. And when choosing a property management firm, it is typical that a property owner develops a **request for proposal (RFP)** to clearly define the scope of work for the companies bidding on the property management assignment. Knowledgeable property owners will look for a diverse range of services, including staffing, engineering, project management, banking, accounting services, operational technologies (including marketing, website, and application assets), tenant relations, property amenities, and other operational services.

The goal of the property owner should be to find the management provider that has the experience and expertise to meet their specific needs and drive value in all aspects of the real estate life cycle.

TALENT

Talent—or the quality of human capital—is key in being able to execute a property owner's vision for property management and occupancy, service delivery, and ultimately, increasing the value of an asset. As such, a property manager must be able to serve as the de facto CEO of a property or portfolio, with a business acumen to deliver on building operations; financial reporting; budgeting; technology; health, safety, and environment (HSE); construction; capital planning; environmental, social, and governance (ESG) performance; and high-touch customer service.

Operations

Operational excellence is delivered through consistent business practices and market-leading policies and procedures, which ensure both the administration of leases and service contracts and the custodial care of the property or portfolio are maintained at the highest level to avoid interruption of services. Disciplined operating practices and a preventive maintenance regimen are critical to preserving the capital equipment and offering the best experience for occupiers—and a maximization of value for owners. Policies and procedures should be developed by those **subject matter experts (SMEs)** within a real estate organization who can articulate best practices for each aspect of a managed property.

A process for audit and governance over these policies and procedures is important to maintain the integrity of the content and changes within the commercial real estate industry. Property management companies will typically develop a team of SMEs to perform regular audits of processes and procedures on a sampling of managed buildings to confirm adherence to said procedures. From a governance perspective, a group of SMEs typically meets several times per year to provide a detailed review of current or proposed policies.

Customer Service

Typically, customers or users of a building or space will only provide feedback if they have had either an exceptionally good or truly awful experience. Word of either experience travels fast, especially online, which puts pressure on the property manager to emphasize high-quality customer service. A handful of bad reviews could have long-term negative ramifications for an asset.

For property management teams, it is imperative to work within a set of service standards so that the expectations are clear to deliver a culture of great customer service. In some cases, building owners will want to create their own service standards and even a service credo, similar to high-end hotels and premier entertainment venues. For example, the Ritz Carlton, known for its high-quality customer service, has the service credo: "We are ladies and gentlemen, serving ladies and gentlemen." This credo is posted in the employee areas of all Ritz Carlton hotels.

Customer service training should be held at least annually for the onsite property management team. This will serve as a reminder of what the customer service expectations are for the building and also train any new employees. The best firms have their own internal training and offer opportunities for enhanced hospitality training at the highest quality assets.

Lease Administration

Lease administration is one of the most important property management responsibilities. The lease governs the relationship between the building owner and the tenant and is the key to the value of the property. The property manager must interpret and enforce the terms of the lease in their capacity as agent for the property owner, help navigate disputes that may arise between owner and tenant, all while maintaining a healthy relationship with the tenant to ensure retention. Property managers need to have an expert grasp and understanding of all lease terms in order to administer the document as intended and serve as the trusted advisor to the building owner.

It is vitally important that when the lease is abstracted, the terms and conditions are summarized in a manner whereby critical milestones are tracked, and the accuracy of the monetary terms are entered into an accounting system that meets the requirements of the property owner.[1] These systems can be hosted by a property management company or by the building owner themselves.

Lease language can vary among different lease types and property types, but the most common lease types in the US are:

- **Net Lease:** Specifies the tenant is directly responsible for all common area maintenance (CAM), tax and insurance expenses (most common in industrial/ logistics leases).
- **Gross Lease:** Specifies the landlord is responsible for all common area maintenance (CAM), tax and insurance expenses, thus the tenant does not directly reimburse the landlord for operating expenses. the rental rates for these leases account for the owner's estimate of building expenses over the term of the lease.
- **Modified Gross Lease:** Specifies tenant pays base rent at the lease inceptions but pays base plus a proportionate share of operating expenses associated with the property in consecutive years.
- **Percentage Lease:** Specifies the tenant pays a base rent plus a percentage of any revenue earned while doing business on the rental premises (most common in retail leases).

OPERATING EXPENSES AND COMMON AREA MAINTENANCE (CAM) EXPENSES

The single most challenging aspect of administering commercial real estate leases in the US is the calculation of **operating expenses (opex)**. With the many different lease types and nuanced language that have been developed over the years, it can be quite complicated to interpret the lease so that operating expenses are both allocated and then calculated accurately.

Office and retail leases tend to be the most complex when it comes to interpreting opex clauses. Landlords often use broad definitions of opex in order to recover as much of the building costs and expenses as possible from tenants. Tenants often negotiate certain exclusions or caps on their expenses, thus creating many unique expense pools at the same property.

Many office leases will also include a gross-up calculation provision within the opex clause. The purpose of the calculation is to stabilize the expenses as if occupancy had reached a certain level from where it may have been when the lease originally commenced. Thus, there could be gross-up provisions at 90, 95, or 100 percent occupancy levels, depending on how the lease was written. The initial calculations during the first year of the lease are critical, as those expense figures will serve as the basis for all future-year calculations.

Budgeting

Preparing an annual operating budget for a property or portfolio is another very important task in a typical property management scope of work. This will include projecting revenues, detailing all operating expenses, and finally developing a capital plan for the coming year and often future years (5 to 15 years).

There are two common approaches to developing commercial property budgets. The first is zero-based budgeting, which is a method for budgeting whereby all expenses must be justified for each new period. The process of a zero base is that every function within the property is analyzed for its needs and costs. The budgets are then built around what is needed for the upcoming period, regardless of whether each budget is higher or lower than the previous one.

The second approach is incremental budgeting, which is the method of taking the prior year's actual figures and applying a fixed percentage increase to expenses without completing a detailed analysis. The incremental budgeting approach would most likely work for industrial/logistics properties but would not be recommended for a more complex piece of real estate, such as an office tower or retail project.

A property management company should have experienced staff to develop annual property budgets as well as provide a budget inclusion reference guide that will stipulate all of the typical expenses that a property should experience in the coming year.

ESG

Property owners are relying more than ever on their property management teams to execute their ESG plans and programming. Property management companies must now be ready to deliver an ESG scope of work that includes utility data collection, utility and waste baselining, annual sustainability reporting, compliance monitoring, and compliance management. This ESG scope is outside of the typical property management scope of services provided in the US, so property owners should expect to pay an additional fee for the ESG scope that they select.

To execute a successful ESG program at a property or for a portfolio, utility and waste data will be required to meet certain data metrics for reporting and compliance. Many jurisdictions across the US have now mandated certain utility metrics to be reported, so it's important that property owners must have language in the tenant's lease that requires them to provide utility usage data in a timely manner. Leases should be written with "Green Language" to hold the tenant accountable for sharing certain information with the property owner, as stipulated in the lease. This is most important at industrial/logistics and retail properties, where the tenant receives their own utility bill, and the transfer can be slower. In office buildings, the data for total building utilities is easier to collect, but some municipalities are pushing for tenant-level detail of usage in office buildings, which will require additional investment by the landlord to submeter each suite.

Amenities

Tenant expectations for building amenities have grown exponentially. Tenants now look at their office spaces as an extension of their homes and have come to expect many of the same conveniences. Property managers must constantly come up with creative ways to keep their properties competitive and provide amenities that will attract usage.

One of the smartest things a building owner can do when thinking about the amenity offering for their building is to ask the tenants what they would like to see. Especially in older buildings that may be undergoing future renovations, this is a great way to engage with tenants and create an opportunity to retain a tenant that may otherwise be looking to relocate to a newer building with more modern amenities.

Those amenities may include services that provide value (e.g., concierge, shoeshine, e-recycling), physical places that enhance the experience (e.g., conference facilities, bike rooms, end-of-trip facilities, fitness, and relaxation), or technology-driven tools that facilitate access and information (e.g., food and beverage ordering, facility scheduling, consumer discounts from building partners, local restaurants, and landmarks). With hospitality-driven services that focus on increased productivity and employee well-being, the property management team can ensure the tenants have everything they need to be at their best.

The use of common spaces has become a real trend in the US, whether that be a lobby area, dedicated open space, or even rooftops and balconies where a tenant can simply grab a cup of coffee and a snack or hold a meeting or take a phone call. Creating connections between the building and the outdoors can be an attractive amenity for tenants. This could include adding outdoor tables and seating, a vegetable garden to purchase produce, or even a walking or running path if the space and weather permit. Fitness centers, wellness rooms, and event spaces are also quite popular with tenants as it gives them the opportunity to step outside quickly and conveniently of their traditional workspace and focus on their personal health and well-being.

Whatever the new trends are in the coming years, it will be important for property managers to remain educated and keep their building owners informed of the changing tenant demands and expectations from their buildings.

NOTE

1. There are a variety of accounting platforms to collect this important lease information that can be utilized, but the two most common in the US among institutional investors are MRI and Yardi.

Closing Out

*What to Know About Disposition,
Representation, and Negotiation*

Cory Saunders, Real Estate Investment Officer, Fidelity Investments

T he sale, or disposition, of a property is the final stage in the investment cycle. Once the decision has been made to sell an asset, the goal of the disposition process is typically to maximize sale proceeds at the lowest risk.

BROKERAGE

Property owners will typically engage a capital markets broker to assist with the disposition process. The role of the broker is to create a competitive marketing process by presenting the property to a wide universe of appropriate buyers and running a process that generates the best competitive terms for the seller.

A seller may have an existing brokerage relationship that it wishes to prioritize, but otherwise it is customary to ask more than one broker to present or pitch its services in connection with a potential disposition. Each broker should provide its perspective on key disposition considerations, including but not limited to:

- Current capital market conditions
- Its team and expertise
- The investment thesis for the property
- Its recommended marketing process and the universe of potential buyers for the property
- A range of pricing that the broker believes is achievable in the market
- Fees for its services
- Other considerations for the seller (e.g., timing, weaknesses, potential alternative strategies)

Brokers are accustomed to such presentations and will typically cover key criteria unprompted, though some sellers elect to ensure a comprehensive response by either posing certain questions or providing brokers with a formal request for proposal (RFP).

Once an owner has chosen a broker, the parties will negotiate and execute an exclusive brokerage agreement. This agreement will set forth, among other matters, a timeframe during which the broker may exclusively market the property and the fees payable to the broker upon successful execution.

PREPARATION

The owner will typically work with the selected broker to prepare a comprehensive financial model that will be shared with prospective buyers. This model should be reviewed by both parties for factual accuracy (e.g., lease data, expenses) prior to finalization. The broker may overlay its own forward-looking assumptions, such as market rents and rental growth, as well as suggest adjustments to expenses to reflect market approach.

It is important to undertake a thorough review of property documentation and materials to ensure that potential buyers have access to the information they will require to underwrite the property and conduct their due diligence. Section 3 of this book covers the due diligence process in further detail, but owners should prepare an organized data room of operational, physical, and legal information. This information should be scrutinized for accuracy prior to release to potential buyers.

In addition to the foregoing, an owner may elect to commission its own property condition report, Phase I report, survey, and/or title commitment to provide to potential buyers. These reports may be independently commissioned by a buyer during its due diligence, but identifying any issues during the competitive stage of the sale process (as opposed to after awarding the property) is best for the seller and eliminates the potential for price adjustments later. In certain circumstances, buyers may elect to rely on a seller's report, shortening the transaction process.

Finally, it is important to consider that prospective buyers will tour the property in connection with the marketing process. For certain asset types, it is important to work with the selected broker to establish an attractive tour route and make targeted improvements to the property to ensure ideal presentation (e.g., landscaping, painting).

MARKETING PROCESS

The selected broker will prepare offering materials for the owner's review. These offering materials typically include a "teaser" and an "offering memorandum." The teaser is a brief, nonconfidential overview of the property and acquisition opportunity. Upon executing a confidentiality agreement (the form of which may be reviewed and approved by an owner), prospective buyers will be granted access to a comprehensive offering memorandum, certain property information (e.g., rent roll, historic financials), and a financial model (if a commercial property).

A sale process will often have several steps, as set forth in Figure 2.6-01. After potential buyers have had a satisfactory period to review the offering materials, the broker will ask interested parties to submit a letter of intent to acquire the property. The letter of intent will include key purchase terms, such as price, deposit amounts and structure, due diligence period, closing conditions and timing, exclusivity terms, and so on.

The broker will collect the letters of intent and prepare a comprehensive matrix to summarize the terms of each offer for the owner. Depending upon the depth of interest, additional rounds of bidding may be held to improve terms for the owner, and at each stage, the broker may release further information about the property to prospective buyers. Once the list has been satisfactorily narrowed, a broker may organize "buyer interviews." This is an opportunity for the seller to meet with potential buyers and better understand the terms and conditions of their offer (e.g., approval process, underwriting assumptions, financing requirements) to help determine the offer with the least amount of associated risk. Brokers may also sometimes ask potential buyers if they wish to improve the terms of their offer during the interview process.

At the conclusion of the process, the broker will consult with the owner and determine the buyer.

FIGURE 2.6-01 **Sales process**

Following the selection of a buyer, the parties will typically execute a letter of intent that memorializes certain key terms of the transaction. This document is typically nonbinding with the exception of confidentiality and exclusivity provisions. The transaction will then move forward (as detailed elsewhere in Section 2 of this book) through closing.

OTHER CONSIDERATIONS

When electing to sell a property, there are certain considerations that may alter the timing or process for a sale. Two common strategies involve a 1031 exchange and a debt assumption.

In a 1031 exchange, an investor uses the proceeds from its sale of a property to acquire a like-kind replacement property. If correctly executed, this allows the seller of a property to defer capital gains taxes on its sale. This approach should involve counsel and tax advisors and requires, among other considerations, execution of a both a purchase and sale on a certain time frame and potential buyer cooperation in the process. It is recommended to establish whether to pursue this strategy prior to launching a disposition process.

In a debt assumption, the seller of the property facilitates the assumption of existing financing by a new buyer. This process will vary depending upon underlying loan documents and typically requires review and consent by the lender, but at a time when prevailing interest rates are higher than the rates on in-place debt at the property, can be accretive to valuation. The buyer customarily pays fees associated with assuming the loan. It is recommended to speak with counsel and potentially the lender prior to informing potential buyers of the opportunity and terms under which the existing loan might be assumed.

Introduction

Commercial Real Estate Finance and Partnerships

Partnerships can offer several advantages for foreign institutional investors looking at commercial real estate investment in the US, including:

1. **Access to Local Expertise:** By partnering with a local real estate company or developer, foreign institutional investors can gain access to their partner's knowledge of the local market, including regulatory and legal requirements, market dynamics, and other factors that can impact the success of their investment.
2. **Sharing of Risks and Resources:** Partnerships allow investors to share the risks and resources associated with a real estate investment, including the financial costs and responsibilities of acquiring and managing the property.
3. **Diversification of Investment:** Partnerships can enable foreign institutional investors to invest in a range of commercial real estate properties across different asset classes and geographies, thereby diversifying their investment portfolio and reducing risk.
4. **Potential for Higher Returns:** By leveraging the local partner's expertise and resources, foreign institutional investors can potentially achieve higher returns on their investment than they would be able to achieve on their own.
5. **Access to Deal Flow:** Partnering with a local real estate company can also provide foreign institutional investors with access to a broader range of investment opportunities and deal flow, increasing their chances of finding a suitable investment that meets their investment criteria.

This section of the *The AFIRE Guide* provides a deep dive into various aspects of real estate finance and partnerships, building on the concepts presented in the previous two sections.

Chapter 3.1 provides a broad overview of various types of commercial real estate loans and debt in the US, including traditional bank loans, bridge loans, mezzanine financing, and other forms of debt. While a commercial real estate loan is a type of commercial real estate debt, not all commercial real estate debt takes the form of a traditional loan.

Chapter 3.2 offers a lender's perspective of real estate finance. Each real estate finance transaction has unique complexities, but typically progresses from inception to closing by following a generally accepted roadmap. Understanding this roadmap and managing expectations from the outset of a deal will significantly improve the chances of a smooth closing for all parties. Chapter 3.3 explores this same roadmap from the borrower's perspective.

Chapter 3.4 explores joint ventures. At the most basic level, a real estate joint venture typically involves a participant with the ability to source and service investments (the operator) and one with capital to invest in the endeavor (the investor). Chapter 3.5 dives deeper, looking at the structures and terms of various joint ventures.

Chapter 3.6 discusses the various types and strategies of commingled funds. Investing in real estate through funds has a number of benefits for investors, including increased diversification, a potentially more favorable tax structure, and easier access to specialist investment strategies, though these benefits typically come at the cost of significantly reduced discretion over the underlying investments—which are explored further in Chapter 3.7.

Chapter 3.8 discusses the restructuring and workouts of real estate loans, especially following economic downturns. Workouts and restructurings become more complicated when there are multiple lenders. Restructuring multilender loans requires one to understand the often-diverging interests of senior and junior lenders and their respective rights in highly structured deals. Chapter 3.9 provides a similar perspective, focusing on bankruptcy issues for foreign investors.

Finally, Chapter 3.10 provides a broad primer for Islamic finance in real estate, or the finance and investment practices employed by individuals and institutions who wish to invest in compliance with Islamic law. These practices emanate from a central core comprising Islamic scriptures, oral traditions, and moral practices.

Real Estate Finance

Loans and Debt

Will McIntosh, PhD, Global Head of Research, Affinius Capital

The commercial real estate (CRE) debt market comprises nearly $5 trillion of outstanding loans, making it one of the largest asset classes within fixed income.[1] Real estate investors have been attracted to the space, as the CRE debt market has dramatically changed following the Global Financial Crisis (GFC), based on a historical profile of strong income generation and risk-adjusted returns while also maintaining downside protection. The rise in institutionalized market participants within CRE debt combined with a generally low interest rate environment also aids in the merits of investing in loans and debt backed by real assets with significant tangible value.

Lest we forget, debt remains the largest part of the capital structure in almost all real estate transactions, and therefore it is an essential aspect of financing a CRE investment once an equity commitment has been secured. As Dr. Peter Linneman and Bruce Kirsch stated in their influential text, "debt, equity, and property values are inextricably linked." Further, they reiterated that "debt capital flows to real estate are cyclical, with rising interest rates increasing lender incentives to deploy funds . . . and with greater debt flows, values tend to rise."[2] Within a multiasset class portfolio, the inclusion of CRE debt can result in enhanced risk-adjusted for investors.

BORROWERS

In many respects, the CRE market for loans and debt is characterized by borrowers and lenders. Borrowers serve as the catalyst for placing debt capital by providing the demand for lenders to loan out excess capital reserves in the case of banks or investor capital in the case of debt funds. Based on the type of borrower combined with the characteristics and demands of the asset(s), users may pursue permanent debt or construction and bridge loans.

Borrowers are motivated to use debt to acquire (or build) property assets since it provides a significant portion of the overall capital to buy an asset, helps diversify their capital sources, provides a meaningful tax shield to income, and has the potential to enhance returns for investors. That being said, introducing leverage into the capital stack comes with an interest rate payment and thus not without additional risk.

CRE has three major types of borrowers: regional developers, construction companies, and institutional property owners (e.g., real estate investment trusts [REITs], real estate operating companies [REOCs], institutional investors):

- **Regional Developers:** Developers represent a significant ongoing source of borrowing demand for CRE loans, and the ability to obtain debt at favorable economic terms is vital to the property development model. In particular, these firms use construction loans to purchase land and build properties until they reach asset stabilization or disposition. Regional developers tend to secure debt financing through a local bank or financial institution based on relationships in their respective market(s).

- **Construction Companies:** Similar to developers, construction companies use debt to provide a large capital base and increase cash liquidity to fund projects for raw materials/equipment, labor, and other overhead and operational costs to build a property asset. Importantly, debt financing allows construction companies to fund the cash flow gap that occurs between the first shovel in the ground until a property is delivered upon completion.

- **Institutional Property Owners:** Property owners are large users of permanent debt given the income-producing nature of stabilized CRE assets as well as their significant tangible value used as collateral for a loan. Property owners use debt to optimize the capital structure and take advantage of the benefits mentioned previously around diversification, taxes, and enhanced returns. Given the cash-flowing abilities of existing assets, property owners can use a variety of debt types and terms, including fixed and floating rates, fully-amortizing or interest-only loans, and so on.

LENDERS

Lending in the CRE industry comes from various public and private sources. This includes national and regional banks, securitization, government-sponsored enterprises (GSEs) and agencies, insurance companies, private debt funds, and publicly traded mortgage REITs. Looking at outstanding commercial real estate mortgages, approximately 60 percent is held by banks, 14 percent by insurance companies, 14 percent by asset-backed securities issuers and finance companies, 7 percent by mortgage REITs, 1 percent by pensions and retirement funds, and 5 percent by other providers of debt financing.[3]

As will be described in more detail later, loan structure and terms will vary depending on lender type as well as their seniority within the overall capital stack. These terms will differ across key areas such as loan-to-value, debt yield, interest coverage and debt service coverage ratios, positive and negative loan covenants, recourse, and cash sweep, among others:

- **Banks (national, regional, local):** Banks are the largest funding source of CRE loans (see Figure 3.1-01), which can be retained on their balance sheets, sold in part or in whole to other financial institutions, or securitized and offered to public market participants. Banks benefit from their relatively low cost of capital and a strong deposit base for financing loans and can therefore lend on a wide variety of projects and assets. Further, some banks specialize in certain types of financial structures, property types, or geographical regions and MSAs. The top originators of US commercial property loans in 2022 were Wells Fargo, J.P. Morgan, Bank of America,

Morgan Stanley, and Citigroup. According to MSCI Real Capital Analytics, banks represented 48 percent of newly originated loans in 2022. Commercial mortgage-backed securities (CMBS) are usually issued by banks and are a type of financial securitization tied to commercial real estate loans. CMBS are agency-rated and separated into different tranches based on risk and payoff priority, thereby offering different yields to purchasers. CMBS can provide borrowers with efficiently priced debt but have additional structural risks, like an inability to modify loans once securitized, unless through a designated special servicer.

- **Insurance Companies:** Similar to banks, insurance companies are advantaged by their low cost of capital and resilient deposit base, facilitating an ability to continuously make CRE loans. Insurance companies find CRE lending an attractive investment opportunity, given the tangible property value collateralizing the loans and premium spreads with historically low loss rates, as well as duration matching of future obligations (e.g., liability-driven investing). These companies tend to follow disciplined underwriting and monitoring of their loan portfolios.
- **Mortgage Companies and REITs:** These companies provide financing for income-producing properties through purchasing or originating mortgages or mortgage-backed securities and generating income from these types of investments. Mortgage REITs raise their funds through shareholders or short-term repurchase agreements. To note, mortgage REITs make loans on both residential and commercial real estate.
- **Private Debt Funds:** Private providers of debt, also known as direct lending, tend to focus on bridge loans or mezzanine debt that are generally short-term and usually with higher interest rates, as this piece of the capital structure will eventually be replaced by more permanent financings from a bank or insurance company.
- **GSEs (Fannie Mae and Freddie Mac):** These government-sponsored entities serve as an essential funding source for the housing sector, which allows commercial multifamily projects and assets to secure more favorable debt pricing. Fannie Mae and Freddie Mac do not directly make the loans but rather purchase and repackage them to maintain a liquid, stable, and affordable housing market in the US.

FIGURE 3.1-01 **Share of commercial real estate loans (by lender type)**

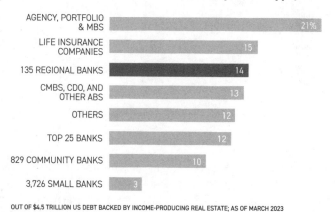

OUT OF $4.5 TRILLION US DEBT BACKED BY INCOME-PRODUCING REAL ESTATE; AS OF MARCH 2023

TYPES OF CRE DEBT

In order to finance a CRE transaction, it takes an entire capital structure of senior debt and common equity, but it can also include areas like mezzanine debt or preferred equity to fill voids in the financial stack. Priority is given to the most senior debt (e.g., a first lien mortgage). To note, an efficient and financially optimized capital structure depends on the asset itself in combination with market cycle, interest rate environment, and ongoing financial evolution. For example (in Figure 3.1-02), a condo developer may have used a simple capital structure of senior debt, mezzanine debt, and common equity in 2006; however, after the GFC, this same condo developer will likely have had to orchestrate a much more complex financial arrangement comprised of additional joint venture capital, preferred debt, and consequently a reduced senior piece relative to LTVs achieved in earlier market cycles.

The dynamic nature of the capital markets gives rise to a strong flow of emerging opportunities in the private debt space for risk-managed capital allocators with a thoughtful investment philosophy and process.

FIGURE 3.1-02 CRE capital structure and financial markets evolution

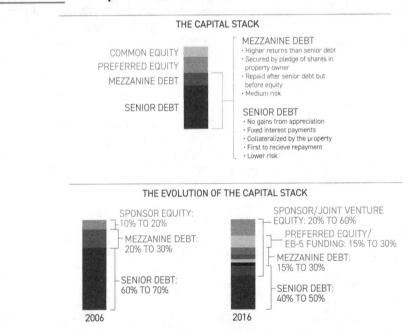

The capital stack is a critical element of all aspects of property development—ground-up and value-add repositioning—and for the acquisition of existing assets. Importantly, it also offers investors the ability to allocate across the risk-return spectrum depending on their return expectations and risk tolerance (see Figure 3.1-03). Further, debt is the largest component of the institutional real estate market—based on estimates of roughly $3.2 trillion in private debt and $1.5 trillion of public debt—and is thus a foundational building block for portfolio construction in the context of the four quadrants of CRE vis-à-vis public and private debt and equity investments. The total return of debt investments is comprised primarily of current yield and less so capital appreciation.

FIGURE 3.1-03 **CRE simple capital structure and risk-return spectrum**

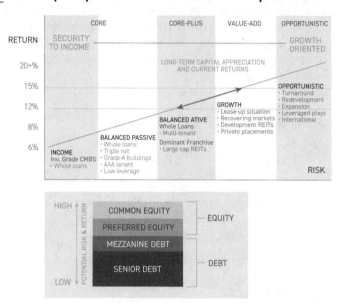

The following sections highlight the key areas within the debt portion for private as well as publicly traded real estate that sophisticated capital allocators and asset owners use.

Whole Mortgages

Whole mortgages represent the most senior portion of the various debt tranches and thus the strongest downside protection if a lender defaults on their loan payments, interest payments, or principal balance, depending on the amortization structure of the loan. Also known as "first liens," whole mortgages comprise the largest part of the entire capital stack—with LTV ratios ranging from 30 to 80 percent on an asset- or portfolio-specific basis—due mainly to their senior priority of claims on company assets. As such, whole mortgages tend to generate the lowest returns provided by a CRE transaction but can be structured with fixed or floating interest rates. Whole mortgages are originated by banks and insurance companies and can be syndicated, with the originators deciding to retain the first lien on their or an affiliates' balance sheet or potentially selling it to another financial institution.

Whole mortgages based on fixed interest rates tend to be more stable; however, floating-rate loans can provide additional upside in the case of a rising interest rate environment.

Floating paper can also be subdivided into additional risk tranches that offer investors higher or lower yields (e.g., A note, B piece) in relation to subordinated positions. DSCRs tend to be well above 1.0× and are made against newer, high-quality commercial properties in the core property sectors. Given all this, whole mortgages have the lowest default rates. Whole mortgages tend to be longer duration fixed-income tools that range from 10 to 15 years in length.

Whole mortgages are managed in a broadly diversified portfolio across factors: counterparty risk, LTV ratios, overall loan and timing between payments, amortization features, repayment/prepayment risk, region/location, industry/economic factors, fixed versus floating rate terms, and so on. This allows banks and insurance companies to make a large number of loans in a systematically risk-managed way, to generate premiums based on a roughly 100 to 200 basis point spread over US Treasuries or in some instances high-quality investment grade corporate credit (see Figure 3.1-04). Spreads are influenced by market competition and cycle and can widen or contract therein.

FIGURE 3.1-04 CRE lending spreads vs. corporate bonds

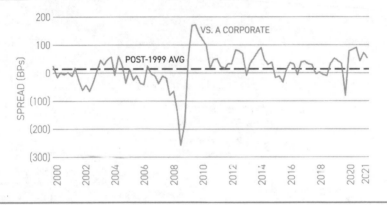

Mezzanine Loans

"Mezzanine" is derived from the Latin word *medianus*, meaning "of the middle." True to its name, mezzanine or "mezz" debt is a tranche in the capital structure that falls between the first mortgage and the equity position. As financial markets have evolved in the wake of the GFC, the mezzanine piece has become an increasingly important financial instrument and helps bridge the gap between the amount of equity that sponsors or owners are willing to commit and the amount a lender is willing to provide for a first mortgage.[4] Depending on the transaction, mezzanine debt can comprise 10 to 30 percent of the overall capital structure after the senior debt. Mezzanine debt shares subordinated debt and preferred equity characteristics and is thus a hybrid security, with the loan collateralized by equity and not the property itself like with a whole mortgage. The term of mezzanine debt is shorter than that of senior debt (e.g., two to three years) given that it's in many regards a transitional financial tool and will likely eventually get refinanced out of the capital structure at asset stabilization with a longer-dated first lien.

Mezzanine debt offers higher returns than whole mortgages due to their risker stance in addition to equity participation if a property sale occurs at or above predetermined thresholds. Mezzanine debt can be managed with a dedicated focus on originating this type of debt tranche in mind, but it can also be allocated to achieve higher yields within a broader debt portfolio or even within equity funds as a means of controlling downside relative to common equity investments.

High-Yield Debt

High-yield debt pushes up the risk-return spectrum, and in taking greater risk, it can offer higher returns, which are generated through several approaches. First, the first mortgage can be carved into multiple pieces (e.g., A note, B and C pieces) and due to subordination can achieve slightly higher returns via the risk of the additional waterfall to claims. Second, these types of loans offer higher returns from yield and appreciation potential based on risks related to higher LTVs, lower coverage ratios, and their subordinated position but participation upon sale. Third, loans can be made on noncore properties to achieve added risk and return. Noncore can include asset types outside of the major sectors (e.g., retail, office, industrial, and multifamily), in secondary and tertiary markets, nonstabilized buildings from the standpoint of occupancy and operating cash flows, among others.[5]

Last, construction and development loans are inherently riskier relative to stabilized cash-flowing assets and can offer a higher yield to reflect this as well as the potential for deferred debt payments. High-yield debt portfolios are also riskier due to a historically higher rate of defaults and less overall diversification than first mortgages. Investors can find these types of strategies compelling as they offer spreads of 200 to 400 basis points over US Treasuries depending on market environment to compensate for the added structural and credit risk.

Commercial Mortgage-Backed Security (CMBS) Bonds

CMBS bonds are another important debt instrument issued by large banks. CMBS bonds are generally collateralized by a diversified pool of underlying mortgages, with most issuances structured as real estate mortgage investment conduits (REMICS). Banks will "warehouse" mortgages over time until the securities are underwritten and sold to investors across different risk tranches that are separately rated by independent agencies (e.g., Moody's, S&P). Tranches can be rated as either investment grade that carry ratings down to BBB as well as noninvestment grade securities, providing a deeper pool of potential buyers that includes mainstream fixed-income funds for the high-quality paper and high-yield debt as well as opportunistic investors like hedge funds.

Other Types of Debt

REITs can also issue bonds at the corporate level that are backed by the entity's operating cash flows and are similar to corporate bonds in their liquidity, investor base, and follow conventional bankruptcy proceedings in the event of default. Given that REITs tend to carry lower debt loads and generate strong cash flow from property leases, unsecured REIT debt can offer investors lower volatility in relation to the universe of corporate commercial paper.

While most loans are made on assets, loans can be issued for a portfolio of CRE assets. Unsecured portfolio-level debt is similar to unsecured REIT debt in the fact they have no claim on the entity's property assets but differ given that a private company usually issues them.

Mortgage REITs, perhaps technically an equity investment based on shareholders owning the corporations that control the underlying debt, own and invest in commercial mortgages. These companies either originate loans directly with property owners or purchase whole mortgages and CMBS bonds in the secondary market.[6] These REITs do not own and operate tangible properties like most equity REITs but are a large provider of debt capital to institutional property investors.

SUMMARIZING DEBT

Loans and debt play an essential role in financing CRE assets. Consequently, the real estate debt opportunity has become an area of increasing interest and capital deployment by institutional investors. Debt backed by tangible property assets can provide strong income generation, added portfolio diversification, and compelling long-term risk-adjusted returns with more limited downside protection when compared to equity investments.

The CRE debt capital markets are characterized by lenders and borrowers of varying sizes and needs. Given this, there is a myriad of different debt types that market participants can use from both a capital structure and investment opportunity perspective. Critically, debt remains the largest part of the capital structure in almost all real estate transactions. As the capital markets have evolved, so too have the debt instruments, allowing debtors to choose from a wide range of terms and structures to suit their property asset or project most efficiently. In summation, debt is an integral part of the capital structure in the CRE industry and therefore closely tied to equity and property values.

NOTES

1. Federal Reserve Flow of Funds, 2021. Note—not including debt funds.
2. Linneman, Peter, and Bruce Kirsch. *Real Estate Finance and Investments: Risks and Opportunities.* Edition 5.1. (Linneman Associates 2018).
3. Ibid.
4. Lynn, David J. *The Advisor's Guide to Commercial Real Estate Investment* (National Underwriter Company 2014).
5. Ibid.
6. Ibid.

Real Estate Finance

The Lender's Perspective

Gary Goodman, Partner, Dentons

Sarah Armendariz, Partner, Dentons

Each real estate finance transaction has unique complexities, but typically progresses from inception to closing by following a generally accepted roadmap. Understanding this road map and managing expectations from the outset of a deal will significantly improve the chances of a smooth closing for all parties.

For lenders, the devil is still in the details, but having the following framework for the big picture is essential for successful transactions.

THE LOAN APPLICATION PROCESS

The loan application process can run from being relatively informal to extremely formal. For example, at the informal end of the spectrum, it is not unusual for a prospective borrower who is a repeat customer of the lender to commence the process with a telephone call to their loan officer, describing in general terms what they want and why they want it. At the other end, a prospective borrower may contact their **mortgage** or **loan broker** to discuss their intentions, at which point the broker will prepare a financing memorandum to circulate to their own various lenders who might have an appetite for such a loan (i.e., term, construction, mezzanine, preferred equity). The lenders will respond through formal avenues and the application will progress.

Given the ever-increasing number of regulations brought to bear on regulated lenders, the loan application has become more formal over time. But regardless of how formal the process, the lender will want to know details such as the address of the property, how the property will be used, who or what will be the borrower and how the agreement will be structured, the amount of equity that will be invested in the project, and the timing of that equity investment.

Additionally, lenders will need to know the expected operating revenues and operating expenses of the project (and the ramp-up period), and whether the loan structure will need to accommodate a ground lease, tenant-in-common arrangement, condominium, or other structure.

133

If the borrower is interested in a construction loan, the lender will need all of the preceding details, as well as the split between hard and soft costs, the construction period, who will be the **general contractor** or **construction manager** and the major trade contractors, how much of the construction budget has been bought out already and when the rest will be bought out, what percentage of the plans and specifications have been completed and coordinated, and details outlining whether the construction contract a fixed-fee contract, a cost-plus contract, or a guaranteed maximum fixed-price contract.

And finally, if the lender is providing a mezzanine loan or a preferred equity investment, they will need all the preceding property details, plus the details of any mortgage debt on the property.

THE LOAN APPROVAL PROCESS

The loan approval process is iterative, and as a lender's underwriting team digs through the information provided during the application phase, they may ask for more detailed information (including financial information) about the borrower, their sponsors and guarantor(s), and the project itself. Lenders will also seek evidence backing up the assertions made by the borrower.

Generally, the lender's underwriting team will not ask for a title survey at this point in the process. However, the lender will then propose terms, and unless those terms exactly match the borrower's expectations, the borrower and the lender will negotiate terms until they come to a mutually acceptable resolution.

Term Sheet or Commitment Letter

Once the borrower and the lender have come to agreement on the principal terms and conditions of the proposed loan, they memorialize their agreement via a term sheet. Originally known as commitment letters, these documents also required borrowers to pay a commitment fee upon acceptance of the letter.[1] Today, commitment letters are typically only used in specific circumstances where the borrower requires (or is required by statute for a specific type of loan, such as bond financing) absolute assurance of the loan being available, subject to the terms and conditions of the commitment letter.

Therefore, it is more common for the borrower and the lender to live with a term sheet, which may or may not be signed or countersigned by the borrower and the lender, but which contains only the most significant terms and conditions of the loan in question. For repeat borrowers, it's common to either have a term from a previous deal between the lender and any borrower affiliates shown as "[TBD]" or "as set forth in the [loan document]"—another mark of relative informality.

Checklist and Status Calls

After finalizing the term sheet, the lender's counsel will prepare a closing checklist for distribution to all parties, at request of the lender. Checklists should essentially cover all deliverables and conditions to closing so that expectations for all parties are clearly communicated from the outset.

Some lenders prefer a single checklist including both legal and business diligence, and others prefer separate legal and business checklists. Either preference works so long as all requirements are tracked to lender's satisfaction.

A typical comprehensive checklist will include the following items (with as much or as little detail as necessary to effectively communicate the status of each):

1. A list of all anticipated loan documents
2. An organizational chart (typically in the form of a flowchart) outlining borrower's organizational structure
3. A list of all required organizational documents evidencing the formation, good standing, operation, and authority of each borrower and guarantor, and any other party in the borrower's or guarantor's authority structure
4. A description of legal opinion letters to be required (typically including enforceability, due formation, authorization, perfection, usury, and local law opinions)
5. A title commitment and loan policy proforma (in accordance with specific title requirements and endorsements to be provided by lender)
6. A survey of the subject property (based on specific survey requirements to be provided by lender)
7. A zoning report or opinion
8. Property-level diligence items such as any management, development, or leasing agreements; documentation of any ground lease or condominium structure; flood certificate; any required tenant estoppels or subordination and nondisturbance agreements; and evidence of utilities serving the property
9. An appraisal
10. Required third-party reports (typically including a Phase I environmental report; a property condition report; and possibly Phase II or geotechnical, soil, seismic, or other reports which may be property-specific)
11. Lender's insurance review and report, typically prepared by a third-party insurance consultant
12. Litigation, bankruptcy, **Uniform Commercial Code**, and judgment searches to be ordered with respect to the borrower, guarantor, and any other relevant parties determined by the lender
13. Financial statements, tax returns, budgets, signatory identification, W-9 forms, and other financial or personal data for the borrower and the guarantor, as may be required by the lender for underwriting and know-your-client compliance purposes
14. A settlement statement, typically prepared by the title company, describing all funds and disbursements associated with the transaction to be handled at closing
15. Other closing conditions, including lender's escrow instruction letter to the title company, delivery to the title company of all invoices and disbursement recipients' wiring instructions, and payment of all fees and expenses associated with the transaction

If the subject loan is for construction purposes, the checklist should include related construction documentation such as plans and specifications; contracts from the general contractor, engineer, and architect; as well as any other major subcontracts; copies of necessary permits and licenses; a construction schedule, draw schedule, and budget; and completion of lender's corresponding plan and cost review.

If the subject loan is to be used for acquiring the subject property, the basic underlying acquisition documents should be added to the checklist, including the purchase agreement, deed, bill of sale, and general assignment.

After circulating the checklist to the lender and borrower teams, including borrower's counsel, the parties typically select a time for an all-hands initial conference call to collectively review the checklist and discuss each party's responsibility for next steps.

The parties frequently choose to schedule a recurring weekly or biweekly checklist conference call to keep all parties on track throughout the transaction. Parties often discuss potential closing dates on the first conference call, which is particularly important if either party has a deadline-driven timeline, such as an upcoming maturity on an existing loan, an outside acquisition date under a purchase agreement, or expiration of a rate lock agreement between the parties. If no hard date must be set, it is helpful to circle a reasonable timeframe for the parties to target, with the understanding that a specific date will be selected as the transaction progresses.

Loan Documents

As the borrower commences collection, preparation, and delivery of due diligence deliverables in accordance with the checklist, lender's counsel will prepare initial draft loan documents.

A typical set of loan documents includes the following:

1. Loan Agreement (which may be a Construction Loan Agreement, or in some jurisdictions, split into Building, Project, and Acquisition Loan Agreements, or a Term Loan Agreement)
2. Promissory Note
3. Security Instrument (Mortgage, Deed of Trust, or Deed to Secure Debt)
4. Assignment of Rents and Leases
5. Collateral Assignment of Agreements
6. Recourse Carve-Out Guaranty
7. Environmental Indemnity Agreement
8. Form UCC-1 Financing Statement (to be filed in the borrower's state of formation)
9. Form UCC-1 Fixture Filing (to be recorded in the real estate records of the county where the property sits, if required by lender or not covered by the Security Instrument)

Depending on the type of property, project, applicable interest rate, and other factors, additional documents may be prudent, such as:

1. Assignment and Subordination of Management Agreement
2. Pledge Agreement
3. Deposit Account Control Agreement
4. Cash Management Agreement
5. Collateral Assignment of Interest Rate Protection Agreement
6. Post-Closing Agreement
7. Other types of guaranties (such as a Payment Guaranty, Completion Guaranty, or an Interest and Carry Costs Guaranty)
8. For construction loans, Assignment of Construction Contracts (and Consents and Certificates of General Contractor, Engineer, and Architect, as applicable) and of Plans and Specifications

Meanwhile, the borrower should also promptly contact the selected title company to start a title search and prepare a title commitment and engage a surveyor as necessary to prepare a new survey or a survey update. Both title and survey can take several weeks to prepare, and are then subject to review, comment, and revision, so it is critical to initiate those processes early in the transaction.

When loan document drafts are available, lender's counsel circulates them to borrower and borrower's counsel for review and comment. The borrower team should then review the loan documents in concert with their counsel and prepare questions and comments to the same.

The borrower's counsel will then convey such comments to the lender team, typically in the form of an electronic redline reflecting specific requested revisions, which, to the extent informative or helpful, may be accompanied by detailed explanations about why such comments are important to the borrower. Such explanations are also often provided in a phone call between counsels after circulation of the borrower's comments. From that point, the parties negotiate the terms and conditions of the loan documents, which process often includes two or more rounds of comments and revisions before the parties come to an agreement. Simultaneously with the negotiation process, the lender and the borrower should continue to finalize and deliver other checklist deliverables.

CLOSING DILIGENCE

As the list of outstanding deliverables shrinks, the parties will choose a specific target closing date (if one was not selected earlier), and in addition to finalizing any outstanding loan documents and other checklist deliverables, various closing-specific requirements must be addressed.

The borrower should ask the title company to prepare a settlement statement, and each party should send all invoices and fee information to the title company for inclusion on the statement and thus payment at closing.

All requirements in Schedule B-I of the title commitment must be satisfied, including delivery to the title company of borrower's final organizational documents and the release or assignment to the lender of any prior mortgages, Form UCC-1 financing statements, or similar interests. The lender's counsel will prepare and circulate signature packages (typically including signature pages in triplicate for all documents, except the promissory note, for which there should be only one) to be executed by each party.

The lender's counsel will provide instructions for delivery of wet-ink originals to both the title company (as to recordable documents only) and the lender's counsel, to be held in escrow until receipt of the borrower's authorization to release the same upon closing. The lender's counsel should also provide an escrow instruction letter to the title company detailing the title company's responsibilities for receiving and recording documents, receiving, and disbursing funds in accordance with the final settlement statement, and ultimately issuing the final loan policy of title insurance, which must conform to an agreed-upon pro forma loan policy, which is typically attached as an exhibit to such escrow instruction letter.

CLOSING

Closings used to be (and can still be, if the parties prefer) held in person, but in recent years (and long before COVID shifted many other processes to remote action), closings have become regularly handled in escrow via the selected title company.

Final versions of recordable documents and UCCs listed in the lender's escrow instruction letter should be dated as of the closing date and provided to the title company to be assembled with original signatures (which the title company should already have in hand). To confirm the versions held by the title company have been correctly compiled, the title company should then scan and email the documents back to the parties for final approval.

The parties will also review the title company's draft settlement statement, provide any necessary comments, and when approved, execute the same. (An emailed copy of signatures to the settlement statement is acceptable.) Once the settlement statement is final, the title company has countersigned the lender's escrow instruction letter, and if any remaining checklist items are imminent, the parties may then decide to wire any necessary funds to the title company in the interest of time. However, only upon satisfaction of all conditions precedent to closing (i.e., receipt of all checklist items) should the lender agree to break escrow and authorize the title company in writing to close and disburse funds in accordance with the lender's escrow instructions. A similar authorization must be provided by the borrower as well.

Once the title company disburses all funds in accordance with the settlement statement, the transaction is considered closed. There will be some post-closing work to be done, such as recording documents, producing final title policies, and other trailing deliverables (which are sometimes memorialized specifically in a post-closing agreement between the borrower and the lender), but the transaction is officially "closed" and the parties can finally celebrate (and focus on the next deal).

NOTE

1. The theory behind a lender requiring a commitment fee is that the lender was actually reserving funds when it issued the commitment letter and should be compensated for reserving those funds for the loan in question.

Real Estate Finance

The Borrower's Perspective

Elliot J. Rishty, Managing Director & US CEO, Vanke

Kai-yan Lee, CEO Europe, Americas, Middle East, JD Property

In general, real estate loans in the US are characterized as either construction loans or permanent loans. The proceeds of construction loans are used to construct or materially modify a project, whereas permanent loans are made once a project has been "stabilized." A project is considered stabilized when the construction has been completed and the completed product has been leased to tenants, thus generating a predictable stream of income.

Construction loans tend to have short terms (one to four years, depending upon the time anticipated to complete and sell or lease up the property) and permanent loans longer terms (typically 5, 10, 15, or even 20 years). Construction loans usually are issued with the expectation that the loan is repaid once the project is sold upon completion or stabilization, or via some takeout financing like a permanent loan replacing the existing construction loan. Some lenders also originate hybrid construction-permanent loans ("mini perm") with features from both types of loans. In addition, there are various iterations of transitionary loans available to borrowers, such as land loans, acquisition loans of yet-to-stabilize assets, and bridge loans that serve the purpose of bridging a timing gap for when a project is neither ready for construction nor stabilization. In this chapter, we focus on construction loans and permanent loans.

Interest rates on construction loans tend to float, often based on a spread over an index such as the prime rate or secured overnight financing rate (SOFR),[1] while permanent loans tend to bear fixed rates. Construction loans are often funded in phases through a draw process over the course of the construction project, usually based on construction progress and requisitions. Depending on the lender's risk appetite and a project's risk profile, a construction loan's proceeds are funded *after* a significant portion of equity has been put into the project; some lenders may be comfortable to fund pari passu along with equity funding into the project. In comparison, permanent loans are typically funded in full at origination. Construction loans tend to require interest-only payments (with no principal payments required), while permanent loans could require principal amortization that may or may not match the term of the loan. Historically banks focused their real estate lending on construction loans, in part because their short-term, floating-rate deposit base lent itself to shorter-term floating-rate lending. The permanent loan arena was dominated by life insurance companies and pension funds, whose long-term financial horizon matched well with long-term fixed-rate real estate lending.

More recently the division between construction and permanent lenders has become blurred and a new group of lenders has emerged, including Wall Street investment banks and nonbank finance companies such as "debt funds." This new group of lenders may originate loans through so-called conduit programs whereby the loans are sold to investors via a securitization process, or they may hold the loans they originate on their balance sheets. In addition, certain lenders may offer construction loan facilities that convert into long-term permanent mortgage loans. While this chapter focuses on traditional lenders and traditional construction/permanent loans, investment banks and nonbank lenders play an important role in today's real estate financing world. It's important to understand the differences between these lenders and their products and the traditional lenders and traditional loans, as they have both advantages (e.g., higher LTV) and disadvantages (e.g., harder to do loan workout) based on your project's financial needs.

THE PROCESS

Identifying a Lender

The first step for a real estate borrower is to identify the lender. For construction loans, a non-US investor should work with its US-based colleagues (local affiliates, development partners, brokers, or attorneys) to identify active construction lenders in the specific market. For permanent loans, the same resources can be utilized to identify lenders who might be approached to offer terms for a potential permanent loan. There are also a number of companies that act as mortgage brokers to assist borrowers in identifying potential lenders. It is common for a borrower to obtain rate and term quotes from several lenders before choosing one, and mortgage brokers will often assist the borrower by organizing this process to "make a market" for the loan that the borrower is seeking. If the loan is a large one, the lead lender may need to identify additional lenders to participate in the loan (either as participants or as colenders, see discussion that follows).

Term Sheet Versus Loan Commitment

Once a lender has been identified, a term sheet or loan commitment setting forth the principal terms of the arrangement under negotiation is typically generated. A term sheet is usually very short (one two pages) and simply sets forth the most fundamental business terms of the loan being offered. A term sheet would typically identify the borrower, the property, the amount and term of the loan, the interest rate, the fees payable to the lender, and the collateral. By its terms, a term sheet generally is not binding upon the lender. The loan commitment is at the other end of the spectrum, running as long as 30 pages and often including many fully negotiated provisions of specific interest to the lender or the borrower. Often, a loan commitment is styled as a binding obligation of the lender to fund the loan upon the satisfaction of the conditions to closing set forth in the loan commitment (although in practice lenders typically include language that significantly undercuts the binding nature of the loan commitment) and generally require the borrower to pay a commitment fee and expense deposit sufficient to pay for the lender's underwriting process and legal expenses.

Occasionally, borrowers are tempted to move beyond the loan commitment to the loan document stage as quickly as possible, choosing not to negotiate the loan commitment in detail in the mistaken belief that issues can be dealt with through negotiation of the actual loan documents. Such borrowers typically find, however, that the lenders are unable or unwilling to revise the terms set forth in the loan commitment. Once the term sheet or loan commitment has been negotiated, the terms therein will be presented to the lender's internal loan committee for approval and, therefore, the lender will resist from modifying terms approved by its committee.

For the borrower, the loan commitment letter (or if there is no commitment letter, the term sheet) is the stage of the process when the borrower has the most negotiating leverage. At this point in time, the lender is still trying to "win the business" and the borrower is not yet financially committed to the lender. As a result, the lender will generally have more flexibility on terms. Once the borrower has signed the commitment letter, paid a commitment fee, and put up a deposit, the leverage shifts significantly in favor of the lender. As such, the borrower should insist on negotiating all important terms in the commitment letter. Even though the terms of the commitment letter are not typically legally binding, it will form the basis for the legally binding loan documents. This is the best point in the process for a borrower to try to control the negotiation and prevent unnecessarily burdensome terms and closing requirements.

The loan committee's approval does not mean that all conditions to closing have been satisfied. Either through its own internal resources or by hiring outside experts, the lender typically will review the borrower's financial status, the physical condition of the property (including its compliance with applicable environmental laws), and the leases, title, and survey. The bulk of this analysis takes place after loan committee approval but prior to closing.

Participating Lenders, Colenders, and Subordinate Lenders

Larger loans often require more than one lender. In a participation structure, the lead lender retains all contractual rights and obligations specified under the loan documents, but has an agreement with each participant lender with respect to a portion of the loan. In the colender structure, each colender becomes a party to the loan documents and has a direct contractual relationship with the borrower. Each lender is directly responsible to the borrower to fund its share of the loan advance, and the lead lender acts as an agent on behalf of itself and the other lenders in administering the loan. A colender arrangement means that the borrower may need to deal with multiple lenders in such matters as negotiating the loan documents or obtaining lender consents that may be required under the loan documents.

In the case of a construction loan, the borrower must also be comfortable that each colender will be capable of meeting its obligations for future advances. It is, therefore, advisable for the borrower to insist that potential colenders meet some financial standards. Loan participants and colenders may maintain a pari passu (i.e., equal priority) relationship with one another, or alternatively, they may create a relationship in which one lender is senior or subordinate to another within the debt stack (i.e., a structure in which one lender is entitled to be repaid ahead of another).

Furthermore, the borrower should be conscious of the increased complexity of lender deliberation and approval process in a participation structure, where lender approval may be subject to simple majority, super majority, or even unanimous approvals among the participating banks. This could significantly increase the risk of not getting lender approval in a timely fashion, or in worse case, at all, for issues important to the borrower. Sometimes this is not due to issues related to the borrower or the project per se, but rather due to misaligned interests among the participant banks. In a colender arrangement, similar challenges also could arise, but the borrower typically has better visibility and can work directly with dissenting colender(s), as the borrower has a direct relationship with each of the colenders. In either case, the borrower should expect more delicate lender deliberation and approval dynamics compared to a single lender loan.

Loan Documents

The principal loan documents in a commercial real estate loan in the US typically include the following:

- The promissory note, which contains the promise to pay and sets forth the basic terms of the loan
- The loan agreement, which sets forth the borrower's representations and warranties, the conditions to closing, the conditions (if any) to further loan advances, the terms of any ongoing financial covenants, reporting obligations, and events of default
- The mortgage, which creates a lien on the real property and associated personal property
- The collateral assignment of leases, which provides the lender with a security interest in the current and future leases on the property
- An environmental indemnity, pursuant to which the borrower (and often a separate creditworthy guarantor affiliated with the borrower) agrees to indemnify the lender for losses incurred as a result of the current or future presence on the property of oil or other hazardous materials
- Uniform Commercial Code financing statements, which are necessary to perfect the lender's lien on certain personal property
- A "nonrecourse carveout guaranty," signed by a creditworthy guarantor affiliated with the borrower, protecting the lender against losses resulting from any "bad acts" of the borrower and the scope of which is typically the subject of extensive negotiation

In the case of construction loans, numerous other closing requirements and loan documents are required to allow the lender to step into the borrower's shoes if a default occurs and to complete construction of the project. Accordingly, collateral assignments of the architect's, engineer's, and construction contracts are typically required. In addition, it is not uncommon for a construction lender to require a completion guaranty from a creditworthy party affiliated with the borrower, as well as a payment guaranty for interest, carrying costs and in some instances, a portion of the loan principal.

The Closing Process

Once the term sheet or loan commitment has been approved by the lender, its legal counsel will typically generate a closing checklist of the documents to be delivered and other requirements to be satisfied in order to close the loan. The lender's counsel will also generate draft loan documents incorporating the terms of the term sheet or loan commitment. The borrower and its counsel review the loan documents to make sure they are consistent with the term sheet or loan commitment, and to check for any other issues of concern. Once the loan documents have been fully negotiated and the closing conditions satisfied, the loan documents will be executed and delivered and the loan proceeds (or in the case of a construction loan, the initial advance) will be funded. Closings of commercial real estate loans in the UStypically occur by mail (by overnight delivery and/or email), often using the title insurance company as the escrow agent.

MAJOR BORROWER ISSUES IN PERMANENT LOAN DOCUMENTS

An exhaustive discussion of borrower issues in real estate loan documents is beyond the scope of this chapter, but a brief description of some of the major issues on which borrowers typically focus is set forth as follows.

Promissory Note

Besides confirming that the basic business terms of the loan have been properly incorporated in the promissory note, the borrower will want to understand whether prepayment or defeasance is permissible and what penalty or payment obligations such a prepayment will entail.

Nonrecourse Carveout Guaranty

The terms of this guaranty are typically heavily negotiated. A borrower will want its guarantor's liability for a breach of the nonrecourse carveout provisions to be limited to the lender's actual loss resulting from such a breach. Lenders sometimes seek to treat a breach of the nonrecourse carveout provisions as a "trigger event" causing the guaranty to require a full payment.

In addition, the scope of the nonrecourse carveouts themselves is negotiated. A borrower will want to define the term "misapplication of revenues" so that distributions made at a time when no event of default exists are not subject to clawback by the lender. Similarly, the borrower will want to make clear that its liability for payment of taxes and insurance is contingent on there being sufficient revenue from the property for that purpose. Lenders sometimes will want the guarantor to guarantee payment of insurance and taxes regardless of the sufficiency of revenues from the property.

As a guiding principle, the nonrecourse carveout guaranty is there to protect a lender from a dishonest or "bad behaving" borrower such as one who might take action to dilute the value of the lender's collateral or undermine the lender's ability to enforce its mortgage; it should not be a source of recovery for the lender in the case of an underperforming investment where a borrower has acted in good faith but for one reason or another the investment has not performed as underwritten. It's important to review this guaranty with that guiding principle in mind. The types of acts that the nonrecourse carveout guaranty cover will, for the most part, fall within the control the party closest to the operation of the property and, therefore, it should be the controlling party that provides such guaranty.

LOAN AGREEMENT

Leasing

The borrower will often seek to define a minor lease based on square footage or rental income so that it can enter into, amend, and terminate such leases without the lender's consent. For leases over any such threshold, the borrower will want the lender to agree that it will not unreasonably withhold its consent, and that its approval will be deemed to have been given if a specified period (such as 20 days) passes without the lender responding to a request from the borrower for approval.

Site Plan Changes

If the borrower knows that it may construct additional improvements on the property or might seek a partial release of a portion of the mortgaged premises, it would be wise to negotiate provisions into the loan agreement to specify the terms under which the lender must approve such changes.

Financial Covenants

If the loan includes a loan-to-value test or debt-service-coverage test, the borrower will want to limit the number of times such tests are administered and make sure that the terms defining the test are clear.

EVENTS OF DEFAULT

For monetary defaults (other than regular monthly payments of interest and principal), a borrower will want written notice and an opportunity to cure.

Financial Reporting

The borrower will want to ensure that provisions calling for monthly, quarterly, and annual property-related and financial reporting are sensible and consistent with its ability to produce information and reports.

Permitted Transfers

The borrower will want to allow for a certain level of transfers of interests other than in the case of general partners and managing members without the lender's consent. In addition, the borrower will want to allow for transfers among existing partners (particularly if there is a buy/sell provision in its operating agreement), or among affiliate companies within the same larger corporate structure. A non-US investor that has partnered with an operating partner will want to make sure that the loan documents do not prohibit it from exercising its rights under the joint venture agreement to replace the operating partner as managing member or general partner. Typically, lenders are receptive to requests for transfer rights to family members, trusts set up for estate-planning purposes, and the like, where the principal maintains operational control of the interest.

Additional Debt

If the borrower anticipates placing subordinate mortgage debt or mezzanine debt on the property, it should negotiate those rights into the loan documents initially. That being said, existing lenders typically will retain the approval right of the specific subordinate or mezzanine debt when it is originated in the future, even if they agree to allow such debt in principle.

Insurance Proceeds Indemnity

The lender's generic loan documents often will not require it to release insurance proceeds to the borrower in the event of a casualty. Borrowers typically can negotiate for the release of insurance proceeds without conditions, in amounts below some threshold usually related to the size of the property, and if certain conditions are satisfied, in the event of a larger casualty. Such conditions might include those typical in construction loans.

What lenders require in terms of a borrower's obligation to deliver an environmental indemnity is an evolving area and in any particular transaction, is largely dependent on the strength of the borrower, the type and environmental condition of the subject property, and the current state of the lending market generally. A borrower is often able to negotiate limits on its environmental indemnification obligations, such as a monetary cap on its liability or an option to purchase an environmental insurance policy, alongside a requirement that the lender first make a claim under such policy before pursuing the borrower under the environmental indemnity. However, over the past several years, lenders have become less likely to accept environmental insurance policies in lieu of indemnification agreements.

In any event, borrowers and indemnitors will want to negotiate indemnification agreements to ensure that they cover only hazardous waste and environmental requirements and not a broader range of land use regulations; that they include a sunset provision so that the indemnitor is not responsible for releases that occur after the lender is in control of the property, for example, following foreclosure or the lender's acceptance of a deed in lieu of foreclosure; that the indemnification does not run to a third-party purchaser at foreclosure; and that the borrower would not be in default merely by virtue of a new release of hazardous waste on the property, as long as the borrower is investigating and remediating the release in accordance with applicable law.

MAJOR BORROWER ISSUES IN A CONSTRUCTION LOAN

Many of the issues set forth previously would also be addressed in construction loan documents. In addition, a number of provisions unique to construction loan documents are of interest to the borrower. These include the following.

Project Budget

The borrower will want language in the construction loan agreement to allow it to reallocate savings from one budget line item to cover cost overruns in other line items. The lender will typically allow this, provided the borrower demonstrates that the savings have actually been realized. In addition, the borrower will want the right to access a contingency line item, whereas the lender's documents often give the lender absolute control over the use of the contingency line item. It is not uncommon for a lender to agree to allow a borrower access to the contingency line item in proportion to the percentage of completion of the project.

Completion Guaranty

The guarantor will want a clear definition of the conditions for release of the guaranty. For example, if leases require the tenants to complete their own improvements, the borrower would want the definition of completion to exclude such tenant improvements. Similarly, in some jurisdictions, a final certificate of occupancy is not issued until all space in the project has been built out and occupied, and occupancy under a temporary certificate of occupancy is customary until that point. In such an instance, the guarantor would not want the loan agreement's definition of completion to require issuance of a final certificate of occupancy.

The guarantor would want the guaranty to be drafted so that it is responsible only for the difference between the actual cost to complete and the unadvanced loan amount. In other words, there should be a credit against the completion costs for the amount of the costs that were intended to be covered by unadvanced loan proceeds. Said differently, the completion guaranty, if designed correctly, should cover the lender for any cost overruns incurred that are above and beyond what is budgeted to be paid for by the loan proceeds for the budget that was intended to be funded by construction loan. Without such a provision the lender could cease funding upon the occurrence of an event of default, and then look to the guarantor fully to complete the project (or to reimburse the lender for its costs of completion) without taking into account the unadvanced loan proceeds.

NOTE

1. The Federal Reserve Board adopted the final rule in December 2022 to implement the transition from LIBOR to SOFR after the cessation of USD LIBOR on June 30, 2023. Most adjustable loans that previously tended to use LIBOR have opted to use SOFR if they were originated in recent years. For loans used LIBOR and with a maturity date after June 30, 2023, they could convert to SOFR before or on June 30, 2023, if they contain adequate benchmark conversion features; whereas those without conversion features or with inadequate conversions feature shall seek counsel for viable solutions.

Sharing the Risk

Considerations for Entering a Joint Venture

Jason Dunn, Director, Goulston & Storrs

The joint venture or partnership form of business arrangement has existed for centuries. Although the structure and terms of a modern real estate joint venture bear little resemblance to those used by medieval merchants, the essence of the arrangement—two or more parties joining forces to provide reciprocal services with the goal of creating mutually beneficial synergies—is the same.

At the most basic level, a real estate joint venture typically involves two types of participants: one with the ability to source and service investments (the operator) and one with (or with access to) capital to invest in the endeavor (the investor). These market participants have a range of investment structures available to them, each with its own characteristics. From these options, market participants often select a joint venture because of the flexibility to create bespoke structures and terms that are best suited for a specific investment mandate or strategy.

At the risk of overgeneralizing, the spectrum of investment structures to deploy capital in private US real estate is as shown in Figure 3.4-01.

FIGURE 3.4-01 **The full spectrum of investment structures**

COMMINGLED FUNDS	CO-INVESTMENTS	JOINT VENTURES	SEPARATE ACCOUNTS	DIRECT OWNERSHIP

Each of these investment structures has its own characteristics in certain key areas, such as (1) number of investors, (2) number of investments, (3) operator versus investor investment discretion, (4) operator and investor control rights, (5) level of coinvestment by the operator, (6) form of operator compensation, and (7) investment hold periods and exit strategies. A joint venture affords the parties a great deal of flexibility to structure their commercial arrangement in these and other areas to best suit their goals. Based on the objectives of the parties, it is common to see one of the following types of investment structures used for joint ventures:

- Single investment, single investor
- Single investment, multiple investors
- Multiple investments, single investor
- Multiple investments, multiple investors

Joint ventures that involve multiple investors, whether for a single investment or multiple investments are often referred to as "club funds." That is because they share with commingled funds the characteristic of multiple investors (hence the "fund" label), but because there are only a few (typically two to four) investors, the arrangement—particularly as it relates to governance—will be bespoke to the group, creating the feel of a "club."

Joint ventures that involve multiple investments are referred to as "programmatic" joint ventures. A variation on the multiple investment/single investor structure described in Figure 3.4-02 involves the establishment of a contract-based investment program in which the parties address certain key topics (such as deal sourcing obligations, exclusivity, investment approval procedures) in a framework agreement, with investments then made through separate investment structures—see the organizational chart in Figure 3.4-03.

FIGURE 3.4-02 **Real estate joint venture structures—single investment**

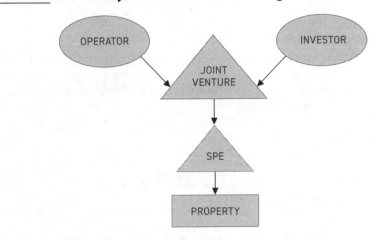

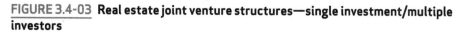

FIGURE 3.4-03 **Real estate joint venture structures—single investment/multiple investors**

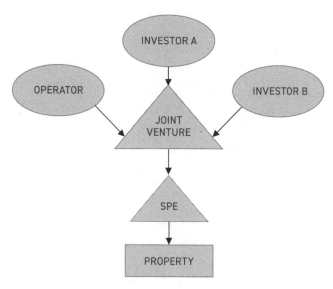

Although programmatic joint ventures can be more complicated to form, they can afford investors certain unique benefits, including a dependable deal flow with known quality operators (often more critical to value creation than access to quality real estate); exclusivity while maintaining investment discretion; access to market information and trends; benefits of pooled economics such as blended results, enhanced alignment of interests, enhanced security for partner defaults, and more; establishment of a substantially capitalized entity that has the capacity to provide credit enhancement as required by project or investment level lenders; more efficient capital deployment, which can be an advantage in competitive bidding situations; operational efficiencies, such as the investor's ability to manage multiple investments through a single business plan; sharing of pursuit costs, perhaps at a negotiated ratio that differs from the ratio in which capital for investments is contributed.

The terms of exclusivity can take many forms. One form is pure exclusive, which means that as long as the exclusive is in effect, the operator may only invest through the venture. Another is preemptive rights, which means that if an investor declines an offered investment opportunity, then the operator may pursue the investment outside of the venture. Last, a noncompete means that when structured with investor preemptive rights, the operator is restricted from pursuing a rejected investment outside of the venture if it is competitive with the venture or venture assets.

But the programmatic form of joint venture investments has its own set of risks and considerations for an investor. This includes:

- Programmatic investments are often larger, more concentrated bets with a single operator (for this reason, it may be best to utilize a programmatic structure once an investor has established a track record with the operator through one-off investments).
- Mistakes and miscalculations may be amplified across a portfolio or operating business.
- J-curve considerations as programmatic investments can involve a significant investment of time and money to establish (which may not be justified if the operator does not produce the anticipated deal flow).
- Programmatic investments may afford less flexibility for making deal-specific modifications; an operator may require reverse exclusivity from its investors, although unusual and not acceptable to many institutional investors.
- A programmatic joint venture may be the means by which the operator establishes a track record for what may ultimately be a larger and more lucrative platform. An investor that invests at an earlier, more risky stage may require follow-on rights to invest in subsequent investment vehicles on favorable terms or options/warrants to invest in the operator's management business.

When selecting the type of entity for a joint venture, the parties to a US joint venture will often utilize a limited liability company, unless there are tax reasons for utilizing a limited partnership structure (e.g., it may not be tax efficient for certain foreign investors to invest in an LLC). The LLC format combines limited liability protection for its members (without having to structure with a general partner that is liable for all partnership liabilities), while providing maximum flexibility in structuring governance and economic terms. Delaware entities are often used because of the well-established body of statutory law and case law and the jurisdiction's sophisticated judiciary.

Several other defining characteristics of a joint venture include:

Tax Attributes: Absent tax sensitivities of particular investors (e.g., foreign investors or US tax-exempt investors) for which a REIT or blocker corporation may be required in the investment structure, the joint venture entity is usually treated as a partnership for tax purposes, with flow-through tax treatment.

Governance: It is common for a joint venture to have a manager or managing member that is charged with managing the entity, subject to negotiated rights of one or more investors to approve or direct actions and decisions. Sometimes, a board structure is used (either with or without a separate manager). In 50-50 (or comparable) joint ventures, comanager structures may be utilized.

Capitalization: Frequently, a joint venture will involve one or more investors putting up most (e.g., 80 percent or more) of the capital required for investments, although there are other situations (e.g., strategic joint ventures, joint ventures involving a contribution of land or other property) where the capitalization may be more even. In some cases, a partner may be obligated to contribute more than its pro rata share of capital for certain purposes.

Another important factor that distinguishes joint ventures from commingled funds and discretionary separate accounts is the investor's level of investment discretion, which is especially relevant in the context of programmatic joint ventures. Investors in programmatic joint ventures typically have discretion over investments and have better control over the amounts and timing of capital outflows. Most often, the investor will have complete discretion over whether or not to invest. More rarely, the operator will have discretion over whether to make an investment without investor approval if the investment satisfies defined investment criteria (which may be more restrictive than typical investment criteria in commingled funds and discretionary separate accounts).

Where an investor has investment discretion, its decision not to invest in offered opportunities could have implications for any exclusivity rights that the investor may have. For example, if an investor declines a certain number of investments satisfying specified investment criteria, or a certain number of qualifying investments within a certain period of time, then the operator could be released from its exclusivity obligations. Joint ventures can also afford parties the flexibility to structure the terms of deal sourcing, exclusivity, and investor discretion so as to counteract certain aspects of fund structures that can lead to misalignment of interests, such as a defined investment period, fees charged only on invested capital after investment period, and so forth.

Returning to governance attributes, when compared to other investment structures (commingled funds, coinvestments, separate accounts), joint ventures can enable the investor to exercise much greater control over some or all aspects of an investment. Often, the operator will have the right and obligation to manage the "day-to-day" affairs of the joint venture.

On the other hand, the investor may have prescribed governance rights of the following types (with investors frequently having some combination of these rights): negative control rights and affirmative control rights. Negative control rights may include the rights to approve major decisions proposed by the operator, such as buying/selling assets, financing, annual business plan/budget, development plan (budget, schedule, plans), material contracts, leases, contracts with the operator or its affiliates, capital calls, admission of additional partners, or fundamental company actions, such as bankruptcy or dissolution/merger. Affirmative control rights, such as rights to control joint venture actions with respect to contracts with the operator or its affiliates and rights to propose or require action with respect to major decisions, such as a sale or financing.

The level of control that an investor has in a joint venture will be influenced by multiple factors, including:

- The history/track record between the parties.
- The investor's internal resources and ability to actively manage.
- The identity of operator (established vs. startup).
- Tax or regulatory constraints on the investor's ability to exercise control over investments.
- The size and type of investments to be made by the joint venture and the level of risk associated with the investments. For example, an investor may require enhanced governance rights for development projects (such as rights to approve plans/change orders, development schedule, development budget, use of contingency/funding of cost overruns) given the heightened risk associated with those investments.

Importantly, a joint venture will almost always provide for the reduction or elimination of the governance rights of either or both parties under certain circumstances, such as investor rights to remove and replace the operator as the manager of the joint venture if any specified "cause" event occurs, and reduction of a party's governance rights if mandatory capital is not contributed when required.

Not unlike commingled funds and other types of investment structures, the operator in a joint venture is often compensated through a combination of carried interest and fees.

Carried interests (or promote) in joint ventures are structured with similar cash flow waterfalls as are encountered in funds and coinvestments, except that it is not as common in multi-investor joint ventures to see investor-specific carried interest terms as it is in the fund context. An operator's carried interest is typically subordinated to a return of and on investor capital (and sometimes, perhaps in the case of returns derived from operating cash flow, just a minimum return on investor capital) by requiring the achievement of specified return "hurdles" before carried interest is distributed. Hurdles are defined with various financial return measures, such as a minimum internal rate of return (IRR) or preferred return or a minimum multiple on invested capital (MOIC). In multiple-investment structures, there are varied approaches on deal-by-deal versus pooled return calculations of carried interest, and in pooled return structures, interim promotes can be used. Other concepts that are encountered in funds and coinvestments—such as clawbacks and tax distributions—are also used in joint ventures. Finally, carried interest is often subject to forfeiture, in whole or in part, upon the occurrence of certain cause-type events.

In addition to carried interest, the operator will often earn fees for services provided to the joint venture or the investor. These may include one or more of the following: asset management fees (usually only in programmatic/multi-investment structures), development management fees, property management fees, leasing management fees, construction management fees, acquisition fees, disposition fees, and financing fees. Although less typical, the investor may also be in the position of receiving fee-based compensation from the joint venture, for example, credit enhancement fees for providing financing-related guaranties.

The operator or its affiliates may also be entitled to be reimbursed for certain expenses incurred on behalf of the joint venture. From the investor's perspective, it will be important to understand the nature and scope of reimbursable expenses to avoid the establishment of additional, unintended, profit centers for the operator. Whether the operator is entitled to recover any of its overhead costs is another important consideration, especially where the operator is receiving fees.

Unlike closed-end funds, joint ventures often do not have a limited term, but instead provide one or more partners with various rights to exit from the investment, either at any time or after a specified lock-in period. These exit rights may be at the level of the joint venture or at the level of underlying investments:

Joint Venture Level Exit Rights: These can include secondary transfers of partner interests (with or without preemptive rights, such as rights of first offer or first refusal in favor of the other partner), buy-sell, put-call, and tag-along/drag-along.

Investment Level Exit Rights: These can include a planned liquidation at a certain time or after achievement of specified objectives, and third-party sale rights (with or without preemptive rights, such as rights of first offer or first refusal, in favor of a partner).

Exit rights and restrictions in a joint venture can be tailored for the specific investment, such as in the development context, restrictions on exercising exit rights until the project is completed or stabilized, tailored restrictions on transfers of upper-tier ownership interests to maintain certain ownership and control attributes for each partner, ability to achieve liquidity quickly and efficiently through a sale of interest to another partner, and tailored hold periods to align with the business plan.

Suffice it to say, there are numerous financial and legal considerations involved when entering a real estate joint venture, and this chapter is just scratching the surface. But perhaps the most important consideration for a successful joint venture is choosing the right partner and ensuring that there is strong alignment of interest. Although this is true in good times, it is perhaps most important when things do not go as planned. In those scenarios, having strong contractual rights will certainly go a long way in protecting each party's interests, but inevitably circumstances will arise that neither party anticipated, and then having a partner that behaves as a true partner and "does the right thing" will be invaluable (See Figures 3.4-04, 3.4-05, and 3.4-06).

FIGURE 3.4-04 **Real estate joint venture structures—programmatic/multiple investments**

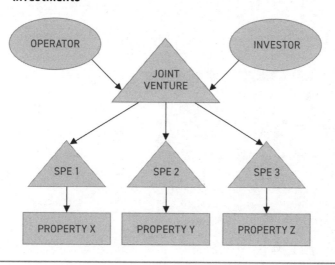

FIGURE 3.4-05 **Real estate joint venture structures—programmatic/multiple investments/multiple investors**

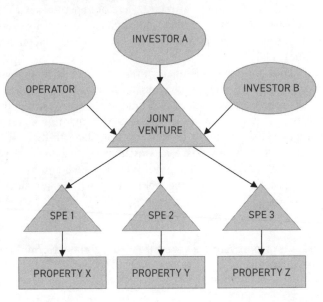

FIGURE 3.4-06 **Real estate joint venture structures—programmatic/multiple investments/multiple investors entities**

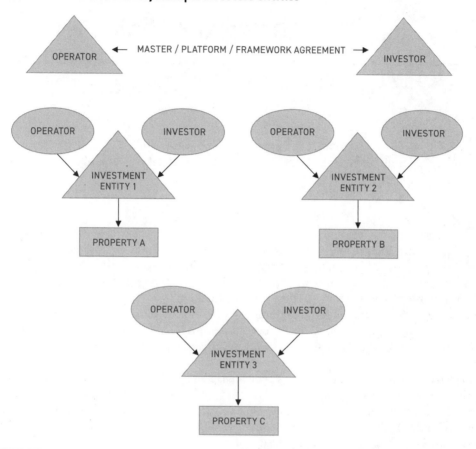

Structuring the Risk

Structures and Terms for Joint Ventures

Joseph L. Pagliari Jr., PhD, CFA, CPA,
Clinical Professor of Real Estate, University of Chicago

The use of joint ventures between institutional investors and operating partners has increased dramatically in the last 20 or so years.[1] The reason, as often suggested, is the potential to generate excess risk-adjusted returns; specifically, the potential benefits include (1) access to "off-market" deals and (2) access to asset- and/or market-specific expertise (i.e., "sharp-shooters").[2] These joint ventures are typically characterized by higher-return/higher-risk strategies, greater leverage, shorter time horizons, and noncore assets.

Because operating partners are believed to be better-suited than institutional investors with regard to providing these skills, a joint venture is often created between the two parties. Such arrangements are a variation of incentive-fee contracts in corporate finance as between principals (shareholders) and agents (senior management). The basic idea is to provide the agent with an incentive to expend (costly) effort and to reduce the principal's monitoring costs. In the context of real estate investing, the incentive takes the form of the operating partner's (or agent's) participation in the venture's residual profits—after payment of all relevant costs as well as the payment of a preferred return to the principals (or money partners).

As a byproduct of such incentive-fee arrangements, certain moral-hazard problems are often created: risk-seeking (or "gambling for redemption"), expending little effort (or "shirking"), empire building, and so on, particularly when the operating partner is unlikely to realize its participation in the residual profits.

A balanced view of joint ventures is agnostic. They are neither inherently good nor bad; instead, they are means to an end. Important matters to consider include:

1. How a JV structure reshapes the return distribution
2. Agency costs (or moral-hazard problems)
3. Improving the alignment of interests between the money partner and the operating partner

The balance of this chapter attempts to sketch some of the major points.

JVS RESHAPE THE RETURN DISTRIBUTION

These incentive-fee structures seem best understood via a simple example.[3] So let's begin assuming that an investor and an operating partner agree to first allocate the venture's profits such that the investors receive a return of their capital plus 12 percent per annum—the "preferred" return (or the "pref")—and that any excess profits are to be allocated 50 percent to the investors and 50 percent to the operating partner.[4] Let's further assume that the venture is expected to produce a gross return of 12 percent and that the standard deviation of that return is 15 percent. To keep matters simple, let's also assume the venture's life is one year and that its returns are normally distributed. An illustration of the venture's expected return and investment operator's participation in the excess profits are illustrated in Figure 3.5-01.

FIGURE 3.5-01 **Illustration of expected fund-level returns with investment manager's promoted interest**

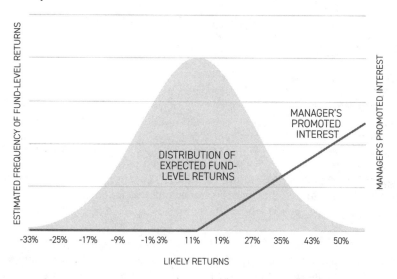

The Scrape and the JVs' Return Distribution

The incentivized nature of these agreements (i.e., returns in excess of the preferred return are shared between the investor and the operating partner) creates optionlike characteristics with regard to the operating partner's promote. Consequently, the operator's participation (sometimes also referred to as the "scrape") truncates the investor's upside, as illustrated in Figure 3.5-02.

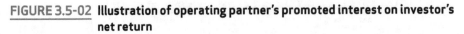

FIGURE 3.5-02 **Illustration of operating partner's promoted interest on investor's net return**

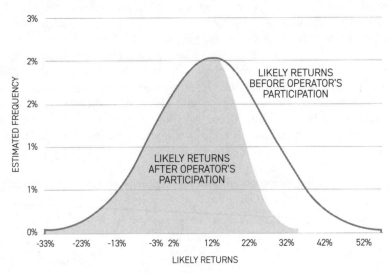

This simple graph communicates two crucial results:

1. The investor's expected net return (9 percent) is lower than the venture's expected gross return (12 percent), even when the preferred return (12 percent) is set equal to the venture's expected gross return (12 percent) because of the expected value of the operator's promote. In other words, even though the preference is set equal to the venture's expected (gross) return, the investor's expected (net) return is substantially reduced.[5]
2. Because the distribution of the investor's net expected return is negatively skewed, the standard deviation understates the investor's risk. In the present example, the calculated standard deviation of the investor's net return (11.9 percent) is lower than the standard deviation of the venture's gross return (15 percent). This result is essentially a statistical illusion because the investor's downside risk is unchanged.[6]

Specific to our example, the operator's carried interest serves to transform the distribution of returns as summarized in Figure 3.5-03.[7]

FIGURE 3.5-03 **Investors' and operators' expected performance**

LIKELY RETURNS:	
Investor-Level Returns Before JV Operator's Promoted Interest	12.0%
Reduction in Return Attributable to JV Operator's Promoted Interest	3.0%
Investor's Net Return:	9.0%
Volatility (Standard Deviation): Investor-Level Volatility of Expected Return	15.0%
Reduction in Volatility Attributable to JV Operator's Promoted Interest	4.5%
Standard Deviation of Investor's Expected Net Return	11.9%

Surely, sophisticated investors appreciate that their upside is truncated in such arrangements; however, they also believe that such arrangements produce incentives in the investment operator that lead, on average, to higher risk-adjusted outcomes. Whether or not this truncation (and, therefore, lowered expected return) is offset by the investment operator's ability to generate positive "alpha" is largely an empirical question. Certain research (e.g., see Bollinger and Pagliari [2019] and Pagliari [2020] with regard to noncore fund performance[8]) suggests otherwise.

Knock-On Effects

The expected value of the operating partner's promoted interest is analogous to a call option in which the operator has a contingent claim on the venture's future profitability; therefore, three relationships are important:

1. **The Level of the Promoted Interest**
   A percentage increase (or decrease) in the level of the promoted interest has a proportionate effect on the expected value of the promoted interest. Using our example, let's assume that we were to increase the promote from 50 to 60 percent (i.e., an increase of 20 percent); in turn, this would proportionately increase the expected value of the promoted interest from 3.0 to 3.6 percent (of the venture's expected 12 percent return).
2. **The Venture's Expected Return Less the Investor's Preferred Return**
   The impact of changing the spread between the venture's expected return and the investor's preferred return is intuitive, but not necessarily straightforward. Figure 3.5-04 examines a range of outcomes in which we fix the preferred return and let the venture-level expected return vary.

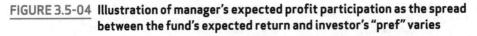

FIGURE 3.5-04 **Illustration of manager's expected profit participation as the spread between the fund's expected return and investor's "pref" varies**

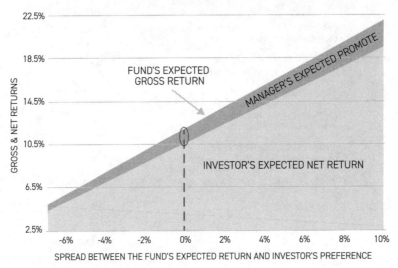

The dashed vertical line highlights the zero percent spread (i.e., the venture's expected return equals the investor's preference) of our earlier example, and the ellipse highlights that 3 percent of the expected venture-level return is the expected value of the operator's promoted interest. Notice that the expected value of the operator's promoted interest increases substantially as the spread widens in a positive manner (i.e., to the right of the dashed line); this pattern (i.e., the preferred return being set lower than the venture's expected gross return) is the more-common relationship found in practice.[9]

3. **The Volatility of Venture-Level Returns**
Like any option, the expected value of the operating partner's promoted interest increases (decreases) as the volatility of the underlying asset increases (decreases). One perspective on this relationship is to consider a range of volatility estimates for venture-level returns against our backdrop of the assumed preferred return (12 percent) and promoted interest (50 percent), while maintaining the venture's expected return (12 percent) (see Figure 3.5-05).

FIGURE 3.5-05 **Illustration of manager's expected participation as the volatility of fund-level returns increases**

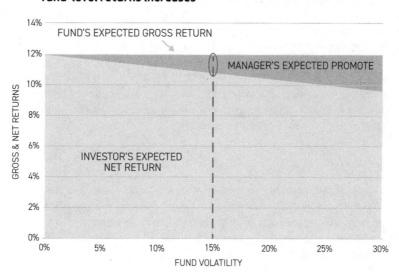

As with any contingent claim, the option value of the promoted interest equals zero when the volatility of venture-level returns is also zero—an unrealistic assumption for commercial real estate investments. (For reference, the dashed vertical line highlights the 15 percent volatility of our earlier examples, and the ellipse highlights that 3 percent of the expected venture-level return is the expected value of the operator's promoted interest.)

Venture Volatility as f(Leverage)

In turn, this stimulates a discussion about the factors contributing to the volatility of venture-level returns. They include the following:

- Property effects (i.e., type, geography, and life-cycle considerations)
- Capital-market effects (e.g., shifting marketwide capitalization rates)
- Operating partner's track record and expertise
- Financial leverage

Of these effects, financial leverage is typically the most impactful—particularly, when one considers ventures using fairly high degrees of leverage. For example, the volatility of venture-level returns doubles as the venture moves from 0 to 50 percent leverage, but also doubles as the venture moves from 50 to 75 percent leverage or from 60 to 80 percent leverage. These latter two examples (50 → 75 percent and 60 → 80 percent) are meant to illustrate the dramatic gearing effects of higher leverage ratios. Changing nothing from our earlier example but the doubling the volatility of expected venture-level returns, we find that the expected value of the promoted interest also doubles, as illustrated previously.

The venture's leverage has two profound effects: (1) it increases the venture's expected (gross) return, and (2) it increases the volatility of that (gross) return, both of which contribute to significantly increasing the expected value of the operating partner's carried interest, at the expense of the investor's net return. Accordingly, investors should be leery of ventures with high degrees of leverage.

Leverage → Law of One Price → JV Pricing

The "law of one" price asserts that two assets with the same pattern of cash flows ought to have the same price. If not, an arbitrage opportunity exists by purchasing the undervalued opportunity and selling the overvalued opportunity.

* * *

The application to this discussion of joint ventures is simply that market efficiency argues that levered core properties, as illustrated in Figure 3.5-06, are the alternative to various joint-ventured noncore alternatives. A joint-ventured noncore venture will be attractive if it is priced above the core-with-leverage alternative (and will be unattractive if priced below the core-with-leverage alternative), as illustrated in Figure 3.5-06.

FIGURE 3.5-06 **Illustration of "law of one price" levered core deal versus JV deal—based upon net returns to each**

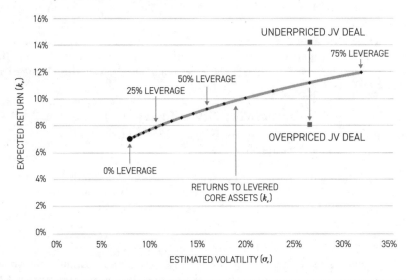

Using the volatility of the venture's gross return and the investor's net expected return, the law of one price can be applied to determine whether or not the noncore JV offers a better risk-adjusted return than the core-with-leverage alternative. It is, of course, axiomatic that this comparison of risk/return alternatives is based on net returns.

AGENCY COSTS AND EFFECTS

Operating partners, like other economic agents (in and outside of real estate), respond rationally to the incentive fees typically found in noncore ventures. As such, operating partners examine their unrealized incentive fee (i.e., after consummating the investment structure, but before the investment concludes). If the fee is "in the money," the operating partners tend to make conservative investment decisions going forward. Conversely, if the fee is "out of the money," the operating partners tend to make aggressive investment decisions going forward.

To better understand this agency effect, consider two contrasting examples: In the first case, the operating partner's promote is in-the-money and—to oversimplify—the operating partner can choose either a conservative or a risky action. The conservative action leaves the operating partner's promote essentially unchanged. On the other hand, the risky action will result in either (1) a substantial worsening of the venture's profitability if the risky matter is unfavorably resolved (with the consequence of the operator's promote expiring worthless), or (2) substantial improvement of the venture's profitability if the risky matter is favorably resolved (with the consequence of the operator's promote substantially increasing, relative to the conservative case). Indeed, it is the out-of-the-money condition that leads to the (previously mentioned) moral-hazard problems of risk-seeking and/or shirking.

Building Blocks: Utility, Effort, and Likelihood

We next need a few building blocks with which we can better appreciate the behavioral aspects of incentive fees. First among them is the idea of utility theory. The basic premise is quite simple: in our case, investors (principals) and operators (agents) prefer bigger gains to smaller gains but at a declining rate, as illustrated in Figure 3.5-07.

FIGURE 3.5-07 **Illustration of utility theory and risk aversion**

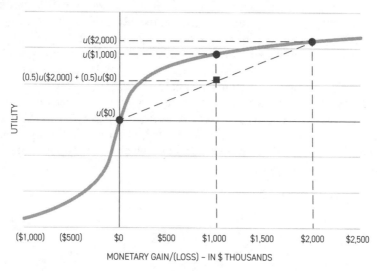

The curve represents the individual's utility over a range of gains and losses. At some point, the utility of future gains begins to slow. This decline in the marginal utility of gains gives rise to risk-averting behavior.[10]

Second, let's consider some positive relationship between the operator's efforts and the venture's asset-level returns. The central idea is that low managerial effort leads to below-market results and high managerial effort leads to above-market results, with some notion that the marginal productivity of effort is declining at high effort levels (i.e., no matter how hard the operator works, there is some inherent limit on returns). However, expending effort is costly to the operator; therefore, the operator must believe it is plausible that its promoted interest will end up "in the money" (i.e., likely to be realized).

Let's now examine these building blocks (i.e., utility, effort, and likelihood) in light of the operator's promoted interest.

Example of Behavioral Effects

To better understand the assertion that the unrealized status (in vs. out of the money) of the operator's promoted interest influences behavior, let's consider the following illustration.

Assume that a significant amount of the venture's properties have leases that are about to expire at some interim date. Further assume that the operator can either execute new (triple-net) leases with strong-credit tenants at $12 per square foot or with weak-credit tenants at $14 per square foot and that the market-clearing capitalization rate is 6 percent in the case of strong-credit tenants and 7 percent in the case of weak-credit tenants. So the current market value of the new lease is $200 per square foot in either case. At the investment's termination date, the strong-credit tenants are still expected to be valued at the market-clearing capitalization rate of 6 percent and, therefore, will continue to be worth $200 per square foot, thereby preserving the operator's promoted interest.

On the other hand, the weak-credit tenants have some economic event[11] that will either be favorably or unfavorably resolved before the venture's termination date. If the economic event is favorably resolved, the market-clearing capitalization rate for these tenants will fall to 6 percent (the same as strong-credit tenants), and therefore, the leased space will increase in value to $233 per square foot, thereby substantially increasing the operator's promoted interest. If the economic event is unfavorably resolved, the market-clearing capitalization rate will jump to 8.4 percent, and therefore, the leased space will decrease in value to $167 per square foot, thereby erasing the operator's promoted interest.[12]

Let's first assume that the venture's performance currently exceeds the investor's preferred return, and accordingly, the operator's promoted interest is "in the money" at some interim date. In this simple example, the operator is best served (in the sense of maximizing expected utility) by selecting the conservative action and thereby preserving its existing in-the-money promoted interest, as shown in Figure 3.5-08.

FIGURE 3.5-08 **Illustration of operator's choice between strong- and weak-credit tenants when operator's interim promote is "in the money"**

		t_1				t_2		
TENANT CREDIT TYPE	LEASE RATE / SQ. FT.	CAPITALIZA- TION RATE	BUILDING VALUE / SQ. FT.		LEASE RATE / SQ. FT.	CAPITAL- IZATION RATE	BUILDING VALUE / SQ. FT.	VALUE OF PROMOTED INTEREST
STRONG	$12.00	6.0%	$200.00		$12.00	6.0%	$200.00	$t_2 = t_1$
WEAK	$14.00	7.0%	$200.00	50%	$14.00	6.0%	$233.33	$t''_2 > t_1$
				50%	$14.00	8.4%	$166.67	$t'_2 < t_1 = 0$

Now assume the same fact pattern as above, except that the operator's promoted interest is "out of the money" at some interim date. If the operator takes the conservative action, it is expected that its promoted interest will remain unchanged, at zero. If the operator takes some risky action, its promoted interest either improves substantially or remains at zero at the venture's termination date. Clearly, the utility of maintaining the existing (out-of-the-money) promote is less than the expected utility[13] of the gamble (i.e., risk-seeking behavior), which results in the promoted interest either improving substantially or remaining at zero. Therefore, the operator takes on the risky action hoping to improve the promoted interest, as indicated in Figure 3.5-09.

FIGURE 3.5-09 **Illustration of manager's choice between strong- and weak-credit tenants when manager's interim promote is "out of the money"**

		t_1				t_2		
TENANT CREDIT TYPE	LEASE RATE / SQ. FT.	CAPITALIZA- TION RATE	BUILDING VALUE / SQ. FT.		LEASE RATE / SQ. FT.	CAPITAL- IZATION RATE	BUILDING VALUE / SQ. FT.	VALUE OF PROMOTED INTEREST
STRONG	$12.00	6.0%	$200.00		$12.00	6.0%	$200.00	$t_2 = t_1 = 0$
WEAK	$14.00	7.0%	$200.00	0.5	$14.00	6.0%	$233.33	$t''_2 > t_1 = 0$
				0.5	$14.00	8.4%	$166.67	$t'_2 = t_1 = 0$

In this simple example, the operator is best served by selecting the risky action—as indicated by the region highlighted via the dashed lines and thereby giving the operator a chance of realizing a substantial promoted interest. This risk-taking is often in conflict with risk-averse investors.

Because of this potential for risk-seeking behavior by the operating partner (particularly when its promote is out of the money), issues of control rights and venture governance are critically important.

Other Financial Considerations → Future Fund Raising

Beyond the contractual aspects of venture agreement with regard to control and governance, there is another force at play with regard to the motivations behind the operating partner's behavior. That other aspect is the impact of the venture's return on the operator's track record and future fundraising efforts. If it is the case that the venture's return at the current level places the operator's performance in the top tier of its competitors, then this level of return may be sufficient for future fundraising efforts. Similarly, if it is the case that losing the gamble on the risky action produces a venture-level return that is merely mediocre with regard to the operator's peers, then this prospect may severely damage the operator's future fundraising efforts. If so, the operator may conclude it is best to select the conservative action, even though the promote will be unrealized, and not jeopardize future fundraising efforts.

As a result, operators are inclined to avoid excessively risky actions and instead, focus their efforts elsewhere (e.g., on other ventures). That is, operators may "limp" (or shirk) through the current venture, trying to avoid excessive underperformance relative to its peers, while concentrating resources and efforts elsewhere. Clearly, this result is suboptimal for the venture's investors.

IMPROVING THE ALIGNMENT OF INTERESTS

What is a rational mechanism for invoking more effort (and therefore, higher expected returns) from the operators (but without unduly compensating the operator or without invoking excessive risk-taking)?

A Reduction in Both the Preferred Return and the Promote

At least one approach to consider is lowering both the investor's preferred return and the operator's promoted interest. As a means of examining this approach, let's consider our earlier example in which the venture's expected return is 12 percent per annum, with volatility of 15 percent, and that the investor receives a preferred return of 12 percent per annum and the operator receives a promoted interest of 50 percent of the residual profits. Under these assumptions, the investor's net expected return is 9.0 percent, and the difference of 3.0 percent (i.e., $0.12 - 0.09 = 0.03$) represents the expected value of the operator's promote. Let's consider this example as the "base case," as indicated in the leftmost column of numbers in Figure 3.5-10. Then let's consider decreasing the preferred return in increments of one percentage point (as we move left to right across the exhibit) and solving for the operator's promote percentage such that the investor's expected net return remains unchanged at 9.0 percent over all pref-and-promote combinations.

FIGURE 3.5-10 **Illustration of the static trade-offs between the investor's preferred return and the operator's promoted interest**

	BASE CASE	SENSITIVITY OF PREFERENCE-&-PROMOTE STRUCTURE												
Venture's (Gross) Return Parameters:														
Average Return (μ_v)	12.0%	12.0%	12.0%	12.0%	12.0%	12.0%	12.0%	12.0%	12.0%	12.0%	12.0%	12.0%	12.0%	
Standard Deviation (σ_v)	15.0%	15.0%	15.0%	15.0%	15.0%	15.0%	15.0%	15.0%	15.0%	15.0%	15.0%	15.0%	15.0%	
JV Allocations:														
Investor's Preference (ψ)	12.0%	11.0%	10.0%	9.0%	8.0%	7.0%	6.0%	5.0%	4.0%	3.0%	2.0%	1.0%	0.0%	
Residual Splits:														
Investor	50.0%	53.9%	57.5%	60.6%	63.5%	66.1%	68.4%	70.4%	72.3%	74.0%	75.6%	77.0%	78.3%	
Operator's (Promote = κ)	50.0%	46.1%	42.5%	39.4%	36.5%	33.9%	31.6%	29.6%	27.7%	26.0%	24.4%	23.0%	21.7%	
Allocation of Venture -Level Returns:														
Expected Returns:														
Average Return (μ_v)	12.0%	12.0%	12.0%	12.0%	12.0%	12.0%	12.0%	12.0%	12.0%	12.0%	12.0%	12.0%	12.0%	
Operator's Promoted Interest ($E[\pi]$)	3.0%	3.0%	3.0%	3.0%	3.0%	3.0%	3.0%	3.0%	3.0%	3.0%	3.0%	3.0%	3.0%	
Investor's Net Return ($E[n]$)	9.0%	9.0%	9.0%	9.0%	9.0%	9.0%	9.0%	9.0%	9.0%	9.0%	9.0%	9.0%	9.0%	
Volatility (Standard Deviation):[a]														
Fund-Level Returns (σ_v)	15.0%	15.0%	15.0%	15.0%	15.0%	15.0%	15.0%	15.0%	15.0%	15.0%	15.0%	15.0%	15.0%	
Manager's Promoted Interest (σ_π)[b]	4.5%	4.2%	4.0%	3.8%	3.6%	3.4%	3.2%	3.1%	2.9%	2.8%	2.7%	2.6%	2.5%	
Investor's Net Return(σ_n)[b]	11.9%	11.9%	11.9%	11.9%	12.0%	12.0%	12.1%	12.2%	12.2%	12.3%	12.4%	12.4%	12.5%	

(a) Unless investor and manager returns are perfectly correlated (which they are not, because of the convex nature of the promoted interest), standard deviations are not additive.

(b) Because of the convex nature of promoted interests, the distributions of investor and manager distributions are no longer symmetrical; consequently, the standard deviation is an imperfect measure of their dispersion.

To help orient the reader: The top highlighted (or shaded) row represents the lowering of the investor's preferred return in increments of one percentage point (such that the investor's preferred return begins at 12 percent and ends at 0 percent). The next highlighted row represents the investment operator's promoted interest (ranging from 50 to 21.7 percent) such that the investor's expected net return of 9.0 percent is unchanged across all pref-and-promote combinations. Of course, this also implies the expected value of the operator's promoted interest also remains constant at 3.0 percent, as shown in the third highlighted row. The bottom highlighted row represents the volatility of the operator's promoted interest. Finally, the four dashed boxes are meant to highlight some of the equivalent pref-and-promote combinations as a means of facilitating the discussion. In an approximate manner, a "50 over a 12" (i.e., a 50 percent promote and a 12 percent preferred return) is equal (in terms of the operator's expected promoted interest) to a "40 over a 9," or a "30 over a 6," or a "25 over a 3," or "20 over zero."[14]

Two important insights can be gleaned from the previous exhibit. These insights can make the reduction in the preferred return and in the promoted interest a "win-win" for both the investor and the operator.

First, the uncertainty of the operator realizing its promoted interest fades as the investor lowers its preferred-return requirement. This is intuitive and statistically observable (see the bottom highlighted row in Figure 3.5-10. Therefore, the risk-averse investment operator should be willing to accept an even lower promoted interest than that in Figure 3.5-10. How much less is a function of the operator's risk aversion.[15] Obviously, a further reduction in the operator's promoted interest improves the investor's expected return—as compared to the base case. Therefore, both parties find it in their best interests to collaborate on lowering the preferred return and the promoted interest beyond those combinations shown.

Second, the previous exhibit treats the venture-level returns as static (or exogenous). They are not. As noted earlier, the venture's expected return is a function of the operator's effort, and, in turn, the operator's effort is a function of the likelihood that the operator's promoted interest will be "in the money." That is, venture-level returns are endogenous. Consider an illustration of this endogeneity, as shown in Figure 3.5-11.

FIGURE 3.5-11 Illustration of market opportunity set vis-à-vis investment-specific returns as a function of manager's effort

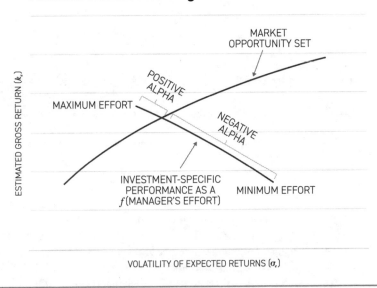

Figure 3.5-11 contrasts the market's opportunity set with an attempt to illustrate that venture-specific returns improve and risk declines as the operator applies more effort. As the venture-specific returns cross the market's opportunity set, the venture produces positive "alpha" (i.e., positive risk-adjusted returns). Again, this increasing application of effort is a

function of lowering the investor's preferred return and thereby improving the likelihood that the operator's realized promote will be in the money.

These two insights suggest that both the investor and the operator can benefit by reducing the preferred return and the promoted interest. The lowered pref improves the chances of the operator realizing its promoted interest; so the operator is willing to accept yet a lower promote, which, in turn, leads to more effort and higher returns on average. In essence, this reduction can create a "win-win" situation for both the investor and the operator. Anecdotally, it seems that market transactions often lead, in the opposite direction, to higher prefs. While this result may permit the investor some initial euphoria, such an arrangement may ultimately be to the detriment of both parties.

Fixed Versus Indexed Preferences

So far, we have expressed the investor's preferred return in terms of a fixed percentage over the life of the investment. Of course, an alternative is to consider a variable percentage that is tied to some underlying index. In so doing, there is a wide variety of choices, reflecting the venture's investment strategy (i.e., its expected risk/return characteristics). In any case, investors would like to avoid paying incentive-management fees for performance, which mirrors an appropriate passive index.

The potential mismatch between a fixed and index-based (or floating) preference is often greatest for ventures with long investment horizons, where the difference between expected and realized market conditions is often greatest. These differences often include a capital-market component (e.g., rising or falling capitalization rates), which is beyond the control of the operator; to reward or penalize the operator for such events is often unfair to both the operator and the investor. Accordingly, an index-based preference serves to remove some of the unintended consequences of a fixed preference, particularly those relating to uncontrollable capital-market effects.

It is often the case that initial expectations about venture-level performance vary from realized performance. With the passage of time, uncertainties about future performance may begin to narrow, while the expectation of likely performance may shift, as illustrated in Figure 3.5-12.

FIGURE 3.5-12 Venture's or fund's evolving expected returns

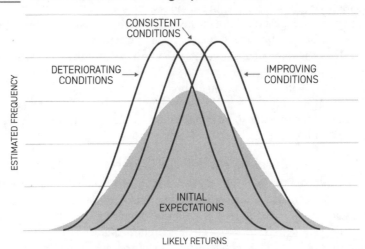

At the risk of oversimplifying, Figure 3.5-12 illustrates three such possibilities with regard to evolving market conditions: those conditions deteriorate, remain consistent, or improve vis-à-vis initial expectations[16] (which are illustrated by the shaded region). If the operator's carried interest (or incentive fee) is designed with a fixed preference, then the two diverging cases (i.e., deteriorating and improving conditions) can create significant imbalances between the investor and the operator (assuming that the operator met the investor's expectations in all other respects).

In the case of improving market conditions and a fixed preference, the operator is unjustly rewarded and the investor unfairly penalized because improving market conditions (e.g., falling capitalization rates) have improved venture-level performance without commensurate effort and expertise from the operator. In other words, the investor paid an incentive fee when the operator failed to outperform the passive benchmark.

The case of deteriorating market conditions and a fixed preference is less straightforward. In such cases, we find that the operator is unfairly penalized because deteriorating market conditions (e.g., rising capitalization rates) have worsened venture-level performance due to no fault of the operator. However, the story does not necessarily end there. As earlier suggested, it is often the case that the operator's effort and expertise are integral components to the venture's future success. It may be the case that without a reasonable likelihood that the operator's carried interest will end up "in the money," the operator will choose to focus its effort and expertise on other ventures (in which the investor(s) may not be involved). Provided that the investor does not find the operator dishonest, incompetent, and/or financially distressed, the investor and the operator may rationally look to renegotiate the fixed preference downward—such that there is now a reasonable likelihood that the operator's carried interest will end up "in the money," and therefore, the operator will choose to focus its effort and expertise on the investor's venture.[17]

The point of examining the deviating cases coupled with a fixed preference is to illustrate the "tails I win/heads you lose" circumstance it might create for the operator. In case of improving conditions, the operator is unjustly enriched when employing a fixed preference; in the case of the deteriorating conditions, the operator's carried interest (or some portion of it) is often preserved by lowering the investor's fixed preference. Much of this circumstance can be avoided by using an index-based (rather than a fixed) preference.

CONCLUSION

This chapter has examined a simple pref-and-promote structure, as typically found in non-core (funds and) ventures—where the operator's effort is generally difficult to discern—to highlight certain economic implications.

First, joint ventures typically impose additional direct costs (e.g., monitoring/supervision and legal complexity) and indirect costs (e.g., issues of control and the risk of a "bad" partner), while also diluting the investor's expected net return—due to the operating partner's carried interest. In exchange for these costs, however, the operating partner is expected to provide certain benefits (e.g., access to "off-market" deals and asset- and/or market-specific expertise). Whether the benefits outweigh the costs ought to be measured in comparison to the investor's core-with-leverage alternatives. Second, these convex incentive-fee structures are likely to produce behavioral effects in the operator. To the extent that the promoted interest is likely to end up "in the money," the operator tends to prefer conservative actions. To the extent that the promoted interest is likely to end up "out of the money," the operator tends to prefer risky actions. However, these behavioral effects are often mitigated by the operator's desires about future fundraising efforts—where adverse reputational effects (due to either excessively conservative or risky actions) may thwart such future efforts.

Third, this chapter proposed that lowering both the investor's preferred return and the operator's promoted interest (expressed as a percentage of profits) may benefit the investor as well as the operator. This win/win situation is the result of the endogenous effects of the operator expending more effort. Additionally, this chapter also proposes that the use of an indexed-based (or floating) preferred return (as opposed to a fixed-rate preference) may create a better alignment of interest between the investor and operator, particularly in those instances in which current conditions move (either favorably or unfavorably) substantially away from the initial expectations.

NOTES

1. This chapter draws heavily on Pagliari (2007, 2013, and 2015), as well as certain other references cited therein.
2. These benefits must, of course, be assessed in the context of the costs of such ventures. These costs include: additional monitoring and supervision costs, additional legal complexities, issues of control, the risk of a "bad" operating partner, and the operating partner's contingent or carried interest.
3. In addition to an infinite array of preference and promote combinations, many other refinements (e.g., "waterfalls" and "catch-up" provisions) are found in practice as well. The intention here is to illustrate a very simple design. However, the exclusion of such refinements does not detract from the main points made herein.

4. In the context of most joint ventures today, a preference of 12 percent is on the upper end of what is typical. Nevertheless, this preference was purposely selected to match the joint venture's expected return, so as to make a subsequent point about the option value of the operator's promoted interest.

5. For some, their first exposure to such contingent-claims examples can be a bit confusing. And while the underlying mathematics is more complicated, let's consider this simple two-outcome possibility as illustrating the expected value of the operator's promote. Assume that the venture will produce either a gross return of 24 percent or 0 percent, with equal probability—such that the venture's expected gross return equals 12 percent. If the venture's gross return equals 24 percent, then the operator's promote equals 6 percent; if the venture's gross return equals 0%, then the operator's promote equals 0 percent. And, as such, the expected value of the operator's promote equals 3 percent (i.e., ½ (6%) + ½ (0%)).

6. Another statistical artifact: the reported standard deviations are not additive.

7. These results were derived by assuming—for analytical convenience—that venture-level returns are normally distributed; however, this assumption is not imperative.

8. The bulk of institutional joint ventures have an investment manager (typically, running a large closed-end, noncore, finite-life fund) investing fund capital alongside an operating partner (who, in the larger picture, contributes little in the way of equity). These investment managers also enjoy a promoted or carried interest in the fund (much like the operating partner enjoys in the venture). As such, the limited partners are "double promoted" (first by the venture and then by the fund).

9. Much less common in practice are instances of the preferred return being set higher than the venture's expected gross return; in the exhibit, these instances are shown to the left of the dashed line.

10. Consider a gamble or a prospect in which an individual will receive either (1) $1 million with certainty (represented by the circle) or (2) either $2 million or $0 (represented by the two squares) with equal probability. The exhibit indicates that the utility of $2 million is less than twice the utility of $1 million, and accordingly, risking a certain $1 million for the chance of winning $2 million but losing everything is unacceptable to this individual.

11. Here, too, there are myriad possibilities; however, let's consider just a few of such events: bringing a new product to market, adjudication of a major lawsuit, the final status of a pending patent, a change in technology, and so on.

12. This is an illustration about risk-taking not skill (which is the persistent ability of an investment manager to produce positive risk-adjusted returns). This illustration presents what is often referred to as a "fair" gamble, wherein the certain outcome equals the expected value of the gamble.

13. While Figure 3.5-09 uses a declining marginal utility of future gains (i.e., risk-averting) to be consistent with the previous section, this result holds regardless of the manager's utility function and, therefore, whether the manager is risk-averting, -seeking or -neutral.

14. From an implementation standpoint, investors and operators may have differing views on expected venture-level (gross) returns impact; consequently, investors and operators may have differing views on what pref-and-promote structures constitute equivalent outcomes.

15. However, specifying the form of the operator's risk aversion and solving for the lower promoted interest is beyond the scope of this chapter.

16. The use of "market conditions" is meant to imply an element of returns about which the manager has little to no control. As a result, the manager's carried interest may be unfairly penalized or unjustly enriched when such conditions significantly diverge from the initial expectations.

17. We should also note that this sort of renegotiation is also found in corporations with stock-option plans for senior management. When it is determined by the corporation's board of directors that the company's share price has fallen due to no (or little) fault of senior management, then the strike price of these options is often reset to a lower value such that senior management now expects that there is a reasonable likelihood that their stock options will end up "in the money," and accordingly, senior management is sufficiently motivated to help improve the fortunes of the company.

Commingled Funds

Types and Strategies

Nick Colley, Global Portfolio Strategist, CBRE IM

Dominic Garcia, Chief Pension Investment Strategist, CBRE IM

Non-US investors may, in addition to making direct property investments and entering into joint ventures with real estate operating companies, elect to invest in commingled funds focused on real estate. Investing via funds has a number of benefits for investors including (1) increased diversification, (2) potentially more favorable tax structure, and (3) easier access to specialist investment strategies. These benefits typically come at the cost of significantly reduced discretion over the underlying investments. Such funds, which are pooled interests in a portfolio of assets, were originally created in the 1970s and focused on core properties. These early funds, while successful, had open-end structures and encountered valuation and liquidity challenges during the late 1980s market downturn. To provide diversity of investment structure, the real estate fund industry evolved to provide closed-end fund structures for investors to access real estate that were modeled on private equity pooled vehicles. Consequently, the commingled fund business has expanded to in excess of $1.4 trillion[1] and has become a staple of diversified investment programs, increasing its significance as a source of capital for the real estate industry.

By investing in commingled funds, investors, or limited partners, assume a passive role and authorize a professional real estate fiduciary to make investment decisions and assemble portfolios on their behalf. In most cases, commingled funds share the following characteristics: their common objective is to invest capital in multiple assets, create value by growing cash flows, and dispose of assets at a profit. They are managed by a sponsor who maintains full discretion over investment decisions and operation of the assets, based on predetermined objectives.

They are structured either as infinite-life, open-end funds or as finite-life, closed-end funds, with standard terms ranging between 6 and 10 years (subject to extensions for optimal disposition). They are comprised of capital contributions from various types of investors, including sovereign wealth funds, endowments and foundations, public and private pension funds, and high-net-worth families or individuals. Ultimately, commingled funds offer value by enabling a symbiotic relationship between classes of holders. The limited partners, who provide investable capital, seek diversification and attractive risk-adjusted returns, but often lack the resources necessary to deploy capital efficiently. The general partners, having developed specialized expertise, provide skilled investment management in exchange for a management fee and in most instances a performance fee.

FUND STRUCTURES

Real estate assets are typically illiquid, heterogenous, and "lumpy," meaning that they are well suited for private securitized investment vehicles as a means for investors to gain access to the asset class. Both open-end and closed-end structures offer the efficiency of sponsor discretion and portfolio diversification but differ in duration of investor commitment.

Open-end funds have no fixed maturity period and are designed for the subscription and redemption of ownership interests at prespecified time frequencies (e.g., monthly, quarterly), allowing for ongoing points of entry and exit for investors, while closed-end funds initiate and complete their investment activities within a defined period, returning capital only upon real-ization of investments. The majority of commingled vehicles are privately held, owing to the relative ease of formation; however, funds may also be listed and traded on a stock exchange. Such listed funds offer investors access to the same real estate cashflows with enhanced liquidity but experience greater volatility in the short term, as pricing is more immediately impacted by non-real-estate forces than private counterparts. It is important to note that pric-ing trends in listed real estate markets often lead the private market by six to nine months, which can present an opportunity for institutional investors to tactically position portfo-lios between public and private investments to capture mispriced real estate risk through a cycle.

Closed-End Funds

By number, the majority of real estate private equity vehicles are closed-end, primarily due to transitional investment strategies appropriate for execution at a certain point in time during a market cycle. Closed-end funds offer a limited number of shareholder interests and a finite life, typically 6 to 10 years, during which investment managers must acquire an asset, execute an asset management plan to improve an asset's cashflow and value, and then realize an asset.

Closed-end funds are best suited to hold investments that require significant operational improvements, development, or adaptive reuse, since value during the renovation period is difficult to gauge accurately. While the portfolio's values will ultimately be realized through disposition, the value of the fund's assets are incrementally marked-to-market, although in a manner that yields less volatility than that of the daily fluctuations in listed markets. By restricting the acceptance of new investors to an initial commitment period, the closed-end fund model provides the sponsor confidence in its supply of capital.

Open-End Funds

An open-end fund is an investment vehicle with an unlimited life that funds its operations through property-level cash-flow generation, asset sales, and additional equity offerings. Unlike closed-end funds, which are typically blind-pool, investors in open-end investment vehicles fund their commitments into a specified portfolio of assets. On average, open-end funds tend to be larger in both total value and number of assets than closed-end funds, providing the necessary scale, diversification, and income-driven performance that inves-tors target from core/core-plus allocations. These funds offer liquidity through redemption provisions based on the fund's net asset value (NAV), which represents the marked-to-market value of the underlying assets, adjusted quarterly and in some cases daily. While liquidity is dependent on the fund's available cash reserves and injections of capital from new investors, open-end funds are permitted to liquidate investments to meet withdrawal requests. A key factor for investors in open-end funds is that capital commitments are invested nearly immediately, allowing the investor to be fully exposed to a diversified property portfolio and begin receiving and/or reinvesting income and capital gains to begin compounding total returns immediately.

INVESTMENT STRATEGIES

The complexity of executing multiple investment strategies, coupled with inefficiencies in the acquisition and operation of real estate, requires specialization and active management by experienced managers to successfully create value. Identifying undervalued and under-managed properties poses significant challenges as opportunities may arise due to evolving economic conditions as well as specific underlying property fundamentals. Value creation depends largely on the detailed understanding of many variables, including property type, market trends, and geographic considerations. As such, experts gain a substantial edge derived from their greater focus on the unique dynamics associated with particular investment opportunities, which leads to more informed acquisition, disposition, and management decisions. Through thoughtful establishment of the investment strategy, careful asset selection, and active operational management, sponsors seek to generate attractive risk-adjusted investment returns.

Commingled funds are typically arranged around a dedicated investment strategy and are categorized by the type of asset, return expectations, and risk tolerance targeted by the investment manager and its investors. The primary categories of funds are discussed as follows.

Core Investing

A core strategy seeks to invest in diversified portfolios of institutionalized real estate sectors, for example, logistics, multifamily, self-storage, life science, and modern office that provide cash flows and modest leverage (up to 30 percent), seeking to deliver relatively stable returns at relatively low risk above inflation. The expected return profile of a core fund is typically 6 to 8 percent (net of fees, discussed in this chapter). Core-plus investing targets a profile of assets and portfolios similar to that in core investing but may employ some components of a value-added strategy to enhance existing income streams. The expected return profile of a core-plus fund is typically 8 to 10 percent (net of fees and carried interest).

Value-Added Investing

Value-added investing is a strategy of moderate risk/return that seeks to acquire assets and increase operating income and/or derisk an asset through significant capital and/or asset management improvements to enhance value. These investors typically employ up to 65 percent leverage and create value through land and building development or redevelopment, releasing, repositioning, and management improvements. Unlike core investing, a significant portion of the expected total return is derived from the realization of the capital appreciation of the underlying asset.

Opportunistic Investing

Opportunistic investing targets higher-risk investments, with commensurately higher return expectations, where the return is generated almost entirely from residual value (limited current income). The objective is to create value through capital appreciation by targeting undervalued assets or taking risks associated with land improvement or new development.

Unlike lower-risk strategies where current income is the main component of the overall total return, opportunistic investing involves enduring considerable market volatility risk, which over a multiple-year hold period may significantly impact the value of the property. Therefore, opportunistic investment requires significant initial capital expenditure, with little or no current income realizations. These funds typically target net returns of 14 percent plus, are often global or international in scope, and may be focused on both emerging and established markets.

Debt-Focused Funds

Debt plays a significant diversifying role in institutional portfolios, providing steady, reliable streams of cash to investors. Additionally, due to its seniority over equity positions within the capital structure, debt provides downside protection against declines in equity value during economic downturns. Debt strategies range from those targeting the most senior, secure tranche of the capital stack to those focused on mezzanine and high-yield credit, with each level exhibiting a higher risk profile. Fund managers seeking to enhance returns often focus on originating or purchasing lower quality issues where risk tolerance and superior underwriting can be used as a competitive advantage. In leveraged capital structures, high-yield debt occupies a position between senior debt (bank lending) and equity capital, and because only a thin layer of equity protects this subordinated debt from impairment, managers seek to earn substantial margins over higher quality alternatives. By embracing credit risk and introducing equity characteristics into the expected payment streams, managers seek outsized returns not only from higher interest rates but also from a combination of equity participation and/or purchase discounts.

Investors in debt-focused funds benefit by receiving income that is at or above comparable public market options, while typically backed by property with floating rates and shorter duration.

Indirect Strategies

Indirect managers select local operating partners on behalf of their limited partners and invest through a range of structures, such as open/closed-end funds, programmatic ventures, coinvestments, and secondaries. By pooling commitments, these sponsors provide economies of scale and focus on manager selection and performance monitoring functions that limited partners might be unable to easily replicate internally. Indirect strategies also offer institutions the ability to gain exposure to unfamiliar market niches and emerging managers. Strategies range in scope from globally diversified to market-, sector-, or property-specific strategies.

A secondaries strategy captures both limited-partner- (LP-) and general-partner- (GP-) led transactions. While there are important differences in the respective execution, both have the common feature of providing fresh capital to an existing investment vehicle. An LP-led transaction is where a limited partner has decided to rebalance their portfolio through the disposal of limited partnership interests. GP-led secondaries refers to transactions where a local operating partner (acting as the general partner) initiates the transaction, often in the context of recapitalizing a portfolio to provide additional time to capture value.

The absence of a liquid market coupled with uncertain valuations can impede the disposal of such interests, and as such, secondary fund managers have emerged as specialists in evaluating and acquiring these interests.

Secondary buyers target these opportunities as a means to access skilled managers and corresponding fund portfolios at discounted valuations (although in rising markets such opportunities may command a premium).

COMPENSATION AND ALIGNMENT

Appropriate organizational structure is a critical element of successful partnership with external sponsors, as it establishes a framework for the alignment of interests among parties. One important aligning factor is coinvestment of equity by the sponsor, which ensures sharing in risk of capital loss. Other structural aspects, such as compensation schemes, are designed to create the incentive to seek appropriate returns while protecting invested capital (managing risk). Value-added and opportunistic fund arrangements typically establish a management fee calculated on the nominal amount of committed or invested capital and an incentive fee (or carried interest) calculated as a portion of the portfolio's profits (typically 15 to 20 percent above a preferred return or "hurdle rate"). By linking the compensation to investment returns, a properly structured compensation structure incentivizes the manager toward risk-adjusted value creation.

Many large global funds are managed by capital allocators, sponsors that provide the equity financing for a local operating partner to acquire and manage assets. These large global or regional allocators focus their attention on macro-level investment theses and portfolio structuring, using their broad-based investment experience, market knowledge, and global network to capitalize on prevailing trends and their corresponding impact on cyclical investments, as shown in Figure 3.6-01.

Allocators' management control over investments is more removed than that of operators, but they often control major decisions. While allocators may lack sector- or market-specific hands-on property management expertise, they provide capital markets and structuring knowledge, fiduciary control, and institutional reporting standards while also offering potential diversification as a risk mitigant, given their ability to nimbly move in and out of markets or sectors as relative value opportunities shift.

Direct operators take a bottom-up approach, focusing their attention on individual properties where they can increase cash flows and create value through improved operations. These sponsors undertake capital improvements and implement efficient business plans directly and typically have extensive experience in the local market.

Another important consideration for investors in higher-returning, drawdown commingled funds (e.g., value-add or opportunistic) is the need to reserve capital to meet current and future capital calls without advance knowledge of, or control over, when they may occur. Consequently, investors are obligated to maintain sufficient liquidity to fund future capital calls, thus possibly incurring a significant opportunity cost. In addition, there is an initial mismatch of cash inflows and outflows, creating a temporarily unfavorable cash stream in the shape of a "J" curve as investors pay management fees on committed equity through the commitment period (typically three to four years) before any investments are made or returns are generated.

FIGURE 3.6-01 **Investment strategies: risk versus return**

TARGET NET IRRs[1,2]	6–8%	9–13%	14%+
	INCOME (CORE)	INCOME + GROWTH (CORE-PLUS/VALUE-ADD)	GROWTH (OPPORTUNISTIC)
DESCRIPTION	Class A, well-occupied properties in prime locations	Properties with refurbishment, repositioning, enhanced property management needs, build to core	Development, distressed situations, complex investments, entity-level investing
RETURN CHARACTERISTICS	Stable, long-duration cash flows with downside protection	Cash flowing but with the opportunity to increase net operating income through an improvement plan	Returns are driven more by residual value than through cash flow
LEVERAGE (LOAN-TO-VALUE)	20–40%	40–65%	50–80%
INCOME (% OF TOTAL RETURN)	60–80%	30–60%	10–30%

Figure 3.6-02 illustrates such a negative net cash position faced by blind-pool fund investors. Alternative asset classes such as real estate provide powerful mechanisms to reduce risk and enhance returns for well-diversified portfolios. Commingled real estate funds are uniquely suited to benefit investors by providing options otherwise available only to the largest investors. Moreover, current income, generated by many types of real estate, can provide a stabilizing influence and reduce the overall volatility of a portfolio. Commingled funds provide investment managers greater execution efficiency, as real estate opportunities often arise amid rapidly changing market conditions and competition among potential acquirers requires the ability to react quickly. A sponsor with discretionary access to a pool of capital is significantly better positioned to pursue such opportunities, ultimately benefiting the limited partners.

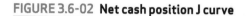

FIGURE 3.6-02 **Net cash position J curve**

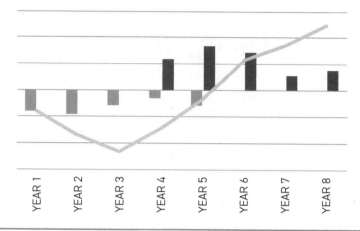

Limited partners must keep a keen eye on a number of issues when investing in commingled funds. Communication and monitoring are important, as limited partners delegate discretion over potential acquisitions and do not have the opportunity to underwrite specific transactions. Additionally, investors should seek to align their interests with those of their general partners through distribution structures, management fees, and sponsor coinvestment.

The commingled form of investing has existed since the 1970s and is widely accepted as a sustainable investment model for institutional real estate. However, like any investment structure, it offers both advantages and disadvantages and continues to evolve and adapt to market conditions and investor preferences. Finally, investors seeking to build a diversified institutional quality portfolio ought to assess their own internal capabilities and objectives to determine the best execution strategy.

For investors with limited internal resources, an indirect strategy may be most beneficial to optimize selection, governance, and oversight of their assets, which is mostly outsourced via investment in a fund or with an operating partner. Additionally, investors ought to assess their own internal risk tolerance in building a portfolio. More allocation to value add and opportunistic strategies produce equity-like risk in a portfolio, whereas core/core-plus risk provides more bondlike risk. For most investors, the optimal allocation is a majority allocation to core/core-plus supplemented by value add and opportunistic to maintain diversification relative to other asset classes in an investor's total portfolio.

NOTE

1. Preqin as of June 30, 2022; includes existing funds that have not been wound up, with funds-of-funds and secondaries funds excluded to avoid double counting, as of publication date.

Commingled Funds

Structures and Terms

Mark Proctor, Partner, Willkie Farr & Gallagher LLP

The purpose of this chapter is to explain the structure and legal terms of a typical US real estate investment fund and to offer a guide to non-US investors as to what they might expect when considering making an investment in such a fund.

The real estate fund industry has experienced significant consolidation since the global financial crisis of 2007–2008. Simultaneously, investors demonstrated an increased interest in real estate as an asset class while inflation was rising. More recently, increases in interest rates aimed at fighting inflation have led to increased interest in credit investments of all kinds, including real estate credit investments. As a result, established real estate fund sponsors have formed larger funds, and many sponsors have faced a more competitive fundraising environment, as compared to the period from the late 1990s through 2007. Sponsors have reacted to the competitive fundraising environment by making concessions to investors, including offering more favorable fee structures. The following discussion reflects the state of the current market.

DISCRETIONARY FUND BASICS

Open-End and Closed-End Funds

Discretionary funds operate as either closed-end funds, with a limited term and liquidation at a predetermined date, or as open-end funds, with an indefinite term, and periodic admission and redemption of investors. Investors are admitted to closed-end funds during a specified period at the beginning of the fund and generally are expected to hold their investments for its entire life. Closed-end funds are expected to sell off their assets and wind down at the end of their terms, which are typically 10 to 12 years. The fund's return to investors is typically expressed as an expected return over the life of the fund and is based on a combination of income from the properties during the life of the fund and anticipated appreciation in the properties that will be realized through liquidation at the end of the term. Depending on the fund's investment strategy, the returns will be driven primarily by income (in the case of core and core-plus funds), or appreciation (in the case of value-add and opportunistic funds). As a general matter, open-end funds tend to employ a core or core-plus investment strategy, since open-end funds tend to favor more liquid assets, which are easier to value and dispose of.

Accordingly, an open-end fund's expected return to investors is largely based on the income generated from the properties held, and from sales and refinancings of the fund's investments.

Structure and Documentation

Most commingled US real estate funds are structured as limited partnerships, with the sponsor or an affiliate of the sponsor serving as the general partner and the investors admitted as limited partners. This traditional structure provides limited liability for the investors and subjects the general partner to unlimited liability for the fund's liabilities, if the fund does not have sufficient capital and/or assets to meet these liabilities. A small number of commingled funds are now structured as limited liability companies, offering limited liability protection to all members, including the sponsor or its affiliate. The advantage of limited partnerships is that they tend to be tax-transparent in most jurisdictions, whereas limited liability companies may not be tax-transparent in all non-US jurisdictions.

Funds may also be structured using one or more REITs, feeder vehicles, parallel partnerships, or other investment vehicles designed to address particular concerns of the sponsor or certain classes of investors. Fund structures are driven by business and tax considerations, investment strategies, the nature of the investors (e.g., tax-exempt, ERISA, US taxable, or non-US), and securities regulation concerns.

Investors considering investment in a fund should expect to receive and plan carefully to review a private placement memorandum (PPM). The PPM will summarize the fund's investment strategy and objective, describe the management team's track record, and provide a term sheet outlining the key terms of an investment therein. It also will set forth risk factors and potential conflicts of interest, and disclose tax, regulatory, securities laws, and other considerations relevant to the fund.

In most cases, an investor will complete a subscription agreement, pursuant to which it makes its contractual commitment to contribute capital to the fund. In addition to the capital commitment, a typical subscription agreement will contain an investor questionnaire and certain representations and warranties to be made by the investor to determine suitability for the fund and to rule out certain tax, securities law, and/or other regulatory concerns. Increasingly, subscription documents are filled out and submitted electronically, which streamlines the onboarding process for investors.

The ultimate terms of any fund will be set forth in the fund's limited partnership agreement, limited liability company agreement, or other governing documents, which investors should review carefully with their legal and tax advisors.

Individual investors in a fund may negotiate side letters with the sponsor of the fund. These letters vary the fund's general terms to address concerns particular to the investor. Side letters frequently deal with tax, regulatory, or reporting issues.

Side letters also are used to grant special rights or privileges to an investor, such as the ability to appoint a representative to the fund's advisory committee, discounted fees, or in open-ended funds, preferential liquidity terms.

Many side letters, and some partnership agreements or other relevant documents, include a "most favored nation" clause stating that if the sponsor grants a special right to one investor, any other investor with an equal or larger capital commitment can elect to receive the same treatment. Most favored nation clauses generally exclude rights that address tax or regulatory concerns that are relevant to a particular investor but not applicable to other investors.

Additionally, many most favored nation clauses exclude a laundry list of other clauses. This list of excluded clauses should be carefully reviewed, and any excluded clauses that are important to an investor should be requested directly in the investor's side letter.

The business deal between the sponsor and the investors is at the core of any investment structure. Despite diverse structures, most commingled real estate investment funds rely on a similar basic set of terms. These basic terms are described in the discussion that follows.

Unless otherwise stated, the discussion applies to both open-end and closed-end funds, and references to a general partner or partnership agreement may be read as applicable to a managing member or sponsor, or limited liability agreement or other governing documents.

ECONOMIC TERMS

Capital Commitments, Capital Calls, and Delinquent Limited Partner Provisions

Most real estate funds call capital from investors on an as-needed basis, rather than requiring investors to fund their full capital commitment at the time of their admission to the fund. The investor's subscription agreement and the partnership agreement (or other governing document) establish the terms under which the investor must make capital contributions to the fund. These include the maximum total amount the investor is required to contribute (the investor's capital commitment), the period during which capital may be called for new investments (the investment or commitment period), and the period within which the investor must make a capital contribution (typically 7 to 10 days after a capital call). Most established open-end funds have "subscription queues" under which investors sign subscription agreements in order to get into line to be admitted into the fund within 6 to 18 months later. In closed-end funds, the investment period is typically in the range of two to five years, but potentially subject to extension by the general partner, sometimes with the consent of the fund's limited partner advisory committee.

During the investment period, the general partner has the right to issue capital calls for any purpose permitted under the fund documents. After the end of the investment period (sometimes called the "harvest period"), the general partner is expected to manage and sell off the fund's investments, and may make capital calls only to pay fees and expenses of the fund, to make investments committed to before the end of the investment period (including investments to complete developments, if applicable) and to make follow-on investments in previously acquired or related properties. Otherwise, the general partner typically may not make capital calls for new investments. Open-end funds do not have a finite investment period—they may make new investments at any time.

An investor's commitment to a fund is a binding contractual obligation and enforceable in court in the event that an investor fails to fund. In addition, the partnership agreement typically will contain an assortment of alternative remedies that the general partner may exercise against a defaulting investor. These remedies include some combination of the right to charge interest on delinquent contributions, the right to suspend or offset distributions to a defaulting investor, the loss of the defaulting investor's right to vote, dilution of the defaulting investor's interest in the fund, the right to cover delinquent contributions with a loan from another investor, or the right to redeem, or sell to a third party, a defaulting investor's interest in the fund at a significant discount.

Subscription Lines of Credit

To provide the fund with working capital and the flexibility to make investments before permanent financing or investors' capital is in place, funds (including open-end funds with subscription queues) frequently will obtain a subscription line of credit from a bank, secured by a collateral assignment of the general partner's right to make capital calls. The lender will loan an amount up to a stated percentage of undrawn capital commitments made by investors that meet the lender's underwriting requirements.

In the event of a default, the lender itself may make capital calls on the limited partners (still subject to the limits of their capital commitments) in order to repay the subscription line. In connection with a subscription line of credit, investors generally will be asked to enter into an "investor letter," confirming their capital commitment to the fund and permitting the lender to exercise the general partner's right to make capital calls in the event of a default. Investors also may be asked for an "investor opinion," issued by their counsel, covering due formation, due authority, due execution, and other matters as may be requested by the lender. A subscription agreement likely will include a commitment on the part of the investor to enter into investor letters and obtain investor opinions, if required by the subscription lender. In recent years, investors have tried to limit the use of subscription lines under the theory that excessive borrowing under a subscription line artificially increases carried interest payable to the general partner (discussed later) while decreasing the return on investors' capital.

General Partner's Capital Commitment

In addition to third-party investors, the general partner or an affiliate of the general partner typically also makes a capital commitment to the fund. Whether the general partner is required to make a capital commitment and the amount of such commitment will be set forth in the PPM and may also be included in the governing documents of the fund. When a sponsor is primarily an investment advisor, the general partner's capital commitment is often in the range of 2 to 5 percent of total capital commitments, although it may, under certain circumstances, be less, particularly in very large funds. In cases where the sponsor also invests in real estate in its own right, such as a public company that raises a fund to invest in a class of assets, the capital commitments of the general partner and its affiliates may be a more significant percentage (often 15 to 20 percent or more) of the fund's total capital commitments. The general partner and its affiliates often do not have the right to vote on matters put to the investors for vote and usually do not pay a management fee or carried interest on their investment in the fund, but their capital commitments are otherwise treated the same as those of any other investors.

In some funds the general partner may be entitled to fund a portion of its capital contributions through a "management fee waiver," which means that the limited partners fund capital contributions on the general partner's behalf, and the management fee is reduced by a corresponding amount so that the net economics to the general partner and limited partners are the same as if the general partner had funded its commitment in cash. This management fee waiver mechanism conveys certain tax benefits to the individuals who invest through the general partner.

Asset Management Fee

In exchange for its services in identifying and evaluating prospective investments, monitoring investments, and determining exit strategies, the fund or the investors pay the general partner, or in some cases, an investment manager that is an affiliate of the general partner, an annual management fee. In the past, most closed-end funds had expressed the management fee as a percentage of committed capital during the investment period and a percentage of invested capital after the investment period. In the wake of the global financial crisis, some general partners have begun to provide instead for a management fee based on a percentage of invested capital throughout the term of the fund. The level of such fees usually ranges from 1 to 2 percent of committed or invested capital per year. In the case of open-end funds, and some closed-end funds, the management fee is a percentage of net asset value or net operating income. In some cases, a fund will offer tiered fees, such that investors with larger capital commitments pay a lower percentage than those with smaller capital commitments. In addition, large "angel" investors, admitted at a first closing, often pay discounted fees.

In some cases, affiliates of the general partner may be entitled to fees for providing services to the fund or its investments, called transaction fees (see the later discussion "Other Fees to Affiliates"). To the extent these fees are charged for providing services that are not real-estate related (such as financing fees, investment banking fees, or capital markets fees), a percentage of these fees (typically 80 to 100 percent) will reduce the management fee.

Distributions and the General Partner Promote

All cash distributed by the fund is distributed to the investors according to a formula, often referred to as the "distribution waterfall," set forth in the governing documents and disclosed in the PPM. Some funds include separate distribution waterfalls for cash generated by the ongoing operation of properties and cash generated by a capital event, such as the disposition of an investment. This feature is more common in credit funds than in funds that invest in equity.

In addition to distributions to investors based on their respective capital commitments and related contributions, the distribution waterfall provides the general partner with a share (typically 15 to 20 percent) of the profits, other than in the case of core funds, where such profit shares are less common. The general partner's share is often referred to as the "promote" or the "carried interest" and is paid separately from any management or other fees paid to the general partner or its affiliates.

In a closed-end fund, the waterfall will return to investors all or a portion of their capital before distributing carried interest. In some funds all invested capital must be returned before the general partner is entitled to a carried interest (this is called a "European" waterfall), whereas in other funds only the capital that funded previously sold or written-off investments must be returned before the general partner is entitled to its carried interest (this is called an "American" or "modified American" waterfall). Once capital has been returned, the investors are usually entitled to receive a specified return on their respective capital contributions (usually 8 or 9 percent), either as a preferred return or internal rate of return (IRR), before the general partner receives its promote.

In some cases where investors receive a preferred return, the general partner is subsequently entitled to a disproportionately large share of incremental profits (typically 50 to 100 percent) until the general partner has received its promote percentage on total profits. This arrangement is often referred to as a "catch-up" and results in the general partner receiving its promote percentage on all profits, not just those above the preferred return, as would be more typical in a joint venture arrangement.

A distribution waterfall with a full return of capital (i.e., a "European" waterfall) with an 8 percent preferred return, a 60/40 catch-up, and a 20 percent promote might read as follows:

Each distribution will be tentatively allocated among the Partners (including the general partner) in proportion to their respective aggregate capital contributions. Then, each limited partner's tentative share of such distribution shall be divided further between such limited partner, on the one hand, and the general partner, on the other hand, as follows:

> **Clause (a)** First, to the limited partner, until the limited partner has received cumulative distributions pursuant to this clause equal to the aggregate capital contributions made by such limited partner;

> **Clause (b)** Second, to the limited partner, until the limited partner has received cumulative distributions pursuant to this clause sufficient to provide an 8 percent cumulative, compounded annual return on amounts returned pursuant to Clause (a) calculated based on the actual date that each such capital contribution was made;

> **Clause (c)** Third, 60 percent to the general partner and 40 percent to the limited partner, until the general partner has received cumulative distributions pursuant to this Clause (c) equal to 20 percent of the sum of (i) cumulative distributions made to date to the limited partner pursuant to Clause (b) and this Clause (c) and (ii) cumulative distributions made to the general partner pursuant to this Clause (c);[1] and

> **Clause (d)** Thereafter; 20 percent to the general partner and 80 percent to the limited partner.

Assume, for example, that a partnership has two limited partners and $200 to distribute; the general partner has made capital contributions in the aggregate amount of $20; Limited Partner A has made capital contributions in the aggregate amount of $30, Limited Partner B has made capital contributions in the aggregate amount of $50; and all capital contributions have been outstanding for a period of one year. In such case, distributions would be made as follows.

Pursuant to the introductory paragraph of the distribution waterfall, the $200 available for distribution would be tentatively allocated among the partners (including the general partner) in proportion to their respective aggregate capital contributions: $40 for the general partner, $60 for Limited Partner A, and $100 for Limited Partner B. Then the amount allocated to the general partner would be distributed to the general partner and the amount allocated to each limited partner would be further allocated between such limited partner and the general partner and distributed as follows.

With respect to Limited Partner A:

> **(a)** First, $30 would be allocated to Limited Partner A to return its aggregate capital contributions;

> **(b)** Second, $2.40 would be allocated to Limited Partner A to provide an 8 percent cumulative, compounded annual return on its aggregate capital contributions;

> **(c)** Third, $0.72 would be allocated to the general partner and $0.48 to Limited Partner A, so that the general partner has received distributions equal to 20 percent of $3.60

($3.60 being the sum of $2.88 in cumulative distributions to Limited Partner A (distributed pursuant to clauses (b) and (c)) and $0.72 in cumulative distributions to the general partner (distributed pursuant to clause (c)); and

(d) Thereafter, out of the remaining $26.40 of the $60 of available distributions initially allocated to Limited Partner A (pursuant to the first paragraph of the distribution waterfall), 20 percent, or $5.28, would be allocated to the general partner and 80 percent, or $21.12, to Limited Partner A.

Then, with respect to Limited Partner B:

(a) First, $50 would be allocated to Limited Partner B to return its aggregate capital contributions;

(b) Second, $4 would be allocated to Limited Partner B to provide an 8 percent cumulative, compounded annual return on its aggregate capital contributions;

(c) Third, $1.20 would be allocated to the general partner and $0.80 to Limited Partner B, so that the general partner has received distributions equal to 20 percent of $6.00 ($6.00 being the sum of $4.80 in cumulative distributions to Limited Partner B distributed pursuant to clauses (b) and (c)) and $1.20 in cumulative distributions made to the general partner (distributed pursuant to clause (c)); and

(d) Thereafter, of the remaining $44 of the $100 of available distributions initially allocated to Limited Partner B (pursuant to the first paragraph of the distribution waterfall), 20 percent, or $8.80, would be allocated to the general partner and 80 percent, or $35.20, to Limited Partner B.

The ultimate distributions thus would be $54 to Limited Partner A, $90 to Limited Partner B, and $56 to the general partner. The general partner's distribution would be the sum of the $40 distributed with respect to its own investment, the $6 in promote distributed with respect to Limited Partner A's investment, and the $10 in promote distributed with respect to Limited Partner B's investment. This example includes the catch-up mechanism set forth in Clause (c), and we assumed that the total amount distributed would be sufficient to satisfy each tier of the waterfall (meaning that distributions would in fact be made pursuant to Clause (d)). So even though each limited partner receives a preferred return before the general partner is paid a promote, the general partner's promote with respect to each limited partner would equal a full 20 percent of the profits distributed to such limited partner (20 percent of the $80 of aggregate profit distributed to limited partners is $16).

If the distribution waterfall did not include a catch-up mechanism, the general partner's promote with respect to each limited partner would be equal to 20 percent of the profits distributed to such limited partner after the 8 percent preferred return had been paid to the limited partner. In the example set forth previously, without the catch-up specified in Clause (c) of the distribution waterfall, the ultimate distributions would be $54.48 to Limited Partner A, $90.80 to Limited Partner B, and $54.72 to the general partner. In this case, the general partner's distribution would include $40 distributed with respect to the general partner's own investment, $5.52 in promote distributed with respect to Limited Partner A's investment, and $9.20 in promote distributed with respect to Limited Partner B's investment.

Because an open-end fund is not expected to liquidate within a specific time period, regular (often quarterly) distributions of cash flow are made pro rata to the investors. Rather than receiving a distribution upon liquidation of the fund, an investor may, subject to certain limitations, request that the fund redeem its shares whenever the investor is ready to exit the investment. An exiting investor's shares are redeemed at the same price an incoming investor would pay to purchase shares in the fund at that time. The sale or redemption price of a share is based on the fund's net asset value, which will be calculated by the general partner at regular intervals, in accordance with the fund's valuation policy and often in reliance on a third-party valuation of the fund's assets.

The general partner's promote in an open-end fund (often called an "incentive allocation") is calculated at regular intervals (usually annually) and distributable to the general partner at such intervals, subject to holdbacks in certain cases (as described later), based on the appreciation in the net asset value of the fund over the relevant interval. In the event that fund's net asset value depreciates over the relevant interval, the amount of the depreciation usually must be returned to investors who experienced a loss before the general partner is entitled to an incentive allocation with respect to those investors.

Other Fees to Affiliates

In addition to the asset-management fee, a fund may pay a variety of fees to the general partner or its affiliates for services provided to the fund. In the event that these fees are paid in respect of real estate services (such as property management, leasing, development, construction management, acquisition or disposition support), the general partner or its affiliate may be able to retain these fees without offset or reduction of the management fee. The partnership agreement generally should require that such services be provided at rates and on terms and conditions comparable to those that would be negotiated with a third party at arm's length or alternatively, should schedule out the fees that will be payable. Transactions between the fund and the general partner or any affiliate of the general partner other than those explicitly disclosed in the PPM or partnership agreement generally will require disclosure to or the approval of the advisory committee, or some other subset of the investors.

Reinvestment Provisions

Some closed-end funds permit the reinvestment of capital, or of capital and profits, by the general partner during the investment period. Funds that permit the general partner to withhold capital for reinvestment often also permit it to recall for reinvestment capital previously distributed during the investment period. These reinvestments are subject to the same timing and investment limitations and controls as are initial investments. Open-end funds generally reinvest substantially all of their capital, except for dividend distributions that they pay periodically, which generally tend to be a small percentage (e.g., 2 percent) of the fund's overall net asset value or income.

General Partner Clawback

If early sales by a closed-end fund generate profits and later sales do not, it is possible that the general partner could receive promote distributions that exceed the promote to which it is ultimately entitled. In most closed-end funds, such situations are addressed through an obligation on the general partner to return to the fund all or part of the promote distributions previously received so that cumulative promote distributions to the general partner do not exceed the percentage of the fund's overall profits to which the general partner is entitled. Such an obligation is referred to as a "general partner clawback." A general partner clawback obligation is generally net of taxes paid by the general partner on the original distributions, although the SEC has recently proposed a rule that would require the general partner to pay back all of its excess carried interest regardless of any taxes it paid. Where the general partner is a single-purpose entity, its clawback obligations may be guaranteed by the sponsor or the individual carried interest recipients (usually on a several basis).

Limited Partner Giveback

Some partnership agreements permit a closed-end fund to recall distributions from investors in order to pay the fund's obligations to the extent that the fund has insufficient capital and assets on hand. This right to recall money distributed to investors is referred to as a "limited-partner giveback" and often survives the termination of the fund for a period of two to three years. The investors' liability should be limited to a percentage (usually between 20 and 30 percent in a commingled fund) of distributions or capital commitments, or to distributions made over a specific period of time prior to the giveback (usually two to three years).

GOVERNANCE TERMS

Investment Limitations

The general partner of a commingled fund has significant discretion to make decisions on behalf of the fund. The general partner's investment decisions are made within the parameters of the investment strategy described in the PPM and certain guidelines and limitations set forth in the partnership agreement.

Investment limitations generally take one of two forms: strategic definition or fund diversification. Limitation by strategic definition relates to the investment strategy and defines the sort of property in which the fund intends to invest. The limitations may restrict the type of asset (retail, industrial, office, multifamily, hotel, etc.); development status (whether the property is under development, stabilized, or in need of renovation or redevelopment); location (a specific country, region, or market [or type of market]); or size of the property to be acquired (either in terms of price or square footage). Fund diversification limitations are intended to allow investment decisions that promote diversification of the fund's portfolio. Such limitations often relate to geographic concentration of assets or the size of individual assets relative to the intended size of the portfolio. As long as the general partner's investment decisions comply with these limitations, the general partner typically need not seek limited partner approval of its investment decisions. The general partner is often permitted to deviate from fund diversification guidelines with the consent of the advisory committee.

Leverage Policy

Most funds include a policy regulating the use of leverage by the fund. Some leverage policies take the form of a simple threshold, usually measured at the time debt is incurred. Organizing documents may specify, for example, that "the fund may not incur indebtedness if, at the time of incurrence, doing so would cause the aggregate indebtedness of the fund to exceed 65 percent of the aggregate gross value of the fund's assets." Other leverage policies go into significantly more detail about what kind of debt may be incurred. Such a detailed policy might address the amount of debt permitted with respect to a single asset or investment, whether and how much floating- or adjustable-rate debt is permissible; whether, and to what extent, debt may be cross-collateralized; whether or not debt may grant recourse to a particular entity; and whether and on what basis the debt must permit substitution of collateral. Since the global financial crisis, investors have become more focused on defining leverage policies and limitations and providing for investor or advisory committee approval of changes or exceptions thereto.

Exclusivity

Some general partners or sponsors offer a fund the exclusive right to acquire a particular type of property during a specified period of time. The type of property subject to the exclusivity coincides with the fund's investment guidelines and restrictions. Exclusivity usually includes several exceptions, intended either to preserve the sponsor's right to engage in transactions that could not be accomplished by investing through the fund or to prevent the fund from acquiring properties inappropriate to its goals and objectives. Typical exceptions include properties acquired in tax-deferred transactions (such as Internal Revenue Code Section 1031 transactions or exchanges for "down-REIT" units in the sponsor); properties adjacent to, or in close proximity with, others owned by the sponsor or its other clients; properties not targeted by the fund due to geography, purchase price, size, or other characteristics usually specified in some detail in the exception; properties that are outside of the scope of the fund's investment restrictions; or properties that the general partner has in good faith determined are not appropriate for the fund.

In some cases where a sponsor has multiple funds, separate accounts, or other investment vehicles that may invest in overlapping property types, the sponsor may rely on an allocation policy to determine which investment vehicle should be offered a specific property. These policies may be based on a set rotation known to each of the investment vehicles or on the decision of an allocation committee, which allows multiple investment vehicles to participate side by side in an investment. A sponsor must disclose its allocation policy to investors and often is required to report regularly how investments have been allocated.

Advisory Committee

Many general partners establish an advisory committee to review and consent to conflicts of interest; review and/or approve certain other matters, such as investment allocations, valuations, and fees paid to affiliates; and advise on other matters in the general partner's discretions. The advisory committee is typically made up of representatives of investors selected by the general partner. Investors with a relatively large investment in the fund may be able to secure a side-letter commitment from the general partner that they will be represented on the advisory committee.

The governing documents of the fund will specify the matters subject to the approval of the advisory committee, including the margin by which such matters must be approved (unanimous, majority-in-interest, or some other percentage) and how votes are allocated (most typically, per-investor). There is significant variation among funds on the issue of which matters will be submitted to the advisory committee, but most require advisory committee approval for conflicts of interest and deviations from specified policies. As oversight by the Securities and Exchange Commission (SEC) over the funds industry has increased, advisory committees have become a much more important tool for approving conflict transactions and providing support for interpretive decisions made by general partners about the terms of fund governing documents.

Transfers of Interest and Redemptions

In both closed- and open-end funds, an investor should expect to have limited rights to transfer its interest. Any transfer of interest will typically require the general partner's written consent, which the partnership agreement typically allows to be given or withheld in the general partner's sole discretion. Transfers to affiliates may be explicitly permitted under some partnership agreements or may be permitted by negotiated side letters. In some cases, the fund may have a right of first refusal over transfers. The transferor and transferee may be required to pay any costs accruing to the general partner and the fund in connection with the transfer and to provide legal opinions with respect thereto.

Investors in an open-end fund usually have a right to apply for redemption of their interests, although they may be required to hold their interests for some specified period of time before such request may be made (this is referred to as a lock-up). If the fund has sufficient cash available when a request for redemption is made, the fund will repurchase the limited partner's interest at a price specified in the partnership agreement. The redemption price is typically based on the fund's net asset value, generally defined as the value of all assets held by the fund, less the amount of its indebtedness, with the value of properties being determined by third-party appraisals conducted on a routine basis. Investors can expect that the definition of net asset value set forth in a partnership agreement will be very detailed, specifying by what means and how often assets will be valued, and how debt is accounted for. The partnership agreement also will specify how to determine whether the fund has sufficient cash available to redeem an investor's interest, and if so, when and on what terms the fund must take actions such as selling or refinancing properties in order to make cash available to redeem investors' interests.

It is often the case that the fund is permitted to use its cash for a number of other purposes, including meeting existing obligations and making new investments, before fulfilling redemption requests. If multiple investors have requested redemption or if the fund has insufficient cash to make a redemption, those requesting redemption will enter a "redemption queue" to be redeemed when the fund has sufficient cash. Investors in the redemption queue are generally redeemed pro rata to the extent of the cash available for redemptions. This pro ration may be based on the relative net asset values of the investors' interests in the fund, or less frequently, the size of their redemption request. Funds may suspend redemptions altogether during times of market stress or when redemption requests exceed a specified percentage of net asset value (this is called a "gate"). Closed-end funds do not permit investors to redeem their interests.

Key Person Provisions

In cases where the general partner's or sponsor's expertise in managing a fund's investments is dependent upon the expertise of a particular individual or group of individuals, the partnership agreement may include a "key person" provision that specifies certain consequences if the key person ceases to devote a specified amount of his or her time to the fund or to maintain a certain level of responsibility with respect thereto. In the case of a group of individuals, the key person provision may be triggered if a specified number of the key persons, or one specified key person and a specified number of other individuals, cease to meet specified commitments. The most common remedy for violation of key person requirements is a suspension of the investment period until such time as the key person requirements are met. In some cases, violation of the provision may trigger a termination of the investment period. If the key person requirements cannot be met within a specified period of time (usually between three months and a year), investors representing a majority interest may have the right to permanently terminate the investment period, to require the fund to liquidate, or in some cases, to remove and replace the general partner. The partnership agreement may also include a mechanism for replacement of a key person by a similarly qualified individual, without triggering any such remedies. An open-end funds may provide for the termination of investor lock-ups following a key person event, instead of terminating the fund's right to make new investments.

Removal of the General Partner

Inasmuch as commingled funds permit the general partner to exercise significant discretion, the ultimate control afforded investors lies in a right to remove a general partner. Nearly all funds permit removal of the general partner "for cause," including, typically, acts of fraud, bad faith, gross negligence, and possibly other acts such as breach of a designated standard of care. In addition, some funds permit investors to remove the general partner without cause; that is, for any reason, or no reason at all.

Removal of the general partner is generally accomplished by a vote of the investors, excluding the general partner and any of that partner's affiliates. A simple majority-in-interest vote may suffice to remove a general partner, particularly for cause, or a significantly higher threshold may be required. A fund typically requires a greater percentile to vote in favor of removal *without cause* than may be required for a removal *for cause.*

Upon removal of the general partner, the partnership agreement may permit the investors to bring in a substitute general partner or may require that the fund liquidate. Often if the general partner is removed without cause, it will be entitled to its full carried interest in respect of investments made prior to its removal, whereas if the general partner is removed for cause, it will forfeit a portion of its carried interest (usually between 25 and 50 percent, although this could be as much as 100 percent).

Liability and Indemnity

Except for certain "disabling conduct" such as fraud or gross negligence, the general partner generally is exculpated and will receive indemnity for all losses incurred in the performance of its duties. The definition of disabling conduct varies among funds. In some, it is limited to fraud, bad faith, or gross negligence. Others impose a standard of care obligation, such as the obligation to act with the same care and skill as a reasonably prudent real estate investment manager.

While the terms of commingled real estate investment funds will vary based on the sponsor's investment strategy, objectives, and negotiations with investors, most funds rely on similar basic terms. When considering investment in any particular fund, non-US investors should review the PPM and partnership agreement (or other governing document) in detail. A review of term sheets for a number of commingled real estate investment funds will reveal a range of idiosyncratic terms, but also general adherence to the basic structure and concepts described in this chapter.

NOTE

1. Note the recursive nature of this provision. This results in the general partner receiving 20 percent of all profit distributions.

Loan Rules

Restructuring and Workouts of Real Estate Loans

Sheri Chromow, SPC Advisors

Tim Little, National Real Estate Department Chair,
Katten Muchin Rosenman LLP

As we emerge from the global COVID pandemic, virtually every real estate market and property type is facing very strong headwinds. The pandemic accelerated negative trends that were already impacting real estate. Retail, already impacted by online shopping, saw many stores fail to survive lockdowns and further growth in online buying. Before COVID, companies were already using less office space per employee, and now landlords will have to adjust to the consequences of remote and hybrid work. Increased interest rates, inflation, and economic uncertainty (and the resultant higher cap rates) are impacting even multifamily prices and threatening the residential market. These factors will create rough seas for real estate in the near term.

However, this real estate downturn will likely look very different than the distress that came after the Great Financial Crisis of 2008. The financial crisis created large reductions in real estate values, but interest rates remained at or near zero. Mortgage loans could not be repaid through sales or refinancing, but debt service could usually be kept current from cash flow. This allowed lenders to adopt an "extend and pretend" strategy—a strategy that bank regulators encouraged and ultimately proved successful in many cases. In contrast, lenders this time around face declining asset values, increasing interest rates, and cash flow deficits making simple extensions without restructuring impractical. This chapter examines real estate loan workouts and restructurings with a focus on the impact that the different conditions characterizing this downturn may have.

DISCOVERING DISTRESS

Lenders should have systems in place to identify early indications that a loan is in distress. Financial reporting by borrower can indicate signs of distress. More often than not, however, distress is directly disclosed by the borrower to "get ahead" of an impending default or because it desires to obtain some concession, waiver, or restructuring from the lender.

Once a lender becomes aware that a loan is in distress, it must take some key initial steps, including:

- Prenegotiation agreement
- Legal diligence
- Property diligence
- Sponsor diligence

Prenegotiation Agreements

The start of the workout process will likely involve a series of fact-finding and discovery discussions between the lender and borrower. The lender should condition its participation in these discussions on the execution of a "prenegotiation agreement" by all involved parties. Prenegotiation agreements specify that the discussions between lender and borrower are not binding unless and until any agreement reached is memorialized in a signed agreement and that no statements during the settlement discussions will be admissible in court. A prenegotiation agreement permits free discussions without concern about statements being used in a subsequent litigation. A prenegotiation agreement does not require that the lender parties agree to a standstill, will provide that no party has any obligation to enter into an agreement, and gives each party the right to withdraw from negotiations at any time and for any or no reason.[1]

For syndicated loans, the agent should also consider having all lenders enter into a "common interest sharing agreement" to extend attorney-client privilege across the syndicate to protect communications between the lenders.

Legal Review

At the same time, a lender should commence a thorough legal review of the loan:

- Is the loan file is complete?
- Have all documents been signed, mortgages recorded, pledged accounts opened, and Uniform Commercial Code financing statements filed (and if necessary, continued)?
- Have final title insurance policies been issued?
- Are there future funding obligations under the loan documents, and what are the conditions to funding?
- What consent and waivers have been issued?
- Does the correspondence (including email files) contain potential agreements, waivers, dealings, or conduct between the parties that might affect the interpretation of the loan documents in a later dispute?
- In syndicated or multitranche loans, what consent rights do other lenders have with respect to a potential workout, and is there any required process?[2]

Finally, the lender team should examine potential recourse to any guarantor. Real estate loans typically include a nonrecourse carveout guaranty pursuant to which a creditworthy affiliate of the borrower guarantees repayment of any losses suffered by the lender as a result of certain specified actions by the borrower or guarantor.[3] The lender team should review any such guaranty to determine whether any specified action has occurred. Potential claims under nonrecourse carveout guaranties can provide valuable leverage in workout negotiations.

Property Review

When a loan is on the threshold of a default, the lender must take a hard look at the underlying property. What are the issues impacting the underlying property? Is the problem one of valuation (i.e., ability to repay/refinance at maturity), cash flow, or both? Is the cash flow expected to continue at current levels? Does the property require additional capital? A thorough assessment of value, cash flow, capital needs, and prospects will likely require accurate and complete current financials and cooperation from the borrower. A borrower's willingness to be forthright and transparent with information can be a useful early indicator of whether continued control by the borrower is advisable.

Sponsor Review

When, like presently, a real estate downturn is triggered by macroeconomic factors, lenders may find that despite a loan being in distress or default, the borrower/sponsor may be in the best position to maximize the lender's ultimate recovery. To help make that determination, lenders should look to the expertise, reputation, and track record of the sponsor, including their history of compliance with the loan documents. Most important, the borrower should submit a business plan detailing the actions that it will take and the approximate timeframe in order to maximize the property value (and the lender's recovery).

WORKING OUT THE LOAN

There are many approaches to working out or restructuring a loan. They include:

- Simple extension (for a maturity default)
- Forbearance
- Short sale
- Restructure

Forbearance

A forbearance agreement contains an acknowledgment of specific default(s) and sets forth the terms on which the lender will forbear from exercising its remedies.[4] The forbearance agreement could also spell out additional rights and remedies of the lender in the event the borrower fails to comply with the agreement's terms. Some lenders even require the borrower to deliver a deed to be held in escrow until an event of default under the forbearance agreement occurs, at which time the deed would be released and recorded—effectively converting into a deed in lieu of foreclosure.[5]

Short Sales

In a "short sale," a lender allows a borrower to market and sell a property even if the ultimate sales price will be less than the loan balance. Generally, the market exacts a discount on property sold out of a "foreclosure," so a short sale may produce a better recovery than a foreclosure followed by a sale by the lender. Borrowers are often willing to undertake such processes (even though they will not get any return of equity from the sale) because they would like to avoid foreclosures in their track records. They can also be incentivized with payments tied to achieving certain pricing levels.

Rescue Capital

In the current environment, many properties may find themselves in need of some type of "rescue capital," a capital infusion for necessary capital projects or leasing costs to fund operating deficits or reserves or to pay down debt and reduce debt service. Borrowers may not have such capital, or even if they do, may not be willing to invest new money that is unlikely to attract an acceptable return. Preferred equity and mezzanine debt could be options for rescue capital, but these forms of investment often require a "current pay" component that could exceed the property's cash flow. They also push the borrower's equity behind a greater amount of leverage, so they may be unacceptable to borrowers.

One additional source for potential rescue capital could be the lender itself. A lender may be able to encourage additional equity investment by the sponsor by converting a portion of its loan into equity or otherwise subordinating such portion to the new money. The immediate reaction of most lenders is to never allow equity recovery before repayment of the debt. However, taking back a property that is currently worth less than the debt will result in an immediate loss for the lender. If a portion of the loan is converted into a subordinate cash flow interest, the ultimate recovery could be greater. Critically, the lender must balance maximizing its recovery with leaving enough on the table to sufficiently motivate the borrower.

If the Workout Fails

If workout negotiations are unsuccessful, at some point the lender(s) will have to proceed against the collateral. The process for "foreclosing a mortgage" varies significantly from state to state. A judicial foreclosure involves an actual litigation and is typically time-consuming and costly. Nonjudicial foreclosures are much quicker but may involve rights of redemption or antideficiency restrictions.[6]

Alternatively, the lender can attempt to negotiate a deed in lieu of foreclosure, whereby the borrower agrees to convey the property to the lender. Deeds in lieu save time and money but do not eliminate subordinate liens.

A lender could also choose to sell its loan in the secondary market. There is a large, relatively liquid market for secondary sale of distressed debt. Distressed real estate loans, however, typically sell at a substantial discount. Those who opt to sell may be more concerned with the speed and certainty of closing than with price. Given the growth in debt funds since the Great Financial Crisis, it will be interesting to see whether they are active buyers, sellers, or both in this cycle.

Suing the Borrower and/or Guarantor

Virtually all large commercial real estate loans are nonrecourse; the lender has recourse to the borrower only to the extent of the borrower's interest in the property. Borrowers themselves are special purpose entities (SPEs) and do not have meaningful assets beyond the property. As a result, the ability to sue a borrower for a "deficiency" after foreclosure is seldom important. If, however, the borrower has committed one of the bad acts specified in the nonrecourse carveout guaranty, the lender can sue the guarantor for any resulting loss (and in some cases, even for the entire debt), but a lender's "loss" from a particular bad act may be difficult to prove.

Typical Borrower Defenses

Borrowers may seek to contest or delay a foreclosure by raising defenses.[7] Borrowers have argued that the lender promised to extend the loan or provide refinancing or that the lender effectively waived a default. During the Great Financial Crisis many borrowers unsuccessfully argued that extension conditions tied to the debt-service coverage ratio (DSCR), which assumed an interest rate, were unreasonable because actual rates at the time were much lower than the assumed rate.[8]

Sources of Lender Liability

Allegations of lender misconduct and potential liability have been plentiful in distressed loan situations. These claims are often raised to create leverage in workout negotiations, but they rarely result in actual liability for the lender. The claims are many but usually fit into one of the following categories:

- Wrongful failure to make required advances or disbursements
- Misconduct in exercising approval rights
- Exercising too much control over the borrower (telling the borrower what to do rather than approving proposed actions)
- Breach of some agreement created by course of conduct outside of the loan documents

TRANCHE WARFARE

Workouts and restructurings become more complicated when there are multiple lenders. Restructuring multilender loans requires one to understand the often diverging interests of senior and junior lenders and their respective rights in highly structured deals. A highly leveraged deal might consist of a senior mortgage loan and one or more mezzanine loans. Different types of lenders (banks, insurance companies, debt funds) may have different regulatory environments and business objectives.

An intercreditor agreement governs the relationship between mortgage and mezzanine lenders and will restrict the lenders' ability to modify the terms of their loans without the other lenders' consent. These restrictions often mean that neither the senior loan nor the mezzanine loan can be restructured without the other lenders' consent.[9]

In syndicated loans, it is not uncommon for a syndicate lender to withhold its consent to a restructuring or short sale in the hope that one or more of the remaining lenders will buy its note and take it out of the deal. To avoid this, care must be taken in forming the syndicate, crafting transfer provisions, and limiting unanimous consent rights.

BANKRUPTCY

Commercial real estate loans are structured to minimize the risk that the borrower will end up as a debtor in a bankruptcy. Lenders require that borrowers be organized as special purpose entities (SPEs), meaning the only permitted business and activities of the borrower entity are those related to owning the applicable property, and use techniques like independent directors or issuing a small ownership interest to the lender to prevent filing. These techniques are useful but not foolproof as the bankruptcy court takes a dim view of restrictions on filing and both independent directors (general growth) and so-called Golden Share (245 Park Avenue) have failed to prevent a bankruptcy.

The most effective bankruptcy protection is that most commercial real estate loans include a nonrecourse carveout guaranty or indemnity from a creditworthy guarantor providing, among other things, that the applicable guarantor will be fully liable for the loan if the borrower files a voluntary petition in bankruptcy or the borrower or sponsor becomes involved in a collusive involuntary filing against the borrower. These "bad-boy" guarantees have been a powerful deterrent to a borrower filing for bankruptcy. They do not work, however, if the guarantor itself is insolvent. Nonetheless, use of nonrecourse carveout guaranties has greatly reduced the number of bankruptcy filings by real estate borrowers.

NOTES

1. Some lenders include provisions in prenegotiation agreements (1) requiring that all attorneys' fees and expenses incurred by the lender in connection with the negotiations will be borne by the borrower and guarantor, (2) whereby the borrower parties acknowledge that the loan documents are enforceable and remain in full force and effect, or (3) waiving any claims the borrower may otherwise want to assert. There is no one formula. Obviously, these type of provisions benefit the lender and could disadvantage the borrower, so they may be resisted by the borrower. Lenders need to balance the benefit of obtaining such a provision against the cost of potential delays in workout discussions until a prenegotiation agreement is signed.
2. Some colender and intercreditor agreements, for example, require the agent to develop and propose a default plan for review and consent by the lenders.
3. The loan could also include (1) a carry guaranty, which is a guaranty to pay specified costs, like debt service, taxes, and insurance, (2) a guaranty of leasing costs, (3) a completion guaranty (either for a construction loan or in connection with a loan for a property that requires a significant capital improvement), or (4) other deal-specific credit support.
4. For example, a lender might impose additional approval requirements, reserves, or cash controls as a condition of forbearance.
5. It should be noted, however, that courts may view deeds in escrow as an impermissible circumvention of foreclosure procedure and refuse to enforce them, as is the case in New York. The risk that it may not be enforced has not deterred many lenders who routinely require a so-called deed in the box as a condition to forbearance.
6. A right of redemption gives the borrower a right to reacquire the property so long as it pays off the loan within a statutory time period (which could extend beyond the foreclosure). An antideficiency statute limits the lender's ability to sue the borrower to recover any difference between the amount of the loan and the value of the foreclosed property.
7. A borrower may, for example, want to delay certain negative tax consequences that will be triggered by a foreclosure to a subsequent tax year.
8. Borrowers might also assert defenses based on any number of legal theories, such as an oral agreement to waive, modify or forbear; fraud; misrepresentation; tortious interference with the borrower's business relationships; negligence; breach of implied covenant of good faith and fair dealing; breach of fiduciary duty; economic duress; unconscionability; overreaching; unequal bargaining position; estoppel; detrimental reliance; and others.
9. For example, typically, the maturity of neither the mortgage loan nor the mezzanine loan can be extended significantly without consent. Maturity extension is a common feature of many workouts.

Understanding Bankruptcy

Issues for Non-US-Based Investors

David Miller, Partner, Pillsbury

Patrick Potter, Partner, Pillsbury

t is always wise to be prepared for the inevitable downturns in the business cycle. From March 2022 through July 2023, the US Federal Reserve increased the federal funds rate 11 times, from 0.25 to 5.50 percent, with concomitant increases in U.S. Treasury and other indexes, resulting in substantially higher interest rates for commercial real estate borrowers in the US. During much of the same time period, the volume of commercial mortgage-backed security (CMBS) issuances has reportedly fallen by 80 percent, with that market being described at times as being "frozen."[1] Even blue chip real estate firms have begun defaulting on billions of dollars of commercial real estate loans.

While as of late summer 2023 certain inflation indicators have improved, many asset values have already sharply declined. Against these headwinds, $1.5 trillion of commercial real estate debt reportedly is scheduled to mature during the next three years. The dominant industry seeking relief under the U.S. Bankruptcy Code since 2020 has been commercial real estate, in sundry classes. In addition, numerous American retail icons have sought (and continue to seek) bankruptcy relief in the US in order to terminate or renegotiate tens of thousands of leases. Presently, there is every reason to believe that some greater number of asset owners will seek bankruptcy or consensual relief, and those deals that are consensually restructured will likely attempt to emulate what could be accomplished under the U.S. Bankruptcy Code without having to actually file for bankruptcy and incur all of the associated costs. For at least these reasons, non-US investors should understand what makes US bankruptcy unique from counterparts in other countries, as well as some of the significant tools available to real estate debtors under US bankruptcy law, and corresponding protections for lenders and other creditors.

US BANKRUPTCY FRAMEWORK

In this section, we briefly introduce concepts that are discussed in more detail in later sections.

The U.S. Bankruptcy Code[2] is the statute governing liquidation and reorganization of debts throughout the US. It is a federal statute, enacted by the U.S. Congress.

Administering the U.S. Bankruptcy Code are the bankruptcy courts, which are physically located in every state and judicial district in the US, including its territories. Appeals of decisions of a bankruptcy court can go to a U.S. District Court or in some instances a bankruptcy appellate panel, comprised of three bankruptcy judges. Further appeals are to the U.S. Court of Appeals for the region where the bankruptcy court is located, and then the highest federal court, the U.S. Supreme Court. All appeals from final judgments are as a matter of right, except for appeals to the Supreme Court, which possesses absolute discretion on the bankruptcy decisions it will review. Binding precedent (meaning case law decisions from a higher court that a lower court must follow and comply with) comes from the Supreme Court and each region's Court of Appeals. All other decisions may be considered persuasive, but nonbinding, authority.

Within the US there also are state statutes and state courts that can affect parties in financial distress, and their creditors, outside of a formal bankruptcy proceeding.

The US (like the United Kingdom) is a common law jurisdiction, with an emphasis on the importance of prior court opinions in deciding future court cases. That is in contrast with code-based jurisdictions. Of course, the distinction is somewhat a matter of degree: the US has codes, and code-based jurisdictions have courts.

Key parties in a US bankruptcy case include (1) the debtor, which is the subject of the bankruptcy case, (2) creditors, some secured (with a perfected lien on property of sufficient value) and some unsecured (with no liens or to the extent of insufficient liens), (3) a case trustee, acting in some but not all cases, and (4) the Office of the U.S. Trustee, a component of the U.S. Department of Justice that facilitates the administration of bankruptcy cases.

A US bankruptcy case is commenced by the filing of a bankruptcy petition in the bankruptcy court. The petition can be filed by the debtor (a voluntary case) or by one or more creditors, depending on the circumstances (an involuntary case). A claim of a creditor is registered by filing of a proof of claim in or otherwise pursuant to the instructions of the bankruptcy court. Creditors may be organized into one or more committees, which may be official (in which case the committee's fees and expenses are paid by the debtor) or unofficial or ad hoc (where the members pay for the committee's fees and expenses).

The U.S. Bankruptcy Code includes chapters governing liquidations and reorganizations of various types of individuals and entities. Our focus is primarily on Chapter 11 of the U.S. Bankruptcy Code, the chapter allowing most forms of business debtors the opportunity to reorganize or to liquidate through going concern sales without the need to cease operations.

UNIQUE CHARACTERISTICS OF US BANKRUPTCIES

Transparency and Disclosure

The the US bankruptcy system operates on a uniquely high level of transparency across all types of bankruptcy, whether commercial or personal. Debtors in bankruptcy in the US are required to file with the bankruptcy court detailed schedules and statements that contain a comprehensive level of detail as to all assets, liabilities, agreements, and many other matters, including prebankruptcy transfers and transactions. While many other countries require similar disclosures from the debtor, that information is not typically made easily available to everyone wishing to review it.

In contrast, with very rare exceptions (usually involving personal identification information such as Social Security numbers, secret business formulas, and the like) every document filed in every bankruptcy case in the US (whether by debtors, creditors, or any other party) is made publicly available to anyone on the globe with internet access. For all cases, the US federal courts maintain a portal (commonly known as ECFs, electronic case files) which anyone can access for a relatively modest fee. In addition, in middle market and larger commercial cases, so-called noticing agents (private service providers) are usually retained by debtors to replicate the court dockets and filings, enabling anyone with internet access to obtain and review all case filings without any log-in credentials or fees.

The level of transparency will likely be meaningful to many non-US investors involved or interested in US bankruptcy, though will vary on a case-by-case basis. Actual involvement by non-US investors in US bankruptcy cases, such as by ownership in the debtor, filing a proof of claim, or involvement as a party or witness in an adversarial proceeding, will be a matter of public record and accessible to anyone interested in examining that information. Non-US investors wanting to avoid such public exposure will benefit from understanding the scope of transparency in US bankruptcy cases. Non-US investors interested in potentially investing or transacting with a reorganizing debtor in bankruptcy, such as by acquiring assets or business lines, will find that accessing public data for a target (separate from obtaining access to a private diligence data room) can be accomplished with relative ease.

No Insolvency Penalty or Insolvency Requirement

Some non-US insolvency regimes require (under potential penalty, including potential criminal sanctions in some cases) that the managers of a company undertake formal steps to announce and declare insolvency within a relatively brief time of becoming aware of such insolvency or its significant likelihood. In countries lacking the debtor-in-possession concept (discussed next), this often means that a third-party fiduciary is appointed to manage the enterprise through the insolvency process. While US managers can be held responsible for acts and omissions that breach a fiduciary duty, company insolvency alone usually is not sufficient to give rise to manager liability, and there is no US requirement (save perhaps reporting requirements under securities laws) that managers announce company insolvency or take actions to place the enterprise into a formal bankruptcy proceeding.

Many non-US insolvency regimes also require enterprise insolvency as a condition to seek formal bankruptcy relief, often requiring proof of such insolvency to be presented to a court before allowing a case to be officially opened and to proceed. In the US, however, there is no insolvency condition to commencing a case seeking any form of bankruptcy relief. Solvent and insolvent enterprises are equally eligible to file for bankruptcy relief, and voluntary bankruptcy cases are opened immediately (without any delay or judicial approval) upon the enterprise's filing of commencement papers, notably the bankruptcy petition. Debtors are required to file for bankruptcy in good faith, which is generally interpreted to mean that the filing is designed to fairly use the provisions available to debtors under the U.S. Bankruptcy Code.

Debtor in Possession

Non-US investors with experience in insolvency regimes outside the US are likely more familiar with the model where managers of an insolvent enterprise are largely if not completely replaced by a third-party fiduciary or insolvency officeholder when the enterprise declares insolvency. The policy considerations for this approach appear to range from lack of confidence in the competency of existing managers to outright lack of trust due in part to concerns about intentional wrongdoing. One thing that the COVID-19 pandemic has highlighted worldwide is that enterprise failure is often not the fault of the business managers. In any event, while this may be changing for some countries, the typical non-US model has historically turned over, to a person acting as a new third-party fiduciary, responsibility for administering the enterprise insolvency.

In contrast, under the US model, there is a strong presumption that managers of a bankrupt enterprise will continue to make all business decisions for the enterprise and will be responsible for managing the enterprise through the reorganization process. The underlying policy is based largely on the belief that the preexisting managers know the enterprise better than newcomers, and that with bankruptcy court and other supervision, existing managers are in the best position to guide the enterprise successfully through the bankruptcy process. That said, the U.S. Bankruptcy Code affords courts the authority to replace managers of a debtor with a trustee, usually upon presentation of evidence of fraud or, short of that, evidence that the existing managers have engaged in more serious malfeasance than merely making imprudent business decisions that led to enterprise insolvency.

Postbankruptcy Financing and Lender Protections

For a variety of reasons, including addressing liquidity crises for operations and paying what are often substantial reorganization costs, new financing is not available to an insolvent enterprise prebankruptcy but becomes available to it in bankruptcy. This is largely because loans made to debtors after commencement of a bankruptcy case are usually granted the highest level of secured priority and often receive other important benefits depending on the circumstances and needs of the case—all approved by the power of a US federal court order. Financing provided after commencement of a bankruptcy case commonly is called DIP financing, for debtor-in possession. A robust and competitive DIP lending industry has existed in US bankruptcy cases for decades. That said, in many larger cases, the DIP lender is the debtor's pre-bankruptcy lender, aiming to leverage its position as part of an overall exit strategy, whereas with smaller or closely held debtors, the DIP lender is often comprised of the principals of the debtor.

While an increasing number of non-US insolvency regimes, particularly those enacted in the last 10 years, allow for financing and lender protections during the bankruptcy case, many remain untested. So confident are DIP lenders in the protections approved by US bankruptcy court orders, that large multinational enterprises with non-US headquarters have, within the last few years, commenced main bankruptcy proceedings in the US, rather than filing main proceedings in their headquarters locales where DIP lenders lack the same high level of confidence that their negotiated rights will be protected and enforced.

Specialized Judges with Adequate Resources

Non-US investors may take comfort that bankruptcy cases in the US are adjudicated in the first instance by specialized bankruptcy judges, rather than generalized commercial judges (often lacking finance and insolvency expertise) or judges whose responsibilities include criminal or other noncommercial matters, as is often the case under insolvency regimes in other countries. Each US bankruptcy judge has their own staff, which usually includes at least two law-school trained clerks to assist with all judicial activities, including case preparation, research, and opinion writing. A host of additional resources exist to support bankruptcy judges (many of whom preside over literally thousands of commercial and consumer cases at any given time) in the administration of their duties. These include the Federal Judiciary Center, which provides continuous training to judges, as well as other federal agencies, such as the Office of the United States Trustee, whose responsibilities include monitoring and taking positions in all forms of bankruptcy proceedings, as warranted. Some bankruptcy judges say that they are also aided by high-caliber, prepared insolvency professionals. While the US is not entirely unique in all of these respects, there are insolvency regimes, particularly those enacted within the last 10 years, where the judiciary is more generalized, overwhelmed by caseloads, and lacking in sufficient resources. These factors inevitably affect the speed and success of insolvency proceedings.

The Cost-Speed Dynamic

US bankruptcy practice evolved from a culture that valued minimizing costs, through use of often lower-caliber and less expensive professional advisors, to an environment that sees value in high-caliber bankruptcy professionals, particularly those advising on large complicated financial reorganizations, who are compensated on the same basis as high-caliber professionals practicing in other disciplines. The net result of this and other factors adds to reorganization costs, making financial reorganization under the US model often considerably more expensive than reorganizations under non-US regimes.

Reactions by financially troubled enterprises (and other stakeholders) to the cost of a bankruptcy proceeding in the US range from (1) undertaking extraordinary efforts (including sometimes accepting risks of greater uncertainty) to avoid bankruptcy altogether to (2) before filing for bankruptcy, prenegotiating the enterprise's reorganization with major creditors to curtail the duration—and cost—of a bankruptcy proceeding. Reorganization professionals and other participants in the US bankruptcy system universally acknowledge that, the longer an enterprise remains in bankruptcy, the more increasingly difficult it becomes to emerge successfully from bankruptcy.

Current debtors and their advisors aspire to emerge successfully from bankruptcy in months, or sometimes days and weeks, rather than a year (or more). Non-US investors learning of a bankruptcy in which their interests are implicated should move expeditiously to protect their rights or risk the possibility of having them inadvertently and promptly compromised.

Precedents and Predictability

The bankruptcy statutes in many countries are spread throughout multiple commercial codes, often mixed within nonbankruptcy statutes and often with disjointed pieces enacted at various points and times rather than as a single, stand-alone, cohesive body of insolvency law as in the US. While newer insolvency regimes in other countries sometimes defy this description, many still incorporate by reference other statutory provisions that must be located and understood for full context. Separately, the legal opinions and decisions from judges adjudicating bankruptcy matters in many countries are often not easily found, making it difficult either to predict what a judge may do when confronted with certain facts, or to cite a comparable decision in an effort to persuade a judge to rule consistently. This latter issue can be particularly prevalent in non-common-law jurisdictions.

Non-US investors may take comfort in knowing that, in the US, nearly all the substantive statutes governing bankruptcy are found in a single, integrated, stand-alone code, the U.S. Bankruptcy Code, which is not commingled with nonbankruptcy statutes. The U.S.

Bankruptcy Code is supplemented by the U.S. Bankruptcy Rules, which govern bankruptcy court procedure, found in a single, concise volume. That said, each bankruptcy court does have its own local rules, and more often than not in the most active districts, each judge has their own chambers rules or guidelines for practice, though local and chambers rules are not constitutionally permitted to contradict the laws and procedures set out in the U.S. Bankruptcy Code or U.S. Bankruptcy Rules.

Further comfort comes from regular reporting in the US of court decisions and easy access to those decisions. This makes future decisions more predictable and should contribute to the efforts of those parties who are genuinely seeking to resolve their disputes without material judicial intervention. The US is a relatively large country with, at any given time, approximately 400 or more acting bankruptcy judges, so naturally there will be differing views of the law and some number of seemingly (if not actually) inconsistent court decisions. That said, precedents and predictability are important features of the US bankruptcy fabric and US law generally. Most bankruptcy judges understand that consistency and predictability can help reduce the number of disputes they are called upon to resolve. Most judges work hard to make their decisions consistent with preexisting decisions on analogous facts, even where preexisting decisions do not constitute binding precedent.

Non-US investors also should take comfort in knowing that, once the judge for a case has been selected—absent unusual circumstances—that judge will be the only judge ruling on matters in the bankruptcy case (short of appeal to a higher court). Additionally, that judge's positions on most or many bankruptcy matters will likely be a matter of public record and easily ascertainable.

SIGNIFICANT TOOLS AVAILABLE TO DEBTORS AND CORRESPONDING CREDITOR PROTECTIONS

Automatic Stay (Moratorium)

The filing of a bankruptcy petition in the US automatically opens a bankruptcy proceeding, creates a bankruptcy estate comprised of all the debtor's assets, regardless of the nature or location of the assets, and acts as an automatic stay of collection actions. This all happens without delay and without the need for any judicial approval or involvement of any kind. Whereas, in some non-US jurisdictions, the debtor must request a court order enjoining creditor-enforcement actions (often referred to as a moratorium), in the US, such an injunction (the automatic stay) arises automatically and immediately, as of the moment the bankruptcy petition is filed. Given the global scope and effect of the US automatic stay and the potential for relief against and recovery from those found to have violated the automatic stay, including compensatory and punitive damages, the best practice for a creditor faced with a US bankruptcy filing is to assume that the stay applies to any action that creditor may contemplate with respect to the debtor, unless and until it is entirely clear that such action can be taken without violating the stay. This may require obtaining a determination by the bankruptcy judge that the stay is inapplicable.

Policies underlying the breadth and immediacy of the automatic stay include (1) ensuring that similarly situated creditors are treated similarly, rather than the fastest and most aggressive creditors obtaining disproportionate recoveries, and (2) affording the debtor a breathing spell for its management to level set and focus on accomplishing the legitimate business objectives permitted by US bankruptcy law, all aimed at preserving enterprise value, jobs, and other business objectives.

As with the bankruptcy estate, the automatic stay in a US bankruptcy case is effective worldwide. Thus, a non-US creditor would violate the US automatic stay even if the creditor attempted to seize, outside of US territory, non-US assets. Whereas a party who does so and never enters the US and never has any assets in the US (or any jurisdiction where a US court order could be ultimately enforced) might avoid being held accountable for such a violation, non-US investors who do invest in or have a presence in the US, and locales where US orders can be enforced, are at risk of financial exposure for violating the US automatic stay.

The automatic stay is not without limits, and counsel should be consulted to explain exceptions and the circumstances when the automatic stay does not apply. Some exceptions related to commercial real estate are addressed later in this chapter. In addition, creditors can request that the court modify (or lift) the automatic stay to authorize a creditor to enforce its rights. While this is the exception rather than the rule, especially during the first 60 to 90 days of a bankruptcy case, the statutory basis for lifting the stay exists when a court finds that the economic value of a secured creditor's lien is eroding (or is already valued at less than the debt), and the likelihood of the debtor successfully and promptly reorganizing is unlikely (e.g., where sufficient creditor support for a reorganization plan is lacking).

Rejecting (Shedding) Burdensome Contracts

A second important tool made available to debtors under the U.S. Bankruptcy Code is the ability to reject executory contracts (generally defined as contracts where the debtor and its counterparty have ongoing performance obligations). If the debtor is a party to a contract where it is selling something for less than market rate (or its cost to do so), or if the debtor is contractually bound to purchase something for more than market rate, then it may decide that the best course of action for the enterprise is to request court approval to reject the contract. Courts apply the so-called business judgment rule to determine whether to approve or deny a debtor's rejection request and will not usually substitute their judicial judgment for that of the debtor's management. As a general proposition, and while there are specific exceptions in the U.S. Bankruptcy Code that must be consulted, once the court approves the rejection, the debtor is relieved of its specific performance obligations, and the counterparty is entitled to assert a breach-of-contract damages claim against the debtor. However, such claim is afforded general unsecured nonpriority status, and often likely to recover few, if any, cents on the dollar.

Use of Cash and Assets During the Case

Chapter 11 debtors are authorized, without the necessity of court approval, to spend unencumbered cash and dispose of assets in the ordinary course of the debtor's business. If the cash serves as collateral for a loan, however, then the debtor must either obtain the secured creditor's consent or obtain approval from the court to spend the cash. All nonordinary course transactions (e.g., selling the entire business or a business line) must be approved by the court after notice and opportunity to object have been given to creditors and parties in interest.

A highly valuable subsidiary tool in this category is the ability of the debtor to sell assets free and clear of all liabilities and claims, such that the buyer obtains pristine clear title to all assets, including successor liability. The processes for accomplishing free-and-clear asset sales have become somewhat routinized, largely predictable, substantially reliable, and usually expedited. Proceeds from the sale of encumbered and financially challenged assets and business lines are paid to secured creditors in order of legal priority, and when there are disputes, held in escrow (and sometimes the registry of the court) pending resolution. These sales are highly powerful tools for extracting assets and business from overleveraging, entanglements, and disputes that could otherwise result in loss of asset value, enterprise value, and jobs, the combined effect of which would otherwise result in negative economic impact.

The Opportunity (Not Guaranty) to Restructure and Discharge Debt

In addition to the benefits described previously, Chapter 11 of the U.S. Bankruptcy Code, affords debtors the opportunity to restructure and emerge from bankruptcy with a balance sheet and debt load that its business and revenue can support. Sometimes this occurs through the free-and-clear asset sale process described earlier, and sometimes it occurs through one of many different forms of recapitalization that may be available to the debtor. When it occurs through the vehicle of a reorganization plan, creditor involvement and support are important.

A reorganization plan is required to propose classes of creditors, with a similar nature and priority of creditors comprising a class. If the rights of creditors are compromised under the plan, then creditors are entitled to vote, by class, on whether to reject or approve a plan. Separate and apart from class voting, affected creditors have standing in their own right to argue a plan should not be approved for failure to satisfy one of the many legal criteria required for plan confirmation. Courts and stakeholders expect that debtors will promptly focus on negotiating with creditors to achieve substantial creditor support for the proposed plan. Ideally, the net result of the debtor's negotiations will be to obtain unanimous class support for plan confirmation, with few if any holdouts maintaining independent objections for the court to resolve. Nevertheless, mechanisms do exist in the U.S. Bankruptcy Code to enable the debtor to obtain plan confirmation (so-called cross-class cramdown) despite one or more dissenting classes of creditors voting to reject the plan.

Obtaining court approval of a cramdown plan in a traditional Chapter 11 proceeding is typically difficult, always requires at least one class of compromised creditors to vote for the plan, and usually requires the contribution of new funds by the debtor's equity holders if they are going to retain their ownership in the reorganized debtor. While the U.S. Bankruptcy Code allows for confirmation cramdown plans, it is generally accepted that the best results in a reorganization in bankruptcy are those achieved by negotiation and consensus and that the threat of cramdown is best used to that end, rather than one that is fully litigated.

THE MORE SIGNIFICANT AND FREQUENTLY USED REAL ESTATE PROVISIONS UNDER THE U.S. BANKRUPTCY CODE

Real Estate Specific Automatic Stay Issues

While the automatic stay applies to prevent a commercial landlord from evicting the debtor tenant, the automatic stay should not prevent eviction where the lease has terminated by the expiration of the stated term of the lease before commencement of or during the bankruptcy case. However, the cautious landlord may find it prudent to nevertheless obtain a ruling from the bankruptcy court that the automatic stay does not apply.

The automatic stay bars the commercial landlord from exercising rights during the bankruptcy case against a cash deposit posted by the debtor tenant, because the cash deposit is property of the bankruptcy estate. In contrast, however, a letter of credit procured by a debtor to support its lease obligations is not property of the estate, and as such, letters of credit are not subject to the automatic stay.

Single Asset Real Estate Debtors

A single asset real estate debtor (SARE) is a debtor (1) which owns a single property or project, (2) for which that property or project generates substantially all of the debtor's gross income, and (3) is not involved in any substantial business other than the operation of that real property or project. The SARE regime was enacted to expedite SARE cases, but SARE debtors are not eligible for the even more streamlined, affordable, and easier to accomplish reorganization process available for smaller businesses with third-party debts under $7.5 million (designated as Subchapter V of Chapter 11), and must instead use traditional Chapter 11, typically making it more expensive and time-consuming and therefore difficult to reorganize. Unlike non-SARE real estate debtors, SARE debtors must either file a confirmable reorganization plan within 90 days after filing the bankruptcy petition or commence debt service payments to its secured lenders at the nondefault contract rate of interest on a principal amount based on the value of the lender's collateral. Otherwise, the secured lender is entitled to prompt relief from the automatic stay to foreclose.

Real Estate Lease Assumption, Rejection, and Assignment Provisions: Debtor as Tenant

The debtor tenant enjoys the right to reject (and effectively terminate) the lease, vacate, turn over possession, and avoid making any further rent payments to the landlord. Alternatively, the debtor tenant may assume the lease (without modification), cure all monetary defaults, and upon proving it has the ability to do so, continue to perform for the duration of the lease. The debtor tenant may also assume the lease and assign the lease to a third party (often done where the rent is below market) despite an antiassignment provision in the lease.

Commercial debtor tenants have an initial four months from the bankruptcy filing to assume or reject a lease. That period can be extended by the court for up to an additional three months. Additional extensions require the landlord's consent. The U.S. Bankruptcy Code contemplates that during this period the debtor tenant will pay the rent that comes due from and after the bankruptcy case is commenced (by the filing of a petition), but not rent that came due before the case was filed (called pre-petition rent). During the COVID-19 pandemic beginning in 2020, many retail landlords sought and obtained substantial and unprecedented judicial relief from rent payment obligations. By and large, the effect was to delay rather than avoid the tenants' payment obligations. Timely payment of rent by debtors in bankruptcy appears to have largely normalized again beginning in 2021.

Where the tenant would be liable for future rent on a lease that has been terminated, the U.S. Bankruptcy Code contains a formula that caps the landlord's claim against the tenant and has been applied to cap the claim against a lease guarantor. The formula in the U.S. Bankruptcy Code has been interpreted by courts inconsistently, using two approaches:

- The **time approach** caps the claim at the rent reserved under the lease for a specified time period (at the next 15 percent of the remaining lease term), so long as that time period is at least one year and no more than three years.
- The **rent approach** caps the claim at 15 percent of the total dollar amount of the rent that would be payable for the entire remaining lease term, so long as that amount is

at least equal to the rent reserved for one year and does not exceed the rent reserved for the next three years of the lease term.

The time approach typically results in a lower claim for the landlord than the rent approach. The issue of which approach applies continues to divide bankruptcy courts and inconsistent decisions will likely continue to result until binding precedent is established by federal courts with higher and greater authority.

Real Estate Lease Assumption, Rejection, and Assignment Provisions: Debtor as Landlord

In some bankruptcy cases, the landlord is the debtor seeking protection. The landlord debtor is entitled to reject the unexpired lease of its nondebtor tenant. Upon rejection of its lease, the tenant (and its successor, assign, or mortgagee) has two options. First, it may treat the lease as terminated by the rejection and file a claim for damages against the debtor landlord, which will be treated as a general unsecured claim and result in payment to the tenant of little to nothing in most cases. That assumes the rejection would amount to a breach sufficient to treat the lease as terminated. Second, and alternatively, and assuming the lease term had commenced, the tenant may remain in possession and retain its rights under the lease for the remaining lease term and any extensions to the extent enforceable under state law. Under the second option, the debtor landlord would be released from ancillary duties contained in the lease (e.g., duties to provide heat, trash disposal, and cleaning staff). In response, the tenant can offset, against the postrejection rent due, the damages caused by the debtor's postrejection nonperformance but the tenant then loses all other rights to claim damages arising from rejection and nonperformance. Instead of rejection, the landlord debtor can also assume and comply with the lease terms, and can also assign the lease to a third-party buyer, who would also be required to comply with the terms of the lease.

NON-US INVESTOR EXPOSURE TO US JUDICIAL SYSTEM

As mentioned previously, non-US investors may become subject to the jurisdiction of federal courts in the US, resulting in potential benefits but also risks. Non-US investors that are active in the US likely understand that their activities may result in a US court asserting personal jurisdiction, making rulings for or against them, and enforcing those rulings against them when and where the court can.

However, not all non-US investors intend or wish to be subject to potential legal process of US courts. Many may believe that they have taken appropriate steps to achieve that objective by engaging in transactions with non-US parties and having transaction documents state that they are governed by non-US law. If, however, a transaction is even minimally performed within the US (e.g., by use of US-dollar-denominated transactions and US correspondent banks), then it is possible that the non-US investor will be subject to personal jurisdiction of courts in the US. Absent a direct conflict between applicable US law and the non-US law, US courts may refuse to dismiss an action against a non-US investor based on extraterritoriality and comity grounds.

In situations where the non-US investor undertakes actions implicating bankruptcy considerations (e.g., setting off against a US debtor's account located outside the US), the likelihood of the non-US investor being dragged into a US bankruptcy court is even greater. US bankruptcy courts hold that the debtor's bankruptcy estate includes property wherever located, whether inside or outside the US, and that the U.S. Bankruptcy Code's automatic stay applies to protect property of the bankruptcy estate, wherever located, from the collection effort of non-US investors, regardless of whether the court possessed personal jurisdiction over the non-US investor. If the non-US investor's assessment of personal jurisdiction, extraterritoriality, and comity turn out to be wrong, and the non-US investor has taken any action that violates the U.S. Bankruptcy Code (e.g., a violation of the automatic stay), then the non-US investor may be subject to sanctions, which if the violation was intentional may include injunctive, compensatory, and punitive sanctions from the US bankruptcy court.

REAL ESTATE TRANSACTION STRUCTURING

Parties have long sought to structure entities and transactions to mitigate the risks of bankruptcy. A sample of the many structures includes:

1. **Bad Acts Guaranties.** One or more principals of a borrower sign a guaranty that includes recourse liability on the guarantor for interfering with the lender's enforcement efforts, including voluntarily initiating a bankruptcy case with respect to the borrower (or colluding with creditors to place the borrower into an involuntary bankruptcy).
2. **SPEs.** Borrower or developer entities are structured as special purpose entities (SPEs) to invest in only one project, with covenants that promise to avoid having that project and entity burdened by obligations unrelated to that one project, with the aim of reducing the likelihood that the borrower will seek or be the subject of a bankruptcy proceeding.
3. **Separate Obligations and Collateral.** Avoiding cross-defaulting or cross-collateralizing multiple projects.
4. **Deposits.** As noted earlier, using letters of credit instead of cash deposits in lease transactions.
5. **Liens.** Ensuring status of a fully secured creditor through a combination of (1) legal diligence to ensure properly created and perfected liens and (2) business diligence and covenants to ensure that value of the security property is and (to the extent possible) remains sufficient to cover the debt that is meant to be secured.
6. **Waiver of Bankruptcy Rights.** Lenders have attempted to get borrowers to contract away all or certain of their bankruptcy rights, including the right to file. With narrow exceptions, most of these efforts have failed when litigated in the bankruptcy courts.

CONCLUSION

Real-estate-centric enterprises can file for bankruptcy in the US with relative ease and without material stigma. Despite the real estate industry's dominant use of bankruptcy in recent years, Chapter 11 continues to be considered as an option of last resort due in large part to the associated expenses. Also, in deciding whether to file for bankruptcy, most enterprises whose debt is supported by nonrecourse guarantees, must consider and manage the risk of converting the guaranty to one of recourse due to the borrower's bankruptcy. Many enterprises ultimately conclude that bankruptcy is not the best path forward and address insolvency by pursuing other options, including transferring collateral assets to the secured lender (by deed in lieu) or cooperating (or at least, not interfering) with a lender's foreclosure. For those unable or unwilling to resolve financial crisis outside of bankruptcy, Chapter 11 can provide a set of clear, concise, and powerful tools designed to afford debtors a breathing spell and an opportunity to financially or operationally restructure and ultimately redeploy their businesses back into the economy.

Some non-US investors will want nothing to do with the US bankruptcy process and the risks that it may pose, and recent case law suggests that this can be accomplished by taking appropriate measures, directly and indirectly, to avoid transactions that can be characterized as invoking US jurisdiction. Even then, care should be given before taking actions taken against a US bankruptcy debtor and its assets. Non-US investors who knowingly subject themselves to the US bankruptcy process can expect a highly transparent, potentially expensive, fast-paced, and sometimes risky process, presumptively run by the enterprise's preexisting management overseen by a single specialized well-supported bankruptcy judge, during which creditor and investor rights are susceptible to material compromise, including extinguishment, with notice that may feel inadequate. In those circumstances, it will be prudent for non-US investors to promptly engage advisors to intercede and endeavor to protect the investor's rights.

NOTES

1. Paul Norris of Conning & Co, quoted in Bloomberg, February 17, 2023.
2. The U.S. Bankruptcy Code is found in Title 11 of the U.S. Bankruptcy Code, 11 U.S.C. §§ 101–1532.

Islamic Finance

Principles and Structures for US Real Estate

Andrew Metcalf, Partner, Corporate Finance and Investments, King & Spalding

slamic, or Shari'ah-compliant, finance refers to finance and investment practices employed by individuals and institutions who wish to invest in compliance with Shari'ah, or Islamic law. These practices emanate from a central core comprising:

1. The Quran, the holy book of Islam
2. The Sunna, practices instituted or approved by the Islamic prophet Muhammad during his lifetime
3. The Hadith, oral traditions relating to the words and deeds of the Prophet Muhammad
4. The *ijma*, or consensus, of Muslim scholars
5. The *qiyas*, reasoned determinations based on analogy to established principles

Probably the best-known feature of Islamic finance is a prohibition against charging interest. This prohibition is not universally shared by Muslims, but it constitutes a central tenet of Islamic finance. It derives from a more general concept, the prohibition of *riba* (translated literally as "excess"). Shari'ah scholars continue to debate riba's exact nature, but generally speaking riba can be described as unearned excess obtained by one party in a transaction or profit earned without giving countervailing value. The concept is further complicated by the Shari'ah's classification of money as solely a medium of exchange, as opposed to an asset with intrinsic value. This characterization implies that money cannot be leased or loaned to someone in the same manner as a true asset, and therefore, that interest, which is tantamount to rent charged for the use of money, is forbidden.

Islamic finance also prohibits impermissible speculation (*maisir*) and uncertainty (*gharar*). These concepts, which overlap to a degree, do not prevent parties from undertaking risks normally associated with business ventures, but do apply to excessive or undue risk. Maisir refers to transactions that depend upon pure chance, instead of effort, to generate a return. The meaning of gharar presents a greater conceptual challenge because it lacks an established definition and encompasses a number of ideas, such as impossibility of delivery, fraud, and uncertainty regarding the object of a contract. Fraud aside, gharar arises when the subject matter of a transaction is so uncertain in terms of identity or assuredness of performance that the transaction amounts to gambling. Some Shari'ah scholars assert that maisir and gharar prohibit life insurance contracts and derivative contracts such as swaps.

Finally, Islamic investors may not invest in companies (or in the case of real estate invest- ments, lease to companies) that are engaged in activities considered harmful or un-Islamic (haram), including gambling and the production of alcohol, pork products, weapons, or por- nography. These restrictions effectively prevent Islamic investors from investing in casinos and some types of hotel properties.

If one had to identify a single theme running through these prohibitions, it would be the encouragement of fair and productive economic activity. This emphasis also manifests itself in Islamic finance's preference for an equitable sharing of risks among economic participants, usually referred to as "profit-and-loss sharing."

Because of this principle, equity investments are generally favored in Islamic finance because equity participants are bound by a shared interest in their venture's success or failure.

However, nonequity financing may also be provided for a venture, if properly structured. In either case, asset-based transactions are preferred because they are thought to provide safe- guards against purely monetary, spurious, activity. Because of this, many Islamic investors consider real estate an ideal investment for both equity and debt providers.

Islamic finance practices are not uniform throughout the Muslim world. Numerous fac- tors contribute to this variety, including divergence in the concepts adhered to by the four main schools of Sunni Islam, geographic differences, and continuing innovation. In practice, the rules followed by any particular Islamic financial institution or Shari'ah-compliant fund are determined by its Shari'ah advisors, who must approve the venture's investments, owner- ship, and financing structures. Shari'ah advisors may take different positions on key issues so that structures or contractual arrangements approved by one advisor may not be acceptable to another. The differences tend to be most pronounced between advisors based in countries that are members of the Gulf Cooperation Council and those based in Southeast Asia. Efforts have been made to encourage more uniformity among Shari'ah advisors, in the hopes of creating a broader-based market. For example, the Accounting and Auditing Organization for Islamic Financial Institutions, a nonprofit organization formed in 1990 and supported by central banks, Islamic financial institutions, and other market participants, issues Shari'ah standards developed in consultation with industry practitioners. However, although these stan- dards have been adopted in many jurisdictions, adoption is not obligatory. Other influential standard-setting bodies include the International Islamic Fiqh Academy of the Organization of Islamic Cooperation, the Shari'ah Supervisory Board of the Islamic Development Bank, and the Islamic Financial Services Board based in Kuala Lumpur, Malaysia. By providing forums for the discussion of standards, these organizations also foster the development of new Islamic finance structures and ideas.

STRUCTURES IN ISLAMIC FINANCE

The central concepts that underlie Islamic finance have existed for over a thousand years, but only recently has modern Islamic finance practice emerged in earnest. Most commen- tators trace the origin of its significant development back to the 1990s. Although Islamic finance still represents a fairly modest percentage of global economic activity, it has grown rapidly in volume, importance, and sophistication since that time. Growth and development trends suggest that Islamic finance transactions may change significantly in the intermediate to long term.

Indeed, a number of commentators and scholars predict and/or advocate for fundamental alterations in current Islamic finance practice. Nonetheless, there are some basic financing structures currently employed for US real estate investments that will remain standard, at least in the short to intermediate term. These investment structures are designed to comply both with Shari'ah, and with US legal, tax, and corporate requirements. Transactional structures will necessarily vary according to the details of each particular investment, but the following discussion outlines the basic parameters of these structures.

Ijara (Lease) Structure

Ijara is by far the most commonly used Islamic finance structure in the US for real estate acquisition financing. It can also be used for financing of corporate acquisitions and asset purchases. An ijara transaction may be analogized to a conventional financing lease, with some structural differences. In an *ijara* transaction, a finance provider leases an asset to an Islamic fund, company, or investor (the venture) in return for the payment of periodic rent. The venture usually has an option to purchase the leased property at the end of the *ijara* term for a preestablished price. The subject asset may be one that the finance provider has either previously acquired or caused to be manufactured.

In theory, a bank or other financial institution acting as finance provider under an *ijara* could own the leased property and lease it to the venture directly. However, because US laws restrict the ability of banks to own and lease real estate, most US ijara structures employ a special purpose company (SPC) to hold title to the real estate assets. The SPC is interposed between the finance provider and the venture, and is typically owned and operated by an independent third party with no financial interest in the ijara or the leased property. In real estate transactions, the SPC will usually finance its acquisition of the leased property by obtaining a conventional mortgage loan from the finance provider. This arrangement affords the finance provider a degree of certainty, allowing it to use familiar loan and security documentation. Following acquisition, the SPC will lease the property to the venture under an ijara. The ijara documentation will contain most of the representations, covenants, and events of default that a lender would expect to have in conventional mortgage documentation. The ijara will also provide for periodic rent payments to the SPC. The ijara's rent provisions will be drafted to ensure that the SPC has sufficient amounts to make all payments due under its conventional mortgage loan with the finance provider. Figure 3.10-01 depicts a typical ijara arrangement.

FIGURE 3.10-01 *Ijara* structure

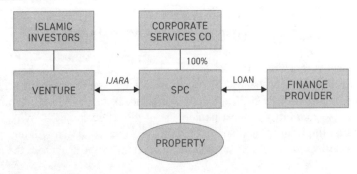

An ijara must satisfy a number of potentially conflicting Shari'ah and US tax requirements, a tension that presents one of the key challenges in structuring these investments. Notwithstanding that the SPC holds title to the leased property, the Venture will typically seek to be treated as the owner of the property for US tax purposes so that it can enjoy tax benefits associated with ownership.

To achieve that tax treatment, US tax law dictates that the ijara and related documentation must allocate to the Venture both the benefits and burdens of ownership of the real property. However, Shari'ah requires that an ijara must assign to the SPC major responsibilities associated with such ownership. Among other things, this Shari'ah requirement seeks to ensure the fair and proper allocation of responsibilities between landlord and tenant. Under typical Shari'ah rules, an ijara should provide that the owner of leased property is responsible for major maintenance and structural repairs for the subject property.

In addition, responsibility for property damage insurance should be allocated to the SPC, as landlord, rather than the Venture, as tenant. This tension between US tax and Shari'ah requirements must, therefore, be carefully addressed.

Finally, just as the ijara between the SPC and the Venture must conform with Shari'ah, any tenant leases that will be assumed or executed by the Venture in its capacity as sublessor must comply.

Although apartment tenant leases often allocate responsibilities between landlord and tenant in a Shari'ah-compliant manner, commercial leases generally contain triple-net provisions that divide these responsibilities differently. Shari'ah-compliant investors have adopted varying approaches to resolve this issue, including where possible, lease modification.

Istisna'a Structure

Although the ijara is the most common structure for US Shari'ah-compliant real estate investment, other arrangements (as well as variations of the ijara structure) are also employed. One such structure, the *istisna'a*, is used primarily to finance real estate development projects. An istisna'a contract is a sales contract for an item that has not yet been produced. The contract can be used to finance the item's production. Under a typical US real estate istisna'a structure, the Venture hires an SPC to construct real property improvements in accordance with specifications provided by the Venture and agrees to purchase or lease those improvements from the SPC upon completion. The SPC arranges for financing to support work undertaken during the construction phase and contracts with a contractor and/or construction manager for such work. Upon completion of construction, the SPC sells the improvements to the Venture or leases them to the Venture under an ijara. The terms of the sale or lease arrangements will vary depending upon the requirements of the project. The SPC uses amounts received from the sale or lease of the developed property to pay its financing obligations incurred during the construction phase. Figure 3.10-02 depicts a typical istisna'a arrangement.

FIGURE 3.10-02 *Istisna'a* **structure**

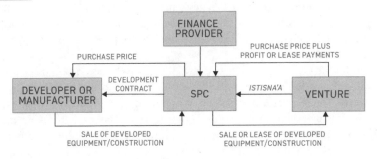

Murabaha Structure

A *murabaha* transaction is essentially a cost-plus financing. It involves the purchase of an asset by an SPC or Islamic financial institution, and the immediate resale of the asset to a Venture at cost plus an agreed profit. Like many other Islamic finance structures, a murabaha can be used to finance the acquisition of a variety of assets other than real property. The asset's purchase price may be paid by the Venture in installments over an agreed period of time, and in real estate transactions the Venture's obligations would usually be secured by a mortgage. Although the murabaha structure has the advantage of placing title to the property with the Venture, prepayment restrictions, transfer taxes, and pricing constraints have limited the use of the murabaha for real estate investments in the US.

However, this structure has been favored in other jurisdictions where the ijara structure presents certain legal problems. Moreover, in recent years, finance providers have adopted the murabaha structure to make mezzanine and mezzanine-style investments in US real estate. In those cases, the equity interest in a property company will usually constitute security for the financing, rather than a mortgage over the property itself. Figure 3.10-03 depicts a typical murabaha arrangement.

FIGURE 3.10-03 *Murabaha* **structure**

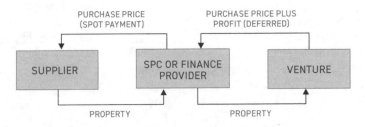

Mudaraba Structure

A *mudaraba* is a quasi-partnership arrangement, in which an investor party (the *rab al mal*) provides capital while a second party (the *mudarib*) provides expertise. Mudaraba is commonly used to establish investment funds that make Shari'ah-compliant investments.

The mudarib typically exercises wide discretion in making investment decisions for the fund and earns a fee, usually based on a share of the fund's profits. The mudaraba parties share profits according to established percentages, which can be highly negotiated. However, only the rab al mal bears the risk of losing its economic investment; the mudarib's losses will be limited to its time, effort, and anticipated income. Mudaraba can be combined with other structures when making an investment. For example, a mudaraba fund can enter into an istisna'a-ijara arrangement with a third-party finance provider to finance the construction of an investment property, and an ijara arrangement for the property's operation. Figure 3.10-04 depicts a typical mudaraba arrangement.

FIGURE 3.10-04 *Mudaraba* structure

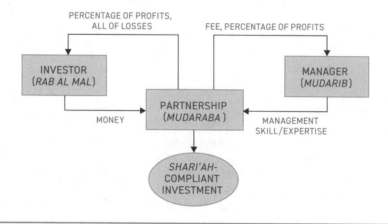

Musharaka Structure

The *musharaka* is a partnership arrangement. Many commentators regard the structure as the purest form of Islamic finance because it features profit-and-loss sharing. Under a musharaka, all partners contribute capital in the form of cash, property, or both. The parties share profits according to an agreed ratio (as with the mudaraba), but the parties also share losses in proportion to their capital investments. All musharaka parties have the right, but not the obligation, to exercise control of the musharaka, although in practice such control is usually exercised by a managing partner.

A variation of the musharaka, the so-called diminishing musharaka, is sometimes used for residential mortgages. Under this arrangement, a finance provider enters into a musharaka arrangement with its customer under which the finance provider contributes cash and the customer contributes property (the residence) and cash. The musharaka will own the residence that constitutes the subject of the transaction. The finance provider receives a periodic payment of return and repayment of its original investment during the term of the agreement. As a result, the finance provider's share in the musharaka diminishes over time as the customer gradually purchases 100 percent of the musharaka interests (and thus the home that is the property of the musharaka). Figure 3.10-05 depicts a typical musharaka arrangement.

FIGURE 3.10-05 *Musharaka* **structure**

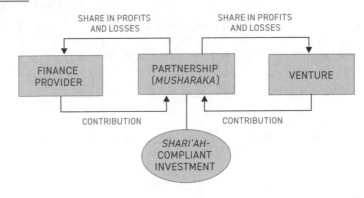

Sukuk

Sukuk are certificates or similar instruments that represent an undivided ownership share in underlying Shari'ah-compliant assets held by the certificate issuer. They are often referred to as Islamic bonds, but differ structurally from bonds in some basic respects. Most important, while conventional bonds represent debt obligations of the bond issuer itself, sukuk represent shares in assets held by the sukuk issuer, including the income generated by such assets. In principle, the sukuk issuer simply passes on the amounts generated by the sukuk assets to the sukuk holders. Nevertheless, sukuk are often analogized to bonds because their payment characteristics often resemble bond returns. For example, if the sukuk issuer owns and leases assets under an ijara in return for payment of a fixed-rate rent, then the holder of sukuk certificates in these assets would receive a bond-like fixed return tied to the assets' ijara. Some sukuk issuances are supported by a guaranty issued by an entity associated with, or otherwise sponsoring, the issuer. Since these guaranties represent the direct obligations of the guarantor, they somewhat blur the distinction between sukuk and conventional bonds, and have proven controversial.

Sukuk have been used for a number of purposes, including by sovereign issuers, by corporations for asset acquisitions, and by sponsors for project finance. Sukuk have not generally been utilized to finance real estate investment pools, but could be utilized for such purposes. Indeed, in the long term, sukuk is likely to be a significant technique for financing investments in asset pools. Figure 3.10-06 depicts a typical sukuk arrangement.

FIGURE 3.10-06 *Sukuk* **structure**

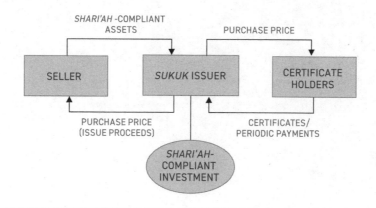

GENERAL STRUCTURING CONSIDERATIONS

All the structures described in this chapter are based on so-called nominate contracts, which are modern incarnations of contracts dating back several centuries and identified in the writings of Islamic legal scholars. Nominate contracts may be combined when structuring transactions, with each contract addressing a distinct capital requirement. Some modern commentators have suggested that using nominate contracts is overly formalistic and should be abandoned in favor of newly developed techniques based on core Islamic financial principles. Given the breadth and diversity of Islamic finance, such new techniques would probably take years to develop and popularize.

As a result, at least for the short to intermediate term, the structures described in this chapter likely will dominate Islamic financial practice. They represent only basic outlines for transactions that are often extremely complicated. Participants must also address a host of US legal issues not covered in this chapter, including tax treatment, bankruptcy, and proper recordation and recognition of ownership rights. Many of these issues arise because of particular Shari'ah requirements and their interaction with US legal concepts. With careful and creative thinking, however, solutions that reconcile the sometimes contrary requirements of Shari'ah and US law can be found.

Introduction

Tax and Regulatory Issues

Foreign institutional investors should be aware of various laws and regulations when investing in US real estate. Some of the main ones discussed in this section of *The AFIRE Guide* include the following:

1. **Foreign Investment in Real Property Tax Act (FIRPTA):** FIRPTA imposes taxes on the sale of US real estate by foreign persons. Foreign investors need to comply with FIRPTA regulations when disposing of US real estate assets.
2. **Committee on Foreign Investment in the United States (CFIUS):** CFIUS is an interagency committee that reviews foreign investment in US companies that may impact national security. Foreign investors need to comply with CFIUS regulations when investing in US companies that own real estate.
3. **Securities Laws:** Foreign investors should comply with US securities laws when investing in real estate through funds or other investment vehicles that are considered securities.
4. **Anti-Money Laundering (AML) Laws:** AML laws require financial institutions, including those involved in real estate transactions, to verify the identity of their customers and report suspicious activities. Foreign investors should be aware of AML regulations and ensure compliance.
5. **Environmental Regulations:** US environmental laws can impact real estate transactions, particularly if the property has a history of environmental contamination. Foreign investors should conduct due diligence on potential environmental risks.
6. **State and Local Regulations:** Real estate is primarily governed by state and local laws in the US. Foreign investors should be aware of state and local regulations that may impact their real estate investment.

Chapter 4.1 examines various securities laws and regulations when funds are raised as part of an offering to investors. It also provides a primer on the legal aspects of financing real estate within the US and the documents that govern these transactions.

Chapter 4.2 discusses the Bank Secrecy Act, Patriot Act, and Office of Foreign Assets Control. Chapter 4.3 discusses US income rules affecting non-US equity and debt investment. And Chapter 4.4 builds on this tax discussion with a close look at the tax implications of FIRPTA.

Chapter 4.5 looks at partnership withholding obligations on effectively connected income (ECI). Chapters 4.6 and 4.7 discuss the Corporate Transparency Act (CTA) and the Agricultural Foreign Investment Disclosure Act (AFIDA), respectively.

Chapter 4.8 explores the regulatory aspects of foreign investment into US real estate investment trusts (REITs). Chapter 4.9 reminds investors of state and local taxes on their investments, which are more varied and specialized than federal regulations and tax expectations. Chapter 4.10 discusses estate and gift taxes, and finally, Chapter 4.11 looks at how real estate agreements are enforced within the US court system.

Raising Capital for US Real Estate

Securities Law Regulations and Recent Developments

AFIRE

Most real estate investors raise capital, whether in the form of debt or equity, to acquire and develop their property. Both forms of capital raising are heavily regulated within the US.

Part one of this chapter provides a summary of the US securities laws and regulations that apply when funds are raised as part of an offering to investors. Part two provides a primer on the legal aspects of financing real estate within the US, as well as a description of the documents that govern these transactions.

US SECURITIES LAWS AFFECTING REAL ESTATE

The issuance and sale of securities is heavily regulated in the US at both the federal and state levels. (The state regulations are known as "blue sky laws.") Violations of these regulations can lead to significant legal liability, both civil and criminal. At the federal level, the primary statutes that create the regulatory framework are the Securities Act of 1933 (the Securities Act) and the Securities Exchange Act of 1934 (the Exchange Act). The Securities Act focuses on the sale of securities, while the Exchange Act is broader and governs the obligations of reporting companies, as well as other related matters.

Securities Act

The Securities Act regulates offerings and sales of securities by requiring issuers to provide investors with information about the investments, including in particular, the issuer's business and finances. One important distinction between US securities laws and other regulatory regimes, including state blue sky laws, is the focus on disclosure as opposed to merit. The primary goal of the securities laws at the federal level is to ensure that investors have information sufficient to allow them to make informed investment decisions. There is no merits-based review of whether the terms of the deal are fair or provide an adequate return to investors.

The Securities Act can be divided into two primary areas: registration and exemptions from registration.

Registration

Section 5 of the Securities Act makes offers and sales of securities unlawful unless (1) the issuer files a registration statement with the Securities and Exchange Commission (SEC) or (2) there is an applicable exemption from registration (as will be discussed). This means that every single offer or sale of securities, including both the initial offering by an issuer and every subsequent resale by persons other than the issuer, must independently either be registered or satisfy an available exemption. Note that the definition of the term "security" has been the subject of extensive discussion and case law.

For our purposes, it is sufficient to state that a security encompasses debt and equity interests in corporations, both public and private, as well as in limited partnerships, limited liability companies, and trusts.

The Securities Act specifies the information that must be included in a registration statement, which includes a prospectus used to market the securities to investors. To prevent fraud, the information in a registration statement must be free from material misstatements or omissions, but it is important to note that the SEC does not explicitly vouch for the accuracy of information in registration statements.

Exemptions from Registration

There are several exemptions from the registration requirements of the Securities Act. (All securities offerings, however, both exempt and not, remain subject to the antifraud provisions of the securities laws, such as Rule 10b-5 under the Exchange Act, as will be discussed.) The two main sources of exemption are Section 3 and Section 4 of the Securities Act. Section 4 exempts certain types of transactions in securities and includes the most commonly used exemptions from registration. Section 3, on the other hand, exempts certain classes of securities themselves, such as issuances by banks, municipalities, and commercial paper.

Section 4(a)(2) and Regulation D

Section 4(a)(2) of the Securities Act states that Section 5 (required registration) shall not apply to "transactions by an issuer not involving any 'public offering.'" This is sometimes known as the "private offering exemption" and along with the safe harbors under Regulation D described later, is the most-commonly used exemption. The term "public offering" does not have a formal definition, but case law and SEC rulings provide guidance for structuring transactions to avoid being deemed public offerings, using the following factors:

1. There's a limited number of offerees.
2. Securities are denominated, offered, and sold in large amounts.
3. Securities contain restrictive legends, if in physical form, and are subject to transfer restrictions.
4. The offering is not made by means of general solicitation or general advertising (except that Rule 506(c) of Regulation D under the Securities Act permits general solicitation and general advertising in transactions where all purchasers are accredited investors).
5. The offering is limited to sophisticated investors, who can "fend for themselves" and make an investment decision without the information typically provided in a registered offering.

6. The purchasers acknowledge that the securities have not been registered, they are sophisticated investors, they are not purchasing with a view to distribute the securities in the US, and resales of the securities are only permitted in reliance on an exemption or effective registration statement.

Regulation D, promulgated under the Securities Act, provides safe harbors under Section 4(a)(2). Fulfilling the requirements of Regulation D ensures that an offering is not a public offering and, therefore, not subject to Section 5.

Apart from solicitation to accredited investors sanctioned by Rule 506(c), general solicitation is generally prohibited in Regulation D offerings. Furthermore, any securities sold using a Regulation D safe harbor are deemed "restricted securities" and, therefore, subject to certain restriction on transfer and resale; they cannot be freely resold.

Rule 504 of Regulation D exempts offerings with an aggregate maximum amount of $1 million during any 12-month period and allows offers and sales to unsophisticated investors. Rule 504 may not be relied upon by issuers that are not reporting companies under the Exchange Act or by blank check companies. (Blank check companies are companies that have no business or purpose apart from engaging in a merger or acquisition with an unidentified entity and are often "penny" or "microcap" stocks.) Rule 505 allows larger offerings, up to $5 million, to an unlimited number of accredited investors and up to 35 nonaccredited investors. The definition of an "accredited investor" generally includes institutional investors and high-net-worth individuals. Rule 505 of Regulation D may not be relied upon by investment companies, and issuers using this rule must provide certain information about the issuer and the securities offered to nonaccredited investors. Rules 504 and 505 were designed to facilitate raising of capital by small businesses and are, therefore, used relatively infrequently, particularly in real estate financing transactions.

Rule 506(b) is the most common method of ensuring that a private placement validly falls within the scope of the Section 4(a)(2) exemption. This rule allows unregistered offerings with no maximum aggregate amount, to an unlimited number of accredited investors and up to 35 "sophisticated investors," that is, investors that have sufficient "knowledge and experience in financial and business matters [to make them] capable of evaluating the merits and risks of the prospective investment." Here, too, certain information about the issuer and the securities offered, typically in the form a private placement memorandum, must be provided to nonaccredited investors.

Regulation 506(c) is a more recent provision, adopted in 2013, as part of the Jumpstart Our Business Startups Act of 2012 (the JOBS Act). This rule allows issuers to use general solicitation in offerings that otherwise satisfy the requirements of Rule 506(b), provided that all purchasers are either accredited investors or the issuer reasonably believes they are. The issuer must take reasonable steps to verify that all purchasers are accredited investors.

Regulation S and Rule 144A

Regulation S provides issuers and resellers with safe harbors to satisfy the exemption from registration for offshore registrants. Rule 903 of Regulation S is generally available to issuers and underwriters, and Rule 904 of Regulation S applies to resales by nonaffiliates of the issuer or underwriters (or other persons acting in a similar capacity). Both rules require the offer and sale to be in an "offshore transaction" and prohibit any "directed selling efforts" in or into the US.

An offshore transaction is defined as one where the offer is not made to a person in the US and is executed either on an offshore or market or when the buyer is or is reasonably believed to be located abroad at the time the buy order is originated. Directed selling efforts in the US, the second prohibition under Regulation S, includes any activity taken, or that could reasonably have the effect of conditioning the US market, for the securities offered. This includes, among other examples, advertising in US publications (including online publications), broadcasts over US media, and mailing offering materials to investors in the US. On the other hand, legally required notices are permitted, if they include legends stating that the securities are not registered and cannot be sold to US persons without an applicable exemption.

In certain situations, Regulation S also imposes, among other requirements, distribution compliance periods, during which resales to US persons are prohibited, as well as agreements by distributors (underwriters) to use certain language and notices and only to sell in compliance with Regulation S.

Regulation 144A, also promulgated under the Securities Act, provides an additional safe harbor exemption from registration for certain secondary offers and sales (i.e., offerings not made by the issuer) to qualified institutional buyers (QIBs). QIBs are generally large institutional investors and must own and invest at least $100 million in securities of unaffiliated entities. Rule 144A is often used alongside Regulation S, whereby securities are offered in reliance on the safe harbors of Regulation S, and those securities are then resold to QIBs under Rule 144A.

RESALES: SECTION 4(A)(1), SECTION "4(A)(1½)," SECTION 4(A)(7), AND RULE 144

Section 4(a)(1) of the Securities Act exempts transactions "by any person other than an issuer, underwriter, or dealer." The primary effect of Section 4(a)(1) is to allow ordinary secondary trading in securities on US exchanges. In the gap between Sections 4(a)(1) and 4(a)(2), an approach developed among securities professionals known as the Section "4(a)(1½)" exemption. The exemption relied on the theory that reselling privately offered securities to investors, where an issuer could have sold securities under Section 4(a)(2), should not be deemed a distribution. Therefore, such a resale ought to be exempt from registration, provided the new investor is subject to the same restrictions as are imposed on the initial purchaser.

The Section 4(a)(1½) exemption has recently been codified in Section 4(a)(7), enacted under the Fixing America's Surface Transportation Act of 2015 (FAST Act). Section 4(a)(7) exempts resale transactions, provided, among other requirements, that:

1. All purchasers are accredited investors.
2. The sale is not conducted using general solicitation or general advertising.
3. For nonreporting issuers, certain information about the issuer must be made available to the seller of the securities and prospective purchasers.
4. The seller is not a subsidiary of the issuer.
5. The class of securities has been authorized and outstanding for at least 90 days prior to the resale transaction.

Securities sold in reliance on Section 4(a)(7) are both restricted securities that are subject to transfer restrictions and covered securities that are exempt from blue sky laws, as will be discussed.

Rule 144, promulgated under the Securities Act, provides a safe harbor for resales of restricted securities. A seller who satisfies the provisions of Rule 144 is not deemed an underwriter and is, therefore, eligible for the exemption provided by Section 4(a)(1) of the Securities Act. Holders may freely resell restricted securities following a required holding period of 6 to 12 months, if among several requirements, the issuer has made available certain current public information and no more than a prescribed amount of securities is sold. In general, nonaffiliates of the issuer may freely resell restricted securities of a reporting company with adequate current public information six months after purchase and may freely resell restricted securities of nonreporting companies one year after purchase.

EXCHANGE ACT

The primary function of the Exchange Act is to govern the obligations of reporting companies (also known as reporting issuers). The main definitions of a reporting company is one (1) whose securities trade on a US securities exchange, (2) whose total assets exceed $10 million and have a class of equity securities held by at least 2,000 persons or 500 nonaccredited investors, or (3) that has conducted a registered offering under the Securities Act. The Exchange Act requires companies to file annual and quarterly reports with the SEC, in addition to current reports regarding certain material events. The Exchange Act also contains provisions that regulate proxy and consent solicitation, as well as restrictions on certain kinds of trading by insiders in the company's securities.

Liability

Several sections of the Securities Act impose significant penalties for violating the act's requirements. Most notable of these are Sections 11 and 12. Section 11 allows buyers to sue the issuer (as well as other participants in the offering, including the issuer's management and the underwriters) for losses due to material misstatements in or omissions from the registration statement. Section 12(a)(1) imposes strict liability for sales of securities in violation of Section 5 of the Securities Act. Sections 11 and 12(a)(1) do not apply to exempt offerings.

Section 12(a)(2) imposes liability for material misstatements in or omissions from the prospectus or any oral communications used for the sale. Section 12(a)(2) applies both to exempt and nonexempt securities offerings.

Another significant liability provision is Section 10(b) of the Exchange Act, which operates in tandem with Rule 10b-5, promulgated under Section 10(b). These provisions generally prohibit fraud or manipulation in connection with the sale and purchase of securities, including material misstatements or omissions with respect thereto.

RECENT DEVELOPMENTS: CROWDFUNDING

One of the significant amendments to the Securities Act included in the JOBS Act created an exemption from registration for "crowdfunded" offerings. Crowdfunding is the use of online means to solicit capital, usually in small amounts, from a dispersed group of investors. Under Section 4(a)(f) of the Securities Act, non-US issuers, however, are not eligible to rely on the new crowdfunding exemption.

Under Section 4(a)(6) and regulation crowdfunding promulgated thereunder, certain offerings are exempt from registration, provided (1) the total amount sold to investors, including by way of crowdfunded offerings, does not exceed $1 million during the preceding 12 months, and (2) the total amount sold to any single investor, including in crowdfunded offerings, is limited to between $2,000 and $100,000, depending on the income and net worth of such investor. In addition, under Section 4(a)(a) of the Securities Act, crowdfunding transactions must be conducted through an intermediary. Such intermediaries must meet certain requirements and must register with the SEC. Finally, the issuer must disclose certain information to investors, including its finances, use of proceeds, capital structure, and other information.

BLUE SKY LAWS: STATE REGULATION OF SECURITIES OFFERINGS

In addition to federal regulation of securities, each US state independently regulates securities. As noted previously, these laws are collectively known as blue sky laws. Blue sky laws generally do not apply to certain covered securities. The term "covered securities" is defined in Section 18(b) of the Securities Act and includes (1) offerings of securities listed on a national securities exchange (as well as securities that have at least the seniority as a class of such listed securities), (2) most securities exempted under Section 3(a) of the Securities Act, (3) offerings in reliance on Rule 506 of Regulation D, and (4) crowdfunding offerings under Section 4(a)(6) of the Securities Act.

There are several notable exceptions to the exemptions from blue sky regulation. States may require issuers to make notice filings with respect to most covered securities. Furthermore, intrastate offerings under Section 3(a)(11) of the Securities Act, conducted entirely within a single US state to residents of that state, are not exempt from blue sky regulation. Therefore, a securities offering effected only within a state to residents of that state may be subject to state, and not federal, regulation.

OTHER RELEVANT LEGAL PROVISIONS

US securities law is a very broad area, encompassing a much greater number of statutes than can be covered in an introductory chapter. Apart from the most important provisions discussed previously, the following is a brief discussion of several additional statutes that need to be considered before proceeding with a securities financing in the US.

The JOBS Act, as modified by the FAST Act, created a new category of issuer: the emerging growth company (EGC). An issuer is categorized as an EGC until the end of the fiscal year in which the fifth anniversary of its IPO occurred, so long as its annual revenues do not exceed $1 billion, it has not issued more than $1 billion in nonconvertible debt over the previous three-year period, and it is not a "large accelerated filer." The primary factor in the definition of large accelerated filer is whether a company's public float is at least $700 million. EGCs may benefit from certain accommodations, including provisions designed to make the initial public offering process less demanding than would otherwise be the case, modified financial reporting disclosure requirements, and facilitation of the process to becoming a public reporting company. For example, EGCs need to provide only two, instead of three, years of financial information in their initial public offering registration statement. The most significant change applicable to EGCs, however, is the exemption from the requirement publicly to file an IPO registration statement. EGCs may instead confidentially submit registration statements (and amendments) to the SEC. An EGC must only publicly file its initial registration statement 15 days before its road show.

The Trust Indenture Act of 1939 (the Trust Indenture Act) supplements the Securities Act in registered offerings of debt securities, requiring debt securities to be issued under an indenture meeting certain requirements. Among other things, the indenture must include information about the trustee and its obligations, as well as any preferences in collection of claims from the issuer. The Trust Indenture Act includes several exemptions from its requirements, including in respect of offerings that are limited to certain amounts (between $10 and $50 million, depending on the structure of the offering).

The Investment Company Act of 1940 regulates "investment companies," defined as companies that are primarily engaged in investing and trading in securities, and offering their own securities to the public. Investment companies are required to disclose information to the public about their investment objectives, structure, and operations. While the Investment Company Act typically applies to mutual funds, it may also apply to certain real estate financing strategies, if those are not structured so as to avoid being deemed an investment company. A company that meets the definition of an investment company is limited in its ability to borrow funds and issue securities. Loans made in violation of the Investment Company Act are legally unenforceable.

Financial institutions in the US are also subject to extensive requirements related to anti-money laundering initiatives, trade sanctions, and related matters. In general, when dealing with a financial institution that will facilitate an offering of securities, customers will be required to submit certain information to verify their identity and generally to assist in compliance with these requirements. These requirements include due diligence procedures, record-keeping, and mandatory reporting of suspicious activity.

Finally, certain aspects of the Volcker Rule may restrict capital-raising efforts in the US. Generally, the Volcker Rule, enacted under the Dodd-Frank Wall Street Reform and Consumer Protection Act of 2010, prohibits certain financial institutions from engaging in proprietary trading in securities and from investing in "covered funds." Covered funds generally include private equity and hedge funds, and certain collateralized loan obligations. REITs, however, are not included within the definition of covered funds.

DEBT FINANCING: INTRODUCTION AND TRANSACTION DOCUMENTS

In the US, real estate investors typically use some form of leverage or debt financing to purchase real property. Given the active real estate financing market, non-US investors may choose to participate as either a lender or a borrower, depending upon their goals for the investment.

A non-US investor may decide to participate as a lender, in order to benefit from favorable tax treatment on interest payments and seniority of debt obligations over equity investments, or to avail itself of debt-related remedies in the event of the borrower's failure to repay. On the other hand, a non-US investor may elect to participate as a borrower if it seeks to limit personal capital at stake, to increase the return on investment, or to garner the support of an experienced financial institution. Regardless of its role in the real estate financing market, the investor should have some understanding of the pertinent laws in the US, including protections for debtors (i.e., borrowers) and rights of creditors (i.e., lenders).

A loan transaction involves several documents executed by the borrower and the lender. In a basic transaction, these documents comprise the loan commitment, promissory note, mortgage or deed of trust, assignment of leases and rents, security agreement, and financing statement.

These documents, along with other issues arising in the life cycle of a loan transaction, are discussed as follows.

Loan Commitment

At the inception of a transaction, the parties will enter into a loan commitment, which may also be referred to as a "term sheet" or "memorandum of understanding." This document informs the parties of the key terms of the contemplated transaction, covering issues such as collateral, loan maturity date, and interest rate. Depending upon the laws governing the transaction, the loan commitment may be binding upon the parties. For the avoidance of doubt, the parties should specify whether the term sheet will be binding and set forth remedies in the instance of breach thereof.

Promissory Note

The promissory note (or note) is the document by which the borrower promises to repay the loan.

The note states, among other things, how much the borrower will pay to the lender on a payment date, how frequently payments will be made, when the principal comes due, and the interest rate owed. The note typically is drafted as a bearer instrument (meaning whoever rightfully holds the note is entitled to payment thereunder), and, therefore, borrowers should ensure that they sign only one note, lest they promise to pay several times over. In addition to other laws governing the note, certain states impose restrictions on the maximum interest rate that a lender may charge. Lenders should pay careful attention to such "usury laws" because violations thereof can result in significant penalties, such as a loss of the lender's right to charge interest on the principal balance of the loan.

Mortgage or Deed of Trust

The mortgage or deed of trust serves two primary functions: first, it secures the lender's interest in the borrower's collateral, that is, the property purchased using the loan proceeds; second, it sets forth other important terms governing the loan transaction. With respect to the first function, the mortgage or deed of trust grants the lender a security interest in the borrower's real property. As a result, if the borrower fails to repay the note, the lender can take possession of the borrower's property, in which case the lender becomes the owner thereof and will typically effectuate a sale of the property to ensure recovery of the funds loaned to the borrower. This process is known as foreclosure, which is discussed in further detail later. With respect to the second function, the mortgage or deed of trust sets forth, among other things, what constitutes an event of default under such agreements and the lender's remedies in the instance thereof. For example, if a borrower misses a payment due under the note, the mortgage or deed of trust will provide that the lender can declare an event of default, accelerate all payments due under the loan (not just the missed payment), foreclose on the lender's security interest, and sell the borrower's property.

Frequently, unsophisticated parties will use the terms "mortgage" and "deed of trust" interchangeably. Although both agreements are intended to accomplish the same result, there are notable differences between the two. In a mortgage, the borrower is the mortgagor and the lender is the mortgagee. The borrower grants a security interest in the mortgaged property to the lender. In a deed of trust, the borrower is the trustor, the lender is the beneficiary, and a third party appointed by the lender to oversee the lender's interests is the trustee. The borrower grants limited legal title to the property to the trustee for the purpose of enforcing or releasing the lender's security interest in accordance with the terms of the deed of trust. Nonetheless, both the mortgage and the deed of trust provide that in the event of a default by the borrower, the mortgagee or trustee, as applicable, will have the right to foreclose and sell the secured property (by judicial or nonjudicial procedure).

Laws at the state and local levels govern the contents of a valid mortgage or deed of trust and the procedures that a lender must follow to foreclose on an interest created by such agreements. In general, foreclosure is the process that lenders invoke to enforce the mortgage or deed of trust, and cause the secured property to be sold free and clear of any subordinate interests therein. Thereafter, the lender may use the proceeds of the sale to reduce the amount it is owed. As stated earlier, state and local laws govern the foreclosure process. Therefore, local counsel should be consulted when entering into and enforcing a mortgage or deed of trust. Local law, and even custom, can have an impact on whether a mortgage or deed of trust is used to confer the security interest.

Although a lender likely would prefer to be the sole holder of a security interest in real property, borrowers will often grant multiple security interests therein. The relationship of a particular lender's interest in secured property to that of another lender is governed by state law. However, the general rule is "first in time, first in right." In other words, the first lender to record its interest against the real property will have priority over other lenders' interests.

Thus, if a senior lender effectuates a foreclosure sale, the property will be sold free and clear of all junior interests and the proceeds of the sale will belong to the senior lender, to the extent of the outstanding amount of its loan. Given this system, lenders must conduct a thorough search of all instruments recorded against the property in the land records to ascertain the priority of interests. (Lenders typically will hire a title company to conduct such a search; the search is documented by a title commitment.) If a lender is concerned about a previously recorded interest, the lender may ask the borrower to secure a release or subordination of such interest. Ultimately, in order for a security interest to be perfected (i.e., legally valid and enforceable against third parties), the conferring instrument must be properly recorded in the local land records in accordance with state and local law.

FORECLOSURE: ENFORCING THE LENDER'S REMEDIES UNDER A MORTGAGE OR DEED OF TRUST

As noted previously, the mortgage or deed of trust sets forth actions and omissions of the borrower that constitute an event of default. In the instance of such an event of default, the lender may seek to realize on its security as a remedy. State law governs the procedure that a lender must follow in order to realize, or foreclose, on its security. The foreclosure process varies depending upon whether the security interest is secured by a mortgage or a deed of trust. In addition, the process varies depending upon whether judicial foreclosure or nonjudicial foreclosure is permissible under state law.

Judicial foreclosure is overseen by a court and generally is a lengthy process that can take several months to resolve. Nonjudicial foreclosure, or foreclosure that occurs pursuant to a power of sale clause, takes place when the mortgage or deed of trust provides that the mortgagee or trustee, respectively, has the power to sell the property in a public auction following a borrower event of default. Such a nonjudicial foreclosure can take place in less than a month, depending upon the jurisdiction in which the property is located. Because this process takes place without judicial oversight, states codify strict notice and advertisement rules to ensure that the borrower, parties with an interest in the property, and the general public are made aware of the impending sale.

Following the foreclosure sale, the proceeds of the sale will be subject to an accounting whereby the funds are allocated to cover the costs of the sale and thereafter distributed to all parties having an interest in the property, in order of their priority. To the extent there are any funds left over after the distribution, those funds are given to the borrower.

DEFICIENCY JUDGMENTS

Commercial loan agreements are generally considered either recourse or nonrecourse. In a recourse loan, the borrower is personally liable for a breach; in nonrecourse loans, the borrower is not subject to such personal liability. With respect to recourse loans, following the foreclosure sale, the lender will have the right to pursue any deficiency between the sale proceeds and the balance of the loan. In order to exercise this right, the lender must sue the borrower for breach of contract and obtain an enforceable judgment. In the case of nonrecourse loans, the lender's only remedy is against the real property itself. Thus, in this instance, after the foreclosure sale proceeds are applied, the lender may not seek a deficiency judgment.

Notwithstanding the above, lenders can create exceptions to the nonrecourse nature of a loan. These carveouts, also known as "bad-boy guaranties," state that in the instance of certain conduct, the lender may seek a deficiency judgment against the borrower. That is to say, the previously nonrecourse loan will become, in effect, a recourse loan. The prohibited conduct can include certain acts of waste and fraud, as well as indications of insolvency.

UNIFORM COMMERCIAL CODE AND
ADDITIONAL SECURITY INTERESTS

In loan transactions involving commercial properties, lenders often receive additional security interests in the borrower's personal property related to, and any lease or rental income derived from, the real property. These interests serve as further collateral under the loan agreement. The interests may be conveyed by a separate security agreement or assignment of leases and rents, or simply by the mortgage or deed of trust. Notwithstanding the conveyance of the security interest, the lender must perfect its interest (i.e., make the interest both legally valid and enforceable against third parties) in the personal property by filing a financing statement pursuant to the Uniform Commercial Code (UCC). After perfecting the security interest, the lender will obtain priority over any subsequently created interests. As its name implies, the UCC is meant to be uniform across all states with respect to its subject matter, that is, securing interests in personal property. However, there are slight variations in the application of the UCC among various states. Accordingly, local counsel should be consulted.

Once the security interest is created, the lender must file a financing statement that puts other creditors on notice as to the lender's security interest in the collateral. This is known as the perfection process. Once perfected, the security interest generally takes precedence over all other subsequently created interests. In general, a financing statement lapses 10 years after the effective date. Thus, a lender will need to file an amendment every 10 years to ensure that its security interest remains perfected.

Similar to the land records, each state maintains a record system for financing statements, which is created pursuant to the UCC and administered by the office of the secretary of state. Before a lender files its financing statement, the lender should conduct a search of such system to assess whether the borrower has granted any preexisting security interests in the collateral. If such interests were granted, the lender may ask the borrower to terminate those security interests, unless the lender is willing to live with a subordinate interest in the personal property. The search may show perfected interests in other types of personal property, such as intangible personal property (e.g., corporate stock). Ultimately, the procedure for perfection varies based upon the type of personal property of concern, in addition to other factors present within each state's version of the UCC.

The UCC and other pertinent state laws draw a distinction between personal property, interests in which are perfected by means of a UCC filing as described above, and fixtures. Fixtures are personal property so closely connected with real property that they, in essence, are viewed by having become a part of the real property. An example is cabinetry installed inside a kitchen at the property. In general, if the removal of the affixed personal property would result in substantial damage to the real property or the item itself, then it constitutes a fixture. To perfect a security interest in a fixture, the lender likely will have to make a filing in the land records, instead of the UCC records.

POSSESSION OF THE REAL PROPERTY AND RECEIVERSHIP

After an event of default, but before foreclosure, a lender may seek to acquire possession of the real property from the borrower. Lenders may do this for several reasons, the primary being that the lender needs to ensure that the property value remains high during the pending foreclosure action. This enables the lender to maximize the sales price of the mortgaged property at the foreclosure sale. The lender may take possession itself or may request a court to appoint a third-party receiver. With respect to the first option, a court will generally permit a lender to take possession of the real property until the borrower exercises its right of redemption (i.e., cures the default by paying off all amounts due under the loan documents) or the property is foreclosed and sold to a third party. The lender's possession is secured either by court order or by the borrower's consent to such possession (typically set forth in a mortgage or deed of trust).

Although a lender-in-possession will have greater control over the real property than would be the case if receiver were appointed, such a lender faces significant obligations and risks. For instance, the lender must prudently manage the property for the borrower's benefit by, among other things, paying for repairs, providing utility services and accounting for receipt of any rental income. The lender must inform the court about these payments and profits. In addition, the lender will face liability for waste or mismanagement and for any injuries suffered by third parties at the property it maintains possession. Because these risks are so great, the lender will often request the court to appoint a receiver to manage the property during the pendency of a foreclosure action.

BANKRUPTCY AND ITS IMPACT ON FORECLOSURE

Bankruptcy is a complex area of law that is beyond the scope of this chapter. Nonetheless, the foreclosure process and bankruptcy are frequently intertwined because borrowers who fail to make loan payments likely face financial constraints that could result in the filing of a bankruptcy petition. Thus, it is helpful to have at least a basic understanding of how bankruptcy affects foreclosure.

Bankruptcy is the process by which a debtor declares its insolvency and either negotiates a plan to repay its debts or liquidates its assets and discontinues operation of its business as a going concern. Fortunately, secured creditors, such as lenders holding security interests in mortgaged property, are treated favorably under bankruptcy law. Nevertheless, when a bankruptcy petition is filed, an automatic stay is triggered that prohibits nearly all actions of creditors to recover debts owed by the debtor. In other words, when a bankruptcy petition is filed, lenders pursuing foreclosure must halt all action against the borrower unless permitted to continue such action by the bankruptcy court (i.e., until the automatic stay is lifted). Until the lifting of the automatic stay, a trustee appointed by the bankruptcy court will manage and oversee the real property in which the lender holds a secured interest. This trustee acts for the benefit of all the debtor's creditors.

RECENT DEVELOPMENTS IN DEBT FINANCING

Following a crackdown on non-US financial institutions, regulators in the US began scrutinizing use of the US markets as a potential safe harbor for money laundering and tax abuse. The current view of the US is that it lags behind most countries in efforts to prevent abuse vis-à-vis real estate investments held by shell companies, such as limited liability companies (LLCs). This environment emanates from both state and federal laws. At the state level, an individual may establish an LLC in any one of several jurisdictions, many of which do not require the registrant to reveal the true beneficial owner of (i.e., the natural person behind) the LLC. At the federal level, banks and other financial institutions are obliged to comply with customer due diligence, also known as "know your customer" laws, which stipulate that such institutions must verify the identity of the institution's customer. In the case of an LLC, however, the customer is the entity itself, not the beneficial owner of the LLC. Moreover, financial institutions typically are not required to identify the beneficial owner of the LLC. Thus, an LLC may open a bank account, obtain debt financing, and purchase real property, all without having to disclose the beneficial owner's identity. Hence, the laws in place allow bad actors to manipulate the system to conceal their ownership of assets using shell companies.

In response to this situation, the U.S. Department of the Treasury (Treasury) has taken two recent steps. First, in early 2016, the Treasury issued a Geographic Targeting Order (GTO) providing that title companies (frequent participants in real estate transactions) are legally obligated to identify and report the beneficial owners of any entity involved in certain residential real estate transactions taking place in Manhattan, New York, and Miami-Dade County, Florida.

Although this GTO is temporary, it represents a step toward preventing abuse through real estate investments. Second, again in early 2016, the Treasury announced that it was close to finalizing a proposed rule that would close the "know your customer" loophole noted previously. Under the new rule, the Treasury will require a financial institution to identify and verify all beneficial owners owning more than a 25 percent interest in a shell company that opens an account at the institution (instead of simply identifying the entity itself as the customer). In addition, the Treasury will require financial institutions to identify and verify all individuals exercising control over such companies. As a result of these measures, borrowers investing in US real estate should anticipate an increased level of scrutiny by US financial institutions and other market participants, such as title companies, in upcoming years.

Planning for Impact

Obligations Under the Bank Secrecy Act, Patriot Act, and Office of Foreign Assets Control

Paul Meyer, Partner, Meyer Brown

The US government has established a series of obligations to deter money laundering, to prevent the financing of terrorism, and to implement various economic and trade sanctions programs. These obligations arise under the Bank Secrecy Act (BSA), the USA PATRIOT Act, and the various economic and trade sanctions laws that are administered by the Office of Foreign Assets Control (OFAC) in the Department of the Treasury. Because of the broad applicability of these obligations, real estate purchases, sales, financings, closing, and settlements are subject to scrutiny by the government and are subject to the possible imposition of severe penalties, both civil and criminal.

While many of the obligations are addressed to "financial institutions," that term is broadly defined and captures many entities and persons beyond banks such as investment companies and persons involved in real estate closings and settlements. BSA coverage includes cash, securities, and assets that are readily convertible into cash or securities. US sanctions obligations apply to all persons subject to US jurisdiction and all assets, both tangible and intangible.

BANK SECRECY ACT

The BSA is the popular name for the Currency and Foreign Transactions Reporting Act of 1970, as amended. As originally promulgated, the BSA was designed to deter the use of financial services institutions as conduits or hiding places for the proceeds of criminal activities. The BSA attempts to identify and disclose suspicious or unusual financial transactions through a series of reporting requirements. Possibly the best-known aspect of the BSA is the requirement to report cash transactions over $10,000, the threshold for which has not changed in decades. This requirement has generated considerable criticism because it often (and increasingly) ensnares innocent transactions and businesses (e.g., a grocery store depositing its daily receipts), but it illustrates the intended breadth of the scrutiny of financial transactions. The BSA has evolved through successive amendments since its original enactment. Foremost among these has been the USA PATRIOT Act, the popular name for the

Uniting and Strengthening America by Providing Appropriate Tools to Restrict, Intercept and Obstruct Terrorism Act of 2001. An outgrowth of the infamous 9/11 attacks on September 11, 2001, the USA PATRIOT Act increased the criminalization of certain financial transactions and greatly expanded the obligations of financial institutions in collecting, analyzing, utilizing, reporting, and sharing financial information. Also notable is the Anti-Money Laundering Act of 2020, which further expanded the scope and granularity of anti-money laundering (AML) obligations under the BSA.

The BSA is implemented by the Financial Crimes Enforcement Network (FinCEN), an organization within the Department of the Treasury, pursuant to a delegation of authority by the secretary of the treasury. FinCEN has very broad authority. It develops and issues regulations implementing the BSA. It serves as the primary interpreter of BSA regulations, subject to limited court review under the Administrative Procedure Act. It monitors financial institution compliance with the BSA and provides guidance to financial institutions. It enforces the regulations and imposes penalties for alleged violations of the regulations.

In addition to the BSA's obvious applicability to banks, credit unions, securities broker-dealers, and the like, it is critical for participants in real estate transactions to recognize that the BSA, as implemented by FinCEN, also covers loan and finance companies, insurance companies, unregistered investment companies, and "persons involved in real estate closings and settlements." This expansive coverage goes far beyond the usual understanding of which business activities are subject to federal financial regulation.

Adding to the complexity is the fact that FinCEN applies its authority with varying degrees of stringency and detail to the various financial system participants that are potentially subject to its control. To date, unregistered investment companies and persons involved in real estate closings or settlements are not obligated to implement currency transaction reporting and suspicious activity reporting. This position remains under review, and, as discussed later, FinCEN has under review a number of proposals to require customer identification programs and AML programs for more participants in the financial services system. Since the BSA does not explicitly restrict FinCEN from widening the universe of participants subject to its requirements, a great portion of the current debate revolves around the definitions of the additional participants who will be directed to more fully implement BSA compliance programs. A core area of dispute is the extent to which various additional categories of institutions are at risk of being utilized by money launderers or for financing terrorism.

Although FinCEN has not fully extended BSA obligations to persons involved in real estate closings or settlements and unregistered investment companies, a number of relevant current obligations must be considered by investors in US real estate. These include:

Geographic Targeting Orders (GTO): The BSA authorizes FinCEN's director to issue GTOs that impose additional recordkeeping and reporting requirements on domestic nonfinancial institutions or a group of domestic nonfinancial trades or businesses located in a specific geographic area. Since 2016, FinCEN has issued a series of increasingly expansive GTOs that require US title insurance companies to identify the natural persons behind legal entities (US and non-US) used in certain "all-cash" purchases of residential real estate. All-cash residential real estate transactions can pose as an AML risk, as they often do not involve the participation of a financial institution that is required to maintain an AML compliance program.

Coin/Currency Reporting: Outside of the BSA's currency transaction reporting obligations, Section 365 of the USA PATRIOT Act requires reporting of the receipt of amounts in excess of $10,000 in connection with a single transaction or related transactions. One challenge for reporters is in determining what transactions are sufficiently related to require aggregation when deciding if the $10,000 threshold has been reached. The best guidance on this question comes from IRS Form 8300 and the related instructions. Because the Internal Revenue Code and the USA PATRIOT Act obligations are so similar, FinCEN requires that an IRS Form 8300 filed at the IRS must also be filed at FinCEN to disclose information about the payor's name, address, and other identifying information, along with information about the date, amount, and nature of the transaction causing the payment. The person reporting receipt of funds has an obligation to verify the identity of the payor and must retain records for five years. Again, the lack of a reporting obligation under current regulations implementing the BSA does not exempt payment recipients from the IRS and USA PATRIOT Act reporting obligations.

Customer Due Diligence (CDD) Rule: The CDD Rule requires covered financial institutions[1] to identify and verify the identity of the natural persons (known as beneficial owners) of legal entity customers when those legal entities open accounts. It requires covered financial institutions to have written policies and procedures that are reasonably designed to identify and verify the identity of customers and beneficial owners, understand the nature and purpose of customer relationships, conduct ongoing monitoring to report suspicious transactions, and (on a risk basis) maintain and update customer information. This requirement has a pervasive effect in the commercial real estate sector because many real estate transfers involve legal entities that hold or are acquiring real estate and need a bank account to facilitate payments.

Beneficial Ownership Information (BOI) Rule: The BOI Rule implementing the Corporate Transparency Act (CTA) requires a broad array of legal entities, both domestic and foreign, to register with FinCEN and disclose their ultimate beneficial owners on an ongoing basis. The BOI Rule is intended to provide law enforcement, regulators, and financial institutions with a single, comprehensive source of BOI to help combat financial crimes. The BOI Rule exempts 23 categories of entities from the regulation.[2] Generally, the categories of exempt entities cover entities that are heavily regulated and have BOI that is more readily available to US regulators, and may cover many real estate-related entities.

Information Sharing: Section 314(a) of the USA PATRIOT Act includes a requirement for the Treasury Department to implement regulations under which the Department will seek information sharing from private institutions. Current FinCEN regulations require financial institutions to cooperate with government information requests "based on credible evidence concerning terrorist activity or money laundering." Since investors in real estate transactions can be treated as financial institutions under the BSA, investors can be subjected to such information sharing demands. On this point, there is a tension in the regulations because as noted previously, persons involved in real estate closings and settlements or unregistered investment companies are not fully subjected to BSA coverage, but the information-sharing regulations do not include a specific statement that the government will not make information requests to such persons. FinCEN also encourages voluntary information sharing between private financial institutions pursuant to Section 314(b) of the USA PATRIOT Act, but this sharing has generally been construed to apply to institutions that are required to have AML programs.

Voluntary Reporting: Quite apart from mandates, FinCEN actively encourages voluntary reporting of suspected terrorism or money laundering activities. However, since the transition to e-filing, it may be difficult for a person to file a suspicious activity report unless they are subject to a mandatory reporting requirement.

POTENTIAL IMPOSITION OF NEW OBLIGATIONS

The limited BSA coverage for persons involved in real estate closings and settlements and unregistered investment companies may not remain limited and is subject to expansion to full coverage. Section 352 of the USA PATRIOT Act establishes extensive requirements for AML programs at financial institutions, including internal procedures, controls, policies, compliance personnel, regular training, and independent audit review of program adequacy. The statute also authorizes the Department of Treasury to establish required minimum standards for such programs.

FinCEN has repeatedly made the industry aware that the current limits on regulation are subject to a "fresh look." As discussed later, FinCEN has initiated the rulemaking process to solicit public comment on how it should impose recordkeeping and reporting requirements on those involved in all-cash real estate transactions. The expansion of BSA regulations to real estate transactions is in line with the Biden administration's broader strategy to combat corruption and illicit finance, which includes preventing actors from hiding their ill-gotten wealth in the US real estate market.

Unregistered Funds: The BSA references unregistered investment companies but does not define this term. In the absence of guidance in the statute and legislative history, unregistered investment companies have remained outside of the implementing regulations, but may be subjected to future rulemaking. Accordingly, investment companies that are not registered under the Investment Company Act of 1940 are temporarily outside of FinCEN's AML program regulations.

For decades, FinCEN has struggled with the boundaries of regulation for unregistered investment companies. In September 2002, AML standards were proposed that would have defined "unregistered investment companies" and subjected them to standards quite similar to those applied to registered investment companies. The proposed scope was quite sweeping and included private equity funds, venture capital funds, and real estate investment trusts. Complex exemptions were also proposed (e.g., offshore funds that are not organized in the US and do not sell to US persons). Considerable opposition materialized, and FinCEN withdrew the proposal when it announced a decision to undertake a more general review of BSA regulation, a project that remains incomplete.

Persons Involved in Real Estate Closings and Settlements: As with unregistered investment companies, the BSA names, but does not define, persons involved in real estate closings and settlements. Also as with unregistered investment companies, FinCEN has labored to define whether and how such persons should be regulated. As early as 2003,

FinCEN sought comments from the public in an effort to define such persons, assess relevant risks, and determine the need to impose AML program obligations.

In 2021, FinCEN issued an advance notice of proposed rulemaking to solicit comments on how it should impose AML recordkeeping and reporting requirements on certain persons participating in all-cash real estate transactions. The requirements contemplated by FinCEN may be applied nationwide to a broad range of real estate transactions, including commercial real estate transactions. They also may impose obligations on market participants that currently are not subject to federal AML compliance obligations, such as real estate developers, managers, lenders, and investment advisors and investment companies involved in real estate. The proposed regulation indicates that FinCEN remains concerned with money laundering vulnerabilities in the US real estate market.

US ECONOMIC SANCTIONS

Although materially different in scope and substance, in many respects US sanctions compliance obligations are similar to US AML compliance obligations. The core sanctions and AML requirements require adequate policies, procedures, and internal controls to detect and prevent unauthorized transactions. The purposes of the US sanctions obligations, however, are different and engage a different set of US government policies. The Office of Foreign Assets Control (OFAC) administers the US government's economic and trade sanctions programs. These programs can selectively or entirely prohibit transactions with entire nations (e.g., North Korea), certain governments or elements of those governments (e.g., a military branch engaged in human rights abuses), private or government-owned entities (e.g., a company that has ties to terrorist activities), and individuals (e.g., a corrupt official or executive). At the broadest level, OFAC administers sanctions that have been imposed by Congress or the president (e.g., Cuba Embargo), and at the most detailed level, OFAC lists individuals and specific types of transactions with those individuals that may not proceed. An OFAC sanctions violation is a predicate offense to criminal money laundering.

To advise the public of what transactions, entities, and persons are blocked, OFAC maintains denied parties lists, the most prominent of which is the listing of specially designated nationals (SDN). The challenge for private parties seeking to avoid unlawful transactions is that the list of persons and entities subject to restrictions is very, very long and changes rapidly. For example, within hours of Russia invading Ukraine, OFAC quickly implemented sanctions against key Russian financial institutions, state-owned enterprises, high-net-worth individuals, and other Russian interests. It also can be difficult for private entities to quickly and independently track and coordinate all of the ways in which the US government announces changes in active sanctions. For example, OFAC issued a finding of violation against a bank for failing to update and search its customer database on the same day that OFAC released a new sanctions requirement. As a result, a number of commercial services have emerged that maintain computerized databases that are made available on a subscription basis and greatly simplify the process of vetting the participants in a proposed transaction.

While OFAC does not mandate specific compliance program standards, it does require all US persons to detect and block prohibited transactions. Further, OFAC has published guidance encouraging US organizations to employ a risk-based approach for their sanctions compliance programs. The standards for establishing an OFAC violation are complex, but it is important to understand that OFAC often asserts essentially a "strict liability" standard in which no showing of intent to commit a violation is required. Because of its regulatory leverage in conjunction with other agencies to essentially bar a defendant from doing business in the US, most allegations of violations are settled with payment of an administrative fine rather than by judgment from a court.

CONCLUSION

The power of the US government to impose penalties through administrative means without obtaining a court judgment absolutely necessitates close attention to US AML and sanctions risks. All participants in real estate transactions that are subject to AML compliance obligations should be attentive to AML, customer identification, and antiterrorism processes and procedures, both to avoid inadvertent violations and to enable any accused person to mitigate potential penalties by showing that due diligence was exercised to detect and prevent such inadvertent violations.

NOTES

1. The CDD rule applies to US banks, mutual funds, brokers or dealers in securities, futures commission merchants, and introducing brokers in commodities.
2. The 23 exempt entities include SEC-reporting issuers, domestic governmental authorities, banks, domestic credit unions, depository institution holding companies, FinCEN-registered money transmitting businesses, SEC-registered broker-dealers, securities exchange or clearing agencies, other Securities Exchange Act of 1934 entities, registered investment companies and advisors, venture capital fund advisors, insurance companies, state licensed insurance producers, Commodity Exchange Act registered entities, certain accounting firms, public utilities, financial market utilities, certain pooled investment vehicles, tax exempt entities, entities assisting tax exempt entities, large operating companies, subsidiaries of certain exempt entities, and inactive businesses.

Tax Rules

US Income Rules Affecting Non-US Equity and Debt Investment

AFIRE

The US is unusual among nations in taxing both its citizens and corporations on their worldwide income regardless of their country of residence. Non-US persons, for example, nonresidents and non-US corporations, conducting economic activities within the US are, by contrast, generally subject to two US taxation regimes.

Under the first regime, a non-US person is subject to US tax on net income that is deemed "effectively connected" with the conduct of a trade or business within the US (effectively connected income, or ECI). If a non-US person is a resident of a country with an income tax treaty with the US, however, the non-US person generally is subject to US tax only on net income "attributable to a permanent establishment" within the US. Income attributable to a US permanent establishment is somewhat narrower than ECI.

Under the second regime, a non-US person is subject to a 30 percent withholding tax on US-sourced, fixed and determinable annual or periodical (FDAP) income that is not effectively connected with the conduct of a US trade or business. In broad terms, FDAP income includes interest, dividends, rents, royalties, and other types of passive income, but does not include gain from the sale or exchange of capital assets or from US real estate. In some cases, the 30 percent withholding tax may be reduced pursuant to the terms of an income tax treaty between the tax home of the non-US person and the US.

ECI

Whether income of a non-US person is taxable as ECI requires an analysis as to whether the non-US person is engaged in the conduct of a US trade or business and if so, to what extent the income of the non-US person is properly viewed as effectively connected with the conduct of such US trade or business. US tax law does not define "trade or business." However, case law and administrative rulings focus on an examination of facts and circumstances in determining whether a non-US person is regularly, continuously, and substantially engaged in a trade or business within the US. The activities looked at include those performed directly by a non-US person and these performed through dependent agents. A partner in a partnership that is engaged in a US trade or business will be subject to US tax on the partner's share of the partnership's ECI.

Generally, a trade or business enterprise must be "active" in order to give rise to ECI. In other words, the non-US person must be regularly and continuously engaged in the underlying activity, rather than merely serving as a passive investor. In addition, the activity must involve the exercise of discretion or business judgment necessary for the production of income, as opposed to simply ministerial and clerical tasks. Activities that advance the purposes for which a non-US corporation was formed will generally meet this standard, and the performance of personal services by a nonresident in the US at any time within a taxable year generally constitutes the conduct of a US trade or business.

Gain or loss derived from the sale of a partnership interest is treated as ECI to the extent that the seller of such interest would have had ECI gain or loss had the partnership sold all of its assets for their fair market value as of the date of sale. If a portion of such sale of an interest in the partnership would be ECI, the transferee will be required to withhold 10 percent of the amount realized on such disposition. If a transferee fails to withhold such amount as required, the partnership may be required to withhold that amount from distributions to the transferee.

REAL ESTATE ACTIVITIES CONSTITUTING US TRADE OR BUSINESS

Facts and circumstances also determine whether the US real estate activities of a non-US person rise to the level of conduct of a US trade or business. Mere ownership of real property or the receipt of income therefrom should not, in and of itself, constitute such conduct. Therefore, ownership of a single piece of US real estate leased to tenants on a triple-net basis generally is not viewed as engaging in a US trade or business. However, ownership of several US real properties, accompanied by substantial, regular, and continuous management activity (whether performed directly or indirectly through an agent) generally does constitute a US trade or business.

A non-US person investing in a US real estate venture that does not constitute a US trade or business must pay a 30 percent tax (without allowance for any deductions) on certain FDAP income (e.g., gross rents) derived from US real estate. When the income results from real estate activities that constitute a US trade or business, however, all of the non-US investor's income that is deemed effectively connected with the investor's US trade or business, computed after all allocable deductions, including interest and depreciation, is subject to the graduated tax rates otherwise applicable to US tax residents.

Non-US persons are permitted to make a "net-basis election" to have income not otherwise effectively connected with a real estate business taxed on a net basis, as if it were ECI. The election enables non-US persons to claim trade or business deductions, including depreciation, against rental income, thereby reducing the tax base, and generally the effective tax rate, on the enterprise.

Non-US persons investing in US real estate through US or non-US partnerships, estates, or trusts that have ECI are themselves deemed to be engaged in a US trade or business. However, a non-US person's ownership of stock in a US corporation engaged in a US real estate trade or business generally does not constitute the conduct of a US trade or business.

CHOICE OF ENTITY

Due in part to the difficulty and cost of making changes, one of the most important initial decisions for a non-US person undertaking a US real estate activity is the form and type of entity through which to operate.

The more common forms of US business entities are:

- Corporation
- Partnership
- Special entity (such as a REIT)
- Branch

It is relatively uncommon for non-US enterprises to operate as a branch without careful planning. From a tax perspective the income of a branch (like that of a US corporation) is initially taxed whether or not distributed. Use of a branch structure may complicate tax planning for the non-US corporation in its home jurisdiction or elsewhere due to the inherent inflexibility of the branch form.

Since the mid-1990s, limited liability companies (LLCs) have become increasingly popular vehicles for holding US real estate. In general, US LLCs are treated as transparent (in the case of a single owner) or as partnerships (where there are multiple owners). Under some circumstances an LLC or a legal partnership can opt to be taxed as a US corporation. Often, individual real property holdings are owned through single-member LLCs, in turn owned under a corporate entity or a master LLC. In such cases, at disposition, the LLC holding the property is sold rather than transferring or selling the specific property, thus avoiding potential reworking of individual leases or contracts on the property. Accordingly, use of LLCs may mitigate certain practical issues encountered when properties are transferred.

US FEDERAL AND STATE TAXES ON ECI

The US federal and state tax income rate structures for individuals are progressive (i.e., the rate of tax varies with the amount of income being taxed). Just as US resident individuals face different tax rates, federal tax rates differ for non-US individuals. State tax rates vary, but in general are also different for non-US individuals as opposed to non-US corporations.

NON-US INDIVIDUALS

Non-US individuals are generally subject to US federal income tax on ECI. To calculate the taxable income from ECI, a non-US individual should first determine his or her gross income from all sources within the US that are effectively connected with his or her trade or business, including rents and gains from the sale of real or personal property located in the US. Once the gross income is determined, the individual should subtract any deductions that are allowed under the Internal Revenue Code, such as interest, depreciation, and other ordinary and necessary expenses incurred in the production of the income. The resulting amount is the taxable income from ECI.

The federal income tax on ECI is then calculated by applying the appropriate tax rate to the taxable income. The 2023 progressive tax rates on the resulting income begin at 10 percent on income up to $11,000. They reach 37 percent on income of $578,125 for unmarried non-US individuals and $693,750 for married non-US individuals.

Unlike non-US corporations, non-US individuals are permitted to apply reduced rates to US capital gains included in ECI. The 2023 US capital gains tax rate for individuals is generally 20 percent, but there in an exemption for capital gains up to $44,625. A special US capital gains tax rate of up to 25 percent applies to any portion of a capital gain attributable to a clawback of prior depreciation expense claimed with respect to real estate. In addition, a special and complicated rule (the alternative minimum tax) applies to non-US individuals if a capital gain is attributable to US real estate.

State taxes are generally imposed on the portion of ECI attributable to a particular state. These rates vary and can be as high as 12.3 percent (e.g., California). Nevada and Florida impose no income tax on individuals. Income taxes levied by cities are relatively rare, with some important exceptions like New York City.

NON-US CORPORATIONS

US tax reform legislation enacted in December 2017, the Tax Cuts and Jobs Act (TCJA), permanently reduced the corporate income tax rate from 35 percent to a flat 21 percent rate for resident and nonresident corporations for tax years beginning after December 2017. The state tax rates vary and can be as high as 8.84 percent (e.g., California). Nevada imposes no income tax on corporations.

Branch Profits Tax and Branch Interest Tax

Non-US corporations are also subject to the branch profits tax and the branch interest tax. The theory underlying these is to align US tax rates for a non-US corporation conducting its business through a US corporate subsidiary with those applicable to one doing business directly or through an entity that is treated as a partnership or disregarded for US tax purposes (i.e., through a branch).

If a non-US corporation owns a US subsidiary corporation, the US corporation is subject to US corporate tax on its worldwide income. In addition, a 30 percent (subject to reduction pursuant to the terms of an applicable tax treaty) withholding tax applies on any dividends paid by the US corporation to its non-US corporate shareholder. Thus, a non-US corporation that conducts its US trade or business through a US corporation bears two levels of US income tax on the distributed earnings from its US business, that is, the profits are first taxed when generated inside the entity and again when they are distributed.

The branch profits tax is imposed at a 30 percent rate (or a lower treaty rate, if applicable) and acts as a substitute for the withholding tax on dividends paid by a US corporation to its non-US shareholder(s). The branch profits tax is imposed (after subtracting any corporate income tax liability) on a non-US corporation's earnings from its US trade or business that are not reinvested in the business by the close of the taxable year, or on earnings that are withdrawn from a US trade or business in a later taxable year. US tax law refers to the base on which the branch profits tax is applied as the "dividend equivalent amount." For purposes of calculating the branch profits tax, the measure of whether the non-US corporation's earnings from the US trade or business have been reinvested in or withdrawn from the US trade or business is measured by the net change in the amount of the non-US corporation's equity (assets minus liabilities) in the US trade or business. An increase in the equity during the taxable year generally is treated as a reinvestment for that year; a decrease in the equity generally is treated as a withdrawal of prior years' earnings that have not been subject to the branch profits tax. The concept underlying this calculation is that the branch profits tax should apply to a base that is equivalent to the amount that the US branch could have distributed to the non-US corporation if it had been operated as a US subsidiary of the non-US corporation.

Similar in intent to the branch profits tax, the branch interest tax seeks to align the treatment of interest paid or accrued by US branches of non-US corporations with the treatment of interest paid or accrued by US subsidiaries of non-US corporations. With certain exceptions, interest paid by a US corporation to a non-US shareholder is subject to a 30 percent (or lower treaty rate) withholding tax. Under the branch interest tax interest paid by a non-US corporation allocable to the US, ECI is treated as though paid by a US corporation and thus is generally subject to the 30 percent (or lower treaty rate) US withholding tax.

The branch interest tax is imposed as a corporate-level tax on the excess of interest deductible by a non-US corporation over interest treated as paid by US businesses operated by the non-US corporation. If the non-US corporation's interest allowable as a tax deduction in computing its ECI exceeds certain interest paid by its US trade or business, the excess is treated as interest paid to the non-US corporation by a wholly owned domestic subsidiary and hence subject to the withholding tax.

ALTERNATIVE MINIMUM TAX

The alternative minimum tax (AMT) is a tax system in the US that applies to certain taxpayers who earn income above a certain level and/or from certain sources. The AMT requires these taxpayers to determine their tax liability twice: once using regular income tax rules and once using AMT rules. They then must pay whichever amount is higher. The AMT generally attempts to eliminate the benefit of certain targeted tax deductions.

For non-US investors, the same AMT rules apply as for US taxpayers. For individuals, the AMT exemption and phaseout amounts are adjusted annually for inflation and are set to return to pre-2017 levels in 2026. The TCJA repealed the AMT for corporations for years after 2017. However, the Inflation Reduction Act of 2022 enacted a new 15 percent corporate alternative minimum tax on the adjusted financial statement income of applicable corporations for taxable years beginning after December 31, 2022. A corporation is generally an applicable corporation if the average annual adjusted financial statement income of the corporation and the other members of its controlled group for a three-tax-year period exceeds $1 billion. Every investor should consider the potential impact of the AMT as part of its overall income-tax planning.

DEPRECIATION

Depreciation is typically the largest tax deduction in real estate operations. US tax law allows a deduction for a portion (based on tables published by the IRS) of the cost of capitalized assets used in a trade or business, or held for the production of income. Depreciation is relatively simple in concept, but the very large number of changes in tax law during the past several years requires attention to detail. Generally, real estate assets are depreciated over 39 years, although there are important exceptions. For example, the depreciable life of residential rental property is generally 27.5 years. Special rules also provide shorter tax lives for restaurants, leasehold improvements, and land improvements such as roads, sidewalks, and landscaping. These rules change regularly and require frequent review of the published tables to ensure that appropriate deductions are claimed each year.

NET OPERATING LOSSES

A net operating loss (NOL) is the excess of a business's tax deductions for the tax year over its taxable income for that year. NOLs can be carried forward indefinitely to offset 20 percent of a taxpayer's taxable income in a subsequent taxable year but cannot be carried back to offset taxable income in prior tax years. Special rules apply to certain types of businesses.

PASSIVE-ACTIVITY LIMITATIONS

Three sets of rules apply to an investor's right to deduct tax losses derived from certain investments:

- Partnership basis limitations
- "At-risk" limitations
- Passive-activity limitations

The basis and at-risk limitations are quantitative tests of whether the investor has sufficient investment in the enterprise to allow a tax deduction. The basis limitations apply where, as is commonly the case, investment is made indirectly, through a partnership. The passive activity rules measure the extent of investor's activity in the business.

A passive activity is any activity involving a trade or business in which the taxpayer does not "materially participate" (i.e., participate on a regular, continuous, and substantial basis). These rules apply to individuals, estates and trusts, personal service corporations, and certain closely held corporations. Rental real estate is presumed to be a passive activity, even if the taxpayer manages the property. The only exception is for real estate professionals or "active participants" in rental real estate who have adjusted gross income of $100,000 or less and net passive loss of $25,000 or less. This deduction phases out $1 for every $2 of modified adjusted gross income above $100,000 until $150,000 when it is completely phased out. By statute, limited partnerships are presumed to be activities in which the limited partners do not materially or actively participate.

In general, unless the taxpayer is "active" (determined, pursuant to applicable regulations, by the number of hours of involvement and other facts and circumstances), these rules defer investment losses until passive activity gains are generated, or until the property is sold or relinquished. Accordingly there are important implications as to how activities and investments are grouped. The rules are complex and require detailed investigation of the property, owners, and their activity and involvement.

LIKE-KIND EXCHANGES

US tax law allows a taxpayer to defer the gain or loss on an exchange of like-kind real property; the tax basis of the newly acquired property is determined by reference to the tax basis of the property exchanged, plus or minus adjustments for cash or liabilities assumed. Partnership or LLC interests are not eligible for like-kind treatment; only the underlying property inside the entity is so eligible (i.e., the owner[s] of the property must be the same before and after the transaction). When US property is to be sold and if the proceeds are to be reinvested into US property of a like kind (including, generally, improved or unimproved land), a tax-deferred exchange can allow reinvestment on a pretax basis. Like kind exchanges are not available for personal property following the enactment of the TCJA. This technique is highly valuable under the right circumstances. Very detailed rules apply, and state tax laws may add additional requirements for deferral.

BUSINESS INTEREST LIMITATION

A "business interest limitation" applies to any interest expense that is not investment interest and is properly allocable to a trade or business. Under this rule, a taxpayer's net business interest deduction is limited to 30 percent of the taxpayer's adjusted taxable income, subject to certain exceptions (the "30 percent limitation"). Any excess deductions are carried forward and may be used in subsequent years, subject to the 30 percent limitation.

In the case of a partnership, this limitation is applied at the partnership level, and any excess business interest may be carried forward to succeeding years until the interest in the partnership is disposed of. A taxpayer must reduce the adjusted basis of their interest in the partnership by the amount of their allocable share of the partnership's excess business interest. If a taxpayer disposes of their interest in the partnership, the adjusted basis in such interest will be increased before the disposition by the amount of the excess business interest allocated to such taxpayer that has not previously been treated as business interest paid or accrued by the taxpayer.

EXCESS BUSINESS LOSS LIMITATION

For taxable years beginning before January 1, 2029, the amount that may be deducted by a noncorporate investor with respect to its aggregate net trade or business losses in a taxable year is limited to certain threshold amounts that are subject to certain inflation adjustments (e.g., for 2023, $289,000 for single filers and $578,000 for joint filers). Any losses disallowed pursuant to the foregoing will be carried forward as a net operating loss, which can be used to offset up to 80 percent of taxable income in a subsequent taxable year.

OTHER LIMITATIONS TO INTEREST DEDUCTION

Under complex IRS regulations, a non-US corporation operating with a US branch may deduct interest expense only to the extent allocable to its US activity. While simple in concept, in practice this limitation is extremely difficult to apply and may result in counterintuitive and unanticipated consequences. Any planned operation in branch form should carefully consider the potential impact of these provisions.

FOREIGN INVESTMENT IN REAL PROPERTY TAX ACT

The Foreign Investment in Real Property Tax Act of 1980 (FIRPTA) applies US tax to a non-US person's disposition of "US real property interests" (including fee and leasehold interests in real property and interests in certain US corporations, as noted later). Specifically, FIRPTA treats any gain from dispositions of US real property interests as ECI and taxes the transaction accordingly. To ensure that the US is able to collect the tax on such gains, FIRPTA also requires withholding on such dispositions. For this purpose, shares in a US corporation, over half the assets of which consist of US real property interests, are included within the definition of US real property interests. A number of states (e.g., California and Hawaii) have versions of FIRPTA applicable to dispositions of real property within their state.

FDAP (FIXED AND DETERMINABLE ANNUAL AND PERIODICAL) INCOME

US tax law imposes a flat 30 percent tax on certain types of US source income realized by a non-US person if the income is not effectively connected with the conduct of a US trade or business. This tax is withheld by the payer at the time of payment on the gross amount of FDAP income. Certain exceptions to this tax on FDAP income apply, as described in the following sections.

INCOME TAX TREATIES

The US has income tax treaties in force with over 40 countries, generally for the purpose of facilitating international trade and investment by removing tax barriers. Most US income tax treaties provide for the reduction of withholding tax rates on certain types of FDAP income. The IRS has stated that US tax treaties have three main functions:

- Preventing the double taxation of income
- Preventing discriminatory tax treatment of a resident of a treaty country
- Permitting reciprocal administration to prevent tax avoidance and evasion

BANK DEPOSITS

Interest earned by a non-US person on US bank deposits is not subject to the 30 percent tax on FDAP income even though the income is from a US source. However, any such interest that is effectively connected with a US trade or business is subject to US tax as ECI.

PORTFOLIO DEBT EXCEPTION

US-source interest received by a non-US person is not subject to 30 percent tax if it is "portfolio interest," including certain interest paid on an obligation that is deemed to be in "registered form." An obligation is in registered form if it is registered as to both principal and stated interest with the issuer or its agent, and its transfer may be effected only through surrender and reissuance of a note evidencing the indebtedness or replacement of a note by a new note. Transfer may also be effected through a book entry system maintained by the issuer or its agent. An obligation that at any time in the future may be converted into one not in registered form is not a registered obligation.

Interest otherwise constituting portfolio interest will be subject to a 30 percent withholding tax if such interest is "contingent" or if paid to a "10 percent shareholder." Interest is generally contingent for this purpose if it is determined by reference to any receipts, income, or change in value of property of the debtor or a person related thereto. The IRS may also deem other types of interest to be contingent if necessary or appropriate to prevent tax avoidance. A 10 percent shareholder is any person who owns, directly or indirectly, 10 percent or more of the combined voting power of all classes of stock of a corporation, or 10 percent or more of a capital or profits interest in a partnership.

CONDUIT ARRANGEMENTS

In an attempt to avoid the related party exception to the portfolio interest exemption, two related parties may interpose an unrelated intermediate party. The IRS, however, has authority to disregard the participation of an intermediate entity in a financing arrangement as a "conduit entity" if, among other requirements, a purpose of the arrangement is deemed to have been avoidance of US federal withholding tax.

The IRS will consider an intermediary to be a conduit entity if it meets three requirements:

1. The participation of the intermediate entity reduces the withholding tax.
2. The participation of the intermediate entity is pursuant to a tax-avoidance plan.
3. The intermediate entity is related to either the financing or the financed entity, or it is unrelated to either but "would not have participated in the financing arrangement on substantially the same terms, but for the fact that the financing entity engaged in the financing transaction with the intermediate entity."

When the IRS finds that a conduit entity has been used, it has the authority to recharacterize the payments and treat them as if they had been made directly to the ultimate non-US person.

COMPLIANCE MATTERS

Partnership Withholding

US tax law requires a partnership to withhold tax on a non-US partner's allocable share of ECI earned by a partnership.

Tax Compliance and Penalties

The US requires an increasing amount of information to be filed annually by taxpayers. Penalties for failure to meet these requirements have increased dramatically.

Careful review and precision are essential as the stakes rise with the IRS's increased interest in transparency and disclosure.

For a US corporation owned by non-US entities, an important annual filing is IRS Form 5472, "Information Return of a 25 Percent Foreign-Owned US Corporation or a Foreign Corporation Engaged in a US Trade or Business." Although this is simply an information return, the penalty for failure to meet the filing requirement is $10,000 for each form. Tax need not be due for the penalty to apply. The IRS automatically assesses this penalty for forms that are not filed on a timely basis, although taxpayers can request relief if they can show reasonable cause for the late filing. Such requests are considered on a case-by-case basis, in light of the specific facts and circumstances.

Other important tax forms may be required, including:

- W-8 forms, including with respect to certification as to certain non-US status, and claims of benefits under income tax treaties
- 1042 forms, dealing with reporting of withholding tax on US-source FDAP income
- Forms 8804, 8805, and 8813, used to reporting withholding tax based on ECI allocable to non-US partners
- Form 114, Report of Non-US Bank and Financial Accounts (FBAR)

Each of these has unique requirements and penalties for failure to file.

Transfer Pricing

Transactions between affiliated entities, especially when crossing international borders, are under increasing scrutiny because of the volume of activity and the possibility for tax abuse. US taxpayers have flexibility to arrange their own affairs as they wish, but they must be mindful of these transfers' pricing rules. Scrutinized transactions include provisions of services, use of intangibles, cost-sharing agreements, and intercompany sales of tangible personal property. Generally, taxpayers are required to employ methods set forth in applicable US tax negotiations in settling intercompany pricing of such transactions in order to forestall an IRS challenge. Taxpayers should have in place contemporaneous documentation supporting the pricing method chosen at the time they file their income tax returns.

Disclosure and Use of Taxpayer Information

US tax law has confidentiality rules designed to protect taxpayers from disclosure of information furnished to tax-return preparers. Enhanced civil and criminal penalties apply to preparers if they disclose or use information in an inappropriate fashion. New requirements also require security controls whenever individual tax-return information is shared across borders.

Other Considerations

Financial statement audits are not required for income tax compliance. They are, however, commonly required to meet loan covenants and may often be required by investors in corporations or other joint ventures.

Foreign Investment in Real Property

Taxation of Non-US Investors Under FIRPTA

Hubert O. Eisenack, Partner, Ernst & Young GmbH WPG

Daniel Tellechea, Director, Ernst & Young GmbH WPG

The Foreign Investment in Real Property Tax Act of 1980 (FIRPTA) created an important exception to the general rule that a foreign person is not subject to US federal income tax ("US tax") on capital gains from US sources. In general, FIRPTA treats the gain or loss of a foreign investor from the disposition of a US real property interest (USRPI) as effectively connected with a US trade or business. As a result, a foreign investor realizing gain or loss on the disposition of a USRPI will generally be subject to US Tax on that gain on a net basis.

The US Tax collection under FIRPTA is enforced through a special set of withholding rules that generally require a transferee or distributee of a USRPI to generally withhold 15 percent of the amount realized upon the disposition (including a distribution) of a USRPI.

The FIRPTA withholding rules have a considerable effect on US-bound real estate investments and affect a wide variety of transfers.

STARTING WITH THE BASICS

Under FIRPTA, the gain or loss incurred by a nonresident alien individual or a foreign corporation (referred to here as "foreign person") on the disposition of a USRPI is treated as effectively connected with a US trade or business (effectively connected income or "ECI"). Such gain or loss is combined with the nonresident alien individual's or foreign corporation's other effectively connected income (if any) and subject to net basis US Tax.

A nonresident alien individual is subject to US Tax at the graduated rates applicable to US persons. Currently, the top individual US Tax rate is 37 percent (through 2025) and 20 percent in the case of long-term capital gains. Foreign corporations are currently subject to a 21 percent US Tax rate. Corporate taxpayers cannot claim a preferential capital gains tax rate. Additionally, a foreign corporation may be subject to a 30 percent branch profits tax (or lower treaty rate) on the earnings from the disposition of a USRPI. However, a gain from the disposition of shares in a US real property holding corporation (USRPHC) is excluded from the earnings that are subject to the branch profits tax.

DEFINITION OF A USRPI AND A USRPHC

A USRPI includes an interest (other than solely as a creditor) in real property located in the US or the US Virgin Islands and in a US corporation that is classified as a USRPHC.

Most direct interests in US real property are USRPIs. This includes fee ownership of land, building improvements, remainder interests in US real property, options to acquire US real property, as well as certain personal property associated with the use of real property. In the case of partnerships, a foreign person who invests in a USRPI through a partnership is subject to US Tax on the gain recognized from such disposition to the extent such gain is attributable to the USRPIs held by the partnership.

A USRPI does not include an interest solely as a creditor. Thus, a mere loan would generally not qualify as a USRPI, unless the creditor has a right, directly or indirectly, to share in the appreciation in value or in the gross or net profits that a USRPI generates. Thus an "equity kicker" type loan, which allows the lender to share in the appreciation in value of the underlying property, would be generally classified as a USRPI.

A corporation will be treated as a USRPHC if the fair market value of its USRPIs equals or exceeds 50 percent of the aggregate fair market value of its USRPIs, foreign real estate assets, and other trade or business assets. It is worth noting that an interest in a US corporation is generally presumed to be a USRPI unless it can be established that such US corporation was not a USRPHC at any time during a specified lookback period—which is the shorter of (1) the five-year period ending on the date of the disposition of the interest or (2) the taxpayer's holding period of the interest. Because of this presumption, foreign persons disposing of a US corporation's stock generally have to determine whether the stock is considered a USRPI as of the date of the disposition and generally also have to follow certain procedures in order to establish whether the stock is considered a USRPI. Failing to take this presumption into account when a foreign person disposes of stock in a US corporation can be a trap for the unwary.

USRPI Exceptions

Several types of interests are excluded from the definition of a USRPI. These include (1) the "cleansing" exception for stock of a former USRPHC, (2) certain publicly traded US corporations, and (3) stock in a "domestically controlled" qualified investment entity (QIE). A QIE is a US real estate investment trust (REIT) or a US regulated investment company (RIC) that is a USRPHC.

Under the "cleansing" exception, stock in a US corporation that was a USRPHC will cease to be a USRPI if such US corporation (1) does not hold any USRPIs on the date of disposition and (2) has disposed of all of its USRPIs in taxable transactions in which the full amount of gain has been recognized. If the "cleansing" exception applies, liquidating distributions from such US corporation will effectively not be subject to US withholding taxation.

However, the cleansing exception does not apply to a corporation that was a QIE at any time during the five-year period before the liquidation (or if shorter, the taxpayer's holding period for the interest).

The term "USRPI" also does not include an interest in certain publicly traded US corporations and QIEs. Specifically, US corporations with at least one class of publicly traded stock that is regularly traded on an established securities market are only treated as USRPHCs to shareholders that own more than 5 percent of the fair market value of such US corporation's stock (or 10 percent in the case of a QIE). Constructive ownership rules apply for purposes of determining the ownership thresholds.

An interest in a "domestically controlled" REIT (DC REIT) is also not considered a USRPI (DC REIT exception) (discussed further on in this chapter).

As foreign investors often invest in US real estate through REITs, the following discussion focuses on the DC REIT rules.

FIRPTA PROVISIONS APPLICABLE TO REITS

A REIT is generally considered a USRPHC due to the nature of its assets. Therefore, the sale of REIT stock is typically subject to FIRPTA. However, exceptions exist for foreign persons owning less than 10 percent of a publicly traded REIT's stock or owing stock in a DC REIT.

The FIRPTA rules provide a "look-through rule" under which a distribution by a REIT to a foreign person is treated as gain from the disposition of a USRPI and is subject to US Tax to the extent the distribution is attributable to gain from the REIT's disposition of USRPIs (capital gain distributions). With certain exceptions, a REIT's foreign shareholders are also subject to US Tax on REIT liquidating distributions following the disposition of all the USRPIs held by the REIT.

As a rule, stock of a REIT that is a DC REIT is not a USRPI (DC REIT Exception). Therefore, gain recognized by a foreign person on the disposition of DC REIT stock is not subject to US Tax. A DC REIT is a REIT in which less than 50 percent of the stock's value was held directly or indirectly by foreign persons at all times during the five-year period ending on the date of the REIT's stock disposition or a taxable distribution by the REIT (or if shorter, the period during which the REIT was in existence).

It is worth noting that the DC REIT Exception only applies to dispositions of stock. Thus, a DC REIT's Capital Gain Distributions are not exempt from US Tax.

Under general US Tax principles, a liquidating distribution is treated as a sale of the underlying stock. Since the stock of a DC REIT is not a USRPI, some taxpayers have taken the position that distributions in complete liquidation of a DC REIT are not subject to US Tax. Nevertheless, the IRS disagreed and has taken the position that liquidating distributions in complete liquidation of a DC REIT are subject to the "look-through rule" described earlier.

The statute and underlying regulations as currently in effect do not explicitly define the terms "held directly or indirectly" for purposes of determining whether a REIT is domestically controlled (see Figure 4.4-01). Therefore, there is considerable uncertainty in practice in this regard, presenting a challenge from an investment structuring perspective.

FIGURE 4.4-01 **Domestically controlled REIT structure**

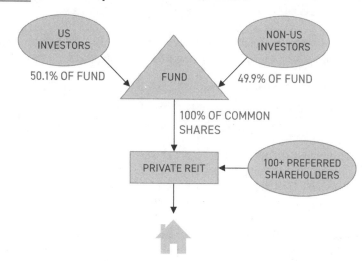

TREATMENT OF NONRECOGNITION TRANSACTIONS

The FIRPTA rules restrict a foreign person's ability to rely on general US Tax nonrecognition provisions upon the transfer or distribution of a USRPI, unless the FIRPTA rules specifically provide an exception for nonrecognition. A nonrecognition provision generally includes any provision under US Tax law for not recognizing gain or loss on a transaction (this includes IRC Sections 332, 351, and 368, among others).

As a general rule, a nonrecognition provision would apply to an exchange of a USRPI only if the sale of the USRPI or the property received for the USRPI in the exchange would be subject to US Tax upon its disposition. Thus, for example, a foreign person would generally be required to recognize gain on an exchange of shares in a USRPHC for shares of a US corporation that is not a USRPHC or shares in a foreign corporation, even though the transaction would otherwise qualify as a tax-free transaction.

The FIRPTA rules provide for certain exceptions that permit foreign persons to qualify for nonrecognition treatment in some types of foreign-to-foreign exchanges. For example, a foreign person may qualify for nonrecognition on the contribution of USRPHC stock to a foreign corporation if certain requirements are satisfied.

The application of these rules must be considered in the context of internal restructurings, reorganizations, liquidations and distributions, and other nonrecognition transactions. Failure to do so could result in gain recognition, withholding tax exposure, penalties, and interest.

SPECIAL REGIMES APPLICABLE TO CERTAIN CLASSES OF TAXPAYERS

This section provides a—nonconclusive—overview of certain FIRPTA rules that are particular to qualified foreign pension funds (QFPFs) and foreign governments.

Qualified Foreign Pension Funds

QFPFs are exempt from FIRPTA taxation and withholding (QFPF Exemption). QFPFs also include corporations and trusts that are wholly owned by one or more QFPFs (Qualified Controlled Entities, QCEs).

It is important to note that a QFPF continues to be subject to US Tax under other US Tax provisions that are applicable to foreign persons. Thus, for example, a QFPF (and a QCE) is still subject to US Tax on non-FIRPTA ECI and is subject to US withholding tax on ordinary distributions from domestic corporations, including REITs, to the extent there is no relief under an applicable income tax treaty.

As a consequence, most QFPFs invest in US real property through US corporations (particularly REITs) in order to take advantage of the QFPF exemption. For example, a QFPF can dispose of REIT stock, including stock in a nondomestically controlled REIT, and USRPHCs without incurring US Tax. Moreover, a QFPF is exempt from US Tax on REIT Capital Gain Distributions. This makes REITs particularly attractive for QFPFs investing in US real estate.

Generally, a foreign pension arrangement qualifies as a QFPF if (1) it is an eligible fund (trust, corporation, or other organization or arrangement), (2) it is organized under foreign (non-US) law, (3) it is established to provide "retirement or pension benefits" to current or former employees, (4) it does not have large beneficiaries, (5) it is subject to government regulation and reporting, and (6) it is entitled to a certain favorable foreign tax treatment. These requirements must be satisfied during a relevant testing period.

The IRS recently issued final regulations (QFPF Final Regulations), which generally retain the framework of the regulations that were initially proposed in 2019, with certain clarifications and additional changes. In particular, the QFPF Final Regulations provide a broader definition of the term "retirement and pension benefits." Such benefits generally include payments made to qualified recipients after reaching a predetermined retirement age or after an event that results in the recipient being permanently unable to work, and includes distributions made to a surviving beneficiary of the qualified recipient. Figure 4.4-02 illustrates this structure.

<u>FIGURE 4.4-02</u> **Sample illustration of QFPF**

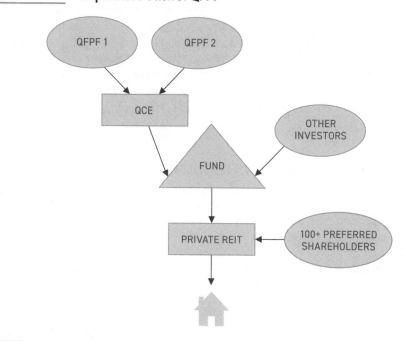

Foreign Governments

US Tax law generally exempts foreign governments and certain of their wholly owned foreign subsidiaries from US Tax on income received from investments in US stocks, bonds, and other securities (Section 892 Exemption).

Income is not subject to the Section 892 Exemption if (1) the respective item of income is derived from the conduct of a commercial activity, or (2) the respective item of income is received by or from a controlled commercial entity (CCE).

The term "commercial activity" includes all activities conducted with a view toward the production of income and gain, but excludes investments in stocks, bonds, and other securities.

A CCE is defined as any entity engaged in commercial activities—whether conducted within or outside the US—that is owned 50 percent or greater, directly or indirectly, or otherwise practically controlled by a foreign government.

Under a special rule, a USRPHC (as well as any foreign corporation that would be treated as a USRPHC if it were a domestic corporation) are treated as engaged in a commercial activity. Therefore, any entity that a foreign government controls and that qualifies as a USRPHC would be automatically treated as a CCE. As noted earlier, a CCE cannot benefit from the Section 892 exemption.

Under current rules, a QFPF or a wholly owned subsidiary of a QFPF that is controlled by a foreign government would be deemed to be a CCE if such entity were treated as a USRPHC. This rule is particularly problematic for government-owned pension funds with US real estate investments.

Recognizing that the purpose of the QFPF Exemption is to encourage US real estate investments by foreign pension funds, the IRS recently issued proposed regulations (Proposed 892 Regulations) that would exclude QFPFs and QCEs from the rules that treat a USRPHC as a CCE. The Proposed 892 Regulations would also exclude a controlled corporation that is a USRPHC solely because of its direct or indirect ownership in one or more other corporations that are not controlled by the foreign government from the definition of a CCE. Therefore, a foreign subsidiary of a foreign government would not be a CCE solely by reason of its ownership in US blockers provided that each US blocker is not otherwise controlled by the foreign government.

FIRPTA WITHHOLDING

In the preceding sections, mainly issues relating to substantive US Tax liabilities under FIRPTA have been addressed. This section provides an overview of FIRPTA withholding tax rules that were enacted to collect the US Tax due (or part of such tax) under FIRPTA (FIRPTA Withholding).

If a foreign person disposes of a USRPI, then the transferee is generally required to deduct and withhold 15 percent of the amount realized on the transaction. However, certain exceptions (discussed later) apply that could exempt the transaction from FIRPTA Withholding.

An important point about FIRPTA Withholding is that a withholding agent is personally liable for the full amount of FIRPTA US Tax required to be withheld, plus penalties and interest.

There are various exceptions to FIRPTA Withholding. Most such exceptions require the withholding agent to obtain certain documentation on or before the date of the transaction to "turn off" FIRPTA Withholding.

Some of the most common exceptions include the following:

Transferor Is Not a Foreign Person: In order to qualify for this exception, the transferor must provide a certification of nonforeign status to the transferee. Since a QFPF is not considered a foreign person for FIRPTA purposes, it can provide a certification of nonforeign status in order to claim an exemption from FIRPTA Withholding. Such certification can also be used by QCEs and foreign partnerships that are wholly owned by QFPFs. In the future, the IRS will issue a revised Form W-8EXP, which will allow QFPFs to certify their status.

Transferred Property Is Not a USRPI: FIRPTA Withholding does not apply if the transferred property is not a USRPI. If the property that is disposed of is a US corporation's stock, the US corporation must certify that the US corporation is not a USRPHC. This is accomplished by obtaining a statement from the US corporation that it has not been a USRPHC during the relevant lookback period or that it qualifies under the "cleansing" exception discussed previously. The certification must be provided to the transferee, and the US corporation must file a copy with the IRS.

If the property that is disposed of is a partnership interest, the transferee is required to withhold 15 percent of the amount realized only if the entire partnership interest is a USRPI. A partnership interest is treated as a USRPI for this purpose if 50 percent or more of the value of the gross assets consists of USRPIs, and 90 percent or more of the value of the gross assets consists of USRPIs plus any cash or cash equivalents (so-called 50/90 partnership). Withholding is not required if the partnership is not a 50/90 partnership and certain reporting requirements are met. Note that a foreign person will be subject to substantive tax under FIRPTA even if the partnership is not a 50/90 partnership.

FIRPTA Nonrecognition Transactions: This is one of the most important exceptions from withholding, particularly in the context of distributions and internal restructurings where no cash is transferred. The transferee or distributee acquiring a USRPI from a foreign person in a qualifying nonrecognition transaction is not required to withhold, provided certain documentation and notice requirements are satisfied. The exception from withholding only applies when the transfer qualifies for nonrecognition treatment with respect to all of the deferred gain.

In addition to the general rule discussed previously, a number of special rules may require corporations to withhold on receipt or distribution of USRPIs, and entities such as partnerships to withhold on foreign owners' distributive share of dispositions of USRPIs. These rules are complex. For instance, if a domestic corporation that is a USRPHC (or that has been a USRPHC during the relevant lookback period) makes a nontaxable return of capital distribution to its foreign shareholder, it is generally required to withhold 15 percent tax on such distribution even though it is not generally subject to US Tax under FIRPTA. Under certain circumstances, such FIRPTA withholding can be reduced or eliminated if the domestic corporation or the foreign shareholder timely obtains a withholding certificate from the IRS.

Partnerships and Income

Partnership Withholding Obligations on Effectively Connected Income

Joshua Kaplan, Managing Director, International Tax, KPMG

Paul Kraut, Tax Partner, KPMG

Non-US persons are subject to US federal income tax on income that is—or is treated as—effectively connected with the conduct of a US trade or business. In response to concerns that non-US partners were not complying with US tax laws, Congress added Section 1446 to the Internal Revenue Code (the Code) in 1986 to require partnerships that are directly or indirectly engaged in a US trade or business to withhold US tax on ECI allocable to non-US partners.[1]

Specifically, Section 1446(a) requires any partnership that has US effectively connected taxable income (ECTI) to withhold, pay, and report US withholding tax on the ECTI allocable to non-US partners at a rate equal to the highest applicable US income tax rate (currently 21 percent for foreign corporations and 37 percent for non-US persons other than corporations). ECTI for this purpose includes gain from the disposition of a US real property interest (USRPI) that is treated as ECI under the Foreign Investment in Real Property Tax Act of 1980 (FIRPTA).[2] A partnership generally must pay quarterly installments of tax withheld under Section 1446(a).

Regulations under Section 1446(a) provide detailed rules for determining how a partnership, including if the partnership has non-US partners and any ECTI allocable to such non-US partners. The regulations compute the amount of withholding tax, identifies who pays the tax, and reports the amounts withheld to its non-US partners and the IRS. The regulations also provide rules addressing tiered partnership structures, rules designed to ease overwithholding, coordination rules with Section 1445 (i.e., FIRPTA withholding), and special rules for publicly traded partnerships and trusts.

This chapter discusses the Section 1446(a) rules applicable to non-publicly traded partnerships. The final section of this chapter also provides a brief overview of the withholding rules in Section 1446(f), which Congress added in the Tax Cuts and Jobs Act of 2017 (TCJA), that require a transferee to withhold tax when a non-US person transfers an interest in a partnership that is engaged in a US trade or business.

DETERMINING EXISTENCE OF NON-US PARTNERS

A partnership must assume that a partner is a non-US person, unless the partner certifies that it is a US person. A non-US person for this purpose generally is a nonresident alien individual, a non-US corporation, a non-US partnership, or a non-US trust or estate. A partnership generally can identify a US partner by obtaining a properly completed IRS Form W-9,[3] and generally can identify a non-US partner by obtaining the applicable IRS Form W-8 certification for the type of investor[4] for non-US individuals, and IRS Form W-8BEN-E for non-US corporations.[5] A certificate on an IRS Form W-8 is generally valid for a period of three years (unless there has been a change in the partner's circumstances) if it contains the partner's name, permanent address and taxpayer identification number, the country under whose laws the partner was formed (if the partner is not an individual), the classification of the partner for US tax purposes, and certain other information.

A partnership generally may rely on a partner's IRS Forms W-9 or W-8, unless the partnership has actual knowledge or reason to know that information on the certificate is incorrect or unreliable. If the partnership has knowledge or reason to know that the information on the certificate is incorrect or unreliable, the partnership must presume the partner is either a non-US individual or a non-US corporation, whichever presumption results in the higher tax. As discussed later, a partnership that improperly relies on a partner certificate to avoid withholding (or withhold at a lower rate) may be liable for withholding tax, along with penalties and interest. Accordingly, it is very important for partnerships to exercise due care in reviewing partner certifications.

DETERMINING ECTI ALLOCABLE TO NON-US PARTNERS

The share of partnership ECTI that is allocable to a particular non-US partner generally is equal to the partner's distributive share of effectively connected partnership gross income and gain, reduced by the partner's distributive share of partnership deductions, other than charitable contributions and excess capital losses, allocable to such gross income and gain. Except as provided in special rules discussed later, a partnership may not take into account partner-level deductions (e.g., itemized deductions, net operating losses, passive losses, etc.) in computing partnership ECTI allocable to a non-US partner, even if the non-US partner is entitled to claim the deductions when computing its tax liability on its US income tax return.

The determination of whether a partnership's activities constitute a US trade or business and, therefore, whether its income constitutes ECI, depends on the facts and circumstances of each case. In situations where there is uncertainty whether a partnership's US real estate rental activities constitute a US trade or business, non-US partners generally may elect under Sections 871(d) or 882(d) to treat as ECI income that otherwise might not constitute ECI. This "net election" generally is advantageous because it enables non-US partners to avoid 30 percent withholding on gross rental income and to claim trade or business deductions (including depreciation) against rental income, thereby reducing the tax base and the tax rate on such income. Income that is treated as ECI pursuant to this election is subject to withholding under Section 1446(a). The net election is made on a partner-by-partner basis, and a non-US partner that makes a Section 871(d) or 882(d) election must furnish to the partnership an IRS Form W-8ECI.[6]

COMPUTING THE AMOUNT OF WITHHOLDING

The amount of Section 1446(a) withholding tax generally equals the non-US partner's allocable share of ECTI multiplied by the "applicable percentage," which is generally the highest rate of US income tax applicable to the type of non-US partner (i.e., the maximum corporate rate for non-US corporations or the maximum individual rate for non-US partners other than corporations).

If a non-US partner is eligible for a preferential tax rate on a particular item of income, the partnership is permitted to consider as the applicable percentage, the highest specified preferential tax rate applicable to the income or gain allocable to the non-US partner. For example, in the case of a non-US individual, a partnership generally may use the highest capital-gains tax rate for long-term capital gains or the maximum tax rate for unrecaptured Section 1250 gain.[7] The partnership is not, however, permitted to use a preferential rate if the rate depends on the corporate or noncorporate status of the non-US partner and the non-US partner has not properly certified its status. Accordingly, to obtain reduced withholding on its allocable share of a partnership's capital gain income, a non-US individual partner must timely certify its status on a valid IRS Form W-8BEN or IRS Form W-8ECI.

PAYING THE TAX

Generally, a partnership must pay the Section 1446(a) tax by making estimated installment payments and providing an IRS Form 8813 on or before the 15th day of the fourth, sixth, ninth, and twelfth months of its taxable year. Any additional Section 1446 tax must be paid with the filing of an annual return (IRS Form 8804) on or before the 15th day of the third month of the following taxable year (or the 15th day of the sixth month of the following taxable year in the case of a non-US partnership that keeps its books and records outside of the US).

A partnership that fails to properly make estimated installment payments will be liable for any underwithholding, along with potential penalties and interest. A partnership that over-withholds during the year may claim a refund for the excess withholding.

REPORTING THE TAX PAID

Reporting Installment Payments

A partnership that is required to make an installment payment of Section 1446(a) tax is required to notify its non-US partners of payments made on the partner's behalf within 10 days of the installment due date or if paid later, the date on which such installment payment is made. No particular form is required for a partnership's notification to a non-US partner, but each notification must include the partnership's name, address, and taxpayer identification number; the partner's name, address, and taxpayer identification number; the annualized ECTI estimated to be allocable to the non-US partner; and the amount of tax paid on behalf of the non-US partner for the current period and any prior periods included in the partnership's tax year.

Annual Return and Notification

Every partnership that has ECTI allocable to a non-US partner must annually file with the IRS an IRS Form 8804.[8] Additionally, every partnership that withholds tax under Section 1446(a) must issue an IRS Form 8805 to each non-US partner on whose behalf it paid Section 1446(a) tax.[9]

Crediting Section 1446(A) Tax Against a Non-US Partner's US Tax Liability

A non-US partner may claim as a credit on its annual US tax return the Section 1446(a) tax paid by the partnership with respect to the ECTI allocable to that partner. The partner may not claim an early refund of these amounts. Generally, the Section 1446(a) tax withheld will be allowed as a credit only if IRS Form 8805 is attached to the non-US partner's return to substantiate the credit, and the name and taxpayer identification number on IRS Form 8805 match the name and taxpayer identification number on the non-US partner's US tax return. The payment of Section 1446(a) tax by the partnership does not excuse a non-US partner from filing a US tax return to report its allocable share of partnership ECTI, even if the amounts withheld are in excess of the actual liability ultimately due.

COORDINATION WITH FIRPTA WITHHOLDING

Section 1445(e)(1) generally requires a *domestic* partnership with one or more foreign partners to withhold tax on the disposition of a USRPI in an amount equal to 21 percent of each foreign partner's distributive share of the gain realized by the partnership on the disposition. Because gain from the disposition of a USRPI also is treated as ECI under FIRPTA, USRPI gains also could be subject to withholding under Section 1446(a). The Section 1446(a) regulations prevent double withholding by providing that Section 1446(a) generally trumps FIRPTA withholding when a domestic partnership with a foreign partner disposes of a USRPI.

If a non-US partnership with non-US partners disposes of a USRPI, the buyer/transferee generally must withhold 15 percent of the amount realized by the non-US partnership under Section 1445(a). The non-US partnership also must withhold under Section 1446(a) on the USRPI gain allocable to its non-US partners. A non-US partnership that is subject to withholding under Section 1445(a) generally may credit some or all of the Section 1445(a) withholding against its Section 1446(a) liability for the year.

TIERED PARTNERSHIP STRUCTURES

The regulations permit a lower-tier partnership (LTP) that receives certain documentation from a partner that is a non-US partnership (an upper-tier partnership or UTP) to look through the UTP to the UTP's partners when computing the LTP's Section 1446(a) withholding obligation with respect to the UTP. The look-through rule is used to determine if a non-US UTP itself has non-US partners, the type of non-US partners, and the amount of ECTI allocable to the non-US partners. A UTP must submit an IRS Form W-8IMY to the LTP, along with IRS Form W-9 or W-8 for each of its partners and certain other information.[10]

A US UTP that is a partner in an LTP may elect to apply the look-through rules to have the LTP withhold and remit the Section 1446(a) tax with respect to ECTI allocable to the UTP's non-US partners, if the UTP provides certain documentation and the LTP consents in writing.

RULES TO EASE OVERWITHHOLDING

To ease overwithholding, the regulations provide procedures that allow a partnership to consider certain partner-level deductions and losses in computing its Section 1446(a) withholding tax obligation with respect to a non-US partner. A non-US partner that meets the requirements of these rules for a particular year must timely provide an IRS Form 8804-C to the partnership to certify the permitted deductions and losses that it reasonably expects to be available to reduce its US income tax liability.[11]

A partnership that reasonably relies on a non-US partner's certification will generally remain liable for underwithholding of Section 1446 tax, but may be excused from liability for additions to tax arising from failure to pay the required amount of quarterly installments. A partnership that relies in whole or in part on a non-US partner's certificate must file an IRS Form 8813, IRS Form 8804, and IRS Form 8805 for the period for which the certificate is considered, even if no Section 1446(a) tax (or installment of such tax) is due with respect to the non-US partner. The partnership must also attach a copy of the IRS Form 8804-C for the non-US partner—and the partnership's computation of Section 1446(a) tax due with respect to the non-US partner—to both IRS Forms 8813 and 8805 for the first period that such certificate is considered in computing the partnership's Section 1446(a) tax (or any installment of it).

SECTION 864(C)(8) AND SECTION 1446(F)

Congress enacted two new provisions in 2017 to subject non-US persons to substantive tax and withholding on dispositions of interests in partnerships that are engaged in a US trade or business. Section 864(c)(8) generally treats a non-US partner's gain or loss on a sale of a partnership interest as effectively connected with a US trade or business to the extent the non-US partner would have been allocated effectively connected gain or loss had the partnership sold its underlying assets. Final regulations issued in 2020 provide detailed rules for determining the amount of a non-US partner's gain or loss that is treated as effectively connected gain or loss. The regulations also provide coordination rules with FIRPTA when a non-US partner disposes of an interest in a partnership that is engaged in a US trade or business and holds USRPIs.

Section 1446(f)(1) and the regulations thereunder generally require the transferee of a partnership interest from a non-US person to withhold a tax equal to 10 percent of the amount realized by the non-US transferor, unless an exception applies. If the transferee fails to withhold the correct amount, Section 1446(f)(4) imposes an obligation on the transferred partnership to deduct and withhold from distributions to the transferee partner an amount equal to the amount the transferee failed to withhold, plus interest. Final regulations issued in 2020 provide detailed rules regarding the scope and application of Section 1446(f), including seven exceptions to Section 1446(f)(1) withholding. The regulations also provide coordination rules with Section 1445 when a non-US partner disposes of an interest in a partnership that is engaged in a US trade or business and holds USRPIs. Section 1446(f)(1) applies to transfers occurring after December 31, 2017. Section 1446(f)(4) applies to transfers occurring on or after January 1, 2023.[12]

NOTES

1. Unless otherwise noted, all Section references are to the Code. Partnerships also are required to withhold under Section 1441 or 1442 on US source dividends, interest, and other "fixed or determinable annual or periodical" income allocable to non-US partners.
2. As discussed further below, ECTI also includes rental income that is treated as ECI pursuant to a partner's "net basis" election under Section 871(d) or 882(d).
3. Internal Revenue Service. "About Form W-9." Accessed May 1, 2023. https://www.irs.gov/forms-pubs/about-form-w-9.
4. Internal Revenue Service. "About Form W-8BEN, Certificate of Foreign Status of Beneficial Owner for United States Tax Withholding and Reporting (Individuals)." Last modified October 29, 2020. https://www.irs.gov/forms-pubs/about-form-w-8-ben.
5. Internal Revenue Service. "About Form W-8BEN-E, Certificate of Status of Beneficial Owner for United States Tax Withholding and Reporting (Entities)." Last modified December 30, 2021. https://www.irs.gov/forms-pubs/about-form-w-8-ben-e.
6. Internal Revenue Service. "About Form W-8-ECI." IRS, March 28, 2019, https://www.irs.gov/forms-pubs/about-form-w-8-eci.
7. Note that current US tax law does not provide preferential tax rates for corporate partners.
8. Internal Revenue Service. "About Form 8804, Annual Return for Partnership Withholding Tax (Section 1446)." Last modified February 2, 2022. https://www.irs.gov/forms-pubs/about-form-8804.
9. Internal Revenue Service. "About Form 8805." Last reviewed or updated March 18, 2021. https://www.irs.gov/forms-pubs/about-form-8805.
10. Internal Revenue Service. "About Form W-8IMY, Certificate of Foreign Intermediary, Foreign Flow-Through Entity, or Certain U.S. Branches for United States Tax Withholding and Reporting." Accessed May 27, 2023. https://www.irs.gov/forms-pubs/about-form-w-8-imy.
11. Internal Revenue Service. "About Form 8804-C, Application for Certification of Partner-Level Tax Consequences." Accessed May 23, 2023. https://www.irs.gov/forms-pubs/about-form-8804-c.
12. See IRS Notice 2021-51.

Beneficial Ownership

The Corporate Transparency Act

Andrew Weiner, Partner, Pillsbury

Brian Montgomery, Senior Counsel, Pillsbury

Congress adopted the Corporate Transparency Act (CTA) in January 2021 to address perceived gaps in the US government's ability to identify and combat the financing of terrorism, money laundering, financial fraud, and tax evasion.[1] The CTA will, for the first time, require many US domestic and foreign entities to file a report with the federal government that identifies their ultimate individual beneficial owners who have substantial ownership interests or can or do exercise substantial control over entities operating in the US. Those reporting requirements are effective January 1, 2024, for entities first formed or qualified to do business in the US and January 1, 2025, for entities existing or qualified as of January 1, 2024. The US government has estimated that 32.6 million companies will be required to submit reports in the first year the CTA is effective, and that approximately 5 million new companies will be required to submit reports each year thereafter.

Congress directed the U.S. Department of the Treasury's Financial Crimes Enforcement Network (FinCEN) to promulgate regulations implementing the CTA. On September 30, 2022, FinCEN published final regulations for the reporting of beneficial ownership information,[2] and as of the date of publication, is in the process of finalizing additional regulations and building a secure registry to which companies will report required information. FinCEN has announced that it will launch the registry by January 1, 2024.

THE CTA APPLIES TO "REPORTING COMPANIES"

The CTA imposes reporting requirements on "domestic reporting companies" formed under US law and "foreign reporting companies" qualified to do business in the US.

A domestic reporting company is defined as a US corporation, limited liability company, or other entity created by the filing of a document with a secretary of state or a similar office under state or tribal law. Similarly, a foreign reporting company is defined as a foreign corporation, limited liability company, or other entity that has registered (qualified) to do business in any US state or tribal jurisdiction by the filing of a document with a secretary of state or a similar state or tribal office. For purposes of these definitions, "state" includes US states as well as the District of Columbia, Puerto Rico, Guam, the U.S. Virgin Islands, and any other US commonwealth, territory, or possession.

Any entity not required to file a formation or qualification document with a state secretary of state or similar state or tribal office is not considered a "reporting company" and is not required to file beneficial ownership information. As a result, sole proprietorships, general partnerships, many trusts, and other similar entities are not required to file with FinCEN. This is not a completely clear distinction, particularly with trusts. The status of trusts was particularly noted by FinCEN as a subject for which it may provide further clarification.

REPORTING COMPANIES MUST REPORT BENEFICIAL OWNERSHIP INFORMATION TO FINCEN

The CTA defines a beneficial owner as an individual who, directly or indirectly, by any instrument, contract, arrangement, understanding, relationship, or mechanism, either (1) exercises "substantial control" over a reporting company or (2) owns or controls at least 25 percent of the ownership interests of a reporting company. FinCEN has interpreted these categories quite broadly, with definitions that are subjective and complex, with a stated intent to maximize the pool of individuals whose identities are required to be reported.

Substantial Control of a Reporting Company

FinCEN broadly defines which individuals have substantial control of a reporting company and are therefore beneficial owners for purposes of the CTA:

Senior Officers. One such category is a company's senior officers, which the regulation specifically defines to include individuals holding the titles of president, chief financial officer, general counsel, chief executive officer, and chief operating officer. However, the individual's role, not his or her title, is ultimately determinative—the regulation provides that any company officer who performs a similar function or has similar authority to the titles just described, de facto or de jure, regardless of the individual's official title, is also deemed a senior officer and therefore a beneficial owner.

Important Decisions. Individuals with authority over the appointment or removal of any senior officer or a majority of the board of directors or similar body or who direct, determine, or have substantial influence over a reporting company's "important decisions" will also be deemed to have substantial control. "Important decisions" include those concerning the nature, scope, and attributes of the company's business; reorganization, dissolution, or merger of the company; major expenditures or investments; issuance of equity; incurrence of significant debt; approval of the company's operating budget; and amendments to its substantial governance documents.

Indirect Control. An individual may exercise substantial control of a reporting company indirectly, including through board representation, control or ownership of voting power or voting rights of a reporting company, control of intermediaries that themselves exercise substantial control of a reporting company, and certain rights associated with financing arrangements.

Ownership Interests of a Reporting Company

An individual will also qualify as a beneficial owner if the individual owns or controls at least 25 percent of the "ownership interests" of a reporting company. FinCEN's regulation broadly defines ownership interest to include any instrument, contract, arrangement, understanding, relationship, or mechanism used to establish ownership. An individual may qualify as a beneficial owner through direct or indirect ownership or control of a reporting company, including indirect ownership or control through intermediary entities, or rights to acquire additional equity.

Ownership interests specifically covered include equity, stock, a preorganization certificate or subscription, and a transferable share of, or voting trust certificate or certificate of deposit for, an equity security, interest in a joint venture, or certificate of interest in a business trust. Such interests qualify as ownership interests under the regulation without regard to whether the instrument is transferable, is classified as stock or anything similar, or represents voting or nonvoting shares. Any capital or profit interest in an entity also qualifies as an ownership interest.

FinCEN's regulation also describes circumstances in which an individual may qualify as holding an ownership interest through a trust or similar arrangement, including as a trustee with authority to dispose of trust assets, as a beneficiary who is the sole permissible recipient of income and principal or has the right to demand a distribution of or withdraw substantially all of the assets from the trust, and as a grantor or settlor who has the right to revoke the trust or otherwise withdraw the assets of the trust.

The term "beneficial owner(s)" excludes (1) minors (if parents or guardians are identified), (2) nominees (if principals are identified), (3) holders of inchoate rights of inheritance (until they vest), (4) employees (excluding senior officers), and (5) creditors (but only if they solely hold the interest and rights of a creditor, and have no options to acquire equity interests or convert debt to equity).

NEWLY CREATED REPORTING COMPANIES MUST REPORT COMPANY APPLICANTS TO FINCEN

Reporting companies formed after January 1, 2024, will be required to report information concerning "company applicants." A company applicant is the individual who directly files the document that creates or registers the reporting company with the secretary of state or similar state or tribal office. In addition, if another individual is primarily responsible for directing or controlling such filing, that individual is also deemed a company applicant.

CERTAIN ENTITIES ARE EXEMPT FROM THE CTA'S REPORTING REQUIREMENTS

The CTA specifically exempts 23 categories of entities from the definition of a reporting company and therefore from the CTA's reporting requirements. Many of the CTA's exemptions are complex, and entities will need to closely analyze the scope of an exemption to determine whether it applies. This is particularly true for foreign entities, because many of the CTA's exemptions will apply to foreign entities in more limited circumstances than to domestic entities. In some cases, a CTA exemption may not apply to foreign entities under any circumstances.

Many of the CTA's exemptions will apply primarily to larger, established entities; in contrast, the CTA may create a more significant burden on smaller or newly established entities. The CTA may also have a larger impact on foreign entities than US entities. The most notable CTA exemption in this category is for entities that qualify as a "large operating company," which is defined as any entity that (1) employs more than 20 full-time employees in the US, (2) has filed a US federal income tax return for the prior year that demonstrates more than $5 million in annual US gross receipts or sales, and (3) has an operating presence at a physical office in the US that the entity owns or leases and does not share with unaffiliated entities. A newly created domestic entity or a foreign entity registering to do business in the US for the first time will not be able to qualify for this exemption, because neither will have a US tax return for the previous year. Even large foreign entities that are already registered to do business in the US, but have a limited US presence, may find it difficult to meet each of these three criteria.

Many of the CTA's exemptions apply to entities that are already regulated by a US government agency, which will also mean in practice that the exemptions apply primarily to larger, well-established US entities. For example, the CTA includes exemptions for certain regulated banks, credit unions, money services businesses, depository institution holding companies, insurance companies, securities issuers, broker-dealers, investment companies, investment advisors, venture capital fund advisors, and entities registered under the Commodity Exchange Act. Foreign companies in these businesses who are regulated elsewhere may not qualify for these exemptions.

Certain pooled investment vehicles are also exempt from the CTA's definition of a reporting company. To qualify, the pooled investment vehicle must be an investment company as defined in the Investment Company Act of 1940 or be operated or advised by a person that meets the requirements of the CTA exemptions for banks, credit unions, securities broker dealers, investment companies, investment advisors, or venture capital fund advisors and if the foreign fund is listed on the operator's/advisor's form ADV (the uniform form used by investment advisors to register with both the SEC and state securities authorities).

The exemption for pooled investment vehicles is more limited for foreign entities. If a foreign entity would be a reporting company but for the pooled investment vehicle exemption, the entity is deemed a reporting company under the CTA and must file required reports. However, the entity's reports must only include information about a single individual who exercises substantial control over the entity. If more than one individual exercises substantial control, the entity must only report information for the individual who has the greatest authority over the strategic management of the entity.

Although certain inactive entities are exempt from the CTA, this exemption will also have limited applicability to foreign investors—an entity will only qualify under this exemption if it is not owned in any part, directly or indirectly, by a foreign person. The entity must also meet several other criteria, including that it was in existence on or before January 1, 2020, and is not engaged in any active business, has not had a change in ownership or sent or received greater than $1,000 in the preceding 12-month period, and does not otherwise hold any assets, whether in the US or abroad.

The CTA also exempts subsidiaries of certain exempt entities. FinCEN has interpreted this exemption to apply only to subsidiaries that are wholly owned by an exempt entity. The

CTA also specifically excludes subsidiaries of certain exempt entities from this exemption, including subsidiaries of money services businesses, pooled investment vehicles, and inactive entities.

An entity that relies on a CTA exemption will need to closely monitor whether it continues to meet the criteria to qualify for the exemption. If an entity ceases to meet an exemption's criteria and is not otherwise exempt, it will need to promptly file the reports required by the CTA with FinCEN. As discussed in more detail later in this chapter, failure to do so could result in significant civil and criminal penalties.

THE CTA'S FILING REQUIREMENTS

Reporting companies must submit initial reports to FinCEN and subsequently submit updated or corrected reports if reported information changes or the company discovers an inaccuracy in reporting information.

Initial Report

The CTA requires reporting companies to file an initial report with FinCEN that must include prescribed information concerning the reporting company and every individual who is a beneficial owner of the reporting company.

Domestic reporting companies created on or after January 1, 2024, and foreign reporting companies that first register to do business with a state or tribal government on or after January 1, 2024, will be required to file an initial report with FinCEN within 30 calendar days of the earlier of the date on which the entity receives actual notice that its creation has become effective or the date on which a secretary of state or similar office first provides public notice, such as through a publicly accessible registry, that the reporting company has been created or registered.

Reporting companies formed or registered before January 1, 2024, will have until January 1, 2025, to file an initial report with FinCEN.

Reporting companies must submit the following information concerning the company in an initial report: full legal name, any trade or "doing business as" name(s), the street address from which the company conducts business in the US, the state or tribal jurisdiction where the company first registers, and its US taxpayer identification number (TIN), or a tax identification number issued by a foreign jurisdiction if the company does have a US TIN.

Reporting companies will also be required to report certain personal information of beneficial owners: full legal name, date of birth, current residential address, a unique identifying number from qualifying identification document (such as a passport), and an image of the qualifying identification document. Reporting companies formed or registered after January 1, 2024, must also file the same information concerning company applicants, except that if the company applicant forms or registers the entity in the course of their business, the reporting company submits the street address of such business rather than their residential address.

Updated and Corrected Reports

Reporting companies will also be required to file updated reports within 30 days of any change to the information previously submitted to FinCEN concerning the reporting company or its beneficial owners. This requirement applies to all changes concerning the required company and beneficial ownership information, including any change to who is a beneficial owner (i.e., an individual ceases to be a beneficial owner or becomes a beneficial owner) and any change to whether an entity meets the criteria to be exempt from reporting to FinCEN. Reporting companies must also promptly correct any inaccuracies in information previously reported to FinCEN. Reporting companies will not be required to submit updated information concerning company applicants.

It will be critically important for reporting companies to establish procedures to effectively monitor changes in beneficial owners and exemption status, as well for providing accurate information in reports to FinCEN. Failure to provide timely and accurate reports to FinCEN could result in civil and criminal liability.

PENALTIES FOR FAILURE TO COMPLY WITH THE CTA'S REQUIREMENTS

Individuals and entities who fail to comply with the CTA's requirements may be subject to significant civil and criminal penalties, including imprisonment. These violations can be generally classified into two categories: failure to report required beneficial ownership information and the unauthorized disclosure or use of beneficial ownership information.

Reporting Violations

The CTA specifies two types of reporting violations, each of which can result in significant civil and criminal penalties. First, it is a violation for an individual or entity to willfully provide, or attempt to provide, false or fraudulent beneficial ownership information to FinCEN, including false or fraudulent documentation. It is also a violation for an individual or entity to willfully fail to report complete or updated beneficial ownership information to FinCEN. Individuals may also be liable for a reporting violation if they cause the failure to report complete or updated beneficial ownership information, or are a senior officer of the reporting company at the time of the failure.

FinCEN did not adopt a broad "good faith" excuse for reporting mistakes. However, FinCEN has clarified that, as a general matter, an inadvertent mistake by a reporting company acting in good faith would likely not constitute a willfully false or fraudulent violation. The analysis of each potential violation will depend on the individual facts and circumstances surrounding the entity's certification and reporting of the beneficial ownership information.

The CTA includes a safe harbor if a person voluntarily corrects inaccurate information in a report within 90 days of submitting the report. To qualify for the safe harbor, the person must file the corrected report within 30 days of becoming aware of, or having reason to know of, the inaccuracy. A person may not qualify for the safe harbor if they attempted to evade the reporting requirements when making the original report or if they had actual knowledge of the inaccuracy when the original report was submitted.

Any person that commits a reporting violation may be liable for a civil penalty of up to $500 for each day that the violation continues or has not been remedied, and may be fined up to $10,000 and imprisoned for up to two years.

Unauthorized Disclosure or Use of Beneficial Ownership Information

Government officials and other persons who misuse beneficial ownership information reported to FinCEN may also be subject to civil and criminal penalties, which exceed those applicable to reporting violations.

DISCLOSURE OF BENEFICIAL OWNERSHIP INFORMATION BY FINCEN

Beneficial ownership information submitted to FinCEN is nonpublic. However, FinCEN is authorized, upon compliance with prescribed procedures (including court orders in some cases), to disclose information to federal and state government agencies (and to qualified foreign governments), for law enforcement and regulatory purposes, including tax collection. The CTA also authorizes FinCEN to disclose beneficial ownership information (BOI) to financial institutions to conduct legally required customer due diligence, provided the financial institutions have their customers' consent.

STATES ARE CONSIDERING SIMILAR LEGISLATION

In June 2023, the New York legislature passed a bill, known as the LLC Transparency Act, which would require limited liability companies to report beneficial ownership information to the New York secretary of state. If signed by New York's governor, the bill would become effective a year thereafter. The New York bill is similar in many respects to the CTA, with two key differences: (1) the bill would create a publicly accessible database of beneficial ownership information reported to the New York secretary of state, and (2) the bill would apply only to limited liability companies.

The California legislature has also introduced similar legislation, although as of the date of publication, the California bills have not been passed by the legislature.

* * *

The effective date of the CTA is quickly approaching. Entities and individuals with US operations or who have invested directly or indirectly in US companies, will need to assess whether they will be subject to reporting. Reporting companies that are subject to the CTA will need to establish policies and procedures to ensure that they timely and accurately report required information to FinCEN. Investors who might be beneficial owners have to consider what to disclose and the consequences of both disclosure and nondisclosure. Failure to do so could expose entities to significant civil and criminal liability and potential reputational risk.

NOTES

1. 12 U.S.C. § 5336.
2. 31 C.F.R. 1010.380, 87 FR 59498.

Farmland

The Agricultural Foreign Investment Disclosure Act

Andrew Weiner, Partner, Pillsbury

Stephanie Mason, Associate, Pillsbury

Samantha Sharma, Senior Associate, Pillsbury

Prior to 1978, the US government did not track or monitor acquisitions and/or holding of US agricultural land by foreign investors. A study published by the U.S. General Accounting Office (GAO) found that in 1978 the federal government did not have access to any reliable data on the amount of US farmland owned by foreign investors. In response to these findings, Congress passed the Agricultural Foreign Investment Disclosure Act (AFIDA) of 1978, requiring all foreign persons who acquire, dispose of, or hold an interest in US agricultural land to disclose such transactions and holdings to the secretary of agriculture (SOA). Furthermore, AFIDA established a nationwide system for collecting information regarding foreign investments and ownership of US agricultural land. The information collected is used by the Economic Research Service (ERS), a component of the U.S. Department of Agriculture (USDA), in the preparation of periodic reports to the U.S. Congress and the president concerning the effect of foreign-owned agricultural land on US family-owned farms and rural communities.

According to the most recent USDA report, as of December 31, 2021, "[f]oreign persons held an interest in approximately 40 million acres of US agricultural land [. . .]. This is 3.1 percent of all privately held agricultural land and 1.8 percent of all land in the United States." This number grows expeditiously each year. The USDA found that "since 2015, foreign holdings have increased an average of 2.2 million acres annually, ranging from 0.8 million acres to 3.3 million acres per year." This growing trend has recently received the attention of the US government, who is concerned with the potential threats of foreign land ownership to national security and food security in the US. However, the federal government has little power to curtail the amount of acreage owned by foreign persons as no current laws exist to restrict such persons from acquiring and holding US agricultural land.

On July 1, 2022, U.S. Representatives Jim Costa (CA-21), Elise Stefanik (NY-21), and Rick Crawford (AR-01), along with U.S. Senators John Tester (D-MT) and Mike Rounds (R-SD) introduced the Promoting Agriculture Safeguards and Security (the PASS) Act. The PASS Act would prohibit "persons who are acting on behalf of or otherwise directed by the government of a prohibited country (defined as China, Russia, Iran, and North Korea) [from] carry[ing] out any merger, acquisition, or takeover that could result in foreign control of a US agricultural company." This act is the first of its kind, and if enacted, the Pass Act could be used to stop or regulate the growing amount of US agricultural land purchased by the stated prohibited countries and other countries, as the US later determines. The data collected by the USDA, in compliance with AFIDA, has proven necessary, as the US government uses it to provide greater insight on the correlation between foreign ownership of US agricultural land in the US and possible threats to national security and food security.

AGRICULTURAL FOREIGN INVESTMENT DISCLOSURE ACT OF 1978

Real estate professionals working with a foreign person to acquire agriculture land in the US must be aware of AFIDA's disclosure requirements. All foreign persons are required to disclose any interest acquired, transferred, or held in US agricultural land to the SOA.[1] However, certain interests in agricultural land are exempt from disclosure, including but not limited to security interests, leaseholds, and contingent future interests.

AFIDA groups "foreign person" into four categories:

1. Any individual, who is not a citizen or national of the US, a citizen of the Northern Mariana Islands or the Trust Territory of the Pacific Islands (collectively, the US territories), or lawfully admitted to the US for permanent residence or paroled into the US under the Immigration and Nationality Act (any foreign individual)
2. Any person, other than an individual or a government, which is created or organized under the laws of a foreign government or which has its principal place of business located outside of the US (any foreign organization)
3. Any foreign government
4. Any person, other than an individual or a government, which is created or organized under the laws of any state, and in which a significant interest or substantial control is directly or indirectly held by foreign individuals, organizations, or governments (i.e., any foreign person that has a significant interest or substantial control [directly or indirectly] in a US organization)
   a. To determine if a person has such significant interest or substantial control to be considered a foreign person under Section 781.2(g)(4), AFIDA requires a foreign individual, organization, or government to hold, directly or indirectly, (i) 10 percent or more interest in a US entity, if acting alone; (ii) 10 percent or more collective interest in an US entity, if acting in concert; or (iii) 50 percent or more collective interest, if the foreign entity is not acting in concert. AFIDA does not define the term "acting in concert." Preparers of Form FAS-153 should reach out to their local FSA county office or the FSA handbook for specific questions regarding their interest in agricultural land.

Once the foreign person determines whether they hold a non-exempt interest in said land, they must next determine if the land is considered "agricultural land." AFIDA is primary concerned with the disclosure of foreign interest in agricultural land. Section 781.2(b) of AFIDA defines "agricultural land" as land in the US totaling 10 or more acres in the aggregate that is used for forestry production or land currently used for, or if currently idle, land last used within the past five years for farming, ranching, or timber production; or 10 or less acres in the aggregate that produce annual gross receipts in excess of $1,000 from the sale of the farm, ranch, or timber products.[2]

FORM FSA-153

All foreign persons who meet AFIDA reporting criteria (i.e., owns a direct or indirect interest in US agricultural land) must file Form FSA-153 with the Farm Service Agency (FSA) county office in the county where the land is located or where the FSA county office administering the program carried out on the land is located. Furthermore, the FSA office in Washington, DC, may permit a foreign person, upon request, to file directly with their office if complex filings are involved.[3] Form FSA-153 requires all foreign persons to provide their legal name, address, citizenship, type of interest, the purchase price, the agricultural purpose of the land, a description of the property and how the property was acquired or transferred, the relationship to the previous owner(s), and the rental agreement. If a foreign person transfers their interest to a third party (either US or foreign owned), the form requires disclosure of the transferee's legal name, address, and citizenship or country of organization, whichever applicable.

It is important to note that Form FSA-153's disclosure requirements are rather inclusive/ expansive, requiring foreign persons to provide the identity of any and all individuals, governments, or organizations that hold an interest in said foreign person, irrespective of whether or not they were included on the original form submitted to the FSA county office. AFIDA permits the USDA to require a foreign person to submit additional information and/or file an additional report to address any discrepancies. Refer to Section 781.3 of the AFIDA for additional guidance on reporting requirements.

Form FSA-153 must be filed within 90 days after (1) the date of acquisition or transfer of interest in agricultural land; (2) the date on which a person, who holds or acquires any interest in US agricultural land, becomes a foreign person; and/or (3) the date on which non-US agricultural land subsequently becomes agricultural land. In addition, foreign person must submit a revised form FSA-153 or a written notification, no later than 90 days after such person ceases being a foreign person or such land ceases being agricultural.

Please note that the information disclosed on form FSA-153 is not exclusive to the USDA or SOA. The USDA is permitted to disclose the provided information to other federal, state, local government agencies; tribal agencies; and nongovernmental entities that have been authorized access to such information by statute or regulation.

PENALTIES

AFIDA applies penalties to any foreign person who violates the reporting obligations set forth within. Such violations include failure to submit a required report, failure to update/ maintain any submitted report with accurate information, and submitting an incomplete or misleading report.

1. **Penalty for a late-filed report:** One-tenth of 1 percent of the fair market value of the foreign person's interest in the agricultural land, for each week or portion thereof that such violation continues, but the total penalty imposed should not exceed 25 percent of the fair market value of the foreign person's interest in the land
2. **Submission of an incomplete or misleading report, failure to submit a report, or failure to maintain accurate reports:** 25 percent of the fair market value of the foreign person's interest in the agricultural land with respect to which such violation occurred

The FSA determines the fair market value of the foreign person's interest in the agricultural land. All penalties previously listed are subject to downward adjustments based on the factors stated in Section 781.4(b)(3) of AFIDA (including but not limited to, the total time the violation existed and the method of discovery of the violation).

If the USDA/FSA finds that a foreign person has violated the reporting obligations, it will send a written notice of apparent liability to the violating party. The written notice of apparent liability includes facts about the violation, the type of violation involved, the amount of the proposed penalty, the fair market value of the foreign person's interest in the subject land, and a summary of the course of actions available to the foreign person. The violating party must respond to the FSA's written notice within 60 days of receipt, or the imposed penalty becomes final. If the violating party fails to respond to the notice of apparent liability or fails to pay the imposed penalty, the case will be referred to the Department of Justice for prosecution to recover the amount of the penalty. The Department of Agriculture is granted the authority to set off the assessed penalties against any disbursements to a foreign person made through their administered programs.

STATE REGULATION AND ACTIONS POINTING TO FUTURE FEDERAL REGULATION

Foreign investment in real property, particularly agricultural land, is increasingly being scrutinized at the federal and state levels. In the FY2022 Consolidated Appropriations Act, Congress directed the USDA to collect data on agricultural land owned by the governments of China, Russia, Iran, or North Korea and analyze the potential impact of such ownership on the US agricultural sector, food security, and rural economies. In the FY2023 Consolidated Appropriations Act, the analysis was expanded to include the impact of foreign investments on family farms, rural communities, and the domestic food supply. The USDA is also tasked with establishing a process for electronically submitting and retaining AFIDA disclosures, including maintaining an internet database of "disaggregated data" from 1978 to date. In addition, foreign investment in real estate is subject to review and control by the Committee on Foreign Investment in the United States (CFIUS) and the Office of Foreign Assets Control at the U.S. Department of Treasury, among others, all of which are outside the scope of this chapter.

As of the date of this chapter, it is reported that at least 20 states have enacted laws prohibiting or restricting, to a greater or lesser extent, foreign ownership of or investments in real property, and at least 12 other states are considering the imposition of similar restrictions. Agricultural land is a common target, and national or food security are frequently cited as concerns. As a recent example, on May 8, 2023, Florida adopted Senate Bill 264 (SB 264), which restricts or limits specified classes of non-US individuals or entities of certain "foreign countries of concern" from purchasing (or having more than a de minimis interest in) agricultural land and certain other real property in Florida. SB 264 is especially restrictive for Chinese investors. SB 264 specifically prohibits direct or indirect ownership of real property by persons or entities from, or associated with, the People's Republic of China or the Chinese Communist Party. "Foreign countries of concern" also include the Russia, Iran, North Korea, Cuba, Venezuela, and the Syrian Arab Republic. Penalties for noncompliance with the prohibitions and prescribed registration requirements of SB 264 may include civil penalties, liens on, and forfeiture of the underlying property.

While the constitutionality of SB 264 is subject to ongoing scrutiny by the courts, the shift toward a more restrictive regime is evident. Notably, on August 16, 2023, the U.S. District Court of the Northern District of Florida affirmed the law's validity, dismissing plaintiffs' claims that it contravened both the U.S. Constitution and the Fair Housing Act. It would be prudent for non-US investors to monitor developments in this area.

NOTES

1. The federal government monitors and tracks any interest in agricultural land acquired, transferred or held by a foreign person except (1) security interests, (2) leaseholds, (3) contingent future interests, (4) non-contingent future interests that do not become possessory upon the termination of the present possessory estate, (5) surface or subsurface easements and rights of way used for purposes unrelated to agricultural production, and (6) an interest solely in mineral rights.
2. Land used for forestry production is considered "agricultural land" when 10 percent of the land is "stocked by trees of any size, including land that formerly had such tree cover and that will be naturally or artificially regenerated." 7 C.F.R. § 781.2(b). In general, farming, ranching, and timber production means growing crops, livestock, or trees.
3. For example, a foreign person might be permitted to file with the DC office if the land being reported is located in more than one county and a foreign person has acquired separate tracts in multiple counties. Filers should review the FSA's AFIDA handbook, which explains that the USDA may grant permission to a foreign person to file their reports directly with the agency.

Real Estate Investment Trusts

Non-US Investment into US REITs

Jonathan Scher, Managing Director, Global Head of Tax,
Madison International Realty

I n 1960, Congress enacted legislation to create real estate investment trusts (REITs), which are generally US corporations (and entities treated as US corporations for US federal income tax purposes) that made a special election to be a REIT. As long as the REIT meets various requirements, including ownership of a certain amount of real estate assets, a REIT may deduct its paid dividends against its taxable income and potentially reduce its federal corporate income tax to zero. Although the 1960 Congress created REITs as a way for small US retail investors to acquire ownership interests in diversified real estate without incurring double taxation otherwise inherent in the US corporate tax system, similar to a mutual fund for stocks and securities, REITs have also become attractive vehicles for non-US investors to reduce their US federal income taxes.

REITS, GENERALLY

REITs are domestic corporations, trusts, or other entities that fulfill certain statutory requirements and elect REIT status. Such statutory requirements consist of both organizational requirements and numerical tests that must be met to ensure compliance with the REIT rules. The organizational requirements include but are not limited to: (1) management authority must be held by one or more trustees or directors; (2) the REIT must have at least 100 shareholders, generally beginning on its second tax year; and (3) greater than 50 percent in value of the entity's stock cannot be owned by 5 or fewer individuals during the last half of each tax year (i.e., the closely held test).

Regarding the various numerical tests, certain thresholds must be met for the assets held by the REIT (tested quarterly) and income generated at or below the REIT (tested annually) to ensure REIT compliance. Generally, at least 75 percent of the gross value of a REIT's total assets at the close of each quarter of a taxable year must consist of "qualifying" real estate assets, cash and cash items, and US federal government securities. The REIT's other assets must meet various numerical tests. In addition, a REIT must satisfy two critical annual income tests: (1) a REIT must derive at least 75 percent of its annual gross income from items including, but not limited to, rents from real property, gain from sales of real property, interests on mortgage obligations secured by real property, dividends from other REITs, and gain from sale of REIT shares; and (2) a REIT must derive at least 95 percent of its income from the aforementioned sources as well as interest and dividends from any source and gains from sale of non-REIT stock or securities.

The REIT must make minimum annual distributions of at least 90 percent of its taxable income to its shareholders. As mentioned previously, an entity that qualifies as a REIT (and thus meets all applicable organizational and numerical tests) is generally able to avoid entity-level federal corporate income tax to the extent the REIT makes a dividend distribution to its shareholders equal to 100 percent of its taxable income each year, since the REIT is entitled to a entity-level deduction equal to the amount of such dividends paid.

Since REITs generally hold pools of real estate investments that can include equity ownership of varied types of properties in multiple locations and/or real estate-related debt interests, a key business advantage to investing in REITs is relatively quick diversification of the investor's portfolio without the need to undertake extended due diligence of each specific property or debt interest.[1] Ownership of publicly traded REITs also provides liquidity. In addition, as described more fully later and the primary focus of this chapter, REITs can provide certain tax benefits to non-US investors investing in US real estate.

TAXATION OF NON-US INVESTORS IN US REAL ESTATE VIA REITS

Non-US investors who own direct interests in US real property (or equity interests in partnerships owning such property) may be deemed engaged in the conduct of a US trade or business and as such are generally (1) taxed as US persons at graduated US federal income tax rates and (2) required to file US income tax returns. The ownership of US corporate stock, by contrast, does not trigger such consequences, as it generally shields or blocks such non-US investors from being treated as engaged in the conduct of a US trade or business. A US corporation that serves such a blocking function is called a "US blocker." The price for the use of a US blocker is typically the US federal corporate income tax paid by the US blocker on its taxable income. If the US blocker is a REIT, however, the corporate-level federal income tax may be reduced to zero by the REIT's dividend distributions.

Unless a tax treaty or statutory exception applies, a non-US REIT shareholder will generally be subject to withholding tax (1) in respect of distributions of REIT operating income and (2) on REIT distributions attributable to the gains from the REIT's sale of US real property interests (USRPIs). Non-US shareholders may also be taxed on gain recognized in respect of sales or other dispositions of certain REIT shares. The following sections will explore further some of these anticipated tax implications and relevant exceptions for certain non-US investors utilizing REITs.

Operating Income

Generally, operating income received by a non-US investor directly investing in US real estate may be considered income effectively connected with the conduct of a US trade or business, which is taxed on a net income basis at graduated rates and generally requires the non-US investor to file a US income tax return. However, as noted previously, when such non-US investor invests in US real property through a REIT, the REIT generally shields such ECI from the non-US shareholder, who avoids a US income tax return filing obligation.

A non-US investor's dividend and interest income from a REIT or other US corporation may be considered fixed, determinable, annual, or periodical (FDAP) income. FDAP income is generally all US-source income that is neither ECI nor capital gain, and non-US investors are subject to a flat 30 percent withholding tax rate on all FDAP income. This tax may be reduced pursuant to the terms of an income tax treaty between the US and the country in which the REIT shareholder is a tax resident or pursuant to a US statutory exemption. Any tax that is withheld by the REIT must be remitted by the REIT to the IRS.

Tax Treaty

Certain older US income tax treaties provide for a reduced US withholding tax rate on all US-source dividends, including REIT dividends, such as the US tax treaties with Poland (1974), Romania (1973), and South Korea (1976). More recent US tax treaties generally provide that the reduced US tax rate on US-source dividends applies only to a limited extent to REIT dividends below certain ownership thresholds, such as the US tax treaties with Germany (1989), the Netherlands (1992), and the United Kingdom (2001). For example, under the German-US income tax treaty, generally the flat 30 percent statutory withholding rate may be reduced to 15 percent, assuming that the investor owns under 10 percent of the REIT.

Some treaties further provide that a non-US pension plan is exempt from US withholding tax on all dividends, including REIT dividends, as long as the pension plan is not related to the dividend payor. For example, dividends received by an exempt Dutch or Canadian pension fund are exempt from US withholding tax under their respective US income tax treaties. The US-Canada income tax treaty, however, contains certain antihybrid rules that may disallow treaty benefits for some types of US REITs.

Sovereign Wealth Funds (SWFs)

Investment in US real estate by SWFs is considered a major source of capital flowing into the US. As a general rule, foreign investors are generally subject to a 30 percent US withholding tax on US-source dividends, including REIT dividends. However, the U.S. Internal Revenue Code (IRC) provides a special rule under Section 892 that exempts foreign governments from US federal income tax on their income from US stocks and securities as long as the foreign government does not own over 50 percent or more (by vote or value) or otherwise have effective practical control of the US corporation or REIT paying the dividend. For this purpose, SWFs are considered part of the foreign government and entitled to the Section 892 exemption. Of particular importance, if a SWF owns less than 50 percent of the vote and value of a REIT (i.e., the REIT is not a "commercially controlled" entity), the SWF is exempt from US withholding tax on any REIT dividends.

CAPITAL GAIN DISTRIBUTIONS

Generally, REIT distributions of asset sales proceeds (sometimes referred to as capital gain distributions) to a non-US investor are taxed under the Foreign Investment in Real Property Tax Act of 1980 (FIRPTA) at the generally applicable rates for capital gains (currently a maximum of 21 percent for corporate investors and 20 percent for long-term capital gain for individual investors). Specifically, these capital gain distributions are attributable to gain from sales or other dispositions of US real property interests (USRPIs) held directly or indirectly by the REIT. USRPIs can include, for example, real estate or debt that is secured by real property and provides for contingent or participating interest based on a share of cash flow or other amounts generated by real property of the debtor. Under special FIRPTA look-through rules applicable to REITs, such distributions are treated as gains recognized by the non-US investor from the sale or exchange of a USRPI to the extent of the investor's pro rata share of the REIT gain. As such, a non-US investor who receives such distributions must also file a US income tax return and pay US federal income tax (and potentially a branch profits tax for a corporate non-US investor) directly with respect to the relevant gain. In addition, under the FIRPTA withholding provisions, a REIT is generally required to withhold 21 percent of all distributions designated as capital gain dividends at the time of payment. The tax withheld is available as a credit against the non-US investor's actual amount of tax ultimately due at the time returns are filed. Tax treaties generally provide no relief from FIRPTA tax on these types of REIT distributions, in contrast to the reduced rates that may be available with respect to REIT dividends attributable to operating income, as described earlier.

TAX ON DISPOSITION OF REIT SHARES

USRPIs include the stock of US real property holding corporations, which are generally corporations whose assets mostly consist of interests in US real property. If the REIT is a USRPHC, a non-US holder of REIT shares will generally be subject to FIRPTA taxation on gain recognized upon a sale or other disposition of the REIT shares. Gains on sale of shares in REITs that are USRPIs will be taxable, in general, in the same manner as REIT capital gain distributions, at applicable capital gain rates. In the case of sales of REIT shares, however, FIRPTA withholding is imposed by the buyer, at a rate of 15 percent of the gross proceeds paid, unless a certificate reducing and/or eliminating such required withholding is obtained.

There are four key exceptions to the general rule that non-US investors are subject to FIRPTA taxation on gains on sale or other dispositions of REIT shares:

1. **Publicly Traded REITs:** A non-US investor would not be taxed on gain resulting from sale of REIT stock if (a) the shares are traded on an "established securities market" and (b) such investor owns no more than 10 percent of the REIT (taking into account for this purpose, stock owned by certain persons related to the investor) over the prior five years. An established securities market includes, for this purpose, (a) a US securities exchange registered under Section 6 of the SEC Act of 1934, (b) a non-US national securities exchange that is officially recognized, sanctioned, or supervised by another governmental authority, or (c) any over-the-counter market. There is some debate over whether this exception applies if a partnership holds more than 10 percent of the REIT's stock, sells the stock, and allocates the gain to partners that indirectly hold not more than 10 percent of the REIT's stock.

Furthermore, capital gain distributions by REITs with shares traded on a US-established securities market are not subject to FIRPTA if paid to shareholders who own no more than 10 percent of the REIT over the prior one year. Instead, the REIT capital gain distributions are taxed in the same way as REIT ordinary dividends (i.e., FDAP income subject to up to 30 percent withholding tax).

2. **Domestically Controlled REITs (DC-REITs):** Gain on disposition of a "domestically controlled" REIT is not taxable to non-US investors under FIRPTA. A REIT is "domestically controlled" if less than 50 percent of the value of its shares was held, directly or indirectly, by non-US persons during the five years before the REIT stock disposition (or since the REIT's inception, if shorter). The DC-REIT exception applies only to gain on the sale of REIT stock and not to the REIT's capital gain distributions from asset sales. Such a rule makes it particularly attractive for non-US investors to acquire shares in REITs owned primarily by US persons so long as the exit strategy is to sell REIT shares.

The Protecting Americans from Tax Hikes (PATH) Act of 2015 contains provisions that in certain instances make it easier for a publicly traded REIT to qualify as a DC-REIT by adding certain presumptions as to US ownership. However, at various points in time, there have been legislative and/or executive proposals that if enacted would make it more difficult for a REIT to qualify as a DC-REIT. For instance, in December 2022, the US Treasury released certain proposed tax regulations for determining the "domestically controlled" status of a REIT. In one private letter ruling (PLR 200923001), for purposes of determining indirect ownership by non-US persons, the IRS took the position that it is only necessary to look through entities that typically do not pay US tax (such as REITs and partnerships) in determining indirect foreign ownership, and therefore it was not necessary to look through a domestic C corporation to its shareholders. The proposed tax regulations, however, provide that a taxpayer must instead look through a "foreign owned domestic corporation" (defined as any nonpublic domestic C corporation owned 25 percent or more directly or indirectly by non-US persons) when determining domestic ownership of a REIT. The position seems to be contrary to PLR 200923001, which could make it more difficult to create DC-REITs and have minority interests in DC-REITs marketed to non-US investors on a tax-advantaged basis.

3. **Qualified Foreign Pension Funds (QFPFs):** Under the PATH Act, QFPFs (or wholly owned foreign entities of such funds) are no longer subject to tax under FIRPTA. A QFPF is generally defined as a trust, corporation, or other organization or arrangement (an eligible fund) that satisfies five requirements, including a purpose requirement that requires the eligible fund to provide retirement or pension benefits to current or former employees. It should be noted that the QFPF is still subject to the regular federal income tax rules on ECI, which may arise from real estate held directly by the QFPF. This change under the PATH Act primarily benefits QFPFs holding their US real property interests indirectly, including through a REIT. Accordingly, QFPFs may dispose of REIT shares or receive REIT capital gain distributions tax-free, regardless of the percentage of stock owned by the QFPF or whether the REIT is domestically controlled. It should be noted, however, that QFPFs are only exempt from FIRPTA, and not US taxation, generally. Thus, QFPFs are still subject to tax on ordinary dividends from REITs, unless a treaty applies.

4. **SWFs:** As mentioned previously, the US IRC provides a special rule under Section 892 that allows tax exemptions for certain foreign governments, including SWFs, that make investments in US stocks and securities. A SWF owning less than 50

percent of the vote and value of a REIT is exempt from tax on any gain resulting from the sale of REIT stock. In this case, similar to the tax exemption provided to QFPFs, the REIT need not be domestically controlled for the SWF to achieve the full tax exemption on gain. However, a SWF is subject to FIRPTA on REIT capital gain distributions from asset sales, while a QFPF is exempt from FIRPTA entirely and is not subject to US federal income tax on REIT capital gain distributions.

Figure 4.8-01 provides a high-level summary of anticipated tax implications to non-US investors investing in US real estate utilizing a REIT.

FIGURE 4.8-01 **Tax implications for non-US investors in US REITs**

TYPE OF INCOME	FOREIGN CORPORATE	FOREIGN GOVERNMENT (SECTION 892)	QFPF	FOREIGN INDIVIDUAL
REIT Dividend (earnings from rental operations)	0% - 30%[1]	0%[2]	-13.8%[1]	-11.4%[4]
Capital Gain Dividend (earnings from sale of underlying real estate assets)	21% / 44.7%[3]	21% / 44.7%[3]	0%	20% / 25%[5]
Capital Gain (from sale of non-domestically controlled REIT shares)	21%	0%[2]	0%	20%
Capital Gain (from sale of domestically controlled REIT shares)	0%	0%	0%	0%

[1] If a foreign investor resides in a jurisdiction that has a tax treaty with the US, the 30% WHT may be reduced to a lower tax rate.

[2] A foreign government (i.e., SWF) owning less than 50% of a US REIT would not be subject to US tax on (i) REIT dividends or (ii) gain on the sale of REIT stock.

[3] Capital gain dividend may be taxed at 21% corporate income tax rate, or in certain cases 44.7% (corporate income tax + branch profits tax, if applicable).

[4] If investor qualifies as a QFPF, then investor is not subject to FIRPTA (i.e., (i) 0% tax on REIT capital gain dividends and (ii) 0% tax on sale of REIT stock).

[5] 25% income tax rate applies to real estate depreciation recapture while 20% federal income tax rate applies to remaining long-term capital gain.

REITS AND TRANSACTIONAL CONSIDERATIONS

In the private equity investment fund business, non-US investors rely on fund managers to implement an optimal tax structure for the acquisition, hold, and exit of US real estate investments. The fund managers have to continuously monitor any changes in tax law during the investment period to maximize the investor's after-tax return. Real estate joint-venture partnerships (JVs) between fund manager and non-US investor will often involve the use of REITs that may help reduce or eliminate US tax leakage for non-US investors making investments in US real property. In certain cases, non-US investors will benefit from investing in funds alongside other US or non-US investors to unlock certain key tax benefits that may not otherwise be available to them if investing alone or direct in US real estate, such as the ability to sell the stock of a DC-REIT without any US federal income taxation.

As discussed previously, various tax regimes may apply (e.g., FDAP, ECI/FIRPTA) to a non-US investor's investment in US real estate. Accordingly, non-US investors may look to negotiate certain tax provisions in the joint-venture agreement (JVA), or side letters thereto, which impose a heightened standard of care (e.g., "commercially reasonable efforts" or "reasonably best efforts") on the fund manager to structure investments in a tax efficient manner and reduce or eliminate the impact of US income tax on the investor's return, where possible. For example, non-US investors may obligate fund manager to ensure (1) REIT compliance with all applicable organizational and numerical tests, (2) no ECI or any related US tax filing obligations for the investor, and (3) exit via sale of DC-REIT stock to achieve exemption from FIRPTA. Given the importance of tax structuring to non-US investors, it is best practice for fund managers to seek advice from tax or accounting firms and counsel on a deal-by-deal basis to ensure that non-US investors are provided all opportunities to achieve intended tax benefits, where applicable.

REFERENCES

Andiorio, Kelly, and Scott Helberg. "The ABCs of REITs." RSM, accessed February 8, 2023, https://rsmus.com/insights/industries/real-estate/abcs-of-reits.html.

"Joint Ventures as REIT Funds," Nareit (Moody's Special Comment), March 29, 2007, https://www.reit.com/sites/default/files/media/Portals/0/Files/Nareit/htdocs/meetings/LawAndAccounting07/secureDocuments/115.pdf.

Ravichandran, Arvind. "Modern FIRPTA: A Transactional Perspective," *Tax Notes Federal 175*, May 16, 2022, https://www.taxnotes.com/tax-notes-international/real-estate-taxation/modern-firpta-transactional-perspective/2022/05/16/7dg4h.

See generally, 26 U.S.C. § 1.

See generally, 26 U.S.C. § 856.

See generally, 26 U.S.C. § 857.

See generally, 26 U.S.C. § 864.

See generally, 26 U.S.C. § 871 (a), (b).

See generally, 26 U.S.C. § 881.

See generally, 26 U.S.C. § 882.

See generally, 26 U.S.C. § 897.

See generally, Treas. Reg. § 1.897-1(d)(3).

See generally, 26 U.S.C. § 884(d).

See generally, 26 U.S.C. § 1445.

See generally, 26 U.S.C. § 1446.

See generally, 26 U.S.C. § 892.

See generally, T.D. 9971.

NOTE

1. However, it may be prudent to perform a certain level of due diligence to confirm the REIT itself has qualified as a REIT since inception and will continue to qualify as a REIT on an ongoing basis.

Keeping It Local

Impact of State and Local Taxes

Bruce Hood, Partner, Withersworldwide (Retired)

Lisa McCann, Special Counsel, Withersworldwide

A non-US investor considering the tax implications of an investment in US real estate typically focuses on US federal income taxes and ignores state and local taxes. There are a number of reasons for this, first and foremost of which is that US federal tax rates are substantially higher than those charged by states and localities.[1] The maximum US federal income tax rates applicable to corporate and individual investors is 35 percent and 39.6 percent (plus a Medicare tax of 3.8 percent in certain circumstances), respectively. Moreover, corporations face a second level of tax applicable to distributions (or deemed distributions) to shareholders, imposed at the rate of 30 percent unless reduced by tax treaty. Most state and local income tax rates, on the other hand, are less than one-quarter of the US federal rates. State taxes are also deductible in computing US federal taxable income, making the effective rate lower still. However, taxes on net income are not the only taxes levied by state and local governments. Some states tax gross income, and others tax a corporation's capital employed in the state.

While almost all states have sales and use taxes (the latter apply to the sale or use of tangible personal property in the state), some also tax various services.[2] Some jurisdictions also impose a tax on rents paid with respect to real estate located within their boundaries. Another type of tax imposed by many states and some cities and counties is a real estate transfer or recording tax. This type of tax is typically expressed as a percentage of the consideration received in connection with a transfer of real estate. Finally, ad valorem real estate taxes are imposed against the value of real estate located within the jurisdictional limits of many state and local taxing authorities.

The overall burden of state and local taxes within the context of non-US investment in US real estate can, therefore, be significant. Perhaps more important, many of them are payable regardless of whether the taxpayer is making a profit. Non-US investors in real estate should also be aware that income tax treaties to which the US is a party (many of which reduce taxation of certain types of income and attempt to eliminate double taxation) do not typically apply to state and local taxes. Finally, except for certain limitations in the U.S. Constitution, no uniformity of taxation is required of US states and localities. This variation can create both pitfalls and opportunities. Attention to state and local tax planning will usually be rewarded.

U.S. CONSTITUTION

The power of states and their political subdivisions to levy taxes is derived from the U.S. Constitution (the Constitution), which confers specific powers on the federal government and permits powers not so conferred to be exercised by the states. The Constitution also limits the powers of both federal and state governments. These limitations include the right to equal protection under the law and the right not to be deprived of life, liberty, or property without due process of law (the due process clause). The due process clause is the principal protection against unlimited state taxation in that it requires a certain minimum level of contact between a person and a state seeking to impose a tax on that person and also requires that a state tax only that portion of a person's activities that are fairly attributable to that state. The courts have also cited the federal government's exclusive authority to regulate interstate and foreign commerce in limiting the exercise of state taxing power.

STATE INCOME TAXES

Just about every state imposes some type of corporate and individual income tax. The principal focus of this discussion will be upon corporate income taxes, since most non-US investors do their investing through corporations so as to avoid direct US tax filing and payment obligations. The highest state corporate tax rates generally range between 5 and 10 percent. While income taxes are for the most part imposed at the state level, some larger cities, like New York, impose them as well.

In order to be subjected to a state's corporate income tax, a corporation must typically be deemed to be doing business in the state or to own income-producing tangible property located there. Ownership of a direct interest in income-producing real estate within a particular state will almost always provide sufficient nexus for that state to tax the owning corporation. The indirect ownership of such real estate, however, such as through another corporation, will not usually result in taxation of the shareholder corporation. While the corporation that actually owns the real estate will be subject to tax, it may be possible to reduce that corporation's taxable income by making tax-deductible payments (such as interest) to the shareholder corporation.

Ownership of real estate through noncorporate entities such as partnerships, limited liability companies (LLCs), and trusts presents more complicated issues. Some states impose a tax on the income of the entity itself. Others tax the owners of the entity on their share of its income attributable to the in-state real estate. Still others differentiate between forms of ownership of the entity. For example, some states tax general partners' partnership income but not that of limited partners. Taxation of income of LLC interests is also not uniform across the states, although most states now follow the federal income tax classification rules for such entities.

As noted earlier, the variations between states' tax rules can present some tax-saving opportunities, among them the use of related-party debt. This mechanism has traditionally been used to reduce federal income taxes when the lender is a non-US entity resident in a country whose tax treaty with the US provides for a reduced rate of withholding tax on interest payments. This technique was curtailed somewhat by "earnings stripping" legislation enacted in the late 1980s (and its reach has potentially expanded with the recent issuance of proposed regulations further restricting use of cross-border related party debt) but is still widely used. A variation is to establish a US corporation in a state (like Delaware) that does not tax passive income as long as the recipient corporation is not conducting an active business there, and then to have that company lend money to the company that owns the real estate. Some states (e.g., Ohio) have enacted laws to limit the deductibility of interest on related-party debt. Others have tried to deal with the issue through unitary tax or combined reporting concepts or by treating the loans as sham transactions that should be ignored. Most states, however, have not been as aggressive as they could be in dealing with the issue. A non-US investor that owns real estate in jurisdictions in which related-party debt can generate state tax savings will in most cases need to use a separate corporation, rather than a tax-transparent entity like a partnership or an LLC, to own the real estate. While from a federal income tax standpoint this creates a more complicated structure, the ability to include the fiscal results of related domestic companies in a consolidated federal income tax return minimizes the complication.

If a corporation owns real estate in more than one state, its tax liability to each state is determined through allocation and apportionment rules. Allocation involves attributing all of the income from a particular activity, such as the ownership of real estate, to the state in which that activity occurs. Apportionment involves applying the percentage of the corporation's overall sales, payroll, and property attributable to a particular state to its entire taxable income. Some states count each factor equally, some double count certain factors (typically sales), and some use fewer than three factors. Some factors, like payroll, can be manipulated, for example, by hiring a management company to perform building services rather than using direct employees. The property factor is usually averaged in some way throughout the year, which can present tax-planning opportunities if a company plans to dispose of more than one property during a particular year. Disposition of property in a high-tax state early in the year and disposition of property in a lower-tax state later in the year will likely yield a lower overall state tax burden than if the order of sale were reversed.

A very simple example of the difference between allocation and apportionment would be that of a taxpayer who owns property in two different states, X and Y. Assume that both states tax income at 5 percent, but that State X allocates all income from real estate to the state in which the real estate is located, and State Y uses a three-factor apportionment method. Finally, assume that the taxpayer has equal amounts of sales, payroll, and property attributable to each state. If the property in State X is sold for a $100 gain and the property in State Y for a $200 gain in the same year, the tax payable in State X would be $5 (5 percent of the $100 of gain allocable to that state). The tax in State Y would be $7.50 (5 percent of the 50 percent of the taxpayer's $300 taxable income apportionable to that state). In this example, the overall tax rate is 4.167 percent, even though the tax rate in each state is 5 percent.

By contrast, an effective tax rate higher than 5 percent would result if the locations of the gains were reversed. The tax payable in State X would be $10 (5 percent of the $200 gain allocable to that state), and the State Y tax liability would still be $7.50 (5 percent times 50 percent of the $300 taxpayer's total taxable income), for an overall effective tax rate of 5.833 percent.

Tax losses carried forward are usually determined differently at the state and local levels than at the federal level. Some jurisdictions have shorter carry-forward periods than those permitted for federal tax losses. In addition, most jurisdictions permit only losses attributable to activities in the state against income allocated or apportioned to the state. This can lead an investor with activities in more than one state to bear a much higher overall state income tax liability in proportion to its federal income tax liability than might be expected. For example, an investor with properties in Illinois and New York, disposing of the property in Illinois in 2000 at a $100 loss and disposing of the property in New York in 2001 at a $100 gain will have its federal taxable income in 2001 fully offset by the $100 loss carried forward from 2000. Its New York income tax liability, however, will be only partially offset, because not all of the loss carried forward will have been attributable to New York activities.

* * *

Another issue that can arise is whether income from the sale of an interest in real estate constitutes "business" or "nonbusiness" income. Many state and local tax systems differentiate between the two, taxing business income on an apportionment basis and nonbusiness income on an allocation basis. If allocation is used, the income from the sale of a direct interest in real estate typically will be attributed in its entirety to the state in which the real estate is located, but income from the sale of an indirect interest, such as an interest in a partnership or an LLC, may be taxed in the owner's state of "commercial domicile," usually where its management is located.

It may be possible under certain circumstances to locate a corporation's management in one of the few states that does not impose any corporate income tax or in a state in which certain types of management activities do not cause a corporation to be subject to tax. Still another possibility is to locate the corporation's management in a state that taxes on an apportionment basis only so that the only factor attributable to that state will be payroll.

Many non-US investors invest in US real estate through real estate investment trusts (REITs). Although a REIT is subject to federal income tax, it is entitled to deduct from its federal taxable income distributions to its shareholders. The shareholders are subject to tax on the distributions. State tax treatment of REITs and their shareholders is not uniform, but most states permit deductions for distributions to shareholders regardless of whether the shareholders are subject to state tax on the distributions.[3]

STATE CAPITAL TAXES

A number of states impose a tax based upon the capital a corporation is deemed to have employed in the states. Some of these impose the capital tax only when it results in a higher tax than the income tax. Capital is typically determined by subtracting the corporation's liabilities from its assets, but there are a multitude of methods for valuing assets, including book value and fair market value.

Some states use a multiple of the value assessed for ad valorem taxes, and others use a multiple of earnings over a specified period of time. A few states use a combination of these methods.

The definition of deductible liabilities is less varied, but some states exclude liabilities to related persons. Some treat deficits in retained earnings as liabilities. Like corporate income taxes, taxes on capital are subject to apportionment based on the corporation's activities in a state.

STATE TAXES ON GROSS INCOME

The most prevalent state tax on gross income is the sales tax, traditionally imposed on receipts from sales of tangible personal property to the ultimate user. The concept of sales tax has been expanded in some states to include fees received for the provision of services. It can also take the form of a tax on rents or on the provision of utilities to tenants. In most cases, taxes on sales are the responsibility of the purchaser but are collected by the seller.

A few states, some cities, and other local taxing authorities impose gross receipts taxes on certain types of businesses carried on within their boundaries. These taxes are borne by the seller and are sometimes called license or privilege taxes.

One gross receipts tax of particular relevance to real estate investors is that imposed on the consideration received in connection with transfers of real estate. These taxes are usually referred to as real estate transfer taxes, recording fees, or deed stamps and vary from less than 1 percent of the sales price to as much as 3 percent. The obligation typically falls on the seller, but in some jurisdictions it is split between seller and purchaser.

States or cities with higher transfer tax rates often have a parallel regime where consideration received for transfers of controlling interests in entities owning real estate located within the state will also be subject to transfer tax. Since these taxes are not collected by the officials who record deeds, as is the case of direct transfers of real estate, they are not as easy to enforce, especially when the change of control takes place several steps removed from the entity that owns the real estate.

Finally, some states impose recording taxes on various real estate–related documents (e.g., long-term leases and mortgages).

AD VALOREM PROPERTY TAXES

Owners of real estate located just about anywhere in the US must deal with ad valorem property taxes levied by local taxing jurisdictions, such as counties, cities, and special-purpose districts, to finance services of a local nature, such as schools and fire and police protection.[4] The rates tend to fluctuate depending upon budgetary requirements and are applied to the value of real property (and sometimes personal property) located within the taxing jurisdiction.

While all property taxes are based upon the value of the subject property, the manner in which that value is determined varies widely. Since the valuation of real estate is a somewhat subjective exercise, taxpayers often initiate legal proceedings to challenge valuations.

It is a fairly uniform practice across the country for tenants in leases of commercial real estate to bear the expense of property taxes. This can be accomplished by having the tenant pay the taxes directly, either into an escrow account or to the taxing authority, or by having the tenant pay additional rent when property taxes increase.

CONCLUSION

While often overlooked, state and local taxes can have a significant impact on the overall return of US real estate investments. The lack of uniformity in the rules governing the states' taxation of multistate activities creates opportunities, not available at the federal income tax level, to manage the tax components of an investment.

NOTES

1. Wood, Robert W. "State and Local Taxation of Foreign Investors in U.S. Real Estate." *Tax Management Real Estate Journal* (2013): 251–261; Rennert, Richard C. "Foreign Investment in U.S. Real Estate: The Impact of Taxation." *The International Lawyer* (1990): 641–650.
2. Hodges, Joseph G. "State Taxation of Nonresident Real Estate Investors: An Overview." *The Real Estate Finance Journal* (1990): 42–51.
3. Colon, Jeffrey M. "State Taxation of Real Estate Investment Trusts." *The Tax Lawyer* (2010): 607–626.
4. Lokken, Lawrence. "State and Local Taxation of Nonresidents' Income from Real Estate." *The Tax Lawyer* (1989): 693–711.

Estates and Gifts

Considerations Regarding Estate and Gift Taxes

Jeffrey Levin, Senior Partner, Squire Patton Boggs

In the US, three types of estate and gift taxes may affect a nonresident alien owning US property at different times and in different ways: gift taxes on transfers of property during life, estate taxes on property owned at death, and generation-skipping transfer (GST) taxes on transfers of property, either during life or at death, to persons in a younger generation.[1]

Gift, estate, and GST taxes are referred to as transfer taxes because they impose a tax on the transfer of property. The donor of a gift, not the receiver, is generally responsible for paying gift taxes; the estate of a decedent, not the receivers of the inheritance, must pay the estate taxes; and the individual or trust that transfers assets to a grandchild (or to a trust for the benefit of only the grandchild and successors) must pay the GST tax. A recipient could have liability if the person with primary liability fails to pay the appropriate tax. These taxes are levied in addition to and independent of any real estate transfer taxes that may be due at the state or local level.[2]

GENERAL GUIDELINES FOR THE ESTATE AND GIFT TAX

Subject to a few exceptions discussed later, a non-resident alien decedent's estate is responsible for US estate tax only on the decedent's property "situated" in the US upon the decedent's death. (For purposes of this discussion, a nonresident alien does not include a non-US citizen, who is domiciled in the US.) A nonresident alien is responsible for gift taxes on lifetime transfers of real and tangible property "situated" in the US If the transfer of such property is to a "skip person" (e.g., a grandchild or someone two or more generations below the transferor), a GST tax could apply as well. Any real estate or tangible property located in the US is considered to have a US situs. Intangible property with a US situs includes stock in US companies, notes receivable from US persons payable to non-US persons, and certain retirement plan benefits, if the sponsor or employer is a US person (unless the services provided by the non-US individual were performed only outside the US For both US estate and gift tax purposes, nonresident aliens are taxed at graduated rates currently ranging from 18 percent on the first taxable $10,000 to 40 percent on taxable transfers in excess of $1,000,000. The GST tax rate is the highest estate tax rate then in effect, currently 40 percent.

In addition, certain US states impose their own gift or estate taxes on transfers on property with a situs in the state. These rates vary greatly. For example, Florida imposes no gift or estate taxes, whereas the estate tax in New York can be as much as 16 percent of the taxable estate. Estate (including state inheritance) taxes paid to a state are deductible for US federal estate tax purposes, but the availability of such deductions for state estate tax purposes varies.

ESTATE AND GIFT TAX TREATIES

Currently the US has estate and gift tax treaties with Australia, Austria, Denmark, Finland, France, Germany, Greece, Ireland, Italy, Japan, the Netherlands, Norway, South Africa, Sweden, Switzerland, and the United Kingdom. In addition, the US-Canada Income Tax Treaty may have an application with respect to US estate taxes and Canadian income taxes. The first step in any analysis is to determine if a treaty would change the general US rules that apply to nonresident aliens. As illustrated later, a nonresident alien domiciled in a country with a US estate tax treaty could be eligible for more favorable US estate tax treatment.

GIFT TAXES

US gift tax laws apply to all direct and indirect transfers of real or tangible property located in the US during the life of a nonresident alien. Unlike the estate and GST tax laws, the US gift tax does not generally apply to a lifetime transfer by a nonresident alien of intangible property, such as stocks, bonds, and notes.

In the case of a US person, US citizen, or US domiciliary, the gift tax applies to any lifetime transfers that are complete gifts made by a US person, regardless of the type of property or the situs of the property transferred.

Annual Exclusion
In 2023, the first $17,000 of outright transfers of real or tangible property by nonresident aliens per donee in each year is excluded from US gift taxes. The amount of the exclusion is indexed annually for inflation. Unlike US persons, nonresident aliens are not allowed to split gifts with a spouse to maximize the use of the annual exclusion.

Gifts to Spouses
A person married to a US citizen may make unlimited gifts to that spouse without incurring gift tax. Annual tax-free outright gifts to a non-US citizen spouse, by contrast, are limited to $175,000 (for 2023). This amount is indexed annually for inflation.

Gift Tax Exemption Does Not Apply to Non-Resident Aliens
For 2023, each US person has a lifetime US federal transfer tax exemption of $12,920,000, which is also indexed for inflation. This exemption amount is currently scheduled to be reduced to approximately half of the then exemption amount commencing January 1, 2026. This exemption does not apply to gifts by nonresident aliens.

ESTATE TAXES

In general, the US gross taxable estate of a nonresident alien consists of all tangible or intangible property situated in the US in which the nonresident alien had an interest at the time of his or her death.

Limited Estate Tax Exemption for Nonresident Alien

As noted previously, each US decedent who dies in 2023 has a lifetime US federal estate tax exemption of $12,920,000 that is reduced by any gift tax exemption used during the decedent's lifetime. As with the gift tax, nonresident alien decedents are not allowed this exemption. Instead, a nonresident alien decedent is entitled to only a $60,000 estate tax exemption. This means that, unless there is an estate tax treaty between the US and the decedent's home country containing a special exemption provision, a nonresident alien decedent can transfer only $60,000 in US-situs property free of US estate tax. Certain estate tax treaties permit a pro rata use of the lifetime exemption amount based on the percentage of the decedent's US-situs property, provided appropriate reporting of the decedent's worldwide assets is made. Any additional US-situs property of more than $60,000 would be subject to US estate taxes.

Bequests to Spouses

A nonresident alien decedent is not entitled to a marital deduction unless the donee spouse is a US citizen on the date of the death of the nonresident alien. Exceptions exist for estate tax purposes if the surviving spouse was a resident at all times after the death of the spouse and becomes a citizen of the US before the estate tax return is filed or if the property is transferred to a qualified domestic trust (QDOT). In these cases, the marital deduction is allowed and no estate tax will be due upon the nonresident alien's death, but they will be due upon the surviving spouse's death.

QDOT

To qualify as a QDOT, a trust must have at least one trustee that is an individual citizen of the US or a US corporation. This trustee must have the right to withhold from a distribution from the trust, other than an income distribution, any US estate taxes imposed on the corpus of the trust. In addition, the decedent's executor must make an election on a US federal estate tax return to treat the trust as a QDOT. A QDOT trust must also satisfy the statutory requirements for a US citizen spouse marital trust, known as a qualified terminal interest trust (QTIP). In this case, however, unlike a QTIP, the property of which is included in the surviving spouse's taxable estate, the federal estate tax due upon the surviving spouse's death is computed as if it were part of the first spouse's taxable estate. Consequently, the lifetime exemption of the surviving spouse, who is a US domiciliary but not a US citizen, could not be used to reduce the US estate tax on the QDOT corpus.

GSTS

In addition to gift and estate taxes, the US imposes a federal GST on transfers made during life or at death to a beneficiary who is more than one generation younger than the donor or decedent. This tax could apply to lifetime or testamentary transfers to a grandchild or to a trust for the grandchild's benefit. In addition, this tax could apply to future trust distributions from a trust that provides for income to be paid to the surviving spouse with the remainder going to a grandchild at the surviving spouse's death. In the latter case, the GST taxes must be paid by the trust upon the surviving spouse's death, not upon the death of the nonresident alien who established the trust. GST taxes are substantial and are levied in addition to gift or estate taxes. A separate lifetime annual exclusion in the same amount as the lifetime estate and gift tax exemption, adjusted for inflation, is also available for the GST tax. For nonresident aliens, the GST tax only applies to US-situs property subject to US estate or gift taxes and the lifetime exclusion is not available.

"COVERED EXPATRIATE"

The previous discussion generally applies to all nonresident aliens. In addition, if the nonresident alien is a "covered expatriate," an additional US transfer tax could apply. A covered expatriate is a former US person who relinquished his or her US citizenship or long-term US resident (green card) status and was subject to a special US exit income tax obligation at the time of expatriation. Gifts and bequests made by a covered expatriate to US persons, if not otherwise subject to US transfer taxes under the preceding rules, are subject to a US tax charge based on the highest estate tax rate then in effect. In this case, the US recipient of the transferred property is responsible for the payment of this transfer tax. This transfer tax applies to any property transferred to a US person regardless of its situs and regardless of when the transferor acquired the property. For example, as explained later, if a covered expatriate, who is now a nonresident alien, transferred the shares of a non-US corporation that owns US real property to a US person, neither the US gift tax nor the US estate tax would generally apply. Because this transfer would be from a covered expatriate, however, this special US tax charge would apply.

"Situated" in the US: Situs of Property

For US transfer tax purposes, property must be situated in the US to be considered US property. The situs depends on the type of property and how it is held.

Real Property

The situs of real property is determined by its physical location. A non-US person who owns US real property and directly transfers it through an estate or as a gift will be subject to US estate and gift taxes on the transfer.[3] The US transfer taxes would be based on the then fair market value of the property. For this purpose, the value of the property would be reduced by any associated nonrecourse mortgage indebtedness. Cooperative apartment corporation shares, and an accompanying proprietary lease for the use of residential property, are treated as intangible property and not as real property.

Tangible Personal Property

Tangible personal property generally includes items one can touch, such as automobiles, artwork, personal items, jewelry, and furniture. The situs of tangible personal property is also determined by its physical location. Thus, a nonresident alien's tangible personal property with a US situs transferred through an estate or as a gift will be subject to US estate and gift taxes. If the tangible personal property is taken out of the US by the nonresident alien prior to the transfer, US transfer taxes would not apply.

Lifetime Gifts of Intangible Property

Generally, the transfer of intangible property during a non-resident alien's lifetime is not subject to US gift taxation. For example, a nonresident alien's lifetime gift of an interest in a non-US or US corporation that owns US real property will be exempt from US gift tax. However, intangible property with a US situs owned by a nonresident alien at the time of the nonresident alien's death may be subject to an estate tax. A nonresident alien owner of US-situs property can therefore significantly reduce the potential estate taxes by making lifetime gifts of US intangible property. Generally, partnership interests are regarded as intangible property, and as such, a gift of a partnership interest is not subject to gift tax. The US tax law, however, in certain circumstances could treat a partner as owner of the underlying partnership assets. In those situations, a gift by a nonresident alien partner could be subject to US gift tax. It is important to note that an interest in a single-member US limited liability company (LLC) that has not made a check-the-box election to be treated as a US corporation is generally treated as a disregarded entity. In that case the sole member of the LLC would be treated as directly owning any US real property owned by the LLC. If the US LLC has at least two members and the company and its members have not made a "check-the-box" election, the nonresident alien's membership interest is generally treated as a partnership interest.

US Corporations

For estate tax purposes, shares of a corporation are deemed to have situs in the jurisdiction in which the corporation is formed or organized. Accordingly, shares of a US corporation have US situs and will be included in the nonresident alien's taxable estate. Therefore, shares of a US corporation owned by a nonresident alien decedent, including shares of a cooperative apartment corporation, are subject to US estate taxes. To transfer shares of US corporations and other US-situs assets of a nonresident alien decedent, the estate's executor/administrator will have to obtain a "transfer certificate" for the transfer agent to transfer ownership of the US-situs assets.

Non-US Corporations

In contrast to shares of a US corporation, shares of a non-US corporation are exempt from US estate taxes because they are deemed to have situs in the country where the corporation is organized. For both estate and gift tax purposes, a non-US corporation is the preferred structure for a nonresident alien to own US real property, provided the IRS does not treat the non-US corporation as merely a conduit or disregard it as a sham. However, one potential drawback to direct ownership by a non-US corporation is the possible application of the US branch profits tax if taxable income is remitted back to the home country. Consequently, to avoid the US branch profits tax, a US corporation owned by a non-US corporation is often interposed as the property owner between the US real property and the non-US corporation. A common estate planning technique is for a nonresident alien to form an offshore company that then forms a US company to hold US-situs assets. While this approach can effectively eliminate exposure to US estate tax, there is a trade-off involving US income taxes due to the difference between individual and corporate tax rates on capital gains. Another advantage of this structure is that at the time of the sale of the property, if the seller does not have any other US real property interests, the seller of the US real estate would not be a US real property holding corporation; consequently, the Foreign Investment in Real Property Tax Act (FIRPTA) 15 percent withholding compliance provisions could be avoided and a US withholding tax on liquidation distributions could be avoided. Companies should always analyze estate tax savings from using a non-US company and the projected US income tax consequences of such a structure.

REITS

Despite their name, real estate investment trusts (REITs) do not fall under the definition of a trust for US tax purposes. Instead, a REIT is treated as a corporation. Therefore, owning shares of a REIT is treated the same as owning shares of any other US corporation for estate tax purposes, including being subject to estate taxes at the owner's death. Special income tax rules apply to REITs that are addressed in another Chapter 4.8.

Partnership and LLC Interests

The law is not entirely clear regarding the situs of a partnership interest for US estate tax purposes, and taxpayers must turn to other sources. As noted earlier, an LLC interest in a US LLC with more than one member is generally treated as a partnership for US tax purposes. An existing IRS ruling and early US estate tax treaties determine situs of a limited partnership interest by whether or not the limited partnership is engaged in a US trade or business regardless of where the limited partnership is organized or the extent of the US business activities. Because owning and operating US rental property is generally regarded as a US trade or business, a limited partnership or LLC is not especially helpful to non-US real estate investors who want to avoid US estate taxes.[4] In addition, if provisions in the partnership agreement or applicable local law deem a limited partnership to terminate upon the death of a partner, a nonresident partner would likely be treated as the owner of his or her share of the partnership's assets and situs rules would apply.

For US gift tax purposes, if the nonresident alien partner or member is considered as an owner of the entity's real property, a US gift tax could be imposed on the transfer of the partnership or membership interest. Given this uncertainty, there is concern among some US tax advisors that a nonresident alien who is a partner or member of a non-US partnership or a non-US LLC that owns US real property could be deemed to own the underlying US real property. Consequently, partnerships and LLCs are not recommended by some advisors. Other US tax advisors view a non-US partnership as an intangible interest with a non-US situs and, therefore, not subject to US transfer taxes. Those advisors often recommend a two-tier partnership structure both to take advantage of favorable US tax rates applicable to individuals on long-term capital gains and to avoid US transfer taxes.

Planning with Trusts

The use of trusts is common in US estate and gift tax planning. Generally, the situs rule for trusts differs for estate tax and gift tax purposes. If a nonresident alien creates a trust that holds US real property, the applicable situs rule for gift tax purposes will depend on the terms of the trust. In a revocable or reversionary trust (one in which the grantor retains rights and powers over the trust income or assets), the nonresident grantor is treated as the owner of any US real property held by the trust. Thus the transfer of property by the nonresident grantor to the trust will be considered as an incomplete gift and not subject to US gift taxes, but any subsequent transfer the nonresident grantor makes of his or her interest in the trust or a trust distribution of the US property will be subject to the US gift tax. In an irrevocable trust (one in which the grantor retains no rights or powers over the trust income or assets), the nonresident alien is not treated as the owner of any US real property held by the trust. Consequently, a transfer by the nonresident alien grantor of US real property would be subject to US gift taxes. The subsequent transfer of the grantor's interest in the trust or a trust distribution of the US property would not be subject to US gift taxes.

A trust is treated as a separate legal entity for US estate tax purposes. Thus the general rule is that the settlor and the beneficiaries of a US trust will not be treated as the owners of the assets held by the trust. However, certain exceptions apply to US citizens and nonresident aliens alike. Specifically, if a decedent makes a gift of US property to a trust within three years of his or her death, the property could be included in his or her estate for US estate tax purposes, depending on the terms of the trust. In addition, any lifetime transfers of property to a trust in which the decedent retained powers over those assets could be subject to US estate taxes and the release of nonresident alien's retained powers during the holder's lifetime could be subject to US gift taxes. An irrevocable nongrantor trust may provide a viable option for avoiding US estate taxes on US real property, but the transfer of the property to the trust could be subject to US gift taxes. In this case, to avoid future US estate taxes, the nonresident alien must be willing to give up all rights, powers, and interests in the US real property transferred to the trust.

If a nonresident alien has family members who are US citizens, there are significant estate and GST tax planning opportunities involving lifetime gifts and the use of US trusts for family members. These trusts can be structured so that the assets they own would not be subject to transfer taxes upon the death of the donor or the beneficiaries.

HOW TO APPLY THESE RULES

The following are two simple examples that demonstrate the application of the general rules discussed previously.

Applying the Gift Tax Rules—Gift of Direct Interest Versus Corporate Shares

Peter, a resident of Hong Kong, wants to invest in an office building located in New York, New York. He has the choice of owning the building directly or forming a corporation to own the building. Peter plans eventually to give the property to his daughter, also a resident of Hong Kong. He decides to buy the building directly and 10 years later gives the property to his daughter. Unfortunately, the transfer of direct ownership of tangible property located in the US is subject to the US gift tax. If Peter had invested in the property through a corporate structure, he would have been deemed to own an intangible asset and the transfer of his shares to his daughter would not have been subject to the gift tax.

If Peter decided to give his direct interest in the building to his grandchild instead of to his daughter, the transfer could be subject to the GST as well. If, however, Peter had transferred the building to a corporation before making a gift of the shares to his daughter or a grandchild, he would have avoided gift or GST taxes, even though he initially had purchased the building directly.

Applying the Estate Tax Rules

Gabriele, a German resident, is a sophisticated investor knowledgeable about the US gift tax rules. Gabriele invests in a US limited partnership that owns a shopping center in Orlando, Florida. Each year through the partnership, Gabriele receives her share of cash and rental income from the operations of the center. She considers her limited partnership interest as intangible property and plans to transfer her interest to her son during her lifetime without any US gift tax. Unfortunately, she dies before she has a chance to make the planned gift. The interest in the partnership becomes part of her US taxable estate, subject to the US estate tax because the partnership interest is considered US-situs intangible property.

Based on 2023 US estate tax rates, if the partnership interest has a value of $310,000, Gabriele's estate would owe approximately $70,800 in US federal estate tax (after considering the $60,000 applicable exclusion available to nonresident aliens). However, because of the US-German Estate Tax Treaty, Gabriele's estate would get a credit on her German estate tax return for any US estate taxes paid, and her US estate would be eligible for a portion of the exclusion available to US citizens. As noted earlier, the exclusion amount available to Gabriele's estate would depend upon the value of her US assets relative to the value of her worldwide net assets. Accordingly, if the partnership interest represented 10 percent of the total value of her worldwide net assets, Gabriele's taxable estate would be reduced by 10 percent of the federal lifetime exemption amount, $1,292,000, resulting in a complete elimination of the US estate tax liability. (Many nonresidents may be reluctant to disclose their worldwide assets to the US government, however, and may choose not to take advantage of this benefit.)

CONCLUSION

The US estate and gift tax laws applied to non-US investors in US real estate are complex.[5] When combined with those of a non-US country, the tax burden on investors who transfer real estate investments to their heirs can be substantial. Proper consideration should be given to these various consequences and to alternative ownership structures to maximize the tax efficiency of an investment.

Non-US investors in US real estate should consider the use of non-US corporations as intermediate vehicles through which to hold their investments, although use of an intermediary entity may cause additional income taxes. Many non-US investors choose to absorb these current costs to avoid having to report their worldwide holdings to the US government, as would be required upon the death of a direct holder of a US real property interest. Investors undertaking such a trade-off should weigh the future US estate and gift tax benefits of these structures against the potential current US income tax costs.

NOTES

1. Jacks, Evelyn. "Property Tax: Owning Multiple Properties, a City Home and a Cottage, Is More Common Nowadays. You Should Explain These Real Estate Tax Consequences to Your Clients." *Advisor's Edge*, vol. 5, no. 8, Newcom Media Inc, 2002, pp. 29–35.
2. The following discussion reflects current US tax law as of February 28, 2023.
3. Sanna, Dina Kapur, and Stephen Ziobrowski. "Foreign-Owned U.S. Real Estate: to Rent or Not to Rent." *Estate Planning*, vol. 41, no. 4, 2014, pp. 3–25.
4. Gagliardi, Elaine Hightower. "Estate Planning Choice of Wealth Management Entity: The Limited Partnership as an Alternative to the Trust." *Creighton Law Review*, vol. 53, no. 4, 2020, pp. 695–705.
5. Beckwith, R. F. (2011). "Estate Tax Considerations for Owning Real Estate in a Foreign Country." *Journal of Financial Service Professionals 65*, no. 2, 29–36.

Enforcement

Real Estate Agreements in the US Court System

Frederick Klein, Partner, DLA Piper

Lisa Goodheart, Partner, Sugarman, Rogers, Barshak & Cohen, P.C.

There is no doubt that enforcing agreements in the court systems of the US is a complex, time-consuming, expensive, inconvenient, and often, uncertain business. This is a fact of particular concern to non-US investors in US real estate because such investments involve various kinds of contracts.[1] Joint venture agreements, brokerage agreements, purchase and sale agreements, leasing agreements, loan agreements, title insurance policies, construction contracts, and asset-management and property-management agreements are only some of the contracts typically required for such investments.[2] Parties entering into such contracts naturally focus on ensuring that the agreements accurately reflect the agreed-upon allocation of rights, risks, and obligations. Given the high stakes and substantial amounts of money involved, however, it is also important to consider what will ensue in the event that either party breaches the agreement, and if so, if litigation follows.[3]

Meanwhile, real estate investors and tenants will at times find it necessary to resort to the US federal bankruptcy court, a separate system designed, at least in theory, to provide debtors suffering from financial distress with a "fresh start" by enabling them, sometimes to the detriment of lenders and landlords, to recast their obligations.

LITIGATION AS A PART OF DOING BUSINESS IN THE COMMERCIAL REAL ESTATE WORLD

Speaking most broadly, participants in the commercial real estate business in the US must be ready, or at least willing, to litigate. For better or worse, litigation is often a necessary part of doing business in this arena. Litigation over all manner of real estate disputes is common. Ready resort to the courts is a time-honored and well-accepted way of resolving disagreements about business arrangements and of seeking to allocate (or reallocate) the costs and other burdens of any problematic set of circumstances. Sophisticated parties who invest in real estate in the US generally do consider the risk of litigation to be a predictable, if unfortunate, by-product of being "in the game."[4]

This anticipation of litigation, or at least of the reasonable prospect of litigation, is reflected in increasingly complex documents that address in ever greater detail such matters as choice of law, choice of forum, the requirement (or not) to pursue some form of alternative resolution in the event of a dispute, methods for calculating damages in the event of a breach, the availability of injunctive relief and other equitable remedies, waivers (or not) of punitive damages, and the recovery of litigation fees and costs by the prevailing party in any suit.[5] Indeed, some real estate agreements seem to have been written by parties fully expecting from the very outset to wind up in court. In many situations, experience has shown that such anticipation is entirely appropriate.

The impact of this litigious culture on the enforcement of real estate agreements can be seen as both positive and negative.[6] On the positive side, the value and usefulness of any contract is based on the willingness of the contracting parties to honor their respective promises. When business pressures become intense, often due to changed circumstances (such as widespread economic stress), that commitment can become strained, sometimes to the breaking point. It is then that the willingness of any party to continue to honor its contractual commitments is naturally influenced by consideration of the negative consequences that can be expected to accompany a breach. The very real prospect of being sued is one of the most obvious and significant negative consequences. Accordingly, parties under pressure often honor their contractual commitments at least in part because they are motivated by a keen desire to avoid litigation. The expense and other negative factors associated with litigation may be a heavier burden for a party to bear than the cost of complying with contractual obligations. Given the many downsides of a court fight (to say nothing of the often enormous expense), a party may conclude that it is better off meeting its commitments than being sued for failure to do so.

On the negative side, the prospect of litigation may also embolden a party to breach an agreement. Typically, it is the very same considerations of expense, delay, inconvenience, uncertainty, and adverse publicity that support a party's decision to take a chance and fail to keep its promise. A breaching party may conclude that it will likely avoid any sanction for failing to meet its commitments, calculating that its counterpart would rather accept the business loss caused by the breach than pursue the matter in court, precisely because bringing suit presents the plaintiff, as well as the defendant, with the burdens of expense, delay, inconvenience, and adverse publicity.

The fact that litigation is frequently used to impede and delay a party in pursuit of its business goals in the US is readily apparent. This phenomenon is particularly evident in the area of land-use litigation, involving appeals from the grants of special permits and variances by local zoning boards. Neighboring landowners or others who challenge a development project may impede or even prevent the project altogether simply by filing a court appeal, because the mere pendency of litigation, regardless of the ultimate merits of the case, can halt the project.

Interested citizens are generally very well aware that the effect of filing such a permit appeal is a critical roadblock to any project. As one Massachusetts developer has commented, "We operate in a world where any idiot can bring a multimillion-dollar development project that a community wants and needs to a grinding halt for the price of a postage stamp [the cost of mailing a permit appeal]." This is unfortunately all too often true. In Massachusetts, as in many other states, it frequently takes several years for a civil case to get to the trial stage, factoring in the initial pleadings phase, pretrial discovery, and motions. If a judgment in the trial court is appealed to the appeals court, the process can easily take another two years or more. Only developers with sufficient stamina and deep enough pockets to persevere for years, market cycles notwithstanding, can effectively do business in this environment.

Developers are the not the only participants in the world of commercial real estate adversely affected by litigation. Disputes involving all of the various contracts typically used to accomplish real estate transactions are subject to resolution in the courts. Joint venturers may have differing goals and interests that lead to litigated disputes about their common undertaking; real estate brokers may litigate disputed claims for commissions; real estate buyers or sellers may have second thoughts about a proposed transaction and seek to litigate their way out of an agreement; landlords and tenants may litigate disputes about their respective rights and obligations under lease agreements; owners and lenders may litigate over financing terms; policyholders may litigate with title insurers over coverage disputes; owners and contractors may litigate over construction defects, cost overruns, delays, or payment issues; owners and property managers may litigate disputes over any number of issues; and on and on. In short, litigation is a familiar item in the toolbox—and a recognized pressure point—that interested parties use with some regularity to achieve their business goals (or to stymie their adversaries) in the world of commercial real estate.

Of course, while the prospect of litigation is an important determinant of business conduct, it is difficult to predict at the outset of a contractual relationship just how that prospect will influence the relationship. Despite the uncertainty, however, the possibility that intractable disputes may later arise usually colors any contract negotiation. Each party's sense of whether it is more or less likely than the other party to seek an "exit strategy" from the contract in the future affects its negotiation of provisions for the termination of the agreement and for the consequences, including details of dispute resolution that will follow a breach or a claim of breach. Ultimately those provisions will impact the dynamic and the outcome of any litigation arising under the contract.

BARRIERS TO THE QUICK, EFFICIENT, AND PREDICTABLE ENFORCEMENT OF RIGHTS

Where courts are ready, willing, and able to enforce contracts, and where parties can obtain judicial enforcement of contracts without undue expense, delay, and uncertainty, breaches are discouraged, business procedures are facilitated, and investment-related expectations are protected. Where the court system does not function efficiently, or where parties are uncertain or unhappily surprised about the costs and consequences of enforcing agreements in the court system, the value of an investment can be damaged dramatically and a contract may ultimately seem to be worth little more than the paper on which it is written. It is thus generally understood that states where the barriers to quick and predictable resolution of contract disputes are lower will be seen as having a climate more conducive to business than other states. Despite this recognition, however, many states have a difficult time reducing such barriers.

Given the significant negative consequences of litigation, and each state's interest in encouraging business within its borders, one might ask why the courts do not function more efficiently to produce prompt, efficient, and predictable results for parties embroiled in contract disputes and other types of civil litigation. There is no simple answer, as there are a number of fairly intractable barriers to the quick, cost-effective, and reliable judicial enforcement of private rights. Among these barriers are institutional causes of delay, due to funding shortages or management problems within the courts; the extraordinary expense of hard-fought civil litigation where big stakes are involved; and the variability of litigation results, which is especially notable in jurisdictions that do not enjoy the advantage of consistently experienced judges steeped in business-law issues.

INSTITUTIONAL CAUSE OF DELAY AND TIMING VARIATIONS ACROSS JURISDICTIONS

Most real estate cases in the US are pursued in the state court system. This is because the federal court system has limited jurisdiction and is available only for cases involving questions of federal law or involving parties of diverse citizenship where over $75,000 is at issue. Real estate contract disputes commonly involve questions not of federal law but of states' common law of contracts, real property, torts or corporate law, or pertinent state statutes. Real estate cases also often do not present the alternative basis for federal court jurisdiction—diversity of citizenship.

The fact that most real estate disputes are resolved in the state court system is significant because state courts generally lack the financial, technological, and various other types of resources available to federal courts. Predictably, overburdened state courts are often slower than federal courts to decide cases. Accordingly, justice may simply take longer in state court than it does in federal court (although this is not the case everywhere).

One of the complicating factors in dealing with real estate on a national level is that the time it takes to get a real estate case resolved in court may differ significantly from jurisdiction to jurisdiction, and between state and federal court within a given jurisdiction. It is often difficult to get reliable and current information about such differences, which can be a critical consideration. There is no substitute for seeking the advice of experienced litigators within the jurisdiction where a property or deal is based, or in the forum that provides the governing law under a given contract. It remains the case, however, that the time it will take to litigate any contract dispute is inherently unpredictable and subject to the influence of myriad variables, an uncertainty that no amount of expert guidance can eliminate. It also remains true that the time it takes to resolve a contract case in any state court is usually much too long to suit at least one of the parties, and more frequently, all of the parties.

THE COSTS OF LITIGATION

The costs of litigation, particularly sophisticated business litigation involving real estate contracts and other complex matters, are substantial and notoriously difficult to cap or even predict.

Private litigants typically pay litigation counsel on an hourly basis, at rates that in the largest metropolitan centers have risen dramatically in recent years. In complex civil cases, substantial resources are frequently devoted to researching and litigating not only the governing law but an array of procedural issues, because as a practical matter, questions of procedure can often be every bit as important in determining the outcome as the substantive legal precedent. Expansive discovery rights and inefficiencies in the court system only serve to escalate the costs of litigation further. For example, a party may incur the substantial cost of preparing for a complex and lengthy trial, perhaps including travel for out-of-town expert witnesses, only to have the trial rescheduled at the last moment by the court. Such an occurrence will require a whole new round of intensive preparations when the case is again called for trial, perhaps many months later. This phenomenon is all too common in state courts within the US.

Moreover, the costs of complex business litigation are difficult to predict and contain, even with the assistance and guidance of experienced counsel. This is true in large part because any litigation effort is driven not only by its own preparation plan but also by the need to respond to discovery requests and motions by the opposing party, to requirements imposed and orders issued by the court, and sometimes to significant newly discovered facts or changed circumstances. Moreover, litigating parties with deep pockets sometimes try to outspend their opponents in litigation, waging a war of attrition, or perhaps more benignly, simply to produce superior work product that will be more persuasive to the ultimate decision-maker. In any event, complex civil litigation is very expensive and unpredictably so. Disputes arising over contracts involving real estate are certainly no exception to this rule.

INCONSISTENCIES IN LITIGATION RESULTS

Another of the complications and frustrations of dealing with contract disputes in the US is that the litigation may progress very differently and produce substantially different results, depending on the forum in which a case is brought. This is true both among judges on the same court, across courts in different states, between state and federal court, and between district, circuit, and appellate levels. In some quarters, for example, there is a perception that federal courts are more inclined than state courts to dispose of cases at the summary judgment stage, based on a determination that there is no genuine issue of material fact and that judgment should be entered for one or the other party as a matter of law. Such perceptions naturally tend to lead to forum shopping by litigants. Many cases, however, are eligible to be brought in only a single forum. Where this is so and a party has comparable cases or similar contracts in different jurisdictions, inconsistencies are particularly frustrating.

Some jurisdictions have established special business courts to handle complex commercial cases, which often require specialized knowledge. The Delaware Court of Chancery, for example, handles only nonjury cases seeking equitable relief and has a long tradition and a well-established reputation as a leader in business jurisprudence and a hospitable forum for business litigants with complex disputes. A number of states (often in limited geographic areas) have adopted specialized business litigation tribunals within the past decade or so.

It is reported that justice moves more swiftly in these specialized business sessions, and a higher percentage of cases settle before trial than is the case in other civil sessions. Business litigants generally prefer the quality of justice they receive from specialized business litigation courts and find the results more predictable, consistent, and rational. Not only are such tribunals not available everywhere, but in some instances they are not available for all categories of commercial cases. In each jurisdiction where litigation is anticipated, it is worth inquiring of litigation counsel whether a specialized business forum will be available.

ALTERNATIVE DISPUTE RESOLUTION

Various methods of dispute resolution, most notably mediation and arbitration, have been used with increasing frequency in recent years as an alternative to traditional litigation for resolving complex business disputes. In mediation, the opposing parties confer privately with the assistance of a trained mediator, who facilitates settlement discussions and tries to assist the parties in reaching their own resolution of a controversy. In arbitration, one or more privately retained decision makers renders a binding decision, in an expedited private proceeding that typically involves limited prehearing discovery and abbreviated motion practice, followed by an evidentiary hearing.

The advantages of mediation and arbitration are considerable in comparison to the experience of full-blown litigation in the courts. Generally, alternative dispute resolution (ADR) methods allow parties to resolve their disputes more quickly and less expensively than does litigation. In addition, the resolution will generally remain confidential so that neither party will have its private business arrangements revealed in a public forum, as happens in litigation.

Certain disadvantages to ADR must be weighed, however. First, a mediated solution inevitably requires compromise, and an aggrieved party that wants the rightness of its position unequivocally and publicly established or that at least wants its "day in court," may prefer to take its chances in the courts. Of course, business litigants with complex, essentially economic, disputes are much less likely to take this view than individuals embroiled in controversies that involve matters of personal principle and reputation.[7] Likewise, there is a perception, correct or not, that arbitration decisions tend to "split the baby" rather than delivering an unequivocal victory to one side or the other, which may be considered a disadvantage.

There is also a more subtle public policy concern about ADR that stems from its inherently private nature. The very confidentiality that most business litigants find appealing in ADR may also have a detrimental long-run impact on the business community at large. ADR providers offer a system of private justice that does not result in publicly available judicial opinions with reasoned explanations for the results in specific cases. As a result, the continuing development of a generally understood body of "business jurisprudence" is hampered and the business community is deprived, to some degree, of the benefit of current and evolving legal precedent, which may guide it in new disputes and new contract negotiations. This may increase the potential for good-faith disputes to arise in areas where the rules of law are not clear, widely understood, or fully developed, or have not been revisited for many years.

This consideration may be of particular significance for certain kinds of business disputes. For example, where one party has an institutional interest in establishing a favorable, public precedent on a particular legal issue that is likely to recur with some regularity, a judicial forum may be preferable to ADR, despite the increased delays, costs, and risks. Moreover, where the availability of a business litigation session enables the parties to know which judge or judges will likely hear their cases, there may be a greater sense of predictability about the course of the proceedings than exists in the ADR context.

LEGAL PRINCIPLES FOR CHALLENGING AND CONSTRUCTIVE AGREEMENTS

State law typically determines disputes over the interpretation and application of real estate contracts in the US. While the law varies from state to state, a number of basic common law principles are generally applicable to contract disputes in US jurisdictions. None of these is universally applicable, and there are various refinements and exceptions that may pertain to any particular case. Still, it is helpful to have a general sense of the typically applicable principles, a few of which are outlined here.

First, as courts faced with contract disputes have been asked to construe what the parties meant by various phrases and terms, litigators for the disputing parties typically offer diametrically opposing (and sometimes quite creative) interpretations. One of the oldest concepts used in the US to resolve such disputes is that if the meaning of the contract can be clearly ascertained from the "four corners" of the document, a court will determine the contractual intent from the written provisions of the contract and go no further. Under this rule, evidence of the parties' negotiations and the drafting history of the contract will not be admitted or considered by the court, unless the contract is deemed to be ambiguous. This rule, which has been the law in most states for generations, can prevent frustration of the parties' clear intent.

Another basic rule that courts in the US often rely on is that ambiguities in a contract will be construed against the party who drafted the document. This notion has become somewhat antiquated in most commercial transactions, where final agreements generally reflect substantial input by attorneys for both parties.

It is not unusual, in documents prepared by sophisticated parties and counsel, to see language that preempts this rule by expressly providing that the document shall not be construed against either party, because it was jointly drafted by two parties with experienced, competent counsel. Meanwhile, a California statute provides that "technical words in a contract must be interpreted as usually understood by persons in the profession or business to which they relate, unless clearly used in a different sense."

When parties simply omit from their contract a term that must be determined in order to rule upon the adequacy of one of the parties' performance, the general rule is that a court will supply a term reasonable under the circumstances. For example, where no time for performance is specified in a contract, it must be performed within a reasonable time after execution. What is a "reasonable time" will depend on the nature of the contract, the probable intention of the parties, and the attendant circumstances.

Where two parties have signed a fully integrated contract, evidence of prior or contemporaneous agreements is inadmissible to vary or contradict the terms of the final and complete written agreement. The basic tenet underlying this rule is that if a court finds the written agreement to have been intended as a complete and exclusive statement of the terms of the parties' agreement, then the writing alone constitutes the contract, and evidence of prior negotiations or side agreements will be ignored in interpreting the final written agreement. Most legal documents will in fact contain an "integration" clause which states explicitly that the document constitutes a complete statement of the parties' entire agreement and that prior writings will be ignored. So in a case where two parties sign a letter of intent for the purchase of an office building and later execute a formal contract, the letter of intent will be ignored in case there is a dispute between the parties as to their intentions. Where a letter of intent is not followed by a formal contract, however, a court may find that the parties are bound by the terms set forth in the letter of intent. This is particularly so in cases where the letter contains no specific language denying the formation of a contract unless and until a detailed formal document is signed.

BANKRUPTCY

The main purpose of the U.S. Bankruptcy Code (the Code), administered exclusively at the federal level to create consistency among the 50 states and the District of Columbia, is to provide debtors burdened by debt with a "fresh start." Two concepts in the Code facilitate this fresh start: the automatic stay that arises upon the filing of a bankruptcy petition and halts, among other things, all collection actions of creditors, and a discharge of all debts that arose before the petition date.

Background/Process

REASONS FOR FILING FOR PROTECTION

A debtor that is insolvent because its liabilities exceed its assets may consider filing for bankruptcy. A debtor that is solvent based on a balance sheet test but is unable to pay its debts as they become due may also seek bankruptcy protection. In addition, a debtor may choose to file for bankruptcy because the automatic stay (described later) prohibits creditor harassment and enjoins most creditor actions against the debtor, while it seeks approval of a reorganization plan that will enable it to emerge from bankruptcy and continue based on its business operations.

DETERMINING UNDER WHICH CHAPTER TO SEEK RELIEF

A business (including a general or limited partnership, joint venture, corporation, or limited liability company) can file a bankruptcy petition under either Chapter 11 or Chapter 7 of the Code. Chapter 7 is filed by a business that no longer intends to operate and chooses to liquidate its assets. Chapter 11 is most often filed by a business that chooses to reorganize its financial affairs. A Chapter 11 reorganization may include liquidation.

Automatic Stay

Filing a bankruptcy petition triggers an automatic stay that prohibits any creditor from attempting to collect from the debtor or the debtor's property. This powerful tool not only prohibits collection activities, but generally requires anyone holding property of the debtor to turn that property over to the debtor-in-possession or trustee. If a creditor willfully violates the automatic stay, a court may award punitive damages and other severe relief. A creditor may seek from the bankruptcy court relief from the automatic stay to gain possession of its collateral and to liquidate the collateral to satisfy its secured claims.[8] The bankruptcy court will consider various factors in determining whether to grant such relief.

The Debtor

In a Chapter 11 case, the debtor usually stays in control of its business or affairs. The goal of the debtor in a Chapter 11 case is to obtain a confirmed plan of reorganization. The plan will describe the treatment that creditors will receive.

U.S. Trustee

The U.S. Trustee is charged with overseeing all bankruptcy cases. A representative of the U.S. Trustee's office conducts a meeting of creditors. The U.S. Trustee's office may also take an active position in the case.

Creditors' Committee

The U.S. Trustee often appoints a creditors' committee soon after the filing of the case.

The committee generally consists of those persons holding the seven largest claims against the debtor or the seven largest amounts of equity securities of the debtor. The committee and its professionals (such as attorneys and accountants) will be entitled to reimbursement of their expenses if they can show that they were beneficial to the estate. Among other activities, the committee consults with the trustee or debtor concerning the administration of the estate and participates in the formulation of a plan of reorganization.

Bankruptcy Process

The bankruptcy case commences with the filing of a petition by the debtor (or as discussed later, of an involuntary case). After filing of the petition, the debtor sends a notice to all creditors and other parties of interest.

The notice also sets the date for a meeting of creditors, to be conducted by the U.S. Trustee, who examines the debtor or its representative under oath. The meeting of creditors allows them to examine the debtor as well.

Once the petition is filed, the automatic stay becomes effective and prevents the continuation or commencement of any actions against the debtor or its property. If a lease has been terminated prior to the filing, but the tenant/debtor remains on the premises, the automatic stay still prohibits any action to recover possession. The landlord may seek relief from the automatic stay in order to obtain possession.

Plan of Reorganization and Disclosure Statement

The ultimate goal of a Chapter 11 proceeding is the formulation and confirmation of a plan of reorganization. In most cases, the debtor has the exclusive right to file a plan of reorganization during the first 90 days after the petition date and has an additional 30 days for soliciting acceptance of the plan by the creditors. Once this exclusivity period has passed, any interested party may file a plan. In many cases, in conjunction with the confirmation of the reorganization plan, the debtor will determine whether to assume or reject leases where it is a tenant. This strategy enables retailers and other tenants to assume some leases and reject others, depending on whether they have value to the debtor's business.

A plan is a contract between the debtor and its creditors concerning the treatment of obligations existing prior to confirmation of the plan. The Code requires that the plan set forth adequate means for its implementation, such as selling assets, modifying contracts, restructuring operations, or liquidating a portion of the operations.

Chapter 7 Cases

A Chapter 7 case consists of the liquidation of the debtor's assets (other than those exempt from creditors under applicable law) in exchange for a discharge of the debtor's prepetition debts. In an asset case, the creditors will receive distributions according to the priority scheme set forth in the Code. At the conclusion of the case, an individual debtor will receive a discharge of prepetition debts but a corporation or partnership will not.

Chapter 11 Cases

In Chapter 11, a debtor tries to reorganize its debts by extending the time in which to pay them and reducing the total amount to be paid.

Generally, a Chapter 11 debtor will remain in charge of the reorganization process and retain control over its business operations and management during the case. The Code, however, provides the court with broad authority over the debtor's operations and allows creditors to carefully to monitor the debtor's financial affairs to ensure that its assets are preserved for the benefit of all of the creditors.

Involuntary Bankruptcy

An involuntary case begins with the filing of a bankruptcy petition by three or more entities holding claims on the debtor that are not contingent as to liability and not subject to a bona fide dispute. If the debtor has fewer than 12 eligible holders of claims, an involuntary petition can be filed by just one qualifying creditor. If the debtor is a partnership, a subset of the general partners can initiate the involuntary filing. Petitioning creditors can be held liable for damages if the involuntary petition is determined to be wrongful or unwarranted; this potential liability serves as a deterrent to involuntary filings.

After the involuntary petition has been filed, but prior to entry of an order for relief, the debtor may continue to operate its business, acquiring and disposing of property without restriction.

However, the court may limit the debtor's ability to dispose of assets of the estate if it believes that the debtor is acting in a manner detrimental to creditors. Despite there being no restrictions on the debtor's right to acquire or dispose of property, the automatic stay is still effective against the debtor's creditors.

An involuntary petition can result if the debtor is generally not paying its debts as they become due (unless such debts are subject to a bona fide dispute) or within 120 days of the filing, a custodian, receiver, or assignee took possession or charge of substantially all of the debtor's property. If the petitioning creditors can prove grounds for relief, the court will enter the order for relief, and the case will proceed in the same manner as a voluntary case. The case may also be dismissed, provided that there is written notice to all creditors and then a hearing. An involuntary Chapter 7 petition may be converted by the debtor to a Chapter 11 petition.

Options Other Than Bankruptcy

This article does not cover scenarios outside of bankruptcy that can arise involving financially troubled borrowers, such as forbearance or workout agreements, foreclosure or deeds in lieu of foreclosure, state-court receivership actions, or liquidation proceedings.

CONFIRMATION AND CRAMDOWN—LENDERS BEWARE!

Classes of creditors vote to accept or reject a plan. If all impaired classes (creditors who will not be paid in full) approve the plan, it will be confirmed consensually. However, so long as even one impaired class votes to accept the plan, it may be confirmed over the objection of other impaired classes through the "cramdown" provisions of the Code. This concept is frequently employed in the case of a secured lender, the value of whose collateral is less than the balance on its loan. In such a situation, the debtor can use the cramdown provisions to attempt to modify the interest rate or the term of the loan.

If one class of impaired creditors votes in favor of the plan *and* the other requirements of confirmation are satisfied, a plan that modifies the terms of an undersecured loan can be approved over the objection of the undersecured creditor. This tool is often used in connection with secured real estate loans where, for example, the property's primary tenant has vacated the premises or the property requires substantial renovations. In a cramdown, the loan terms can be modified to reflect market conditions and the debtor's ability to pay.

If the court confirms the plan of reorganization, the debtor's prepetition obligations are discharged and creditors are bound by the provisions of the plan, regardless of how they voted on it. Once the plan has been confirmed, the debtor is vested with all of the property of the estate and required to carry out the confirmed plan.

EXECUTORY CONTRACTS AND UNEXPIRED LEASES

An executory contract is defined as a contract, including a lease, under which the obligations of both parties are so far unperformed that the failure of either to complete performance would constitute a material breach excusing the performance of the other party. Upon the filing of a bankruptcy petition, the trustee or debtor-in-possession may either assume, assume and assign, or reject executory contracts.

Assumption of an executory contract or unexpired lease has two functions: the bankruptcy estate is obligated, as an expense of administration, to complete performance, and the estate is entitled to the benefits of performance from the nondebtor party. In deciding whether to assume a contract, the trustee or debtor-in-possession should determine whether the cost of further performance by the debtor estate exceeds the benefit to be received from the nondebtor party. If the contract is profitable, the trustee or debtor-in-possession would be expected to assume the contract, thereby obtaining the nondebtor's contract performance in exchange for that of the debtor estate.

Rejection, on the other hand, is the estate's decision not to undertake further performance of the contract but to breach it. By rejecting the contract, the estate incurs liability for the breach in the form of a claim for contract damages, which is unsecured.

The nondebtor party cannot force the debtor to perform under the contract or lease prior to its assumption. In addition, the Code requires a trustee or debtor timely to perform all the obligations of the debtor from and after the petition date under any unexpired lease until the lease is assumed or rejected. If the debtor fails to perform its obligations, a landlord or other creditor can file a motion to compel performance, including all payments due. Promptly seeking this relief can make a significant difference in the ultimate result for a creditor in a Chapter 11 proceeding, particularly when there is a question about the debtor's ultimate ability to reorganize.

Executory contracts and unexpired leases are deemed rejected if not assumed within 60 days of the petition date (although a court can extend this deadline and often does). Landlords should be mindful that during this prerejection period, the debtor-tenant is required to comply with all current obligations under the lease. In the case of a deemed rejection, the real property should be immediately surrendered to the landlord. At any time a landlord may file with the court a motion to compel the debtor to assume or reject the executory contract or unexpired lease.

In a Chapter 11 proceeding, the trustee or debtor-in-possession may assume or reject an executory contract at any time prior to confirmation unless, upon the request of a party to the contract or lease, the court orders that the trustee or debtor determine within a specified time whether to assume or reject the contract or lease.

In a Chapter 7 case, the trustee has 60 days from the date of the bankruptcy filing (or of conversion from Chapter 11) to assume or reject an executory contract or unexpired lease. However, the court may extend this time for cause if a request is made within the initial period. If the trustee fails to assume the contract, it is deemed rejected.

In order to assume a lease or other executory contract, the trustee or debtor-in-possession must cure, or provide adequate assurance that it will promptly cure, any existing defaults, including those that existed on the petition date, and provide adequate assurance of future performance under the lease.

A landlord should pay particular attention to notices regarding the assumption of leases. Generally, a debtor will file a motion to assume (or to assume and assign) a contract or lease, along with a proposal to cure any payment defaults. The landlord may then object to the motion. The parties will either resolve their dispute between themselves or a court will do so for them. Since the debtor will frequently propose a cure amount of zero, the landlord must object or it could waive any claim for additional amounts due. A debtor may also assume a contract and then assign it to a third party, which invokes requirements for assumption.

The rejection of an executory contract constitutes a breach, which is deemed to occur immediately before the filing of the petition. Under the Code, a landlord's claim for damages arising out of the termination of a lease for real property is limited to the "rent reserved by such lease," without acceleration, for the greater of one year, or 15 percent, not to exceed three years, of the remaining term of the lease. In most cases, the landlord is entitled to a claim for one year's rent (plus additional rent, etc.) under the lease, plus any amount due as of the petition date.

A landlord's claim upon breach through rejection is reduced by the amount of any security deposit it holds. Depending on where the case is filed, the claim may also be reduced by the amount of a letter of credit provided in lieu of a security deposit. One federal appeals court recently ruled that a landlord's claim for damages upon the rejection would be reduced by the amount of a security deposit in the form of a letter of credit. Many jurisdictions have not definitively addressed this issue. The claim arising out of the rejection or breach of the lease is a general unsecured claim in the bankruptcy case.

While a trustee or debtor-in-possession may assume or reject an executory contract, it may not modify the contract without the agreement of the nondebtor party. Thus, the debtor must assume the entire contract, not just its favorable parts.

IMPORTANT CONSIDERATIONS UPON A TENANT'S BANKRUPTCY FILING

An informed landlord will keep the following in mind when a tenant files for bankruptcy:

- The automatic stay will limit the landlord's remedies.
- If the lease terminated before the bankruptcy filing and the tenant remains as a holdover tenant, the landlord should consider seeking relief from the automatic stay to obtain possession.
- Under the Code, all rent that accrues after the bankruptcy filing must be paid currently.
- Be mindful of the deadlines, particularly those to file a proof of claim and to assume or reject executory contracts.
- Do not apply a security deposit without advice of counsel.
- The debtor may assume or reject an executory contract, but modification of the lease requires agreement by the landlord.

PROTECTING THE LANDLORD IF A TENANT MAY BE FILING FOR BANKRUPTCY SOON

A landlord can take a number of steps to minimize its exposure before a tenant files for bankruptcy. The proper steps depend on the circumstances of each case, but the following are good overall guidelines:

- **Monitor Defaults:** This may include issuing timely notices of default in accordance with the lease and applicable state law. The landlord also should consider pursuing actions for possession early in the tenant's delinquency.
- **Payment and Application of Rents:** When a tenant is in financial trouble and bankruptcy is likely, if there are arrearages, it may be preferable for a landlord to apply payments to current rent due rather than to arrearages. Payments on current amounts due are less likely to be set aside as preferential transfers. Of course, state law may affect how the rent must be applied.
- **Obtaining Possession:** If the lease is terminated before the bankruptcy filing and the landlord obtains possession, the tenant likely will have no interest in the property upon the filing of bankruptcy. To that extent, the landlord will not be affected by the automatic stay.
- **Application of Security Deposit:** It can be advantageous for a landlord to exercise its rights with respect to a security deposit or letter of credit before the filing of a bankruptcy case, subject to the terms of the lease, the security deposit, the letter of credit, and state law. Once a tenant files for bankruptcy, the landlord should not apply a security deposit without obtaining relief from the automatic stay.

If a tenant files for bankruptcy, a landlord cannot, without consent of the bankruptcy court: issue a default, demand, or collection notice for rent that came due prior to the filing; issue an invoice for rent due (including a year-end reconciliation that covers a prepetition year, if there is a balance due); issue a notice of termination of a lease; commence or continue a suit for possession; commence or continue a suit for back rent; apply a security deposit or draw down a letter of credit; or enforce a judgment for possession or for money.

CONCLUSION

Litigating contract disputes involving real estate matters in the US court system is often frustrating, confusing, and complex. Lengthy delays in resolving cases, the high cost of litigation, and unpredictable variations in the ultimate outcomes characterize the experience, and variations between various courts adds to the risks and uncertainties, particularly for those who do business on a regional, national, or international basis. These negative impacts can be significantly compounded by the potential that an adverse party may be able to change the operative terms of the pertinent contract in the bankruptcy forum.

For all of these reasons, methods such as mediation and arbitration are increasingly popular for resolving real estate and other commercial contract disputes. At the same time, however, contracting parties need to have a shared understanding of the consequences of a default, which comes ultimately from a well-developed public body of pertinent case law. As a result, the real estate and business communities have a certain irreducible dependence on the state court litigation system, which uniquely serves to develop and make public the rules of law by which their transactions will proceed and their ventures will operate.

NOTES

1. Meyers, Charles J., and Richard R. Powell. "Specific Performance of Real Estate Contracts: The Ultimate Remedy." *Tennessee Law Review*, vol. 45, no. 549 (1978).
2. Nelson, Grant S. "The Essential Elements of a Real Estate Contract." *University of Richmond Law Review* vol 27, no. 1 (1992); Powell, Richard R. "Enforcing Real Estate Contracts: Specific Performance and Liquidated Damages." *John Marshall Law Review* vol. 27, no. 237 (1994).
3. Thomas, Jeffrey E. "Specific Performance of Real Estate Contracts: An Analysis of State Laws and Court Practices." *Real Property, Probate and Trust Journal* vol. 23, no. 111 (1988).
4. Dennis, Roger J. "Controlling the Performance Risk of Real Estate Contracts." *Oklahoma Law Review* vol. 46, no. 59 (1993).
5. Stein, Gregory M. "Efficient Remedies for Breach of Contract," *Journal of Legal Studies*, vol. 30, no. 287 (2001).
6. Hill, R. Keith. "Enforcing Agreements to Agree: The Search for a Reasonable Standard." *Real Property, Probate and Trust Journal* vol. 251 (1987).
7. Cooter, Robert E., and Daniel L. Rubinfeld. "Economic Analysis of Legal Disputes and Their Resolution." *Journal of Legal Studies* vol 27, no. 453 (1998).
8. Smith, James C., and Diane E. Thome. "Liquidated Damages Clauses in Real Estate Contracts: An Examination of Enforcement Issues." *John Marshall Law Review*, vol. 27, no. 251 (1994).

GLOSSARY

Agricultural Foreign Investment Disclosure Act (AFIDA)

Signed into law in 1978, AFIDA requires that a foreign person who acquires, disposes of, or holds an interest in US agricultural land must disclose such transactions and holdings to the U.S. Secretary of Agriculture. The goal of the act is to maintain a nationwide system for collecting information pertaining to the foreign ownership of US agricultural land.

Alternative minimum tax (AMT)

The AMT is a method to calculate taxes for people whose income exceeds a certain level. It was passed in 1969 and was intended to close loopholes that allow them to reduce or eliminate tax payments. Generally, a taxpayer pays more taxes as their income rises. Previously, certain high-income taxpayers were able to avoid paying income tax by structuring their income to qualify for as many exemptions as possible. The alternative tax calculation limits the number of exemptions that can be claimed by an individual and uses a different rate structure with the goal of increasing the amount of income subject to tax.

Anti-money laundering (AML)

"Anti-money laundering" is a term that refers to an extensive network of legislation that is aimed at uncovering efforts to "launder money," a practice that attempts to make illicit funds appear as legitimate income. Common crimes relating to money laundering include tax evasion, drug trafficking, and public corruption. AML requires banks and financial institutions develop sophisticated customer due diligence plans to catch suspicious transactions and assess money laundering risks. The first set of anti-money laundering laws in the US were established under the Bank Secrecy Act of 1970, but many other regulations have been added in the subsequent years to close more common loopholes.

Bank Secrecy Act (BSA)

A US law passed in 1970 requiring financial institutions in the US to assist US government agencies in detecting and preventing money laundering, a practice that attempts to make illicit funds appear as legitimate income. Previously, banks did not have any documentation system for transactions involving cash over $10,000, which allowed suspicious transactions to go unnoticed. Now, businesses must file Form 8300 with the IRS if they receive more than $10,000 cash from one buyer, and banks must provide regulators with currency transaction reports as well as other documentation. While not every cash transaction over $10,000 is considered suspect and therefore reported, the law is relatively vague about what qualifies as "suspicious," leading to a huge volume of data being reported annually.

Blocker corporation

A blocker corporation is a Type C corporation that acts as an off-shore vehicle to allow tax-exempt individuals to protect their investments from taxation when they participate in private equity or with hedge funds. The "blocker" entity acts as a barrier between the investors and the investment, helping convert any gains from that investment into corporate dividends distributed by the blocker. Dividends, interest, and capital gains are generally not subject to federal taxes for non-US and non-tax-exempt investors.

Blocker, Cayman

A Cayman blocker is so named because fund-managed blockers are often organized in the Cayman Islands, largely due to low operating costs and the absence of a corporate income tax for the island territories.

Blue sky laws

State-level antifraud regulations that require issuers of securities to be registered and to disclose details of their offerings. These work in addition to federal securities laws to require companies to register their offerings of securities before they can be sold in a particular state, unless a specific exemption is available. Blue sky laws can also license brokerage firms, their brokers, and investment advisor representatives.

Branch profits tax

A tax that treats US operation of foreign corporations in much the same manner as US corporations owned by foreign persons by imposing a 30 percent branch profits tax on the corporation's earnings, profits, and interest payments to foreign lenders. It also requires the tax to apply if the amount of interest deducted by the branch on its US tax return exceeds the amount of interest actually paid during the year.

Broker

The term "broker" has a few different meanings in real estate, but an investment broker can be a firm or individual that engages in the business of buying and selling securities, including stocks, bonds, mutual funds, exchange-traded funds (ETFs), and certain other investment products. Brokers can advise clients on buying, selling, or holding investments and may periodically monitor investments in some accounts. Typically, brokers are paid a commission fee by clients for each purchase or sale of an investment.

Building Owners and Managers Association (BOMA)

The leading trade organization for commercial real estate professionals based in the US and founded in 1907. BOMA represents owners, managers, service providers, and other property professionals of all commercial building types, including office, industrial, medical, corporate, and mixed-use. The organization is engaged in legislative advocacy efforts on behalf of CRE as an industry, as well as providing thought leadership and advice to members. They also maintain a comprehensive set of standards for measuring buildings and best practice guidelines for developers.

Capital expense (Capex)

Capital expenses are funds used by a company to acquire, upgrade, and maintain physical assets such as property. This type of financial outlay is made by companies to add a future economic benefit to a project or operation. These expenses are then recorded on a company's balance sheet instead of expensed on an income statement. Capitalizing an asset requires the company to spread the cost of the expenditure over the useful life of the asset.

Central business district (CBD)

The commercial and business center of a city that contains commercial space and offices, sometimes referred to as a financial district or a "downtown" sector. CBDs are the center of economic activity in a city, and shops that have locations there are usually paying high premiums for the location. CBDs look very different from city to city depending on the development, economic, and political history of the area, but all feature certain characteristics, such as being the most densely populated and economically active neighborhoods of a city.

Class A, B, and C (buildings)

Some sectors, such as office, rely on a system of three classes to organize properties. Class A is made up of buildings with both excellent construction and a great location, placing their rents well above average and offering a definite market presence. Class B includes buildings with great construction but lacking a great location, which compete for a wide range of users with rents in the average range of the market. Class C consists of buildings with subpar construction and location, giving them the reputation of "fixer-uppers." Some organizations, such as BOMA (see Building Owners and Managers Association) have laid out quantifiable standards that define each class, but definitions vary across the industry.

Commercial mortgage-backed security (CMBS)

A security backed by mortgages on commercial properties instead of residential properties. These fixed-income investments can provide liquidity to real estate investors and commercial lenders at the same time. There are no standard rules for the structure of CMBS, so valuations can be difficult, but there is an advantage of a prepayment risk when compared to residential mortgage-backed securities (RMBS).

Commingled fund

A portfolio made up of assets from several accounts that are blended together. The portfolio/fund owner uses this design to reduce the cost of managing constituent accounts separately. These pooled funds are generally not publicly listed or available to individual retail investors.

Committee on Foreign Investment in the United States (CFIUS)

An interagency committee authorized to review certain transactions involving foreign investment in the US and certain real estate sales. The committee comprises nine Cabinet members, two ex officio members, and other members as appointed by the president. The committee is primarily tasked with assisting the president on such foreign economic matters, but after increasing scrutiny on the committee's methods in the early 2000s, the Trump administration passed the Foreign Investment Risk Review Modernization Act of 2018 to revise the foreign investment review process, and then in 2020 the U.S. Treasury also passed down final guidelines that require CFIUS to operate with increased security measures for evaluating large foreign real estate transactions in relation to national security.

Construction manager

Also known as general contractors or project managers, construction managers coordinate and supervise building projects, including public, residential, commercial, and industrial structures. They are an integral part of the development process by remaining onsite to oversee construction tasks.

Controlled Commercial Entity (CCE)

Any business or organization in which a foreign government holds 50 percent or more of the company's shares, giving the government practical control. Tax exemptions generally applicable to a foreign government's income from investments in certain securities do not apply to income received by (or directly/indirectly received from) a controlled commercial entity, despite the foreign government's control.

Core (investment)

A term referring to the central investments of a long-term portfolio—in the case of real estate, these investments are usually properties. These properties are typically fully leased buildings in high-quality locations that require minimal upgrades. Core holdings are those that have a history of reliable service and consistent returns.

Core-plus (investment)

A portfolio management style using a low-to-moderate risk profile that permits managers to augment a core base of holdings with assets that have greater risks, such as those that need light property improvements, better management efficiency, or increased quality of tenants. The properties will produce ample cash flow, but still need some capital to be diverted to necessary improvements.

Corporate Transparency Act (CTA)

Enacted in 2021, the Corporate Transparency Act is an expansion of anti-money laundering laws like the Bank Secrecy Act intended to help prevent and combat money laundering, financing anti-American interests, tax fraud, and more illicit activities. The CTA establishes uniform beneficial ownership information reporting requirements for certain types of corporations, limited liability companies, and other similar entities created in or registered to do business in the US. It also authorizes FinCEN (see FinCEN) to collect that information and disclose it to authorized government authorities and financial institutions.

COVID-19

COVID-19 is a shortened title for the coronavirus disease strain discovered in 2019, an infectious respiratory illness caused by the SARS-CoV-2 virus. COVID-19 caused a global pandemic beginning in 2020 and continues to evolve today.

Currency and Foreign Transactions Reporting Act

Also known as the "Bank Secrecy Act," this 1970 act requires US financial institutions to assist government agencies to detect and prevent money laundering by contributing to FinCEN. FinCEN, or the Financial Crimes Enforcement Network, is a department that safeguards the financial system from illicit use, combats money laundering and its related crimes, and promotes national security through the strategic use of financial authorities and the collection, analysis, and dissemination of financial intelligence. FinCEN acts as the main administrator of the Currency and Foreign Transactions

Reporting Act (see also Anti-money laundering, Bank Secrecy Act, Financial Crimes Enforcement Network).

Data center (property type)

Data centers are highly specialized facilities that house servers, storage devices, switches, routers, and fiber optic transmission equipment. Sometimes mixed in with industrial properties, data centers are tech-specific but usually housed in similarly large and commercial buildings. However, data centers have a higher need for power, making it necessary for operators to determine fees on kilowatts of power used or provisioned. Despite these infrastructure costs, data centers' capacity for data has made them an attractive sector to many investors.

Diversification

The practice of limiting exposure to any one type of asset by spreading investments both among and within different asset classes. This form of asset allocation is done to manage risk and boost performance. It can be achieved by purchasing multiple stocks in several companies or sectors at the same time, investing in pooled funds such as mutual funds, or buying bonds from different issuers.

Easement

The right to cross or otherwise use a property owner's land for a specified purpose, an easement bestows a nonpossessory interest on the easement holder in the property of the landowner. The easement holder's interest is limited and specified to the terms of the agreement. A positive easement might prevent the property owner from making any changes to the property that would block the easement holder from using it, such as adding a fence blocking the holder's access point. A negative easement might prevent an owner from developing a property in such a way that it negatively effects the easement owner, such as a neighbor who wants to protect their property's view.

Economic cycle

Refers to the overall state of the economy as it goes through four stages in a cyclical pattern: expansion, peak, contraction, and trough. An expansion is a period of time in which the economy displays rapid growth, lower interest rates, and production increases. The "peak" refers to the apex of the expansion, or the height of the economic growth. A peak may see prices and economic indicators stabilize for a short period before reversing to the downside. Following a peak is usually a contraction, which happens when growth slows, employment falls, and prices stagnate. As the contraction continues, the economy will settle into a trough, in which supply and demand hit their lowest. If the economy stays in the trough state for long, it will become a depression. The National Bureau of Economic Research (NBER) is the definitive source for the official dates of US economic cycles.

Effectively connected income (ECI)

All income sources within the US connected with the conduct of trade or business by a foreign person engaging in trade or business is considered effectively connected income by the IRS. ECI is taxed at a graduated or lesser rate under a tax treaty. Taxpayers must be engaged in a trade or business during the tax year to treat income as ECI and use the reduced rate.

Emblements

Emblements are the agricultural crops (e.g., corn, wheat, soy, carrots) produced by labor and cultivation, rather than naturally occurring (e.g., grass, trees, wild berries, crabapples, black walnuts). Emblements are generally considered as personal property belonging to the tenant responsible for cultivation.

Employee Retirement Income Security Act (ERISA)

Passed in 1974, ERISA is a federal law that sets minimum standards for most voluntarily established retirement and health plans in private industry, excluding governmental agencies, churches, or plans meant to comply with worker's comp, unemployment, or disability laws. Under ERISA, plans are required to provide insured individuals with plan information like features and pricing, and establish a grievance and appeals process for participation, vesting, and benefit accrual and funding. The act also sets minimum standards for participation, vesting, and benefit accrual and funding; provides fiduciary responsibilities for those who manage and control plan assets; gives participants the right to sue for benefits and breaches of fiduciary duty; and if a defined benefit plan is terminated, ensures payment of certain benefits through a federally chartered corporation known as the Pension Benefit Guaranty Corporation.

Environmental site assessment (ESA)

A report prepared for a real estate holding that identifies potential or existing environmental contamination liabilities. Under the Comprehensive Environmental Response, Compensation, and Liability Act (as amended by the Superfund Amendments and Reauthorization Act of 1986), property owners may be held liable for environmental contamination found on the property, whether the owner created it or not. Potential buyers of a new property conduct an ESA to assess the condition of the property to determine any liabilities before the sale occurs.

Environmental, social, and governance (ESG)

An investment strategy that uses a set of standards—environmental, social, and governance—for a company's behavior used by progressive investors to screen potential investments. "Environmental" refers to a company's strategy for dealing with climate change; "social" refers to an organization's relationships with employees, suppliers, customers, and other communities where it operates; and "governance" refers to company leadership, executive pay, audits, and shareholder rights. While ESG is a strong strategy to safeguard portfolios from holding companies that engage in problematic behaviors, some companies have been insincere in touting their ESG accomplishments, misleading investors.

Exchange Act

The Securities and Exchange Act of 1934 mostly regulates securities transactions in the secondary market. Most of these sales take place between parties who are not the original issuer, including trades that investors funnel through brokerage companies. So the Exchange Act requires companies to disclose information that investors need to make investment decisions, including annual reports, important events, and information about company leadership. It also regulates exchanges on which securities are sold and establishes severe penalties on organizations that defraud investors or take part in trading strategies that use illegally obtained information an average investor wouldn't have, like insider trading.

Financial Crimes Enforcement Network (FinCEN)

Established in 1990 by the U.S. Department of the Treasury, FinCEN is a government bureau that maintains a network to prevent money laundering and other financial crimes. FinCEN tracks suspicious persons by researching mandatory disclosures for financial institutions established by various anti-money laundering legislation. FinCEN is made up of three main contributors—law-enforcement agencies, the regulatory community, and the financial services community. Data collected by the network is compiled to make recommendations on the distribution of resources where there is greater risk of financial crime (see Anti-money laundering, Bank Secrecy Act, Corporate Transparency Act, Currency and Foreign Transactions Reporting Act).

Foreclosure, judicial and nonjudicial

Foreclosure is a legal process in which a lender attempts to recover the balance of a loan from a borrower who's gone into default. A judicial foreclosure uses the courts to file a lawsuit for the unrecovered amount—this step can only be taken when the loan has been past due for 120 days. A nonjudicial foreclosure doesn't use a lawsuit, making it faster and cheaper for a lender. The nonjudicial process is only available in certain states and is sometimes called statutory foreclosure, typically using a foreclosure trustee, a neutral third party who is sometimes listed in the deed of a property, to proceed with foreclosing. In some states, the trustee will give the owner a warning to pay default balances before foreclosure, while others will simply send a notice of sale after foreclosure. The entire process can be executed within a few months.

Foreign Investment in Real Property Tax Act (FIRPTA)

A tax law that imposes US income tax on foreign persons selling US real estate: specifically, if a US taxpayer buys real estate from a foreign person, they may be required to withhold 10 percent of the amount realized from the sale (usually the amount realized is the same as the purchase price). If a purchase falls under FIRPTA, then within 20 days of the sale, the taxpayer will be required to file Form 8288 and submit their withholding. Exceptions to this requirement include residences for $300,000 or less or properties not considered US real property interests. Exemptions can also be secured with a withholding certificate from the IRS, which is granted in certain circumstances.

Fund, closed-end (CEF)

A mutual fund that doesn't continuously offer its shares for sale, but instead sells a fixed number of shares at one time to maximize income potential for regular distributions. A CEF is designed to translate total returns into predictable and tax-advantageous income over time. Closed-end funds are able to invest in specialized corners of the market where open-end funds may not be able to absorb the risk. This allows fund managers to employ a leverage-based strategy of borrowing to gain greater investment exposure and potential opportunities.

Fund, open-end

A mutual fund that can issue unlimited new shares, priced daily on their net asset value (NAV). A diversified portfolio of pooled money, the fund sponsor sells shares directly to investors. When a share is purchased, a fund will create a new replacement share, but when a share is sold, it will be taken out of circulation. Shares are priced based on the value of the fund's underlying securities. There are various types of open-end funds, such as some mutual funds, hedge funds, and exchange-traded funds. These funds are much more common than their alternative, close-ended funds, and usually make up the bulk of company-sponsored retirement plans.

General contractor

A person or company responsible for overseeing a construction project, usually directly contracted by the project owner or investor. General contractors schedule and manage subcontractors as well as direct the broader project and its progress. They are usually hired as an independent contractor on a project-by-project basis.

General partner (GP)

Generally refers to the firm managing a private equity fund, which is arranged as a general partnership with third-party investors being limited partners. In addition to providing capital and managing daily operations, a general partner is also following new investment opportunities, developing new strategies with management to maximize value, and liquidating so that distributions can be made to limited partners.

Generation, baby boomer

People born in the years following World War II, or mid-1940s to early 1960s. This is the generation following the Silent Generation and preceding Generation X. Historically, the baby boomers were the largest generational group, until millennials eventually took their place. As a result of their numbers, they have strong buying power.

Generation, Generation X

People born between the early 1960s and the late 1970s. This generation follows the baby boom and precedes the millennials. Despite the economic affluence of their parent generation, Gen X is set to become the first generation to be in a worse financial position before retirement than their parents.

Generation, Generation Z

People born between the early 1990s and the early twenty-first century. Generation Z follows the millennials. It is the most diverse generation in the US so far and tends to be more socially progressive than former generations.

Generation, millennial

People born between the early 1980s and the late 1990s, this generation was born after Generation X and before Generation Z. Named for the turn of the twenty-first century, millennials are the largest generation in living US history. They are often considered the first generation to be raised with electronics thoroughly involved in their lives.

Great Financial Crisis (GFC)

A severe economic crisis occurring between 2007 and 2008 that would turn into the worst financial crisis since the Great Depression after the housing market crashed. The crash was attributed to a housing bubble created when subprime mortgages were vastly over-represented in mortgage-backed securities, causing a recession when the bubble burst. Major financial institutions were left holding trillions in worthless investments as a result.

Gross leasable area (GLA)

The total usable area of a building or office space for the tenants, or the total usable floor space that generates income. This comprises all common areas, elevators, bathrooms, stairwells, and other shared spaces the tenant may not regularly occupy. A tenant's occupied square footage is referred to as the net rentable area of the building.

Healthcare (property type)

A real estate sector including hospitals, doctors' and medical office buildings, drugstores, retail medical facilities, and similar properties. As the baby boomer generation grew older and legislation changed, the need for more medical facilities became apparent, but the COVID-19 pandemic catapulted the sector into the front of many portfolios.

Heating, venting, and air conditioning (HVAC)

The use of various technologies to control the temperature, humidity, and purity of the air in an enclosed space. The HVAC system of a property is the most critical device to maintain and monitor, especially in extreme climates where air-conditioning may be needed year-round. An HVAC system can incur large financial losses if it fails entirely, so a property owner needs to ensure proper maintenance is done to protect the system.

High-net-worth individual (HNW)

Someone with liquid assets of at least $1 million. Because these people have access to additional benefits and opportunities usually closed to people with lower incomes, these individuals often seek the assistance of financial professionals to manage their money. Private wealth managers seek clients of similar assets because their portfolios often require extra work to manage.

Industrial (property type)

A category of property types that includes large commercial spaces for the production and shipment of goods. There are three main categories of industrial buildings: manufacturing buildings are focused toward the manufacturing of goods and consist of less than 20 percent of office space, have loading docks for trucks, and clear heights of at least 10 feet; storage and distribution sites comprise buildings focused on logistics, or the process of getting products to consumers; flex space properties are meant to be more flexible to tenants and usually feature more office space, at least 30 percent of the available space.

Internal rate of return (IRR)

A metric that estimates the annual rate of growth that an investment is expected to generate by making the net present value (NPV) of all cash flows equal to zero in a discounted cash flow analysis. While this calculation uses the same equation as NPV, it is specifically the annual return that makes the NPV equal to zero, while the NPV is the actual dollar value of the project (see Net present value).

Internal Revenue Code (IRC)

Also known as Title 26 of US Code, the Internal Revenue Code is a body of legislation that houses federal tax law, comprising laws from as early as 1874 through today. It saw major amendments in 1939 (when it was originally compiled in one place), 1954, and 1986 (both were overhauls of the system). It first became known as the IRC after the 1986 changes. The IRC comprises several important concepts to US economic law, but in the realm of real estate, its most important contribution is the establishment of real estate investment trusts (REITs) (see Real estate investment trusts) as a business type, laid out in Section 856 of the IRC.

Internal Revenue Service (IRS)

A federal agency that administers and enforces the US federal tax laws, primarily existing to fund the U.S. Department of the Treasury. The IRS does not deal with revenue laws relating to the industries of alcohol, tobacco, firearms, and explosives. First formed in 1862, its stated mission is to collect the proper amount of tax revenue, at the least cost to the public, by efficiently applying tax law.

International Investment and Trade in Services Survey Act (IITSSA)

Passed in 1976, this act requires that US businesses report all foreign investment if a foreign entity owns 10 percent or more of the voting interest in the US entity, whether their control is direct or indirect. Required forms include the Quarterly Survey of Foreign Direct Investment in the US, which reports the relationship between the business and foreign investor, as well as the Annual Survey to report annual financial and operating data of US entities, and the Benchmark Survey, which is filed once every five years to report whether the entity had at least 10 percent foreign-based ownership at the end of the prior calendar year. The act is administered and enforced by the Bureau of Economic Analysis of the Department of Commerce. Some exemptions exist, such as investment that is under $1 million, any investment in real estate that is under 200 acres, or any investment that is in real estate intended for personal use only.

Investment philosophy

A set of beliefs and principles that guide an investor's decision-making process. Less of a set of rules, an investment philosophy contains several guidelines and strategies taking into account one's goals, risk tolerance, time horizon, and expectations. Popular philosophies include growth investing, value investing, and technical or fundamental analysis. Some individual investors even trademark their own strategies.

Joint venture (JV)

A real estate venture where two or more investors pool their resources and knowledge for a development project or investment. Each partner is liable for profits, losses, and costs associated. However, the venture is its own organization, separate from the participant's other business interests. While they are technically considered partnerships under colloquial definitions, a joint venture can take on any legal structure.

Know-your-client (KYC)

Refers to the mandatory process of identifying and verifying the client's identity when opening an account as well as periodically, over time as part of international anti-money laundering efforts (see Anti-money laundering). The process includes ID, face, document, and biometric verification. Banks may refuse to open an account or halt a business relationship if the client fails to meet minimum KYC requirements.

Lease, appurtenant

A lease in which a real property is improved by an appurtenant who grants ownership of certain items to a person who owns the property in legal transactions. The appurtenance, or improvement, could be a permanent attachment like a physical addition of a fence or deck, or it could be nonphysical, such as a lease or easement (see Easement).

Lease, gross

A lease where a tenant pays a set amount periodically for renting the property exclusively. The fee encompasses all of the costs associated with property ownership, such as taxes, insurance, and utilities, but the lease will include incidental charges incurred by the tenant as well. These are the most common leases used in the commercial property market.

Lease, ground

An agreement in which a tenant is permitted to develop a property during the lease, usually meant to allow the lessee to make land improvements on behalf of the property owner, who takes back the land after the lease period is over. Generally commercial agreements between landlords, these agreements typically last 50 to 99 years. Tenants who can't afford their own property often opt for a ground lease to build experience, while the landlord earns income on the property.

Lease, net

A lease in which a lessee pays a portion of property expenses that would usually be paid by the property owner, such as taxes, insurance fees, and maintenance costs in addition to rent. Common in commercial real estate, these agreements expect tenants to cover some costs related to a piece of property as if they were the actual owner. A single-net lease requires tenants to pay property taxes specifically, while a double-net lease requires both taxes and insurance. Many net leases allow tenants to pay a lower rent in exchange for taking on additional expenses.

Lease, space

A legal document between a tenant and a landlord that governs the leasing of commercial real estate. In a commercial lease, the space must be used specifically for business to qualify as a commercial space. While a residential property may be partly used for commercial purposes such as office space, a commercial space is only to be used for business—this is usually written into the lease. Commercial space leases also include more information than a residential lease, such as occupancy limits, property expenses for required renovations or modifications needed for business, as well as maintenance procedures, property taxes, insurance, utilities, and who will pay for them.

Lease, triple-net (NNN)

A commercial lease where the lessee pays extra fees in addition to rent and utilities. These expenses are in addition to rent and utilities. While any net lease expects tenants to take on some additional fees outside of rent, a triple-net lease is one that specifically requires tenants to cover three additional fees: insurance, maintenance, and taxes.

Triple-net leases have grown into popular investment vehicles because they offer stable and low-risk income.

Leasehold estate

A legal term for a property rental that does not grant ownership but grants the tenant certain rights to use the property for a specified amount of time in exchange for a payment to the property owner. The leasehold may grant tenants interest in the property, but it does not grant any ownership.

Letter of intent (LOI)

A nonbinding agreement that outlines the sale or lease terms and conditions. The letter outlines the chief terms of a prospective deal, usually used in business transactions to allow two parties to organize the higher-level details before resolving the finer points. LOIs often include nondisclosure agreements and no-solicitation provisions.

Leverage

The practice of using borrowed money or debt to increase a return on investment, such as paying a down payment to own a property. This technique is often used by companies to expand potential for returns while also reducing risk. When properties are purchased as an investment, sellers are sometimes willing to finance some of the price to allow purchasers the ability to buy without using their own funds.

Life sciences (property type)

An asset class dedicated to providing both lab and office space for tenants who study and develop biomedical technology. Life sciences properties can be converted from traditional office or industrial spaces or may be built specifically for this purpose. Top life sciences markets are centered around universities with a strong involvement in research for the industry, as they provide the best access to relevant talent.

Limited liability corporation (LLC)

A business structure that protects its owners from personal liability for its debts or liabilities. A real estate LLC offers investors a way to buy, sell, and rent property separate from themselves as individuals. Further, LLCs may be partnerships, allowing investors to work with several investors to purchase properties. Partners in an LLC are liable up to their amount of initial investment.

Limited partner (LP)

A partner in a business who does not partake in managing the business directly, usually as part of a limited partnership agreement. Limited partners hold liability up to the amount of their initial investments. If the limited partner is a part of a limited liability partnership (LLP), there is no general partner who holds unlimited liability, so all partners are limited. However, if the company is a limited partnership, there is a general partner who holds unlimited liability while limited partners have additional protections.

Live-work-play

Multifamily developments that include spaces for housing, stores, office spaces, gyms, dining, schools and other living conveniences for tenants. This offers amenities such as convenience, walkability, and community. With a variety of businesses so close, work is readily available for residents. Further, mixed-use neighborhoods offer a chance to include several types of housing, including single and multifamily.

Loan-to-value ratio (LTV)

The amount of a mortgage compared with the value of its property. If a mortgage has a particularly high down payment, the property likely has a low LTV ratio. Mortgage lenders may use the LTV in deciding whether to lend and to determine if they will require private mortgage insurance.

London Interbank Offered Rate (LIBOR)

An interest rate average calculated from estimates submitted by the leading banks in London. Long considered a benchmark for global banks to use when lending among themselves, the rate is calculated daily by the Intercontinental Exchange, a US company that operates various exchanges. Controversy surrounding LIBOR has led to questions around its trustworthiness as an accurate benchmark, causing the Federal Reserve and several British authorities to decide to replace it with the Secured Overnight Financing Rate (SOFR), a benchmark for dollar-denominated derivatives and loans.

Market, primary

Also known as gateway or establishment markets, primary markets are metro areas with populations of over 5 million people and the highest available transaction volume. Primary markets don't offer the fast growth of a secondary market, but they offer significant opportunities for real estate by creating far more economic activity than secondary markets.

Market, secondary

Also known as magnet markets, secondary markets consist of metro areas with between 2 and 5 million people which boasts a large volume of sales. These cities see population rates that are higher than the national average, as well as a younger population made up mostly of millennials and Gen-Xers (see Generation, millennials, and Generation, Generation X).

Market, tertiary

Also known as emerging markets, a tertiary market is a smaller metro area that lacks the density and infrastructure found in primary and secondary markets. Cost of living is generally lower, which leads to a steady stream of population growth and job opportunities. Since the COVID-19 pandemic, many tertiary markets are seeing record rates of growth, solidifying tertiary markets as a growing sector.

Metropolitan statistical area

A core area of a city that contains a substantial population, as well as adjacent communities having a high degree of economic and social integration with that center. The US Office of Management and Budget (OMB) determines metropolitan areas based on U.S. Census data. The first statistical areas were defined in 1949 by the Bureau of Budget and have undergone several amendments in the years since. Currently, a "Core based statistical area" is comprised of metropolitan and micropolitan statistical areas, which are divided based on population.

Mezzanine loan

A form of financing that combines debt and equity. Lenders provide subordinated loans (less-senior than traditional), and they potentially have relatively high interest rates and flexible repayment terms. This gives lenders the ability to convert the debt to an equity interest in the company in case of default, generally after venture capital companies and other senior lenders are paid. Risk is shared between senior debt and equity.

Mixed-use (property type)

Properties used for a variety of purposes, including commercial, residential, retail, office, or parking space. This property type combines several property types in one investment. Usually, the development contains complementary properties, such as a hotel that also holds retail stores and a gym, or an apartment complex in very close proximity to restaurants.

Mortgage

An agreement between a lender and lendee that allows the lendee to purchase or refinance a property and gives the lender the ability to seize the property if not repaid. The amount of payment per month is determined by the length of the loan, the interest rate, and the value of the property. Lendees also have the ability to refinance the loan later on if interest rates change or become untenable.

Multifamily residential (property type)

A property that contains several separate housing units for residential inhabitants within one building or several buildings at one property, such as duplexes, apartment complexes, or others. If the owner chooses to live in one of the units, it's an owner-occupied property. Most property types under this category can be funded with a traditional mortgage, while others may require a commercial loan depending on size and price.

National Council of Real Estate Investment Fiduciaries (NCREIF)

The National Council of Real Estate Investment Fiduciaries aims to inform concerned parties on the actual performance of the real estate industry by collecting data, analyzing it, and presenting it in its relevant forms to the target audience. NCREIF operates as a nonpartisan collector, validator, aggregator, converter, and disseminator of commercial real estate performance and benchmarking information. Members include investment managers, investors, consultants, appraisers, academics, researchers, and other professionals in the real estate investment management industry.

NCREIF Property Index (NPI)

Released quarterly by the National Council of Real Estate Investment Fiduciaries, this data provides returns for institutional grade real estate held in a fiduciary environment in the US. The objective is to provide a measurement of property-level returns to increase knowledge of the asset class of real estate.

Negotiated-rate state

The amount a plan or issuer has contractually agreed to pay an in-network provider for covered items and services.

Net effective rent (NER)

A metric calculated by dividing the total gross rent of the lease by the number of months, including any discounts, offers, or promotions. It implies a discount has been applied to the apartment on rent, usually a free month. For instance, a landlord may advertise that the apartment has a "net effective rent" of $1,500, but because that price includes one free month of rent, the actual rent is $1,625. Mostly, this metric is used to advertise rentals.

Net operating loss (NOL)

A loss in which tax deductions are more than a company's income for the year. This means the NOL can be deducted from previous years' incomes on tax returns. To be able to claim that exemption, the loss must be caused by deductions from the business or another approved reason. Partnerships and S corporations generally can't use an NOL exemption.

Net present value (NPV)

How much an investment is worth throughout its lifetime, discounted to today's value. This is used to help calculate the internal rate of return and is used to represent the actual dollar value of a project. In other words, it helps determine whether the property will be profitable down the line. The NPV is calculated using a discounted cash flow valuation, which includes the discount rate, cash flows, and the number of periods.

Office (property type)

This type consists of properties in the office sector, which are designated low-, mid-, and high-rise based on their size. They're also sorted into three Classes: Class A consists of buildings with great construction and location, Class B properties are well-constructed but in a bad location, and Class C contains those with both poor construction and location (see Class A, B, and C buildings).

Office of Foreign Assets Control (OFAC)

The financial intelligence and enforcement agency of the U.S. Treasury Department administers and enforces economic trade sanctions in support of US national security and foreign policy objectives. OFAC acts under presidential national emergency powers, as well as authority granted by specific legislation, to impose controls on transactions and freeze assets under US jurisdiction.

Operating company (opco)

A subsidiary company that is responsible for the day-to-day management of a business without directly owning the property itself, usually as part of an operating company/ property company deal (see Property company). An opco/propco deal involves two or more companies, one of which is a property company that owns all of the assets, including real estate, and the other an operating company, which uses the assets to generate sales. These deals allow all financing and credit rating related issues for both companies to remain separate while fulfilling each end of the deal. The arrangement allows the operating company to keep any debt off their books.

Operating expense (opex)

An expense incurred through normal business operations like rent, equipment, inventory, marketing, payroll, and so on. These are shorter-term expenses for the day-to-day operation of a business as opposed to capital expenses, which are larger, long-term investments in the future of a property. Operating expenses are expensed on an income statement and can be deducted from income so long as the business is for-profit.

Opportunistic (investment)

Investment strategy that involves developing a plot of land, redeveloping an existing property, or carrying out renovations to reposition the property as a more premium asset. Because of its longer investment horizon, there is an added risk to the investment. Construction delays and other issues may lead to a very long development phase before the investment begins generating income.

Ordinary dividends

Shares of a company's profits passed on to the shareholders periodically, this is the regular payment of dividend income on a stock. Dividends are considered ordinary more often than not, but sometimes they may be considered "qualified" because they meet certain tax laws to be eligible for the lower capital gains rate.

Overlease

Within the language of a sublease, references to the original, underlying lease a tenant and landlord have are called the "overlease." A sublease is an arrangement in which a third party is signed onto an additional leasing agreement for a set period of time during the original leasing period.

PATRIOT Act

The US PATRIOT Act is a 2001 US act that creates new abilities for law enforcement to detect and prevent terrorism directly following 9/11. As part of the goal to enhance law enforcement investigatory tools, several sections of the PATRIOT Act revised the Bank Secrecy Act to grant many new abilities to FinCEN (see FinCEN) to subject foreign jurisdictions to additional scrutiny and increase requirements for reporting suspicions of money laundering. It also added new prohibitions on US correspondent accounts with foreign shell banks and regulations governing concentration of accounts by financial institutions to ensure such accounts are not used to obscure the identity of the customer. The additions were aimed at preventing terrorist groups from being funded by illicit US funds.

Preferred equity investment

An investment in which all cash flow or profits are paid back to the preferred investors (after all debt has been repaid) until they receive the agreed-upon "preferred return." This type of financing is employed as part of the aggregate capital raise for a given real estate project, making it a form of bridge financing similar to mezzanine debt (see Mezzanine loan). Capital raised in a preferred equity position serves to bridge the gap between a senior loan and the common equity portion of the capital stack.

Private placement memorandum (PPM)

A securities disclosure document used by a company (issuer) that is engaged in a private offering of securities. The PPM is a comprehensive document outlining material details of an offering. It provides important risk disclosures, strategies, management teams, investment criteria, and more information about the issuer's securities. It protects the issuer against claims of misrepresentation or omission.

Property company (propco)

A subsidiary company created specifically by a parent company (see Operating company) to manage profitable real estate while the operating company does the work of generating income. These arrangements are often pursued to secure better financing and ease credit rating issues for the operating company. Since the propco and opco are part of the same group of companies, operating companies never actually give up ownership of the property.

Property condition report

An evaluation of the capital expenses that will likely be required to maintain an asset in the short term and long term. The report is designed to assess the physical condition of a property after a walk-through survey as well as identify areas for improvement, such as site improvements, facades, roofs, mechanical/plumbing/electrical, and so on. The property's needs are often categorized based on immediacy of need.

Proptech

A broad range of products, services, and systems that use technology to enhance the ways people interact with a commercial property. Proptech can be used in all sorts of properties, including office, multifamily, industrial, and more sectors. Billions have been invested into companies who aim to develop new proptech solutions for real estate clients.

Protecting Americans from Tax Hikes Act (PATH)

Passed in 2015, the Protecting Americans from Tax Hikes Act (PATH) expanded or renewed tax credits for individuals, families, and businesses while implementing measures to prevent fraudulent claims for those credits. The act primarily affects people who qualify for the earned income tax credit or the additional child tax credit, refunds for which aren't issued before February 15, giving the IRS additional time to evaluate fraud. These tax credits were also made permanently available to taxpayers under the PATH Act, while it expanded the work opportunity tax credit. A tax credit is more valuable to the average taxpayer than a tax deduction, because it reduces the taxes owed dollar for dollar.

Published-rate state

The amount a provider typically charges for their items and services.

Qualified Controlled Entity (QCE)

An organization that was created under the laws of a foreign country, was established (by such foreign country or one or more employers) to provide retirement or pension benefits to participants or beneficiaries that are current or former employees of one or more employers for services rendered, does not have a single participant or beneficiary with a right to more than 5 percent of its assets or income (the 5 percent limitation), or is subject to government regulation controlling which annual information about its beneficiaries is provided to the relevant tax authorities in the country in which it is established or operates (the information reporting requirement). Another qualifying case would be if, under the laws of the country in which it is established and operates,

(1) contributions to the company that would otherwise be subject to tax under such laws are deductible or excluded from gross income or taxed at a reduced rate, or (2) taxation of a company's investment income (if any) is deferred or subject to a reduced rate (the "foreign tax treatment").

Qualified domestic trust (QDOT)

A type of trust that allows taxpayers who survive a deceased spouse to take the marital deduction on estate taxes, even if the surviving spouse isn't a US citizen. Normally, a US-citizen surviving spouse can take the marital deduction and a noncitizen surviving spouse cannot, but a QDOT allows the marital deduction when the assets are included inside the trust before the spouse's death. Any assets not included in the trust will be subject to estate taxes.

Qualified foreign pension fund (QFPF)

Any trust, corporation, or other organization or arrangement that satisfies certain requirements: the organization was created under the law of a country other than the US, the company is established to provide retirement funds or pension benefits to beneficiaries that are current/former employees, the association does not have a single participant or beneficiary with a right to more than 5 percent of its assets, it is subject to government regulation with respect to which annual information about its beneficiaries is provided, and under the laws of the country in which the company was established or operates, contributions are taxed and taxation of any investment income is deferred or taxed at a reduced rate.

Qualified investment entity (QIE)

An REIT or RIC that was held directly or indirectly by less than 50 percent of foreign persons during the testing period. Generally, a distribution from a QIE is taxed as if it were a gain related to a sale by the foreign corporation receiving the distribution. However, any distribution by a REIT on a stock traded on a securities market in the US is not treated as a gain from a sale of a real property interest if the shareholder did not own more than 5 percent of that stock at any time during the year—this applies to QIEs as well.

Real estate investment trust (REIT)

A company that owns or finances income-producing real estate across a range of property sectors. The company is managed by one or more trustees or directors, and the beneficial ownership is evidenced by transferable shares the owners receive. Typically, this would be a taxed domestic corporation like any other, but REITs qualify for some exemptions. To qualify as an REIT, the company must also be owned by 100 or more people, and the vast majority of income for the year must be derived from real-estate related activities, like dividends, interest, rents, and so on.

Request for proposal (RFP)

A document that announces a project, describes it, and solicits bids from qualified contractors to complete it. Most organizations and governments use them to launch projects. The entity requesting the bid is typically responsible for evaluating the feasibility of the bids submitted, the financial health of the bidding companies, and each bidder's ability to support the project. Without a formal document, it's likely a less organized process could fail to lay out the best plan for a project.

Research and development (R&D)

"Research and development" is a term that encompasses all activities that companies undertake to innovate and introduce new products and services. This is the first stage of development of a new product. When undertaking a new project, companies should be aware of how R&D costs can materially impact their income statements and balance sheets. In real estate, R&D is a critical part of the building process, when experts are tasked with ensuring building standards measure up to laws and regulations. This will also have a significant impact on income statements for an investment undergoing a large construction project or other development.

Retail (property type)

Properties used to market and sell consumer goods and services. Retail is usually classified under eight categories of buildings. This includes malls, lifestyle centers, factory outlets, power centers, community centers, neighborhood centers, convenience centers, and mixed-use properties. Malls are usually enclosed with several stores under one roof. Lifestyle centers are like upscale malls, but don't require department stores to anchor them and also don't typically exist under one roof. Factory outlets are usually outdoors and feature outlet stores for national brands, ranging from mid-priced to luxury designers. Power centers are generally comprised of three big-box stores, generally discounters, large specialty chains, or home-improvement stores. Community centers are often referred to as strip malls or shopping centers. Neighborhood centers are smaller versions of a community center and feature one large anchor store. Convenience stores are small properties with convenience-based retailers such as dry cleaners or nail salons, and often weather economic recessions fairly well. Mixed-use retail combines retail space, office, and multifamily residences among other businesses.

Rights, air

The ability to occupy the vertical air space above a plot of real estate. This includes any space above a property, which might mean the upper stories of a building, power lines, or sometimes a region of air space above the property. For commercial and residential real estate in cities, this is especially important for developers looking to build vertical structures like skyscrapers to combat issues finding ground space.

Rights, farming

Refers to the right to farm on a piece of land. In some situations, it's beneficial for owners of agriculturally viable plots of land to allow farmers to plant crops there. Lenders usually use an agricultural lease to allow these individuals the right to use their agricultural real property, such as land, equipment, or livestock in exchange for rent. This provides a mode of entry for beginner producers and established farmers wishing to expand their production.

Rights, mineral

Ownership rights that allow an owner the right to exploit minerals from underneath a property. "Minerals" can apply to liquid, solid, or gaseous minerals, such as gold, oil, natural gas, and other natural deposits. These are often separate from surface rights and aren't always possessed by a property owner. Some minerals aren't included, such as limestone, sand, gravel, and subsurface water.

Rights, subterranean

Refers to the legal rights a landowner has to the resources and materials located beneath their land. In other words, legal ownership over anything that lies in the ground beneath the property. While most property owners have surface rights to anything on the surface of their property, some don't have rights to the land below ground. This could mean they don't have the right to extract resources under their land.

Rights, timber

Allows an individual to own all or part of trees on a property without actually owning the ground where they grow. Some investors designate plots of forests that are designed for use by railroad companies and other industries that require timber, and plots are referred to as "timberland." Tenants pay for the right to use matured trees for their businesses.

Risk-adjusted returns

A calculation of the potential profit from an investment that takes into account the degree of risk assumed by the investor. The risk is measured by comparing the risk of the investment to a virtually risk-free investment, such as US Treasuries. The risk may be represented by a number or a rating depending on the metric used to calculate it. Risk-adjusted returns are applied to stocks, funds, and portfolios to determine if the risk was worth the income to investors.

Securities Act

Also referred to as the Truth in Securities Act, this 1933 act requires investors receive financial and other significant information concerning securities being offered for public sale. Congress primarily targeted securities markets and issuers to ensure issuers are disclosing material information to the public before sale, as well as preventing fraud in the securities market. The act requires disclosure through a mandatory registration process in any sale of securities, excluding exemptions. Regulations are primarily aimed at primary market offerings.

Self-storage (property type)

Self-storage retail properties that offer spaces for customers to rent. This category features three types of occupancy that are used to evaluate a property's performance in this sector. The first is physical occupancy, which refers to the number of occupied units at a self-storage property. The second is square-foot occupancy, which is the number of rentable square feet occupied at a facility, also expressed as a percentage. Last, economic occupancy is the percentage of potential income being received from available units (in other words, the market rate that could potentially be charged versus what is actually being paid by tenants currently).

Single-family rental (property type) (SFR)

Houses or apartments that are designed to be rented by a single family or individual. Homes can take many forms, such as detached homes, townhomes, flats, and are not occupied by the property owner. This offers reliable income in the form of rent, as well as a stable customer base in that demand for homes is usually high. These properties are popular among newer investors who are looking to secure stable investments to begin growing a portfolio.

Sovereign wealth fund (SWF)

A government-owned investment fund that is comprised of a country's economic reserves, such as state-owned natural resource revenues, trade surpluses, bank reserves that may accumulate from budgeting excesses, foreign currency operations, money from privatizations, and governmental transfer payments. Usually, funds are targeted toward a specific purpose or project, similar to the private sector's use of venture capital. The funds are generally meant to improve a country's economy.

Student housing (property type)

A multifamily rental property in which 40 percent or more of the units are leased to undergraduate or graduate students. A student with sufficient income to pay rent does not count toward the student unit concentration required. Student residents and their property owners often have different needs than typical multifamily tenants, such as smaller kitchens, shared units with private bedrooms, and less cosmetic amenities like patios or balconies.

Subject matter expert (SME)

An individual with qualifications and experience in a particular field or work process. A SME's responsibility is to ensure the facts and details are correct so that the project's deliverables will meet the needs of the stakeholders, legislation, politics, standards, and best practices.

Sublease

A new contract between a tenant and a sublessee, conveying all or part of the estate for a shorter term than that for which the lessee holds originally. In the commercial sector, a retail or business tenant may sublet or assign space to help with costs and to avoid being penalized for leaving a lease early. At times, transferring leasing rights is the only way to avoid being penalized for not meeting lease obligations.

Sunbelt

A section of the US from California to Florida, the region experiences growth when businesses and populations move into southern states from the north. Since the COVID-19 pandemic (see COVID-19), the Sunbelt has been growing exponentially, allowing for significant developments in southern cities across the region.

Talent

Skilled or high-potential employees. When speaking about groups of people, such as the "talent pool" of a city, talent can also refer to the population of skilled workers for a certain sector in that area.

Title

A formal document outlining the rights an owner holds over a piece of property. Mostly, titles are used to confirm ownership, but they may also include information about any liens on the property, usage rights, easements, and natural resource rights, among other things. A title is distinct from a deed, as deeds transfer ownership between two parties, essentially transferring a title from one individual to another.

Truth in Lending Act (TILA)

Passed in 1968, the TILA is an act that protects against inaccurate and unfair credit billing and credit card practices. The main changes implemented by TILA require lenders to provide lendees with loan cost information to allow consumers to better comparison shop. Loans that are subject to TILA allow consumers a right of recession, or a three-day period to reconsider the decision and back out of a loan without losing any money.

Uniform Commercial Code (UCC)

A comprehensive set of laws governing all commercial transactions in the US. This is not a set of federal laws, but instead a uniformly adopted state law to allow for smooth interstate business transactions. The code was developed by the Uniform Law Commission around the turn of the twentieth century and was further developed until the 1950s when states began to adopt it, starting with Pennsylvania. Now often referred to as the "backbone of American commerce," all 50 states have adopted the code to give businesses the ability to enter into contracts with the knowledge that courts will enforce the contact terms identically in any state.

U.S. Bankruptcy Code

Also referred to as Title 11 of the US Code, the Bankruptcy Code governs the procedures that businesses and individuals must follow when filing for bankruptcy. All bankruptcy cases are handled in federal courts and follow the procedures outlined in the Code. Businesses may file under Chapter 7, Liquidation, of the Code, which allows their assets to be seized to pay their debts, or they may file Chapter 11, Reorganization, which allows the debtor to keep their assets and have the duties of a trustee while a plan of reorganization is created to decide how to pay debtors. Chapter 11 is much preferred for most businesses, as it protects the debtor from losing as many assets.

U.S. Bureau of Economic Analysis (BEA)

Formed in 1903, the BEA is a federal agency that provides macroeconomic and industry statistics, primarily about the gross domestic product (GDP) and trade balance of the US. The BEA offers granular GDP data, including breakdowns of GDP by state, metropolitan area, and industry, as well as tracking personal incomes, corporate profits, balance of payments, and more. Their stats are critical for planning, investment, monetary policy, and more based on the performance of the US economy.

U.S. Department of Housing and Urban Development (HUD)

A department of the federal government that administers housing and urban development laws. Homes are also provided directly to citizens via the Housing Choice Voucher Program. The department was formed after the U.S. Housing Act of 1937 provided for federal subsidies to be used for local housing agencies to create housing for low-income families, establishing HUD to oversee how the subsidies are distributed and aid local governments in construction and maintenance.

U.S. Environmental Protection Agency (EPA)

This agency is tasked with environmental protection matters and sets environmental regulations to protect nature and the public from harmful emissions or chemicals. Among their primary goals are verifying that the US has clean air, land, and water and all regulations are based in accurate climate science. Many of these regulations directly affect real estate by applying to suppliers and construction. For instance, the EPA's Residential Lead-Based Paint Hazard Reduction Act of 1992 made sweeping changes to construction and design of residential homes for sale or lease nationwide and continues to be enforced on pre-1978 buildings today. Outside of actual legislation, the agency also engages in industry supervision to address land use concerns and protect fragile ecosystems.

U.S. real property holding corporation (USRPHC)

Per IRS regulation, a foreign or domestic corporation is a USRPHC if the fair market value of its real property interest (USRPI) is at least 50 percent of the sum of the fair market value of (1) its total USRPIs, (2) its total interest in real property located outside the US (FRPI), and (3) any other assets used in business. In the past, foreign individuals disposed of real property interests without paying income taxes, but FIRPTA (see Foreign Investment in US Real Property Tax Act) revised this in 1980 by treating a gain or loss on a disposition as connected to a US trade or business. This created the designation of a US real property holding corporation.

US real property interest (USRPI)

An interest in real property (including an interest a natural deposit of some kind) located in the US or its territories, as well as certain personal property that is associated with the use of the property, such as machinery. Per IRS regulations, foreign corporations must account for the net gain or loss of US real property, including dispositions of interests, so USPRI is a categorization of those property interests for reporting purposes.

U.S. Securities and Exchange Commission (SEC)

Formed after the Wall Street Crash of 1929, the purpose of the U.S. Securities and Exchange Commission is to protect capital markets from manipulation. The SEC regulates public disclosures for markets and works to protect investors from fraud and other manipulation. It does this by bringing civil court cases against those perpetrating fraud and contributing to the Justice Department's intelligence on criminal situations, as well as overseeing securities markets, exchanges, firms, and more. Due to their oversight, investors are required to have access to registration statements, financial reports, and other forms for a potential investment through the SEC's online database, EDGAR.

Value-add (investment)

Refers to a strategy of investment that emphasizes properties with an existing cash flow and seeks to grow that profit by improving or repositioning the property. Also known as value-oriented real estate, a value-add investment already generates an income before the renovations are done, but isn't at its maximum earning potential. By doing necessary renovations, the value of the property is appreciated while generating additional income at the same time.

Workouts, debt

Short for "workout agreement," a workout is a contract between a lender and borrower to renegotiate a defaulted loan. The workout allows the borrower to waive any existing default fees and avoid foreclosure, but it also allows the lender to recover some losses, making it mutually beneficial. This is usually only allowed in situations where it will serve both the borrower and lender, and some lenders aren't willing to lose part of their initial investment.

INDEX

ABOUT THE CONTRIBUTORS

Sarah Armendariz, Partner, Dentons

Sarah is a member of Dentons' Real Estate practice group and is based in Kansas City, Missouri. Her practice focuses on sophisticated commercial real estate lending, and she represents both foreign and domestic financial institutions, including real estate investment trusts (REITs), commercial banks, mortgage lenders, and life insurance companies. She is skilled in all phases of a transaction, including complex negotiations, due diligence and closings. She also frequently represents agent banks in syndicated loans and in dealing with the colenders not only during the syndication process, but also during the term of the loan. Sarah also represents participating banks and prospective colender who seek to join existing bank groups.

dentons.com

Zeb Bradford, Chief Investment Officer, Metzler Real Estate

As Metzler's Chief Investment Officer, Zeb Bradford manages the firm's overall investment activities. He excels at building and managing industry relationships and leveraging resources to achieve optimal return on investment. Since 2012, he has led his team in executing more than $6.3 billion in transactions across the major US markets. Since the early 1990s, Mr. Zeb has successfully negotiated over $10 billion in a variety of transaction types, identifying creative methods to add value to client investment strategies. Zeb is a regular speaker for organizations such as Private Equity Real Estate, the Association of Foreign Investors in Real Estate, Expo Real, and Urban Land Institute.

metzlerna.com

Gunnar Branson, Chief Executive Officer, AFIRE

As CEO of AFIRE, Gunnar Branson brings nearly three decades of experience across commercial real estate, professional services, education, and association leadership. Prior to joining AFIRE in 2018, he served as CEO of the National Association of Real Estate Investment Managers (NAREIM), and before that he led strategy and marketing for Fortune 500 and other innovative mid-market companies. As a recognized thought leader, Gunnar is a regular speaker, panelist, and spokesperson for the global real estate and investing community, focused on institutional investing, urbanism, sustainability, and future trends. Gunnar also hosts The AFIRE Podcast and is the author of *Chasing Lights*.

afire.org

Sheri P. Chromow, Founder, SPC Advisors

Sheri P. Chromow is the founder of SPC Advisors, a firm representing Chinese institutions in structured finance transactions collateralized by commercial real estate and corporate assets. A career attorney, she is a strategic leader with expertise in many areas. She excels in providing strategy and tactics, building consensus, and closing complex transactions across corporate and international cultures. Chromow often advises on legal issues relating to real estate, hospitality, finance, sustainability, joint ventures, opportunity funds, structuring, and negotiating transactions. She is skilled in managing financing and debt restructuring involving complex structures subject to securitization, syndication, and participations. She also provides advisory/board assistance on governance, risk management, cybersecurity, ESG issues, private equity, and diversity. She has experience developing extensive relationships and acting as advisor to European and Asian banking institutions deploying capital in the US, as well as counseling foreign investors on debt and equity investments in the US.

SPC Advisors

Trey Clark, Director, Chief Investment Officer (US), Vanke

Since 2015, Trey has been responsible for real estate investments and expansion of Vanke US on the West Coast, specifically within the primary markets of Seattle, Los Angeles, and the San Francisco Bay area. Prior to joining Vanke US, Trey worked in acquisitions and development at MacFarlane Partners and in distressed debt and real estate opportunities with Sequoia Equities. Trey holds an MBA from the Haas School of Business at the University of California, Berkeley, where he focused on real estate and finance. Trey enjoys wine and biking and is passionate about real estate markets, world history, and solar energy.

vanke.us

Nick Colley, Global Portfolio Strategist, CBRE Investment Management

Nick Colley is Global Portfolio Strategist for CBRE Investment Management. In this role, Nick collaborates with Client Solutions officers, the Insights & Intelligence group, and investment teams globally to deliver real assets portfolio solutions for investors. Nick joined the firm in 2021 from Property Funds Research, where he led the development of their in-house investment processes, underwrote a wide range of real estate and social infrastructure funds, developed portfolio models, and led the implementation of advisory mandates for institutional investors. Prior to that, he also served as a Global Property Analyst at Aberdeen Asset Management. Nick began his career in the industry in 2008. Nick earned a BA from the University of Southampton and an MS in real estate management from Oxford Brookes University. He holds an Investment Management Certificate and is a chartered financial analyst and member of the Society of Property Researchers.

cbreim.com

Jason E. Dunn, Director, Goulston & Storrs

As Director at Goulston & Storrs, Jason Dunn has a wide-ranging practice that encompasses all aspects of commercial real assets, with a focus on representing domestic and foreign institutional clients in equity and debt investments in North American real estate and infrastructure through funds, coinvestments, joint ventures, and REITs. Through his representation of tax-exempt and international investors, Jason is experienced with tax and ERISA transaction structures. Jason's commercial real estate and infrastructure practice also includes public-private partnerships, acquisitions and dispositions, occupancy and ground leases, sale-leasebacks, development, and financing. Jason is a Co-Chair of the firm's International Investors group.

goulstonstorrs.com

Hubert Eisenack, Tax Partner, Ernst & Young

Hubert Eisenack is a Tax Partner at Ernst & Young, an international accounting firm offering assurance, tax, and strategy services. Previously, he served as Director for KPMG AG, an audit, tax, and advisory firm. Eisenack specialized in advising cross-border transactions, real estate asset management, funds, and companies. He holds an ML in American Law from Boston University.

ey.com

Kris Ferranti, Partner, Shearman & Sterling

Kris Ferranti is a partner in the Real Estate practice at Clifford Chance. He has extensive experience representing a diverse range of clients, including financial institutions, sovereign wealth funds, investment funds, family offices, and individual and institutional investors and developers in complex commercial real estate transactions. His experience spans real estate acquisitions, dispositions, joint ventures, development projects, foreign investment, financings, ground and space leasing, real estate fund and co-investment formation, and LP investments into funds. Kris has contributed to several publications, including the American Bar Association, American College of Real Estate Lawyers, American Law Institute, Commercial Property Executive, Corporate Real Estate Journal, Family Office Real Estate Magazine, Law360, Lexis Nexis, National Real Estate Investor, Real Estate Finance & Investment, Thomson Reuters Practical Law, and Wolters Kluwer. He is a regular speaker, frequently appearing at seminars and conferences on various real estate subjects, sharing his insights and expertise with the wider industry. Kris is a Fellow of the American College of Real Estate Lawyers (ACREL), which is the premier organization of US real estate lawyers and admission is by invitation only after a rigorous screening process.

shearman.com

Dominic Garcia, Chief Pension Investment Strategist, CBRE Investment Management

Dominic Garcia is Chief Pension Investment Strategist for CBRE Investment Management. In this role, he is focused on developing solutions for pension funds looking to expand their investments in infrastructure. Dominic, who has 16 years' experience in the investment and pension industry, joined the firm from the Public Employees Retirement System of New Mexico, where he served as Chief Investment Officer. In that role, Dominic worked with stakeholders on enhancing plan sustainability, established a risk budget and delegation of investment authority to staff, and created a risk-based approach to portfolio management. Prior to his role at New Mexico, Dominic served on the Investment Committee and was a Senior Funds Alpha Manager for the State of Wisconsin Investment Board. Dominic earned a

BA in Political Science and Spanish from the University of New Mexico and an MPP degree in Public Finance from the University of Chicago. An industry-respected thought leader and speaker on pension portfolio construction, governance, and sustainability, Dominic serves on multiple research and advisory boards and has garnered various industry awards.

cbreim.com

Zev D. Gewurz, Director, Goulston & Storrs

Zev Gewurz is a real estate attorney who represents institutional and private equity lenders, foreign and US-based investors, as well as owners and real estate developers across the US and abroad. He advises clients on portfolio acquisitions and dispositions, joint venture structuring, complex financings, mezzanine and participating debt transactions, and distressed debt workouts and sales. Zev has an outstanding reputation for excellent work and deep experience in handling sophisticated matters. He currently serves as Co-Chair of the firm's Real Estate Group and International Investors Group.

goulstonstorrs.com

Gary Goodman, Partner, Dentons

Gary Goodman is a Real Estate partner at Dentons with extensive experience in real estate financing transactions, representing domestic and foreign institutional lenders and borrowers in fee and leasehold construction and term financings, refinancings, mezzanine financings, and workouts. Gary routinely represents agent banks in syndicated loans and in dealing with the colenders not only during the syndication process, but also during the term of the loan. He also represents prospective colenders and participating banks who are considering becoming part of existing bank groups. He has extensive experience representing various firms and agencies in a variety of restructuring and lending processes.

dentons.com

Jacques Gordon, Lecturer, MIT Center for Real Estate

Jacques Gordon (MIT '87) joined the MIT Center for Real Estate (CRE) as the first "Executive-in-Residence" for the fall academic semester of 2023. Previously, Jacques was a Global Strategist for LaSalle Investment Management, a global real estate investment manager with $82 billion in assets under management. He announced his retirement from LaSalle and will continue to serve on the boards of the JLL Income Property Trust, The Real Estate Research Institute, and The Institute for Urban Research at the University of Pennsylvania. He currently co-chairs the Social Impact committee at PREA and serves as a founding member of LaSalle's Climate Risk Task Force.

cre.mit.edu

Richard Grossmann, P.C., Partner, Real Estate, Kirkland & Ellis

Richard A. Grossmann is a partner in the Real Estate Practice Group in the New York office of Kirkland & Ellis LLP. He represents both US and non-US clients in complex commercial real estate transactions, including joint ventures and other equity capital arrangements, acquisitions, dispositions, financing, and M&A transactions involving real estate and real estate-related businesses. He has experience representing hedge funds, private equity funds, and logistics-focused investment management. Previously, Grossmann worked with Debevoise & Plimpton as well as Kirkland & Ellis LLPs.

kirkland.com

Bruce E. Hood, Partner, Withersworldwide

Bruce is a partner in the international corporate tax team at Withersworldwide. He represents clients on taxation matters at the federal, state, and local levels, principally in international, real estate, corporate and partnership taxation. He has advised clients on taxable and tax-free mergers and acquisitions, partnership formation and restructuring, preimmigration tax planning, tax-free exchanges of real estate, REIT formation, and operation. Bruce also has significant experience in FIRPTA planning, compliance, and all types of matters pertaining to income tax treaties. The Dutch and South American regions have been major areas of concentration for Bruce's active role in the firm's Latin American and European teams. His clients include high-net-worth individuals and their businesses as well as a number of the world's largest pension funds.

withersworldwide.com

Shiukay Hung, Partner, Co-Chair, National REIT Tax Practice, DLA Piper

Shiukay Hung is Co-Chair of DLA Piper's National REIT Tax Practice and a partner in DLA Piper's Investment Management and Real Estate Capital Markets Practice resident in the New York office. His primary focus is the real estate industry and particularly REITs (e.g., private REITs, public nontraded REITs/NAV REITs, US listed REITs, and Singapore-listed REITs). His REIT practice is recognized by *The Legal 500 USA 2022*. Drawing upon his experience as a lawyer in Canada and Asia, Shiukay is particularly sensitive to the tax considerations of non-US investors. He is a frequent legal commentator and has spoken before various audiences and media outlets including *Bloomberg*, *Law360*, the American Bar Association, *Tax Notes*, the American Institute of CPAs, the Harvard Law School Association of New York City, Strafford, the *Private Equity Law Report*, and the Tax Executives Institute. He has also written for *LexisNexis* and the *Real Estate Finance Journal*.

dlapiper.com

Brian Jennings, Senior Managing Director, CBRE

As Senior Managing Director for the Property Management US Business Operations Team, Brian Jennings ensures operational excellence and consistency. Prior to his current position, Brian joined the Property Management Global Operations team in February 2013 and served as the Consulting General Manager for Shanghai Tower in Shanghai, China. Mr. Jennings' commercial real estate experience encompasses more than 33 years of management and leasing responsibilities for leading properties and portfolios. Prior to his current position, Brian joined the Property Management Global Operations team in February 2013 and served as the

Consulting General Manager for Shanghai Tower in Shanghai, China. Mr. Jennings' commercial real estate experience encompasses more than 33 years of management and leasing responsibilities for leading properties and portfolios.

cbre.com

Michelle M. Jewett, Partner, Mayer Brown

Michelle Jewett is a partner in Mayer Brown's New York office and a member of the Tax Transactions & Consulting practice. She focuses on all areas of federal income taxation, offering deep experience in private investment funds and real estate investment trusts as well as mergers and acquisitions, partnerships, energy and infrastructure, financial restructuring, financial instruments, and intellectual property, both domestically and internationally. Michelle contributes pro bono service forming and advising 501(c)(3) organizations on a variety of issues, including hybrid for-profit/not-for-profit structures, unrelated business income tax concerns, and the commerciality doctrine. Michelle is recognized as an Up and Coming lawyer by *Chambers USA*, has been named a Rising Star by *Law360* and *IFLR1000*, recommended as a leading lawyer by *The Legal 500*, and included in Euromoney Legal Media Group Americas Women in Business Law Awards Shortlist for Best in Tax.

mayerbrown.com

Joshua Kaplan, Managing Director, KPMG

Joshua Kaplan is a Managing Director in the International Tax group of the Washington National Tax practice of KPMG LLP and is based in Philadelphia. Mr. Kaplan received an LLM in taxation from New York University School of Law, a JD cum laude from The George Washington University School of Law, and a BA from the University of Michigan. He is admitted to practice in New York and the District of Columbia..

kpmg.com

Paul Kraut, Tax Partner, KPMG

Paul Kraut is a Tax Partner at KPMG LLP based in New York City and is a practicing CPA. Mr. Kraut graduated magna cum laude from the State University of New York at Buffalo with a BS in Accounting in 2003 and received his MS in Taxation from St John's University in 2013. For the last 10 years, Mr. Kraut has been providing US tax compliance and US tax advisory services to global real estate and private equity funds.

kpmg.com

Jeffrey Levin, Senior Partner, Squire Patton Boggs

Senior Partner Jeffrey Levin's practice includes federal, state, and local taxation; estate planning, trusts, and estates administration; charitable giving; and succession planning for closely held businesses. His practice concentrates on income, estate, and gift tax planning for US and non-US clients and the use of domestic and foreign trusts. His US tax practice also includes guidance on various individual, entity, and fiduciary state and local income and sales and use tax compliance considerations. As part of overall and multigenerational estate planning, Jeffrey advises closely held family businesses and family limited partnerships on their tax and related business matters. In addition, he advises on fiduciary income and estate tax planning, compliance, and administration. He also advises US and non-US clients on tax consequences of ownership of US real property.

squirepattonboggs.com

Andy Lusk, Chief Investment Officer, Lionstone Investments

As Lionstone's Chief Investment Officer, Andy Lusk serves as chair of the Investment Committee and oversees the Acquisitions, Research and Analytics, Investment Risk, and Portfolio Management teams. Mr. Lusk and his team deploy approximately $1.0 billion of capital per year utilizing advanced analytic capabilities to pinpoint long-term demand, constrained supply, and attractive pricing. As Head of Corporate Strategy, he is responsible for the development of long-range strategic initiatives and growth strategies to improve the firm's overall performance. Prior to joining Lionstone in 2011, he worked in the Real Estate Investment Banking group at Goldman Sachs where he helped execute various strategic advisory transactions and capital raises. Previously Mr. Lusk worked in acquisitions at LaSalle Investment Management. Mr. Lusk is a graduate of Dartmouth College and received an MBA from The University of Texas.

lionstoneinvestments.com

Stephanie Mason, Associate, Pillsbury

Stephanie Mason, an associate in Pillsbury's Real Estate practice, advises clients on a variety of commercial real estate transactions, including financing, acquisitions, dispositions and leasing. Stephanie focuses her practice on all aspects of real estate. She has experience drafting complex commercial agreements, such as loan documents, JV agreements and purchase agreements. Prior to joining Pillsbury, Stephanie worked as an associate for Stroock & Stroock & Lavan LLP (2021–2022). During law school, Stephanie was the managing editor for the *Human and Civil Rights Law Review* and a student attorney in the Alternative Dispute Resolution Clinic.

pillsburylaw.com

Lisa McCann, Special Counsel, Withersworldwide

Lisa is special counsel in the international corporate tax team. She focuses on advising clients on US and foreign tax planning and compliance. Her clients include individuals, trusts, and various business entities. She has experience helping clients with tax audits and voluntary disclosures. She enjoys helping clients navigate through complex tax laws. McCann started her career as a Certified Public Accountant; having always loved numbers and math, it was a perfect career path for her. While working in public accounting, she became very interested in the tax aspect of accounting and was intrigued by the tax laws. She decided to pursue a law degree and focus on tax law. She still enjoys working with numbers and helping clients navigate through the complex tax laws.

withersworldwide.com

Andrew Metcalf, Partner, King & Spalding

Andrew Metcalf, Partner, specializes in Islamic finance and investment transactions. As a partner in the Islamic Finance and Investment practice, Andrew represents clients in a wide variety of Shari'ah-compliant financial transactions and investments, as well as conventional financing. Andrew represents Middle Eastern clients in an array of Shari'ah-compliant finance and investment transactions, including private equity acquisitions, real estate transactions, working capital financing, structured and subordinated financings, and letter of credit/ guaranty facilities. In addition, Andrew advises financial institutions and their customers in domestic and international finance transactions, including secured and unsecured credit facilities, asset-based loan facilities, structured financings, project financings, bridge financings, acquisition credits, participations, syndications, subordinated debt facilities, letter of credit facilities, and other credit-related transactions.

kslaw.com

David Miller, Partner, Pillsbury Law

David Miller, a Pillsbury Real Estate partner, has closed billions of dollars in public-private partnerships, financings and other complex transactions for US and international clients. David has decades of experience in public-private partnerships involving office buildings, high-rise biomedical laboratory facilities, military housing developments, transportation and telecommunications facilities, and large mixed-use real estate developments. Supervising interdisciplinary teams of Pillsbury lawyers, he represents government entities, private enterprises, and international investors in financings, public debt offerings, redevelopment projects, joint ventures, and the purchase, sale, and lease of US properties. Several of his transactions have received "Deal of the Year" awards from industry publications and organizations.

pillsburylaw.com/en

Sunil A. Misser, Chief Executive Officer, AccountAbility

Sunil (Sunny) A. Misser is the Chief Executive Officer of AccountAbility. Prior to joining AccountAbility, Mr. Misser was the Global Managing Partner of the Sustainability Advisory Business at PricewaterhouseCoopers (PwC). Before that, he was Global Strategy Leader for PwC's Assurance and Business Advisory Services—the firm's accounting, risk management, and consulting operation. He also served as the New York Metro leader for the Governance, Risk, and Compliance practice. During his career, Mr. Misser has been a strategic business advisor to CEOs, boards, and senior executives at Fortune 500 companies and multilateral organizations (MLOs). Previously, Mr. Misser worked in industry, operations, and advanced manufacturing, with Mars, Inc., and Honeywell. He holds an MS in Management from the Massachusetts Institute of Technology (MIT), Sloan School of Management, with a concentration in International Business and Technology. He also has an MS in Industrial Engineering from Lehigh University and a BS in Mechanical Engineering from M.S. University.

accountability.org

Brian Montgomery, Senior Counsel, Pillsbury

Brian Montgomery is a Senior Counsel in Pillsbury's Financial Industry Group, representing and advising banks, nonbank financial institutions, fintech companies, and other businesses on regulatory and compliance matters and advising how to navigate regulatory issues in bringing innovative financial products and services to market. Brian also counsels clients on compliance with cybersecurity, information technology, and third-party risk management requirements. Brian previously served in senior positions at the New York Department of Financial Services and headed the department's program examining compliance of regulated institutions with federal and state laws.

pillsburylaw.com

Jonathan Y. Newman, Partner, Shearman & Sterling

Jon Newman is a partner in the Real Estate practice at Clifford Chance. He specializes in real estate acquisitions and dispositions, joint ventures and financing transactions, including construction, mortgage, mezzanine, and preferred equity financings of US real estate. Further, his experience spans LP investments into real estate funds and foreign investment into US real estate. He also advises on Shari'a compliant investment, with a particular emphasis on structuring real estate acquisitions and fund investments in a Shari'a compliant manner. Jon regularly represents landlords and tenants in ground leases and in commercial leasing transactions, as well as sponsors and capital investors in multifamily, commercial, hospitality and industrial property acquisitions, financings and dispositions. Jon received his JD from the University of Pennsylvania and BA from the University of Michigan.

shearman.com

Hans Nordby, Head of Analytics and Research, Lionstone Investments

As head of Lionstone's Analytics and Research team, Hans Nordby is responsible for leading the firm's proprietary analytics and data-driven research platform. He joined Lionstone in 2020, bringing more than 20 years of industry experience to the firm. Previously, he led the Portfolio Strategy division at CoStar Group, and its predecessor Property & Portfolio Research, where he drove the development of analytic tools that harness the power of big data for use by the commercial real estate industry. He is a graduate of the University of Minnesota and holds an MBA from Indiana University.

lionstoneinvestments.com

Joseph L. Pagliari, PhD, Clinical Professor of Real Estate, University of Chicago, Booth School of Business

As a Professor of Real Estate, Joseph L. Pagliari Jr., PhD, CFA, and CPA focuses his research and teaching efforts—based on over 40 years of industry experience—on issues broadly surrounding institutional real estate investment, attempting to answer important questions from a rigorous theoretical and empirical perspective. Pagliari is board member of the Real Estate Research Institute (RERI) and also a member of numerous academic and professional associations, including the American Real Estate Society (ARES), the American Real Estate and

Urban Economics Association (AREUEA), the Homer Hoyt Institute (where he is a Hoyt Fellow), the National Association of Real Estate Trusts (NAREIT), the National Council of Real Estate Investment Fiduciaries (NCREIF), the Pension Real Estate Association (PREA), and the Urban Land Institute (ULI). Pagliari earned a BA in Finance from the University of Illinois–Urbana in 1979. He earned an MBA from DePaul University–Chicago in 1982 and a PhD in finance from the University of Illinois–Urbana in 2002.

chicagobooth.edu

Patrick J. Potter, Partner, Pillsbury Law

Patrick Potter provides clients with innovative and practical solutions to business problems in the commercial real estate, healthcare, and hospitality sectors. Patrick handles primarily distressed real estate, healthcare, and hospitality transactions, Chapter 11 proceedings, restructurings, workouts, and recovery efforts. His experience encompasses representing debtors and creditors in complex bankruptcy proceedings across the US and Puerto Rico. Patrick's clients include real estate and hospitality lenders and owners (including REITs), landlords and tenants, and medical and healthcare companies. Patrick regularly represents CMBS borrowers as well as mezzanine (and other structurally subordinated) lenders, real estate lenders in workouts, and Chapter 11 proceedings. He also has extensive international experience, including insolvency work in several MENA countries, including Saudi Arabia, Bahrain, UAE, Yemen, Morocco, and Tunisia.

pillsburylaw.com/en

Mark Proctor, Partner, Asset Management, Willkie Farr & Gallagher

Mark Proctor is a partner in the Asset Management Department. Mark advises private fund managers on structuring, establishing, and operating private investment funds, including blind pools, coinvestment funds, pledge funds, single investment funds, and other investment vehicles. Mark also represents fund managers on their internal structuring and compensation matters, and frequently advises clients in connection with coinvestments and seed investments in asset managers, as well as buyers and sellers in secondary market transactions involving private fund interests and portfolios of assets held by private funds. Mark's practice extends beyond fund managers to include institutional investors and family offices in connection with their investments in various private equity vehicles.

willkie.com

Sara Queen, Head of Investment Strategies, MetLife Investment Management

Sara Queen is head of equity strategies for MetLife Investment Management's (MIM) Real Estate group. Sara joined MIM in March 2021. Before joining MIM, she was with Mapletree Investments, a global real estate development, investment, and capital management company headquartered in Singapore, where she was head of the company's North America business. Sara currently serves as the board chair for Solar One, an organization that provides education and resources that create more sustainable and resilient urban environments. Sara holds a BA in economics and history from Wellesley College. She also has an MBA from Harvard Business School.

investments.metlife.com

Elliot J. Rishty, Managing Director, Chief Investment Officer US, Vanke US

Elliot J. Rishty leads all aspects of Vanke's US business, overseeing management of Vanke's operations and investment program throughout the US and leading efforts to develop and implement a strategic vision for Vanke's expansion in the US market. Mr. Rishty brings a unique perspective and broad range of experience to the company, having served in various leadership roles since first joining Vanke in 2016, initially as US General Counsel and, subsequently, as its US Chief Operating Officer. Prior to joining Vanke in 2016, Elliot served as Real Estate Counsel for the Hearst Corporation, where he was responsible for all legal matters relating to the corporation's real estate portfolio and operational needs. Previously, he was an Associate in the Real Estate Department of Willkie Farr & Gallagher. Elliot obtained his JD from Harvard Law School and his BA in Economics from Rutgers University.

vanke.us

Cory Saunders, Vice President, Head of Washington, DC, Office, Pembroke Institute

As Vice President and Head of the Washington, DC, Office, Cory is responsible for managing Pembroke's real estate investments in San Francisco, Seattle, and Washington, DC, and for sourcing and evaluating new investment opportunities across the US. He also provides strategic support to the firm's Tokyo office. Prior to establishing Pembroke's Washington, DC, office in 2014, Cory worked in the firm's Boston office where he was responsible for the global valuation process, sourcing, and underwriting new acquisitions in North America and supporting the evaluation of investment opportunities in Japan, Europe, and Australia. Prior to joining Pembroke, Cory was an associate at a private real estate investment and merchant banking firm, responsible for structuring and analyzing Latin American investment opportunities, as well as underwriting acquisition opportunities.

pembroke.co.uk

Jonathan Scher, Managing Director, Global Head of Tax, Madison International Realty

Mr. Scher serves as Managing Director, Global Head of Tax at Madison International Realty with primary responsibilities including tax structuring, coordination of REIT due diligence, oversight of the tax reporting function, and advising on both US and local tax implications of real estate transactions for Madison and its investors. Mr. Scher has close to 15 years of transaction tax experience. Prior to joining Madison, Jonathan worked in-house at Tishman Speyer Properties in the transaction tax group where he provided tax advice in connection with the acquisition, disposition, and restructuring of US and non-US real estate investments and was instrumental in building out the group's risk management function. Mr. Scher also worked at Ernst & Young as part of both the M&A Transaction Advisory Services group and the Real Estate Tax Services group where he specialized in tax structuring, buy-side/sell-side tax due diligence and REIT compliance. Mr. Scher graduated with a BS in finance from the University of Maryland and has a JD from Hofstra Law. He is currently licensed to practice law in both New York and New Jersey.

madisonint.com

Samantha Sharma, Senior Associate, Pillsbury

Samantha Sharma is a real estate associate at Pillsbury, representing lenders, owners, investors, and tenants since 2015 in all areas of real estate law and practice. Her experience includes drafting and negotiation of complex commercial agreements, such as loan documents for the origination, acquisition, and syndication of commercial real estate loans, purchase agreements, and joint venture agreements for the acquisition, disposition, or development of commercial real property, lease agreements for office, industrial, retail and restaurant space, and advising the boards of cooperative corporations and condominiums. She graduated from Fairfield University and Touro Law Center.

pillsburylaw.com

John L. Sullivan, Partner, Chair, US Real Estate, Co-Chair, Global Real Estate, Co-Chair, US Real Estate Sector, DLA Piper

John Sullivan has a broad-ranging practice that encompasses all aspects of commercial real estate. His clients include institutional real estate investment advisors, US and non-US pension funds, sovereign wealth funds, real estate investment funds, and family offices. In addition to being Chair of the US Real Estate practice and Co-Chair of the Global Real Estate Practice, John is a member of DLA Piper's US Executive Committee and Policy Committee. He is recognized as a thought leader with respect to real estate joint ventures, and he is a guest lecturer on that topic at the MIT Real Estate Center and Columbia Business School. He also has substantial experience representing both lenders and borrowers in complex real estate loan workouts and restructurings throughout the US.

dlapiper.com/en-us

Daniel Tellechea, Director, EY

Daniel Tellechea is an international tax director at EY specializing in US inbound tax planning and compliance matters, with a focus on real estate and private equity funds. He joined EY as a senior tax manager in 2014, following nearly eight years as a senior tax manager at KPMG. After received a BS in accounting and finance from the University of Arizona in 1999, he joined Keegan, Linscott & Kenon in 2000, where he served as an assistant tax manager.

ey.com

Benjamin van Loon, Senior Communications Director, AFIRE

Benjamin van Loon is Managing Director and Editor-in-Chief for AFIRE, responsible for strategy, innovation, technical operations, communications, and thought leadership, including serving as editor-in-chief of *Summit Journal*, AFIRE's quarterly journal. Previously, Ben held several marketing communications and strategy leadership roles for global organizations across urban planning and architecture, economic development, public relations, professional services, and business journalism. An active writer and editor, Ben holds a master's degree from Northeastern Illinois University, where he also teaches strategic communications and public relations.

benvanloon.com, afire.org

Andrew Weiner, Partner, Pillsbury

Andrew Weiner is a real estate partner at Pillsbury Winthrop Shaw Pittman LLP (Pillsbury), practicing in New York City since 1976. His practice is national and global, with a concentration in New York. He represents domestic and foreign clients in equity, debt, and leasing transactions, including joint ventures, distressed real estate, and the hospitality and REIT sectors. He is a fellow of the American College of Real Estate Lawyers. Andy graduated from Yale College and Harvard Law School. He served at the NYC Department of City Planning, the Urban Land Institute, and the Ralph Nader Congress Project, and as Chair of the Real Property Law Committee of Lex Mundi.

pillsbury.com